Full-Stack Web Development with Jakarta EE and Vue.js

Your One-Stop Guide to Building Modern Full-Stack Applications with Jakarta EE and Vue.js

Daniel Andres Pelaez Lopez

Apress®

Full-Stack Web Development with Jakarta EE and Vue.js

Daniel Andres Pelaez Lopez
Medellin, Colombia

ISBN-13 (pbk): 978-1-4842-6341-9   ISBN-13 (electronic): 978-1-4842-6342-6
https://doi.org/10.1007/978-1-4842-6342-6

Managing Director, Apress Media LLC: Welmoed Spahr
Acquisitions Editor: Louise Corrigan
Development Editor: James Markham
Coordinating Editor: Nancy Chen

Cover designed by eStudioCalamar

Cover image designed by Freepik (www.freepik.com)

Distributed to the book trade worldwide by Springer Science+Business Media New York, 1 New York Plaza, New York, NY 10004. Phone 1-800-SPRINGER, fax (201) 348-4505, e-mail orders-ny@springer-sbm.com, or visit www.springeronline.com. Apress Media, LLC is a California LLC and the sole member (owner) is Springer Science + Business Media Finance Inc (SSBM Finance Inc). SSBM Finance Inc is a **Delaware** corporation.

For information on translations, please e-mail booktranslations@springernature.com; for reprint, paperback, or audio rights, please e-mail bookpermissions@springernature.com.

Apress titles may be purchased in bulk for academic, corporate, or promotional use. eBook versions and licenses are also available for most titles. For more information, reference our Print and eBook Bulk Sales web page at http://www.apress.com/bulk-sales.

Any source code or other supplementary material referenced by the author in this book is available to readers on GitHub via the book's product page, located at www.apress.com/9781484263419. For more detailed information, please visit http://www.apress.com/source-code.

Printed on acid-free paper

*To my family, who gave me the push to move forward
when I needed it the most.*

Table of Contents

About the Author

Daniel Andres Pelaez Lopez is a software craftsman with 12 years of experience working in the software industry across a variety of domains including the finance, aerospace, entertainment, and government sectors.

Passionate about IT architectures and software development at all levels, from solution design to software implementation. He likes to solve difficult problems using high technology applying not common solutions.

He worked as a contractor for Fortune 500 companies like Southwest Airlines and Disney, solving hard problems using the Java ecosystem and participating on the overall solution architecture. Currently working on Hourly, a fast growing startup, creating the next generation of payroll systems.

He holds a Bachelor's Degree on Computer Science from the University of Quindio, Colombia, and a Master's Degree on IT Architectures from the University of los Andes, Colombia.

He has participated in all stages of development from software architecture to implementation, from front-end to back-end, using Vue.js, React.js, Java, JavaEE, Spring, AWS infrastructure, and more.

He blogs at Coders Tower: `https://coderstower.com/` and can be found on Twitter @danielpelaezlo.

About the Technical Reviewer

Massimo Nardone has more than 23 years of experience in security, web/mobile development, cloud, and IT architecture. His true IT passions are security and Android. He has been programming and teaching how to program with Android, Perl, PHP, Java, VB, Python, C/C++, and MySQL for more than 20 years.

He holds a Master of Science degree in Computing Science from the University of Salerno, Italy. He has worked as a project manager, software engineer, research engineer, chief security architect, information security manager, PCI/SCADA auditor, and senior lead IT security/cloud/SCADA architect for many years.

Technical skills include security, Android, cloud, Java, MySQL, Drupal, Cobol, Perl, web and mobile development, MongoDB, D3, Joomla, Couchbase, C/C++, WebGL, Python, Pro Rails, Django CMS, Jekyll, Scratch, etc.

Massimo worked as a visiting lecturer and supervisor for exercises at the Networking Laboratory of the Helsinki University of Technology (Aalto University). He holds four international patents (PKI, SIP, SAML, and Proxy areas).

He currently works at the Chief Information Security Office (CISO) for Cargotec Oyj and he is a member of ISACA Finland chapter board.

Massimo has reviewed more than 40 IT books for different publishing companies, and he is the coauthor of *Pro Android Games* (Apress, 2015).

Acknowledgments

Thanks to the whole software community; without your efforts day to day, I wouldn't have enough knowledge to write this book.

Introduction

Full-stack development has been a trending term the last years, but what does full-stack development really mean? I will try to answer that question in the following paragraphs and link it with this book.

When I started my career as a software engineer, 12 years ago, the technologies I used were Java EE for the back end, using MVC with JSF, HTML, jQuery, over a server like Jboss or Weblogic. Everything was server side.

In those times, as a back-end developer, I needed to code on the front-end side also. I learned JavaScript and CSS to render a page that consumes the back-end logic.

Today, things have changed. We have a lot of back-end frameworks, like Spring, Jakarta EE, Micronaut, Quarks, only to mention a few. And on the front-end side, we also have Vue.js, Reac.js, Angular.js, and so on.

The distinction over front end and back end is greater today than before. The front-end frameworks are not server side anymore; they are client side.

This moved the industry to "create" new specialized roles: we have front-end developers and back-end developers. As the frameworks in both sides get bigger and more complex each year, mastering both sides at the same time is hard.

However, companies become complex also, having a lot of software components, in different languages, using different frameworks. Companies started to have problems finding talent and retain it, as they will need to hire a lot of developers with different roles to pull off even one project. Companies started to search for workers with more complex roles: engineers with abilities to master both sides of the coin, front-end and back-end.

This conflict between software engineers' abilities and companies' interests opens a new concept: Full-Stack Engineer.

A Full-Stack Engineer is someone who has "mastered" front-end and back-end sides, or at least, that's what people think. This new "role" allows companies to hire lees engineers, and the engineers are able to apply their knowledge more broadly.

Full-Stack Engineer is a pretty interesting concept because it looks familiar. If the previous definition was true, 10 years ago I was a Full-Stack Engineer, and maybe all of my peers were also Full-Stack Engineer.

I cannot say if the previous definition of Full-Stack Engineer is true or not, but what I can say is this: don't get locked in by one technology or one language or framework; be open to learning both sides of the coin. Maybe you won't master both, but, in the end that's what a software engineer does: build software to solve problems, and it doesn't matter which toolset you use.

I prefer to call myself a software engineer as this opens an entire world of possibilities.

In this book, you will see the journey of a full-stack/software engineer: from learning how to set up a development environment, to monitoring an application in production.

In Chapters 1 and Chapter 2, you will see how to set up your environment to use Jakarta EE as a back-end framework and Vue.js as a front-end framework.

Chapter 3 shows you how to build a proof of concept, using only Vue.js, creating a whole application for user management.

Chapter 4 shows you a fictional delivery company named Daniel's Delivery, its current state, and where they want to be. You will see an analysis of how to move from Daniel's Delivery today, to where they want to be, using high-level requirements, stories and quality attributes, ending with a new software architecture. The next chapters will solve Daniel's Delivery problems, using Jakarta EE and Vue.js.

In Chapter 5, you start modeling the data for Daniel's Delivery and create a back end using JakartaEE to connect to a database, and finally, you will see how to create unit and integration tests.

In Chapter 6, you will see the high-level requirements for Daniel's Delivery, breaking them over wireframes and mapping them to Vue.js components. Finally, you will see the Vue.js implementation for the shopping cart.

In Chapter 7, you will see how to expose and modify your data using JAX-RS and RESTful services in the Jakarta EE back-end, and of course, unit and integration tests.

In Chapter 8 you will connect Vue.js and JakartaEE using RESTful services through the Axios framework and handling exceptions.

In Chapter 9, you will learn the basics of securing a full-stack application, starting from authentication and authorization, and ending with a configuration using Keycloak for OAuth2 and OIDC protocols.

In Chapter 10, you will use the concepts of Chapter 9 to secure Daniel's Delivery application, from the front-end to the back-end, using Keycloak.

In Chapter 11, you will learn some of the good practices of building full-stack applications, from decoupling, security, and databases, to RESTful design.

In Chapter 12, you will design and implement the cloud architecture for Daniel's Delivery using AWS as an infrastructure provider.

In Chapter 13, you will define a continuous integration and deployment strategy for the front-end and back-end sides.

And finally, in Chapter 14 you will learn how to monitor your AWS infrastructure to detect errors or improvements.

## CHAPTER 1

Full-Stack Web Development with Jakarta EE

In this chapter, we are going to cover the basics of full-stack development with Jakarta EE, talking about general concepts and the environment's installation, so that you will understand where and how to start your full-stack project in a hands-on manner.

The following topics will be covered in this chapter:

- Understanding Java EE and Jakarta EE basics

- Using GlassFish application server as an example

- Environment installation

- Understanding Jakarta EE project structure

Technical Requirements

- Java 1.8

- Netbeans 11

- Eclipse GlassFish

- Java Enterprise Edition

- Jakarta Enterprise Edition

We are not going to cover Java 1.8 installation in this chapter.

You can check the whole project and code at https://github.com/Apress/full-stack-web-development-with-jakartaee-and-vue.js/tree/master/CH1/.

1

© Daniel Andres Pelaez Lopez 2021
D. A. P. Lopez, *Full-Stack Web Development with Jakarta EE and Vue.js*,
https://doi.org/10.1007/978-1-4842-6342-6_1

Using Jakarta Enterprise Edition as a Back-End Layer

The first design we will create in our heads for a software project splits the responsibilities into at least two segments: front-end and back-end.

There are a lot of back-end technologies in different languages and with different features. In this book, we are going to cover Jakarta Enterprise Edition as our back-end framework.

Java Enterprise Edition

Java Enterprise Edition is an enterprise standard created by Sun Microsystems (later bought by Oracle Inc.) that uses different specifications to enrich web applications, from database access to RESTful services. There you will find:

- Well-known standards and specifications like JAX-RS or JPA. A programming models based on layers.

- Highly featured application servers supporting those standards.

- A well-constituted community of developers and companies using the specification.

Note   We are not going to cover the details of how the specification is created and validated in this book. However, I suggest you read more about this interesting process through different people and organizations here: `https://javaee.github.io/javaee-spec/`.

Java EE applications have been in the market for a long time, from **J2EE 1.2** (December 12, 1999) until today, with the current version being **Java EE 8** (August 31, 2017). You can have a look at the list of version releases at `https://en.wikipedia.org/wiki/Java_Platform,_Enterprise_Edition`.

Note   For the purposes of this book, we assume you have a basic understanding of Java EE applications.

Today, a lot of companies have their systems over the **Java EE** platform due to their robust application servers and pretty good support. However, its evolution has been slow and other frameworks in the Java ecosystem have shown up, like Spring or Play.

For its own reasons, Oracle Inc. made the choice to open source the **Java EE** specification. You will learn more details about this in the next section.

Jakarta Enterprise Edition

Java EE has been a great tool to build enterprise applications using Java. However, its evolution has been slower in comparison to other similar frameworks like Spring Framework.

As it was slowly evolving, the leading software vendors (including Oracle Inc.), who supports and implements **Java EE**, collaborated to move **Java EE** as open source and named **Jakarta EE**, handled by the Eclipse Foundation, to boost up its development and evolution.

Tip   Java EE is the Oracle trademark; that's why the name was changed. You can find more information here: `https://blogs.oracle.com/theaquarium/the-road-to-jakarta-ee`

In September 2019, **Jakarta EE 8** was released by the Eclipse Foundation. In addition, Eclipse released the **Eclipse GlassFish 5.1** application server fully compatible with **Jakarta EE 8**. This first release was not a huge technical one but was more about negotiations, processes, and specifications related to the open sourcing strategy. Also, the Eclipse Foundation released the first Java API specification, changing from the `javax.*` namespace (**Java EE**) to `jakarta.*` namespace (**Jakarta EE**).

Jakarta EE won't stop here, as new versions are being planned for release.

Note   You can find more information here: `https://www.infoworld.com/article/3437783/eclipse-jakarta-ee-arrives.html`

From here, we are going to use **Jakarta EE** as a specification reference.

Using Eclipse GlassFish Application Server: An Open Source Jakarta EE Reference Implementation

An application server is a comprehensive framework that allows us to create web applications, giving us a set of tools and APIs to facilitate our job. **Jakarta EE** is a set of specifications defined for application servers. So, in the market, at the time I wrote this book, you find **Eclipse GlassFish**, **OpenLiberty,** and **WildFly** as servers supporting Jakarta EE. You can find more information here: `https://jakarta.ee/compatibility`.

Note   For Java EE, there are more servers like JBoss, Tomcat EE, WebLogic, and so on.

The **Eclipse GlassFish** application server is a fully compliant server for **Jakarta EE** standards and specifications. GlassFish is usually the first server that gets updated when a new **Jakarta EE** specification arrives.

We are going to install GlassFish through Netbeans IDE in the following section.

Using Apache Netbeans IDE

Netbeans is the default IDE used when developing an application using Java EE. It has the latest Java EE integrations and plugins and is up to date with the current specification; however, it is not upgraded yet to use Jakarta EE by default.

Until Netbeans 8.2, Oracle Inc. handled and sponsored it. After that version, Oracle released the IDE as an open source project to Apache. We have now the 11 incubating version, which has enough features to work with Jakarta EE

For the purposes of this book, we are going to use Netbeans as a default IDE; however, you can choose one at your discretion or just use your favorite one.

Note   For more information on Netbeans and Java EE compatibility, you can have a look at the questions posted at `https://stackoverflow.com/questions/45852077/netbeans-how-to-add-a-javaee-version` and `https://stackoverflow.com/questions/46528103/upgrade-netbeans-to-jee-8`.

Tip   At the time of writing this book, Intellj IDE supports Java EE in the Ultimate edition.

Netbeans 11.1 was released while we were writing this book; however, it is in an unstable state. You can see more information here: `https://netbeans.apache.org/download/nb111/index.html`.

Installing Apache Netbeans

We are going to use the Netbeans 11 version. For the setup and installation, the following steps need to be performed:

1. Download the installer for your specific SO from `https://netbeans.apache.org/download/nb110/nb110.html`.

2. Unzip the file. You will find the folders shown in Figure 1-1.

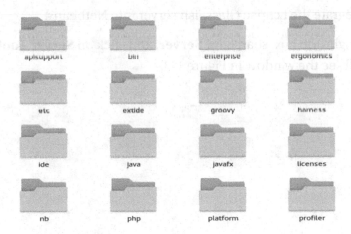

Figure 1-1. *Netbeans installation folder*

3. Move to the **bin** folder and run NetBeans using the right runner for your OS. You will see the window in Figure 1-2.

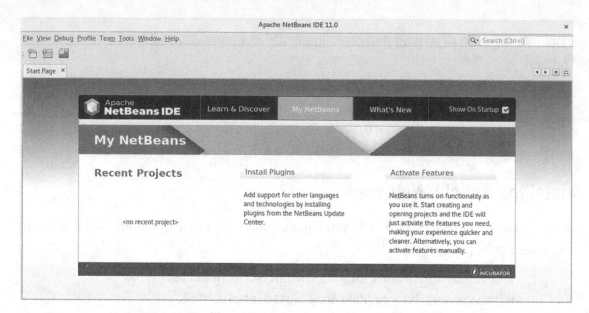

Figure 1-2. *Netbeans home*

Now, let's integrate the Eclipse GlassFish server into Netbeans.

1. In the right-top box, search for **Server**, and click on **Server Tools**. You will see the window in Figure 1-3.

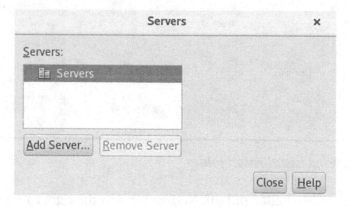

Figure 1-3. *Window to aggregate a server*

2. Now, click on **Add Server**, and then select **GlassFish Server** as shown in Figure 1-4.

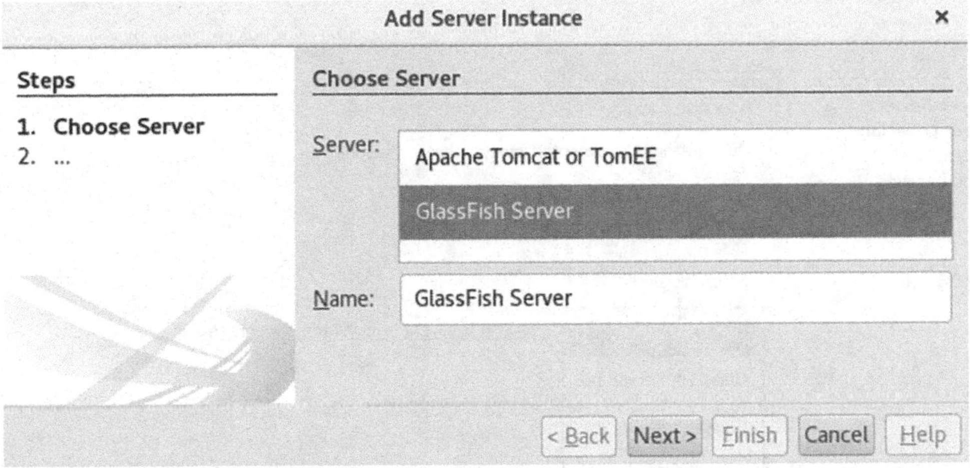

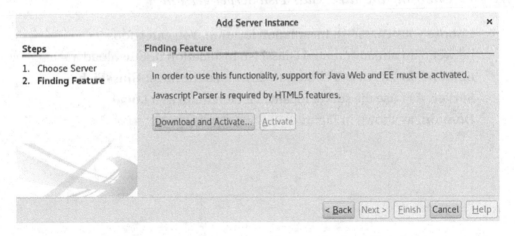

Figure 1-4. *Selecting GlassFish Server configuration*

3. Click on **Download and Activate ...** to start downloading the support for Java EE and Web, as shown in Figure 1-5.

Figure 1-5. *Downloading and activating the Java Web and EE support*

4. After your download is completed and you have activated the features, click on **Next**. This will bring up the screen in Figure 1-6.

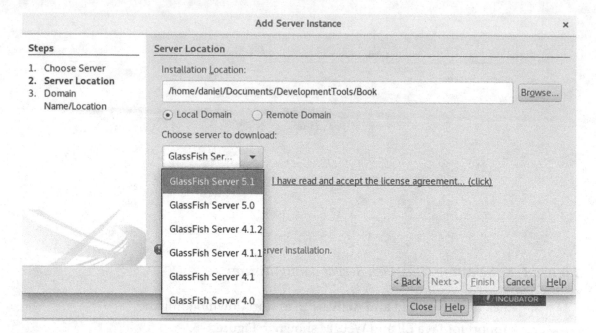

Figure 1-6. *Choosing the latest GlassFish Server version*

5. Choose your GlassFish installation location. You can choose
    between an already created GlassFish installation or download a
    new one. In this case, I choose to download the latest **GlassFish
    Server**. As I use the server locally, I let it remain as a **Local
    Domain**, as shown in Figure 1-7.

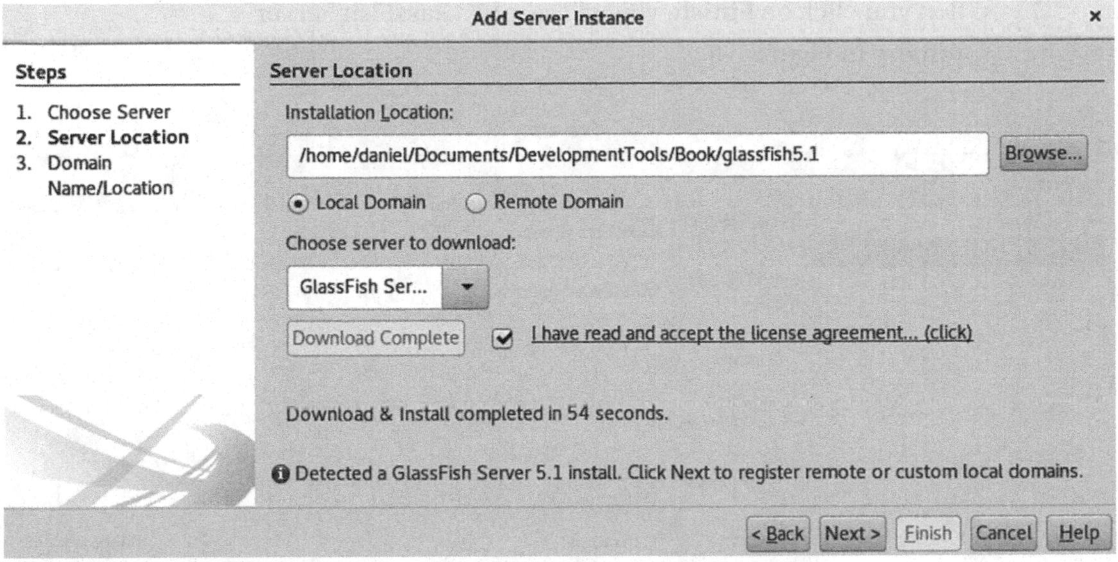

Add Server Instance   ✕

Steps

1. Choose Server
2. **Server Location**
3. Domain
   Name/Location

Server Location

Installation Location:

/home/daniel/Documents/DevelopmentTools/Book/glassfish5.1 | Browse... |

⦿ Local Domain   ○ Remote Domain

Choose server to download:

| GlassFish Ser... ▾ |

| Download Complete | ☑ I have read and accept the license agreement... (click)

Download & Install completed in 54 seconds.

ℹ Detected a GlassFish Server 5.1 install. Click Next to register remote or custom local domains.

| < Back | Next > | Finish | Cancel | Help |

Figure 1-7. *Setting the location of the GlassFish installation*

6. Now, set up the environment as **local** and use **root** as a user and
   password for now. Use the default domain as **domain1** that is
   given by GlassFish, as shown in Figure 1-8.

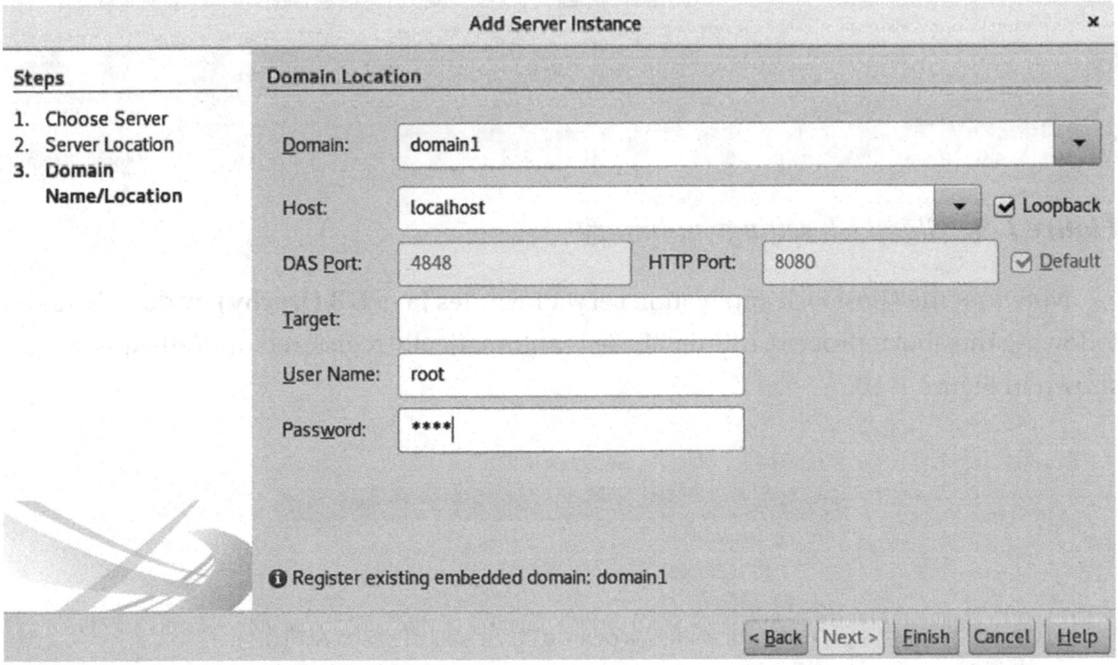

Add Server Instance   ✕

Steps

1. Choose Server
2. Server Location
3. **Domain
   Name/Location**

Domain Location

Domain: | domain1   ▾ |

Host: | localhost   ▾ | ☑ Loopback

DAS Port: | 4848 | HTTP Port: | 8080 | ☑ Default

Target: | |

User Name: | root |

Password: | •••• |

ℹ Register existing embedded domain: domain1

| < Back | Next > | Finish | Cancel | Help |

Figure 1-8. *Setting the domain, host, user name, and password to access GlassFish*

7. When you click on **Finish**, you will see the GlassFish Server
   summary in Figure 1-9.

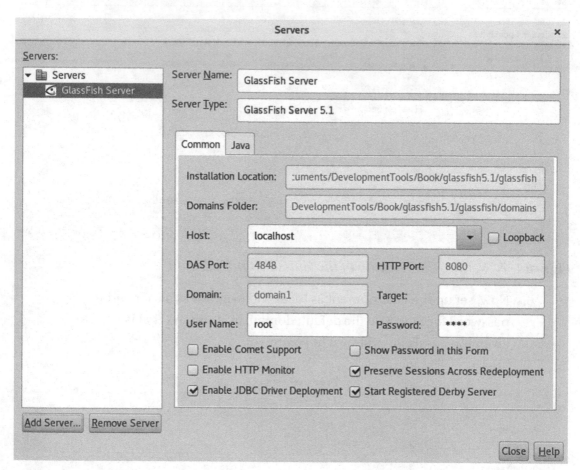

Figure 1-9. *GlassFish settings summary*

Note that the GlassFish application server includes **Java DB (Derby)** by default, and following the above process, this database is automatically registered on Netbeans, as shown in Figure 1-10.

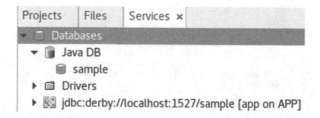

Figure 1-10. *Derby database by default*

10

In the following section, we are going to discuss what a Jakarta EE project looks like.

Jakarta EE Project Structure

Now you are going to create a new Java EE project. Remember, Netbeans 11 cannot create Jakarta EE projects, only Java EE 7. So, we are going to use Java EE 7 and upgrade the project to the Jakarta EE at hand.

1. Navigate to **File | New Project**, select **Java with Maven** for category, and **Enterprise Application** for projects as shown in Figure 1-11.

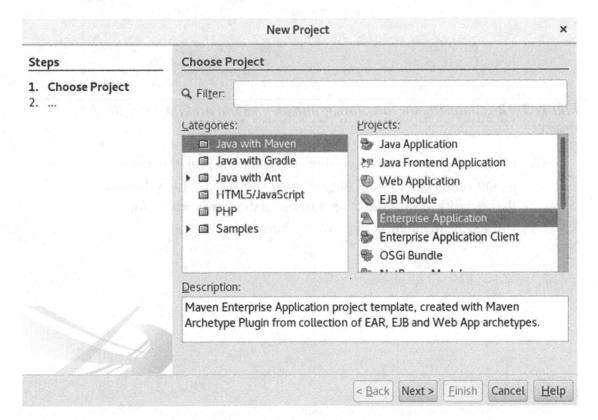

Figure 1-11. *Choosing the category and project type for the new project*

2. Now, define the basic project data like name, location, and so on. Once this is done, click on **Next**, as shown in Figure 1-12.

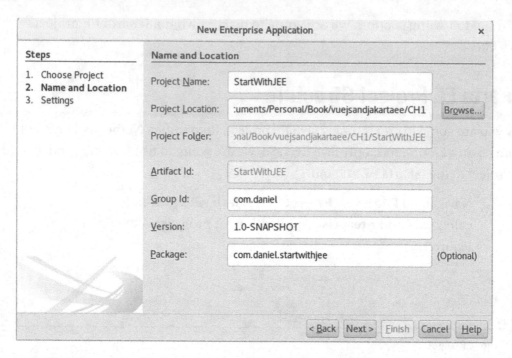

Figure 1-12. *Choosing the location, group id, version, and package for the new project*

3. Choose the latest **Java EE** version and define the projects' names,
    as shown in Figure 1-13. I suggest you do not change the suffix due
    to the clarity of what the main purpose of those projects is. You
    will see the meaning of those names later.

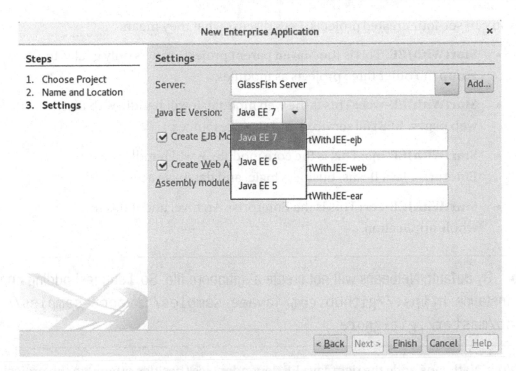

Figure 1-13. Choosing the Java EE version and the default names for each project

4. Now, you will see this project structure in Figure 1-14.

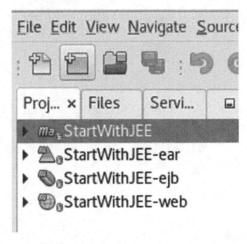

Figure 1-14. View of the generated projects

You can see four created projects. Let's discuss what they mean:

- **StartWithJEE:** This is the Maven parent project, and its only goal is to group the other three projects as modules.

- **StartWithJEE-web:** This is the web module. It will handle web files, web pages, RESTful services, and static resources.

- **StartWithJEE-ejb:** This is the core module. It will handle the Enterprise Java Beans, business logic, and database access.

- **StartWithJEE-ear:** This is the Enterprise Archive, and it has the whole application.

Tip   By default, Netbeans will not create a .gitignore file. So, I suggest adding one, for instance: `https://github.com/javaee-samples/javaee8-samples/blob/master/.gitignore`

Now, Netbeans adds the right Java EE dependencies (besides others) to the project as you see in Figure 1-15.

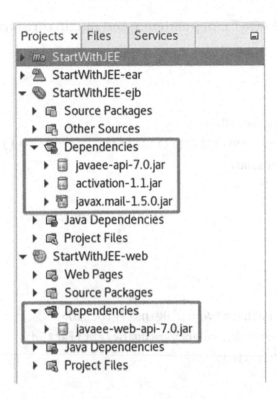

Figure 1-15. *Java EE dependencies for StartWIthJEE-ejb and StartWIthJEE-web projects*

We found two important dependencies there:

- **javaee-api-7.0:** Java EE general specification, like EJBs.

- **jarjavaee-web-api-7.0.jar:** Java EE web specification, like filters and servlets.

As you can see, those are Java EE 7 APIs, as we created the project using the Java EE 7 specification.

As we want to use Jakarta EE, we need to update some dependencies in the new project. Listing 1-1 provides a fragment of the current pom.xml for StartWithJEE-web.

Listing 1-1. Previous Java EE dependency and plugin on StartWithJEE-web/pom.xml

```
</dependencies>
  <dependency>
    <groupId>javax</groupId>
    <artifactId>javaee-web-api</artifactId>          <!--(1)-->
    <version>7.0</version>
    <scope>provided</scope>
  </dependency>
</dependencies>
<build>
  <plugins>
    <plugin>
      <groupId>org.apache.maven.plugins</groupId>
      <artifactId>maven-dependency-plugin</artifactId>            <!--(2)-->
      <version>2.6</version>
      <executions>
        <execution>
          <phase>validate</phase>
          <goals>
            <goal>copy</goal>
          </goals>
          <configuration>
          <outputDirectory>${endorsed.dir}</outputDirectory>
          <silent>true</silent>
          <artifactItems>
            <artifactItem>
              <groupId>javax</groupId>
              <artifactId>javaee-endorsed-api</artifactId>
              <version>7.0</version>
              <type>jar</type>
            </artifactItem>
          </artifactItems>
        </configuration>
```

```
    </execution>
   </executions>
  </plugin>
 </plugins>
</build>
```

The following is a description of the code sample:

1. Here we see the Java EE 7 web dependency. We must update it
    using the new Jakarta EE API as Listing 1-2 provides.

Listing 1-2. New Jakarta EE dependency on StartWithJEE-web/pom.xml

```
<dependency>
  <groupId>jakarta.platform</groupId>
  <artifactId>jakarta.jakartaee-api</artifactId>
  <version>{set latest version}</version>
  <scope>provided</scope>
</dependency>
```

2. Here, there is a plugin using the endorsed Java EE 7 web
    libraries to copy them on the final executable. Jakarta EE does
    not have endorsed libraries, so let's remove this plugin from the
    StartWithJEE-web/pom.xml file.

Now, we must update the pom.xml in the StartWithJEE-ejb. Listing 1-3 provides a
fragment of the current pom.xml for StartWithJEE-ejb.

Listing 1-3. Previous Java EE dependency on StartWithJEE-ejb/pom.xml

```
<dependencies>
  <dependency>
    <groupId>javax</groupId>
    <artifactId>javaee-api</artifactId>          <!--(1)-->
    <version>7.0</version>
    <scope>provided</scope>
  </dependency>
</dependencies>
```

```xml
<build>
  <plugins>
   <plugin>
    <groupId>org.apache.maven.plugins</groupId>
    <artifactId>maven-dependency-plugin</artifactId>          <!--(2)-->
    <version>2.6</version>
    <executions>
     <execution>
      <phase>validate</phase>
       <goals>
        <goal>copy</goal>
       </goals>
      <configuration>
      <outputDirectory>${endorsed.dir}</outputDirectory>
      <silent>true</silent>
      <artifactItems>
       <artifactItem>
        <groupId>javax</groupId>
        <artifactId>javaee-endorsed-api</artifactId>
        <version>7.0</version>
        <type>jar</type>
       </artifactItem>
      </artifactItems>
     </configuration>
    </execution>
   </executions>
  </plugin>
 </plugins>
</build>
```

The following is a description of the code sample:

1. Here we see the Java EE 7 dependency. We must update it using
   the new Jakarta EE API as Listing 1-4 provides.

Listing 1-4. New Jakarta EE dependency on StartWithJEE-ejb/pom.xml

```
<dependency>
  <groupId>jakarta.platform</groupId>
  <artifactId>jakarta.jakartaee-api</artifactId>
  <version>{set latest version}</version>
  <scope>provided</scope>
</dependency>
```

2. Here, there is a plugin using the endorsed Java EE 7 web
    libraries to copy them on the final executable. Jakarta EE does
    not have endorsed libraries, so let's remove this plugin from the
    StartWithJEE-ejb/pom.xml file.

Now, let's refresh the Maven dependencies, and you will see the updated libraries as shown in Figure 1-16.

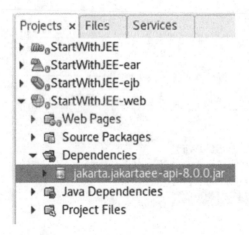

Figure 1-16. *After updating Maven dependencies, you see the new API version*

After the poms files are updated, we can build the application:

1. First, **Clean and Build** the StartWithJEE-ejb project using the
    right-click menu, as shown in Figure 1-17.

Figure 1-17. *Menu to clean and build the StartWithJEE-ejb project*

2. And then **Clean and Build** the StartWithJEE-web project, as you
    see in Figure 1-18.

Figure 1-18. *Menu to clean and build the StartWithJEE-web project*

3. Finally, **Clean and Build** the Maven parent project StartWithJEE,
    as shown in Figure 1-19.

File Edit View Navigate Source Refactor Run
<default con...
Projects
Files
Services
New
Build
Clean and Build
Build with Dependencies
Clean
Generate Javadoc
Run

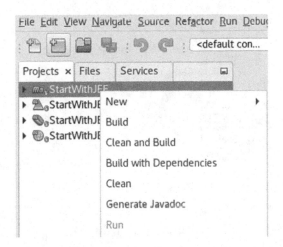

Figure 1-19. Menu to clean and build the StartWithJEE8 project

You will see an output like that shown in Figure 1-20.

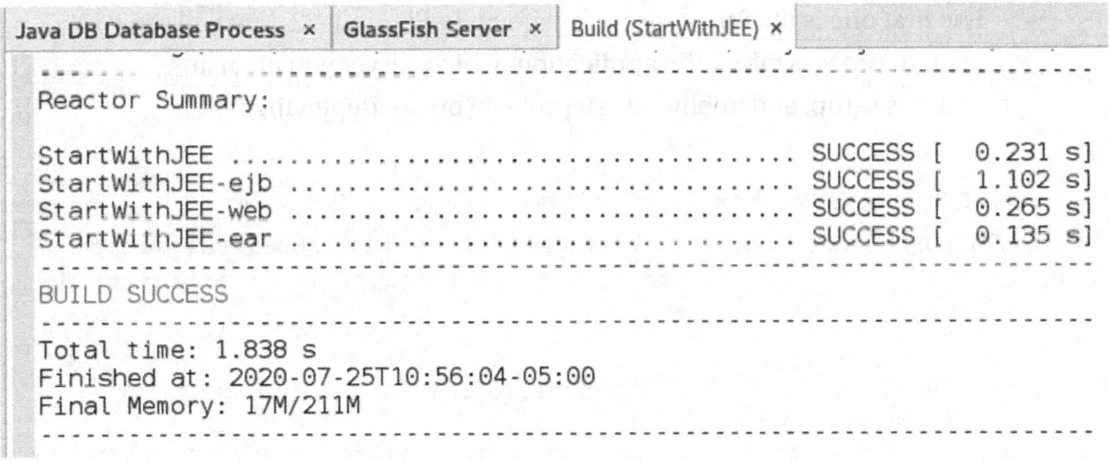

Java DB Database Process
GlassFish Server
Build (StartWithJEE)
Reactor Summary:
StartWithJEE .... SUCCESS [0.231 s]
StartWithJEE-ejb .... SUCCESS [1.102 s]
StartWithJEE-web .... SUCCESS [0.265 s]
StartWithJEE-ear .... SUCCESS [0.135 s]
BUILD SUCCESS
Total time: 1.838 s
Finished at: 2020-07-25T10:56:04-05:00
Final Memory: 17M/211M

Figure 1-20. Console output after clean and build the StartWithJEE project

Now we have the new project ready to run in the following section.

Running the Jakarta EE Project

Let's run our project. We will do so by right-clicking over StartWithJEE-ear and then selecting Run, as shown in Figure 1-21.

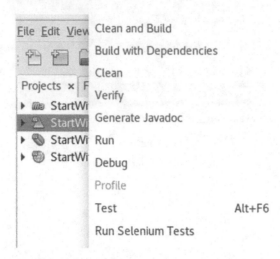

Figure 1-21. *Running the StartWithJEE-ear project*

Three output consoles will be opened:

- The first one is the Run console, as shown in Figure 1-22. You will see the IDE process to run the application, which server you are using and this setup, and finally, which project you are deploying.

Figure 1-22. *Console output for the artifact generation and deployment*

- The second output console is the Java DB (Derby) process, like in Figure 1-23.

```
Output ×
Run (StartWithJEE8-ear) ×   Java DB Database Process ×   GlassFish Server ×
    Sat May 04 11:12:02 COT 2019 : Security manager installed using the Basic server security policy.
    Sat May 04 11:12:02 COT 2019 : Apache Derby Network Server - 10.14.2.0 - (1828579) started and
```

Figure 1-23. *Console output for Java DB process*

- The third output console is the GlassFish server log, shown in
  Figure 1-24. You will see the deployment process and what the web
  context has.

```
Java DB Database Process ×   GlassFish Server ×   Run (StartWithJEE-ear) ×
WARN:     WELD-000146: BeforeBeanDiscovery.addAnnotatedType(AnnotatedType<?>) used for class org.glassfish
WARN:     WELD-000146: BeforeBeanDiscovery.addAnnotatedType(AnnotatedType<?>) used for class org.glassfish
WARN:     WELD-000146: BeforeBeanDiscovery.addAnnotatedType(AnnotatedType<?>) used for class org.glassfish
WARN:     WELD-000146: BeforeBeanDiscovery.addAnnotatedType(AnnotatedType<?>) used for class org.glassfish
WARN:     WELD-000146: BeforeBeanDiscovery.addAnnotatedType(AnnotatedType<?>) used for class org.glassfish
WARN:     WELD-000146: BeforeBeanDiscovery.addAnnotatedType(AnnotatedType<?>) used for class org.glassfish
WARN:     WELD-000146: BeforeBeanDiscovery.addAnnotatedType(AnnotatedType<?>) used for class com.sun.faces
WARN:     WELD-000146: BeforeBeanDiscovery.addAnnotatedType(AnnotatedType<?>) used for class org.glassfish
WARN:     WELD-000146: BeforeBeanDiscovery.addAnnotatedType(AnnotatedType<?>) used for class org.glassfish
WARN:     WELD-000146: BeforeBeanDiscovery.addAnnotatedType(AnnotatedType<?>) used for class org.glassfish
WARN:     WELD-000146: BeforeBeanDiscovery.addAnnotatedType(AnnotatedType<?>) used for class org.glassfish
Info:     Initializing Soteria 1.0.1 for context '/StartWithJEE-web'
Info:     Loading application [StartWithJEE-ear#StartWithJEE-web-1.0-SNAPSHOT.war] at [/StartWithJEE-web]
Info:     StartWithJEE-ear was successfully deployed in 553 milliseconds.
```

Figure 1-24. *Console output for GlassFish Server*

Now the application is running and can be accessed through
`http://localhost:8080/StartWithJEE-web/`, as shown in Figure 1-25.

Hello World!

Figure 1-25. *Hello World page for the running application*

We just set our back-end environment using Jakarta EE, Netbeans 11, and
GlassFish 5.1. We are ready to move to the upper layer, our Vue.js front end.

Summary

Jakarta EE is a pretty good option to choose when you need a back-end framework. It solves plenty of the basic problems you might find while creating any full-stack application.

In this chapter, we saw which software we need to run a Jakarta EE application, how to install the basic elements to start to code it, the structure of a Jakarta EE project, and how to run the project.

In the following chapters, we are going to see details about what Vue.js offers us as a front-end framework.

Extended Knowledge

1. Why is Oracle changing the JavaEE name to Jakarta?

2. Can we add more projects to an EAR than just WEB and EJB?

3. How do we disable Java DB (Derby) to start at the same time as the GlassFish server?

4. Which servers exist to work with Jakarta EE?

CHAPTER 2

Vue.js as a Front-End Layer

In this chapter, we are going to cover the basics of full-stack development with Vue.js, as a front-end layer, talking about the general concepts and environment installation so that you will understand where to start your full-stack project in a hands-on manner.

The following topics will be covered in this chapter:

- Understanding Vue.js basics

- Using the CLI to create a project

- Using Visual Studio Code to open the project and run it

- Installing plugins to help us to work with Vue.js

- Debugging a Vue.js application through Visual Studio Code or Google Chrome

Technical Requirements

For this chapter, we are going to require the following:

- Node.js 10.13.0

- Npm 6.7.0

- Nvm 0.34.0

- Visual Studio Code 1.33.1

We are not going to cover Visual Studio Code installation in this chapter.

You can check the whole project and code at `https://github.com/Apress/full-stack-web-development-with-jakartaee-and-vue.js/tree/master/CH2`.

© Daniel Andres Pelaez Lopez 2021
D. A. P. Lopez, *Full-Stack Web Development with Jakarta EE and Vue.js*,
https://doi.org/10.1007/978-1-4842-6342-6_2

Vue.js

The front-end layer has changed a lot in the last few years, from server-side render using JSP to client-side render using JavaScript, or enhanced versions named single page applications.

Single page applications are a relatively new concept, where the whole front-end application is on the client side, in this case, in the browser. That means the server just serves the initial HTML page (single page) with a set of JavaScript libraries, and the browsers put those together to create the view.

The single page application usually communicates with the back-end layer using RESTful services. Also, there are other alternatives likes WebSockets or events.

Vue.js is a popular single page application framework. Vue.js is defined as:

> *Vue (pronounced /vju:/, like view) is a progressive framework for building user interfaces. Unlike other monolithic frameworks, Vue is designed from the ground up to be incrementally adoptable.*

—https://vuejs.org/v2/guide/

We are going to use NPM as a package manager for our Vue.js application. So, let's see what NPM is in the following section.

Understanding NodeJS and NPM

NodeJS is a JavaScript runtime, offering the option to run JavaScript applications outside a web browser. It uses the Google Chrome engine as its core.

Tip To compare with something back-end related, NodeJS is to JavaScript as the JVM is to Java.

For our case, we will use NodeJS as a part of the dependency management infrastructure with NPM and NVM.

For dependency management, we mean the library dependencies any project can have, for instance, HTTPs communication or UI enhancements. We will see this in detail in the following sections.

Installing NodeJS through NVM

As the JVM, we can have different NodeJS versions in a machine to peform different tests or create backward-compatible applications.

NVM is a NodeJS Version Manager, a software that allows you to handle different NodeJS versions in your machine.

So, let's start with the NVM and NodeJS installation:

1. Install NVM. We won't show the details about this, but you can
    follow the installation instructions here: `https://github.com/`
    `nvm-sh/nvm`

2. After the installation, you can verify the version with the following
    command, as shown in Figure 2-1.

    `nvm--version`

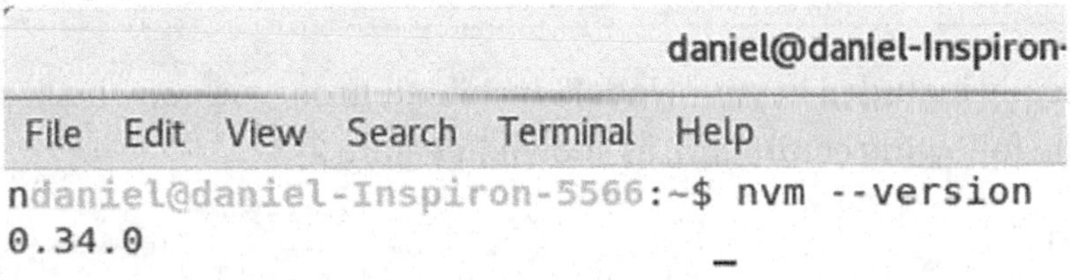

Figure 2-1. *Checking the NVM version*

3. Now, let's install the NodeJS environment:

    `nvm install 11.3.0`

4. To verify the installation, run the following command, as shown in
    Figure 2-2.

    `node --version`

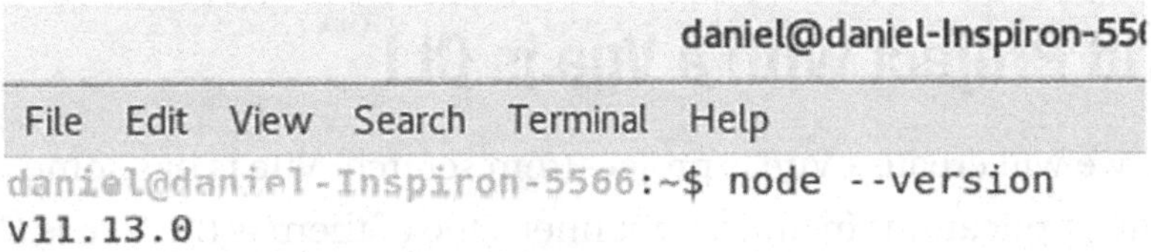

Figure 2-2. *Checking the NodeJS version*

After this process, we have NVM to help us control multiple NodeJS versions, and we have one NodeJS version installed.

As NodeJS is just a JavaScript runtime, we will need to add external libraries and frameworks to build JavaScript applications. NPM will help us with that.

Understanding NPM

In a NodeJS environment, you can have multiple plugins or frameworks to help you in your JavaScript development process, like ESLint for static code analysis or Vue.js CLI, which we are going to discuss in the following sections.

NPM is the NodeJS Package Manager; it means you can use it to install, update, or remove any framework you want to have in your application.

Tip   To compare with something back-end related, NPM is the Maven framework for JavaScript developers.

NPM is already included in your NodeJS installation, so, you can check your current version with the following command, as shown in Figure 2-3.

```
npm --version
```

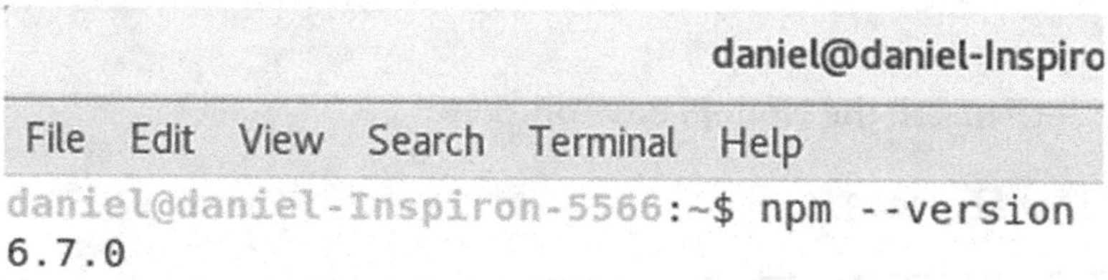

Figure 2-3. *Checking the NPM version*

Now we are ready to move to our first Vue.js application.

Hello World Project with a Vue.js CLI

In this section, we will create a Vue.js project from scratch. Vue.js has some utilities that help us to create applications in an easy manner. One of them is the Vue.js CLI.

Vue.js CLI (Command-Line Interface) gives us some useful features:

- **CLI**: Provides the vue command allowing you to create and prototype ideas; moreover, it gives you a graphical user interface to handle your projects.

- **CLI Service**: Built over webpack, it gives you some useful commands and scripts to run and build your application.

- **CLI Plugins**: They are NPM packages to enhance your application like unit testing or TypeScript transpilation.

Installing Vue.js CLI

To install the CLI, use the following command, as shown in Figure 2-4.

```
npm install -g @vue/cli
```

Figure 2-4. Installing Vue.js CLI

You can check if you have the right version (3.x) or not with the following command, as you can see in Figure 2-5.

```
vue --version
```

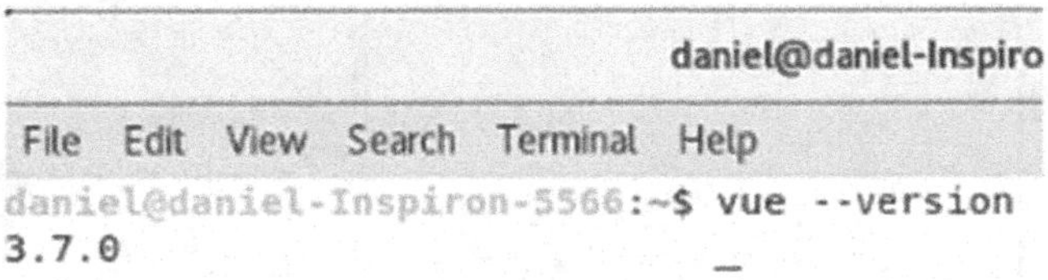

Figure 2-5. Checking Vue.js CLI version

Note   At the time we wrote this book, the Vue.js CLI latest version was 3.7.0.

Creating a New Project

We can use the CLI to create a basic project. We can choose for a Web UI or a CMD (Command Line) to follow the instructions. In this case, we are going to use Web UI:

1. Run the following command, as shown in Figure 2-6.

    ```
    vue ui
    ```

```
daniel@daniel-Inspiron-5566: ~/Documents/Personal/Book/Code/Hands-On-Full-Stack-Web-Deve...    ×

 File   Edit   View   Search   Terminal   Help
daniel@daniel-Inspiron-5566:~/Documents/Personal/Book/Code/Hands-On-Full-Stack-W
eb-Development-with-Java-EE-and-Vue.js/CH1$ vue ui
🚀  Starting GUI...
🎉  Ready on http://localhost:8000
```

Figure 2-6. *Starting the Web UI tool to create a Vue.js project*

2. That command starts a server where you can handle the Vue.js projects and setup. Let's access the address: `http://localhost:8080`, as you see in Figure 2-7. You will see the existing projects and you can create new ones. Those will be located on the folder you set in the bottom.

Figure 2-7. *Home page for the Vue.js CLI UI*

3. Let's create a new project. Click on the **Create** option, shown
    in Figure 2-8. You can choose where you want the project to be
    created, and click on **Create a new project here**.

Figure 2-8. *Initial setup to create a new Vue.js project*

4. You start to add the details, like the location, which package
    manager to use (by default is NPM), and additional options (let's
    leave them by default), as shown in Figure 2-9. Click **Next**.

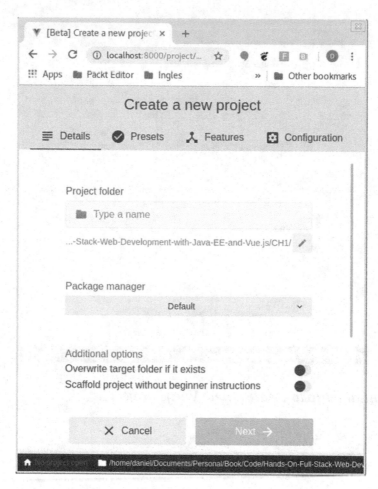

Figure 2-9. *Defining location and package manager for the new Vue.js project*

5. Now, you can add plugins to your application. Let's click on the
    Manual option and **Next** button. This will allow us to customize
    some plugins we need, like in Figure 2-10.

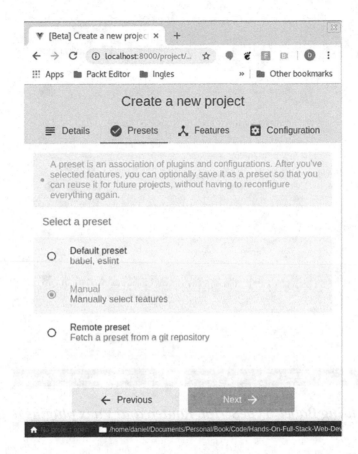

Figure 2-10. *Setting the plugins for the new Vue.js project manually*

6. We are going to use Babel, TypeScript, Router, and Vuex plugins,
    so, let's check those options, as shown in Figure 2-11 and click
    Next.

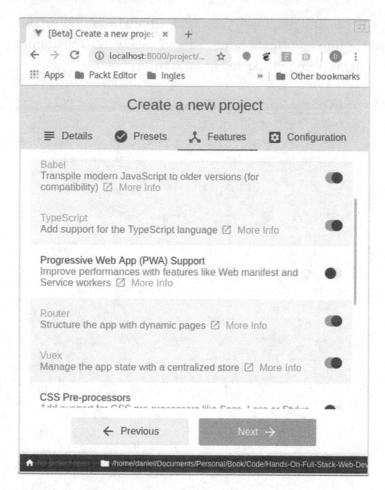

Figure 2-11. *Adding Babel, TypeScript, Router, and Vuex plugins to the new Vue.js project*

Note   We are going to talk about Babel, TypeScript, Router, and Vuex plugins in the following chapters.

---

7.   Choose the Pick a linter / formatter config as ESLing + Standard
     Config, as shown in Figure 2-12, and click on **Create Project**.

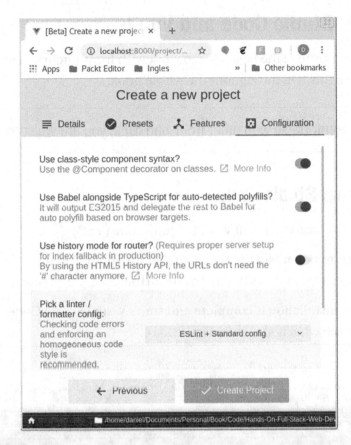

Figure 2-12. *Adding ESLing + Standar Config to the new Vue.js project*

8. After the process finishes, you will see a confirmation message like in Figure 2-13.

Figure 2-13. *Confirmation message for the creation of the new Vue.js project*

Now, we are ready to use the Visual Studio Code as our IDE.

Using Visual Studio Code and Vue.js

Visual Studio Code is one of the best IDEs to work with front-end frameworks like Vue.js. We are going to use this IDE throughout the whole book.

Tip   If you are comfortable with other front-end IDEs, you are welcome to use them.

Installing Visual Studio Code

The following are the steps to install Visual Studio Code (VSC):

1. You need to download the right installer for your OS here: `https://code.visualstudio.com/download`.

2. After the installation is complete and starts Visual Studio Code, you will see what is shown in Figure 2-14.

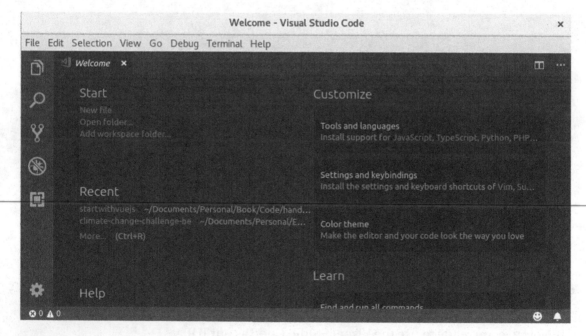

Figure 2-14. *Visual Studio Code welcome window*

3. Figure 2-15 shows the version we are going to use throughout this book.

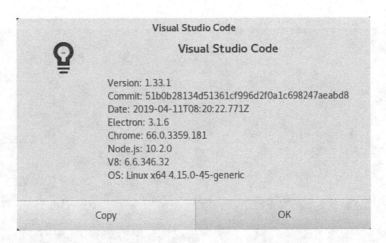

Figure 2-15. Visual Studio Code version

Now, let's use it in the following section.

Open a Vue.js Project

When you open the Vue.js project using Visual Studio Code, you will see what appears in Figure 2-16.

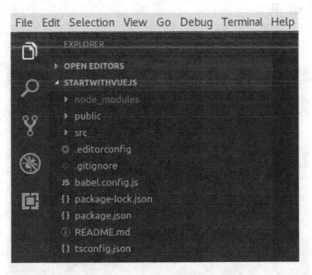

Figure 2-16. New Vue.js project open in Visual Studio Code

Now, let's open the *App.vue* file into *src/*, as shown in Figure 2-17.

Figure 2-17. *APP.vue doesn't have a format in VSC*

As you can see, the file is open as a text file, without a format. Visual Studio Code detects your frameworks and asks you to download some plugins to improve your experience, as shown in Figure 2-18. In this case, it found a Vue.js extension (Vetur plugin), so click on **Install**.

Figure 2-18. *Vetur plugin installed in VSC*

You will see the Vetur plugin marked as Installed.

Vue.js Project Structure

The Vue.js project structure is similar to other single page application frameworks. Figure 2-19 shows the main files and folders.

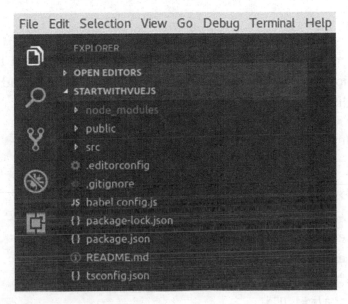

Figure 2-19. *Vue.js project structure*

In the following sections, we will cover each file and folder in detail.

General Node.js Elements

First, let's check some of the default files the project has related to Node.js:

- **dist**: This is the production folder, where the final executable of the application is. This is similar to a target folder on Gradle or build folder on Maven. node_modules: this is the dependencies folder. You will find any framework/utility dependency that your project needs.

- **babel.config.js**: Babel is a TypeScript transpilation plugin and here is its configuration.

- **tsconfig.json**: This defines that this is a TypeScript project. You will find root files and compiler options.

- **package.json**: This is like the pom.xml file on Maven. You will find the plugin dependencies and configurations.

- **package-lock.json**: This is a snapshot of your dependencies over time.

Public Folder

In the public folder, you will find the *index.html*, as shown in Listing 2-1 This is the single page of your application. This page bootstraps the whole application and is going to be the only html file in the project.

Listing 2-1. index.html file in the new Vue.js project

```
<!DOCTYPE html>
<html lang="en">
  <head>                        <!--(1)-->
    <meta charset="utf-8">
    <meta http-equiv="X-UA-Compatible" content="IE=edge">
    <meta name="viewport" content="width=device-width,
    initial-   scale=1.0">
    <link rel="icon" href="<%= BASE_URL %>favicon.ico">
    <title>startwithvuejs</title>
  </head>
  <body>
    <noscript>
<strong>We're sorry but startwithvuejs doesn't work properly without
JavaScript enabled. Please enable it to continue.</strong>
</noscript>
    <div id="app"></div>                <!--(2)-->
    <!-- built files will be auto injected -->
  </body>
</html>
```

The following is a description of the code sample:

1. Here, the head tag doesn't have any JavaScript/CSS files linked, but they will be linked when you build your application. Those scripts will be the joining of plugins, frameworks, and Vue.js technology.

2. Here, Vue.js is going to use the div element to inject the whole application. Remember, the browser will use Vue.js scripts and plugins to create the HTML on the fly. That HTML will be injected in this *div* element.

src Folder

The *src* folder has the content as in Figure 2-20.

Figure 2-20. *src folder content in the Vue.js projects*

We will discuss this content in the following sections.

assets Folder

assets save images/logos or any other media element.

main.ts File

Listing 2-2 shows the Vue.js main, which is the bootstrap file of the application as we see in Listing 2-2.

Listing 2-2. main.ts file in the new Vue.js project

```
import Vue from 'vue'            // (1)
import App from './App.vue'      // (2)
import router from './router'    // (3)
import store from './store'      // (3.1)

Vue.config.productionTip = false // (4)

new Vue({                        // (5)
    router,                      // (5.1)
    store,                       // (5.2)
    render: h => h(App)
}).$mount('#app')
```

The following is a description of the code sample:

1. Here, we import the Vue.js framework. Remember, Vue.js is a set of plugins and JavaScripts.

2. Here, we import the first Vue.js component of the application, named *App*.

Note   We are going to discuss Vue.js components in the following sections.

---

3. These imports are related to Router and Vuex plugins. We chose them when we created the application.

4. This disables the production warning when you start your application. It looks something like this in the console:

You are running Vue in development mode.

Caution   Make sure to turn on production mode when deploying for production. See more tips at `https://vuejs.org/guide/deployment.html`.

5. And finally, this is equivalent to the main method in Java. This starts up your application, adding plugins (router and store), and injects it into *#app* element in your *index.html*. Remember, the #app is the id we set to a div tag in the index.html file.

App.vue

This is the wrapper component for our application. As you can see, it has the extension vue. This means, this file is a Vue.js component and has a defined structure, as you see in Listing 2-3.

Listing 2-3. App.vue file in the new Vue.js project

```
<template>                                        <!--(1)-->
 <div id="app">
   <div id="nav">
     <router-link to="/">Home</router-link> |
     <router-link to="/about">About</router-link>
   </div>
   <router-view/>
   </div>
</template>
<script>                                           <!--(2)-->
</script>
<style>                                             <!--(3)-->
  #app {
  font-family: 'Avenir', Helvetica, Arial, sans-serif;
  -webkit-font-smoothing: antialiased;
  -moz-osx-font-smoothing: grayscale; text-align: center;
  color: #2c3e50;
  }
```

```
#nav {
padding: 30px;
}
#nav a {
font-weight: bold; color: #2c3e50;
}
#nav a.router-link-exact-active { color: #42b983;
}
</style>
```

This file defines the initial App component in the application. There are three sections in a Vue.js file:

1. Here, we have the HTML code and Vue.js directives, templating, and so on.

2. Here, you find the component code, using TypeScript, your business logic, your components, and functions. By default, this script tag is not included.

3. Here, we have the specific CSS styling for the component.

We are going to talk in detail about these components in the following sections.

Note   There are other files we will cover in the following chapters.

Running a Vue.js Project

Vue.js projects run using NPM, so let's start:

1. Open a Terminal in the Visual Studio Code on **View | Terminal**, as shown in Figure 2-21. You can use the terminal application that you are familiar with. Through this book, we are going to use the Visual Studio Code Terminal.

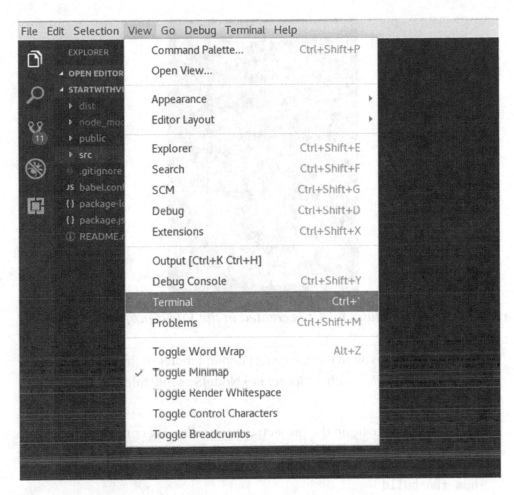

Figure 2-21. *Open a Terminal in VSC*

2. After that, you need to download the project dependencies, like
    when you do that using Maven. In this case, you need to run the
    following command:

    ```
    npm install
    ```

This is going to create a new folder named *node_modules* as you can see in Figure 2-22.

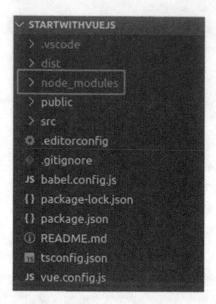

Figure 2-22. *node_modules folder is created in the Vue.js project*

This folder keeps all of the JavaScript dependencies of the project.
To compare, *node_modules* folder is a NodeJS as *.m2* folder is a
Maven folder.

3. Now, you need to build the project; use the following command,
    as shown in Figure 2-23.

    ```
    npm run build
    ```

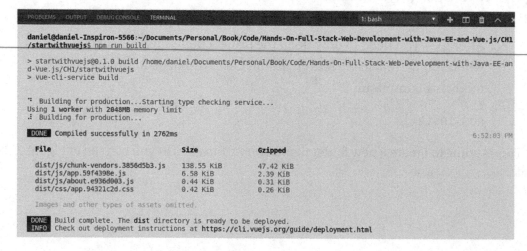

Figure 2-23. *Building the Vue.js project*

Tip   Vue.js is ready to deploy your new changes on the fly, so you will not need to frequently use the npm run build.

4. To run the project, you just need to execute the following command, as you see in Figure 2-24.

   ```
   npm run serve
   ```

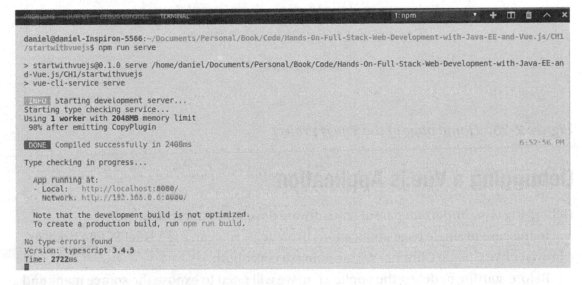

Figure 2-24. Running the Vue.js project

That command is going to start a local server and deploy the Vue. js application there.

5. The application will run on http://localhost:8080 so, let's access it as shown in Figure 2-25.

Figure 2-25. *Home page of the Vue.js project*

Debugging a Vue.js Application

Debugging is an important part of any software development process.

In the case of single page applications like Vue.js, you can use Visual Studio Code or a browser like Google Chrome. We are going to cover both.

Before starting to debug the application, we will need to expose the source maps and add some code to the default Vue.js project.

Exposing Source Maps

Source maps are files where you find the mapping between the transpiled files and our vue files, and they are needed to debug our application.

Note   We are using Vue.js with TypeScript support. TypeScript is not supported by the browsers yet, only JavaScript, so, we need to transpile (transform) the Vue.js source code from TypeScript to JavaScript.

Let's create a new file named *vue.config.js* on the root project, as shown in Figure 2-26.

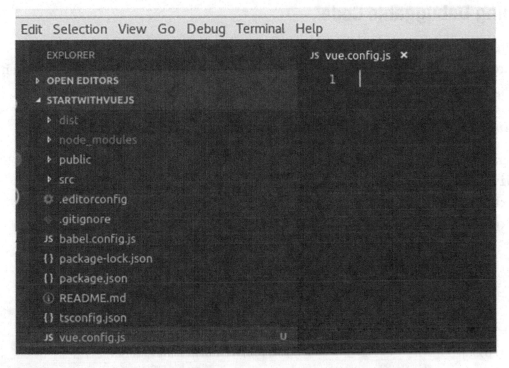

Figure 2-26. *Adding vue.config.js config file to the root of the Vue.js project*

Now, add the content in Listing 2-4.

Listing 2-4. module.exports code to allow source mapping

```
module.exports = { configureWebpack: {
    devtool: 'source-map'
  }
}
```

That piece of code tells webpack to create and deploy the source map files.

Note   Webpack is a framework that allows us to build web modules, in this case, single page applications.

Adding Debuggable Code

We are going to modify a little of the generated project to allow us to test the debug feature. In this case, we change the **src | components | HelloWord.vue** file as shown in Listing 2-5.

Listing 2-5. HelloWorld.vue updated component for debugging pourposes

```
<template>
  <div class="hello">
    <h1>{{ defineMessage }}</h1>                    <!--(1)-->
    <p>
      For a guide and recipes on how to configure / customize this
      project,<br>
      check out the
      <a href="https://cli.vuejs.org" target="_blank" rel="noopener">
      vue-cli documentation</a>.
    </p>
    <h3>Installed CLI Plugins</h3>
    <ul>
      <li><a href="https://github.com/vuejs/vue-cli/tree/dev/
      packages/%40vue/cli-plugin-babel" target="_blank"
      rel="noopener">babel</a></li>
      <li><a href="https://github.com/vuejs/vue-cli/tree/dev/packages/
      %40vue/cli-plugin-typescript" target="_blank" rel="noopener">
      typescript</a></li>
      <li><a href="https://github.com/vuejs/vue-cli/tree/
      dev/packages/%40vue/cli-plugin-eslint" target="_blank"
      rel="noopener">eslint</a></li>
    </ul>
    <h3>Essential Links</h3>
    <ul>
      <li><a href="https://vuejs.org" target="_blank" rel="noopener">
      Core Docs</a></li>
      <li><a href="https://forum.vuejs.org" target="_blank" rel="noopener">
      Forum</a></li>
```

```
      <li><a href="https://chat.vuejs.org" target="_blank" rel="noopener">
      Community Chat</a></li>
      <li><a href="https://twitter.com/vuejs" target="_blank"
      rel="noopener">Twitter</a></li>
      <li><a href="https://news.vuejs.org" target="_blank" rel="noopener">
      News</a></li>
    </ul>
    <h3>Ecosystem</h3>
    <ul>
      <li><a href="https://router.vuejs.org" target="_blank"
      rel="noopener">vue-router</a></li>
      <li><a href="https://vuex.vuejs.org" target="_blank"
      rel="noopener">vuex</a></li>
      <li><a href="https://github.com/vuejs/vue-devtools#vue-devtools"
      target="_blank" rel="noopener">vue-devtools</a></li>
      <li><a href="https://vue-loader.vuejs.org" target="_blank"
      rel="noopener">vue-loader</a></li>
      <li><a href="https://github.com/vuejs/awesome-vue" target="_blank"
      rel="noopener">awesome-vue</a></li>
    </ul>
  </div>
</template>

<script lang="ts">
import { Component, Prop, Vue } from 'vue-property-decorator'

@Component
export default class HelloWorld extends Vue {
  @Prop() private msg!: string;

  get defineMessage () {                                 // (2)
    return this.msg + ", yeeeaahhh"
  }
}
</script>

<!-- Add "scoped" attribute to limit CSS to this component only -->
```

```
<style scoped>
h3 {
  margin: 40px 0 0;
}
ul {
  list-style-type: none;
  padding: 0;
}
li {
  display: inline-block;
  margin: 0 10px;
}
a {
  color: #42b983;
}
</style>
```

The following is a description of the code sample:

1. This is a call to a new method, named defineMessage.

2. This is a new method we added to allow debugging. It is just a test code.

For now, it does not matter if you understand what this means, as we will cover it in the following chapters.

Visual Studio Code Debugger

Let's start debugging with Visual Studio Code. The following are the steps to do it:

1. In the extensions section, you will find, as recommended,
   Debugger for Chrome, so let's install it, as shown in Figure 2-27.
   There is another plugin for Firefox if you prefer that browser.

Figure 2-27. *Plugin for Chrome in VSC*

The detail about the plugin is like that in Figure 2-28.

Figure 2-28. *Detail of the Plugin for Chrome in VSC*

You will see a confirmation message as shown in Figure 2-29.

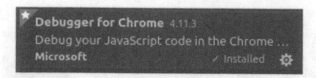

Figure 2-29. *Confirmation message for the installation of the Plugin for Chrome in VSC*

2.   Now, move to **Debug | Start** Debugging, as shown in Figure 2-30.

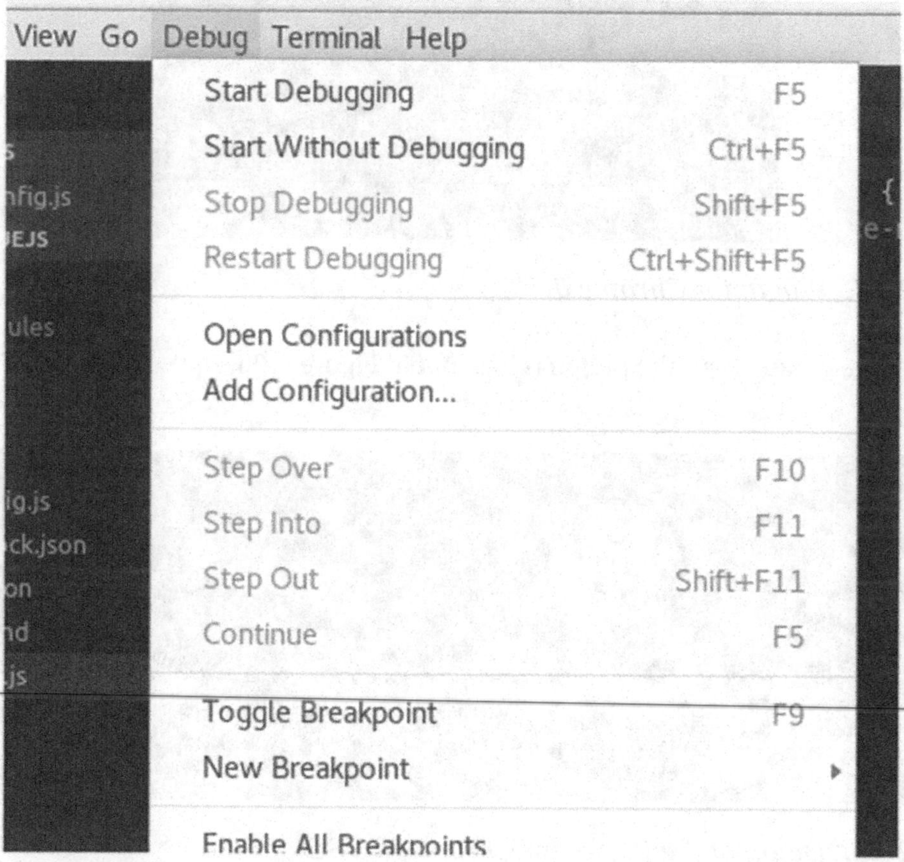

View	Go	Debug	Terminal	Help
		Start Debugging		F5
		Start Without Debugging		Ctrl+F5
		Stop Debugging		Shift+F5
		Restart Debugging		Ctrl+Shift+F5
		Open Configurations		
		Add Configuration...		
		Step Over		F10
		Step Into		F11
		Step Out		Shift+F11
		Continue		F5
		Toggle Breakpoint		F9
		New Breakpoint		▶
		Enable All Breakpoints		

Figure 2-30. *Starting the debugging in VSC*

3.   Choose Chrome as an environment, like in Figure 2-31.

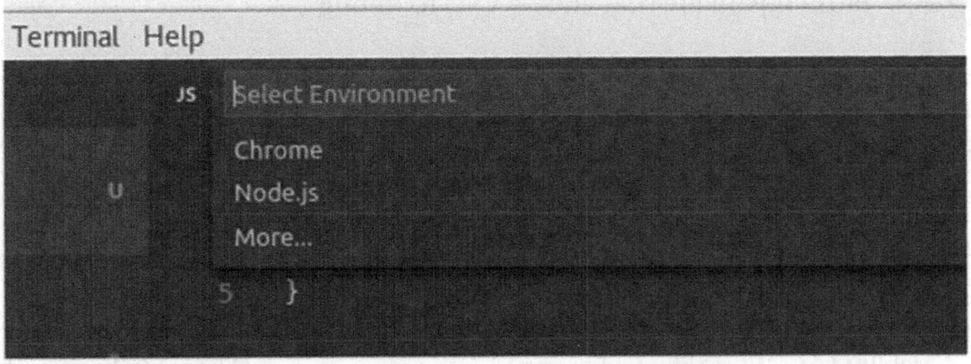

Figure 2-31. *Setting Chrome as debugger in VSC*

4.   Visual Studio Code is going to open a file named *launch.json*, as shown in Figure 2-32. Here, we are going to tell VSC how to talk with Google Chrome to debug our application.

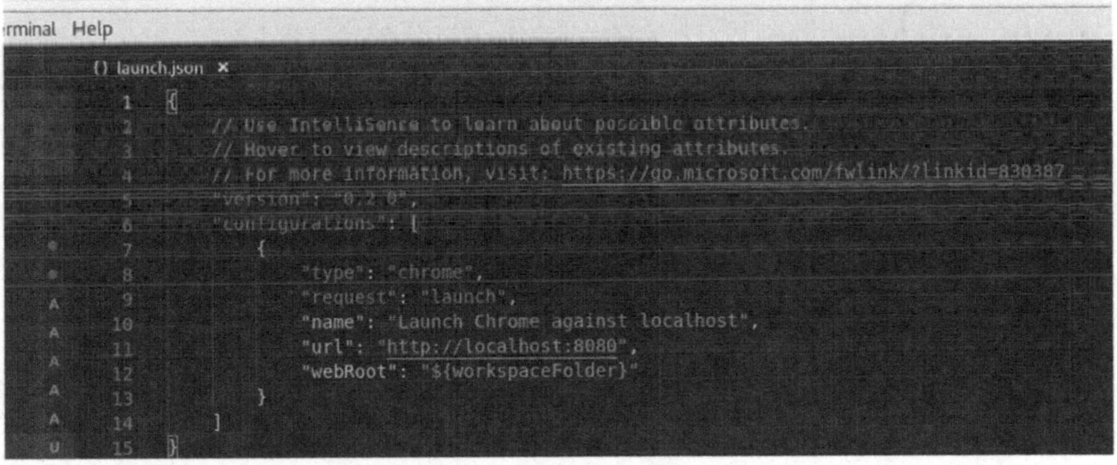

Figure 2-32. *Setting Chrome as debugger in VSC*

5.   Let's replace the file content with the right configuration, for instance, Listing 2-6.

Listing 2-6. launch.json file that allows VSC to debug

```json
{
  "version": "0.2.0", "configurations": [
    {
      "type": "chrome",
      "request": "launch",
      "name": "vuejs: chrome",
      "url": "http://localhost:8080",
      "webRoot": "${workspaceFolder}",                "breakOnLoad": true,
        "sourceMaps": true,
        "disableNetworkCache": true,
        "sourceMapPathOverrides": {
                  "webpack:///*": "${webRoot}/*",
                  "webpack:///./*": "${webRoot}/*",
                  "webpack:///src/*": "${webRoot}/src/*"
          }
    }
  ]
}
```

6. Now, set a breakpoint in *HelloWorld.vue* on line **42** where the data function returns a string. It should look like a filled red circle, as shown in Figure 2-33.

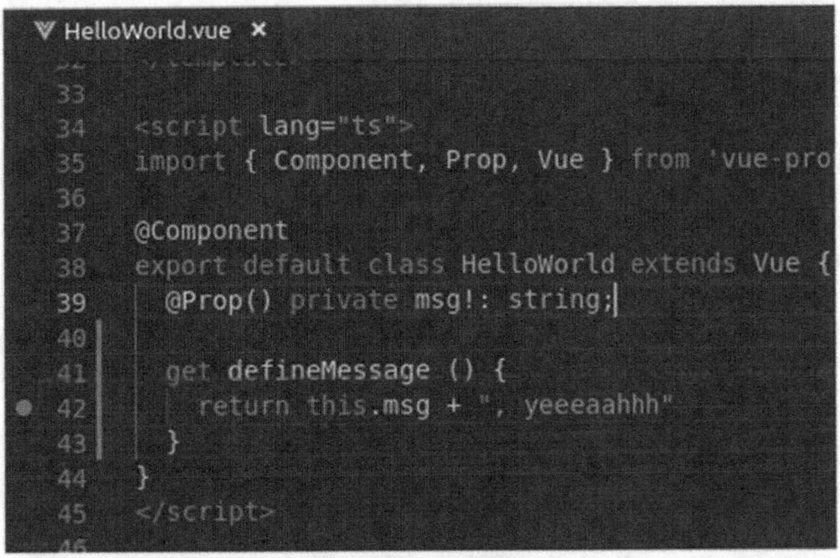

```
V HelloWorld.vue  ✕

33
34    <script lang="ts">
35    import { Component, Prop, Vue } from 'vue-pro
36
37    @Component
38    export default class HelloWorld extends Vue {
39      @Prop() private msg!: string;
40
41      get defineMessage () {
42        return this.msg + ", yeeeaahhh"
43      }
44    }
45    </script>
```

Figure 2-33. *Setting the debug breakpoint in VCS*

The little red dot is where the debug was set.

7. Run the application as we saw in the previous chapter and access
    it through the browser. You will see how VSC hits the breakpoint,
    as shown in Figure 2-34.

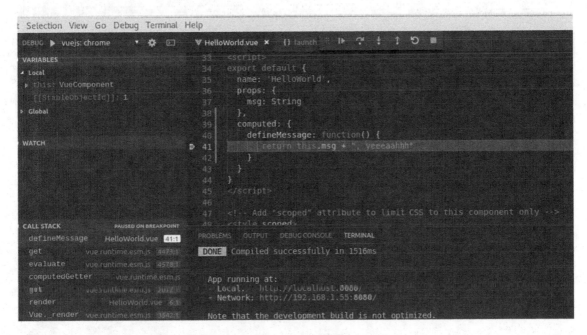

Figure 2-34. *Hitting the debug breakpoint in VCS*

You can access the request state, call stack, and watch variables on the call.

Google Chrome Debug

Let's start debugging with Google Chrome. The following are the steps to do it:

1. In the Chrome browser, hit **F12**, and it will open the debugger console, as shown in Figure 2-35.

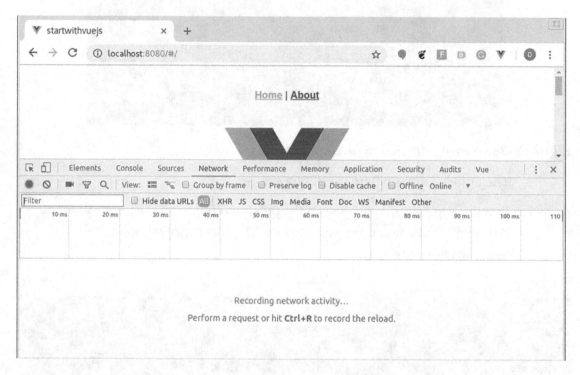

Figure 2-35. *Open the development window in Google Chrome*

2. Move to the tab Sources, search on the left for the **webpack | . | src | components**, and you will find *HelloWord.vue* file. Set a breakpoint in the *defineMessage* method, as you see in Figure 2-36.

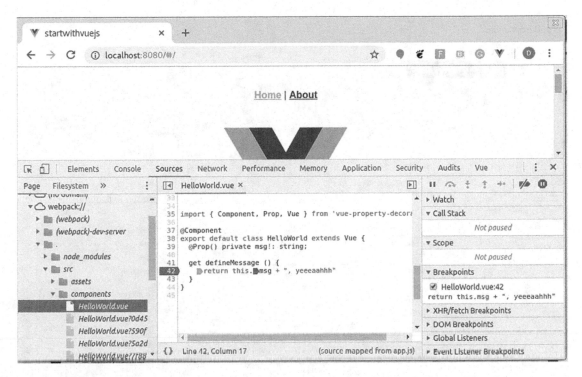

Figure 2-36. *Setting a breakpoint in the method defineMessage in Google Chrome*

The purple arrow on the left side is the breakpoint.

Tip   You might need to scroll down on that file to find the source code.

---

3. After that you can put a breakpoint, reload the page, and you will
   hit the debugger process, as shown in Figure 2-37.

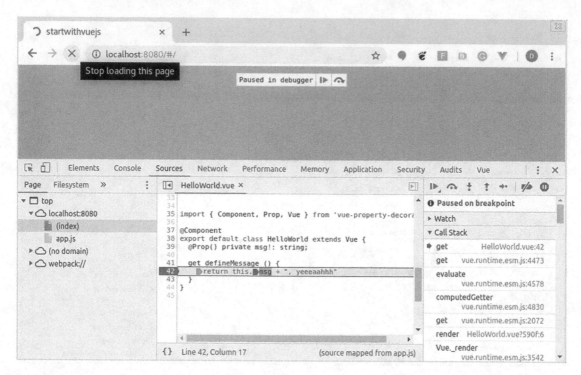

Figure 2-37. *Hitting a breakpoint in the method defineMessage in Google Chrome*

Vue.js DevTools Plugin

Vue.js has a Google Chrome plugin that allows us to see the components' trees and queries and modify their data.

1. Install the plugin here: `https://github.com/vuejs/vue-devtools`. The plugin looks like what is shown in Figure 2-38.

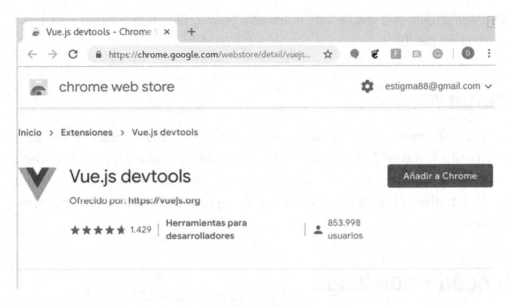

Figure 2-38. *Vue.js devtools plugin official page*

2.   After the installation, you can find DevTools as a new tab on the debugger console (F12), as shown in Figure 2-39.

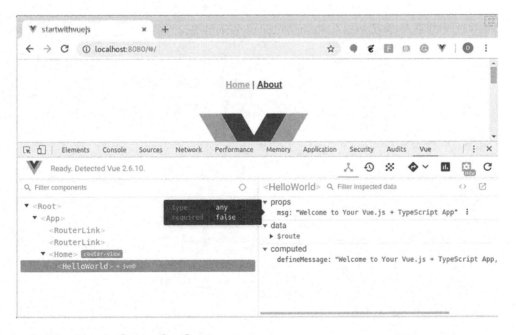

Figure 2-39. *Vue.js devtools plugin*

With this plugin, you will be able to see how your application is structured and change data on the fly.

Summary

As a front-end framework, we choose Vue.js. Vue.js is easy to install and starts to be productive in a fast way. In this chapter, we saw how to set up a Vue.js environment, what the Vue.js project structure looks like, how to run it, and how to debug a front-end application. In the following chapter, we are going to see a business case example using Vue.js.

Extended Knowledge

1. How does a source map work?

2. Can I use Vue.js without .vue files and webpack?

3. Which other IDEs are there to work with Vue.js?

## CHAPTER 3

Getting Started with Vue.Js

In this chapter, we are going to talk about Vue.js, a progressive framework for building user interfaces. We will learn how to build a Vue.js application; the basics of its structure and definitions; how to interact with the final user; and finally, how to create reusable components. We are going to use those features to create a user management application having basic CRUD operations. By the end of this chapter, you will have gained the basic knowledge to build a single page application using Vue.js and mocking data.

The following topics will be covered in this chapter:

- Defining some CRUD requirements

- Creating business entities using TypeScript

- Creating storage using Vuex with mock data

- Routing through URL to new components

- Defining Vue.js components using declarative rendering, methods, and lifecycle events

- Using props, handling user input, conditional rendering, and emitted events

- Creating a user management application

© Daniel Andres Pelaez Lopez 2021
D. A. P. Lopez, *Full-Stack Web Development with Jakarta EE and Vue.js*,
https://doi.org/10.1007/978-1-4842-6342-6_3

Technical Requirements

To follow the instructions in this chapter, you will need the following:

- Node.js 10.13.0

- Npm 6.7.0

- Nvm 0.34.0

- Visual Studio Code 1.33.1

You can check the whole project and code at `https://github.com/Apress/` `full-stack-web-development-with-jakartaee-and-vue.js/tree/` `master/CH3/startwithvuejs`.

Creating Our Business Entities Using TypeScript

We are going to build a user management application from scratch. The following are the requirements for that application:

- A user can have an email, name, password, and role

- The user's role could be ADMIN or USER

- We need to see the whole list of users

- We need to create a new user

- We need to update an existing user

- We need to remove an existing user

- The users should persist only for the time the server is up

Now, let's start defining our business entities for those requirements. We will first start with defining the role enum.

Note   We are using TypeScript to get a more robust code. We won't explain it in this book. For more information, you can check `https://www.typescriptlang.` `org/docs/home.html`.

Defining the Role.ts Enum

Well, let's define the Role.ts enum (Listing 3-1).

Listing 3-1. Role.ts enum

```
export enum Role {
  USER = 'USER',
  ADMIN = 'ADMIN'
}
```

We assign this string representation to each value; otherwise, you get an incremental number by default.

Defining the User.ts Entity

Let's define our *User.ts* entity as follows (Listing 3-2).

Listing 3-2. User.ts entity

```
import { Role } from '../entities/Role'        // (1)

export class User {
  name: string = ''                            // (2.1)
  email: string = ''                           // (2.2)
  password: string = ''                        // (2.3)
  role: Role = Role.USER                       // (2.4)

  static emptyUser () {                        // (3.1)
    let user:User = new User()
    return user
  }

  static newUser (name: string,
                  email: string,
                  password: string,
                  role: Role) {                // (3.2)
    let user:User = new User()
```

```
    user.name = name
    user.email = email
    user.password = password
    user.role = role

    return user
  }

  copyUser (userToCopy: User) {                    // (4)
    this.name = userToCopy.name
    this.email = userToCopy.email
    this.password = userToCopy.password
    this.role = userToCopy.role
  }
}
```

The following is a description of the code sample:

1. Here, we import the role enum to be used in our user entity.

2. Here, we define the user properties: name, email, password, and role.

3. For this, we define two factory methods: one to build an empty user and another to create a new one with its properties.

Tip   Having factory methods to build entities is a good practice because you can define them with a good intent in the method's name and you can control how the entity is built. For more information, see `https://coderstower.com/2019/06/25/the-object-instantiation-nightmare-the-factory-method-pattern/`.

---

4. Finally, define one method to update an existing user from the data of another user.

Tip   The copyUser method is going to help us a lot in handling reactive properties on Vue.js. We are going to discuss those properties in the following sections.

Defining the State.ts Entity

The state entity is a special one. We are going to use it to save our users using Vuex (we are going to talk about Vuex in the following sections). The code sample is as follows:

```
import { User } from '../entities/User'          // (1)

export class State {                             // (2)
  users: User[] = [];
}
```

The following is a description of the code sample:

1. First, we import our user entity.

2. Then we define a property as an array of users.

With this, we have now created all the required business entities and we are prepared for creating our storage.

Creating the Storage Using Vuex

We need to save our data somewhere. For that purpose, we are going to use Vuex.

Vuex is a storage framework. It helps us to handle the application's state across our Vue.js components so that you can access it anywhere. The storage is saved on memory, which means that if you close your browser, the storage is gone.

Note   We added the Vuex plugin when we created our Vue.js project in Chapter 1, "Full-Stack Web Development with Jakarta EE and Vue.Js." You can revisit that chapter for more information.

Vuex is set up on a file named store.js. By default, this file has only a basic structure. The following stora.js file has an enhanced structure (Listing 3-3).

Listing 3-3. store.ts configuration for Vuex

```
import Vue from 'vue'
import Vuex from 'vuex'
import { User } from './entities/User'          // (1.1)
import { Role } from './entities/Role'          // (1.2)
import { State } from './entities/State'        // (1.3)

const stateBase: State = {                       // (2)
  users: [
    User.newUser('Daniel Pelaez',
              'danielpelaez@email.com',
              'password123', Role.ADMIN),
    User.newUser('Hector Hurtado',
              'hectorhurtado@email.com',
              'password123', Role.USER),
    User.newUser('William Agreda',
              'williamagreda@email.com',
              'password123', Role.USER),
    User.newUser('Roger Salazar',
              'rogersalazar@email.com',
              'password123', Role.USER)
  ]
}
export default new Vuex.Store<State>({           // (3)
  state: stateBase,                              // (4)
  mutations: {
    saveUser (state:State, user:User) {          // (5.1)
      state.users.push(user)
    },
    removeUser (state:State, userToRemove:User) {    // (5.2)
      const index = state.users.findIndex(user => user.email ===
      userToRemove.email)
```

```
      Vue.delete(state.users, index)
    },
    updateUser (state:State, userToUpdate:User) {    // (5.3)
      let user:User | undefined = state.users.find(user => user.email ===
      userToUpdate.email)

      user!.copyUser(userToUpdate)
    }
  },
  actions: {

  },
  getters: {
    getUserByEmail: (state) => (email:string) => {    // (6)
      return state.users.find(user => user.email === email)
    }
  }
})
```

The following is a description of the code sample:

1. Here, we add new imports about our entities; remember, we are going to store them in Vuex.

2. Later, we define our init data using the state, user, and role entities. We just created four users. This is going to be our users base and that is how the data will be saved.

3. Next, we define a type of storage. In this case, the type is the state entity.

4. Now, we can assign directly our stateBase to the Vuex state.

5. Here, we add mutations. First, mutations define how we are going to modify the Vuex state, in this case, our array of users. We created three operations: saveUser, removeUser, and updateUser. Let's check them one by one.

    a. saveUser takes the users array and pushes to it a new user.

b. removeUser goes through the users list, and find the user we want to remove, with its email, then we use Vue.delete and the index, to remove the user from the list. Vue.js is a reactive framework, which means any change in the objects/arrays handled by Vue.js, will generate a event, and therefore, a change of state. However, Vue.js cannot detect when a property or value from an object/array is removed, so they created the Vue.delete method to handle that common scenario. We are going to use the users array in a Vue.js component, so this array is going to be marked as reactive; that is why we use the Vue.delete method.

c. updateUser finds the user with its email, and later it uses the User. copy method to update the current user data with the new one.

6. Finally, we are going to add a new section named getters. A getter is a method to query the state; in this case, we added the getUserByEmail method, who based on a user's email, finds the whole user's data.

With this, we have our "database" ready to use for the Vue.js components we are going to create in the following section.

Defining the Vue.js Components

Now, for our requirements, we defined that we need the following components to meet those requirements:

- UserList.vue is going to display the whole list of users currently saved.

- UserForm.vue is the form used to create or update a user.

- UserNew.vue uses the UserForm.vue in a new mode.

- UserUpdate.vue uses the UserForm.vue in an update mode.

- User.vue is our main page about user features.

Figure 3-1 illustrates how those components interact with each other.

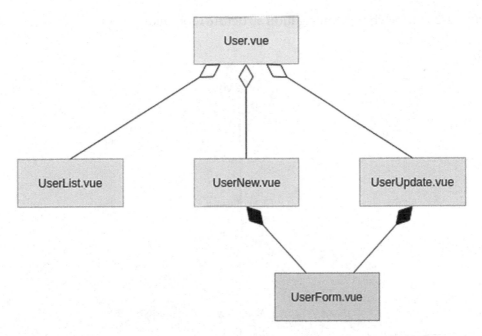

Figure 3-1. *Composition diagram of the User components. The bold arrows mean composition and the white arrows mean aggregation*

Each of those components uses different Vue.js features, which we are going to discuss in detail.

Defining the Navigation Structure

Let's define the navigation structure for each component - whether it is routable and how we are going to access it:

- User.vue: We are going to access it through /user path. This is our root path for the user module.

- UserList.vue: We are going to access it through the /user path.

- UserNew.vue: We are going to access it through the /user/new path.

- UserUpdate.vue: We are going to access it through the /user/:email path. The last part of the path is a param named email. There we must add the email of the user we are going to update.

Figure 3-2 shows what the navigation structure looks like.

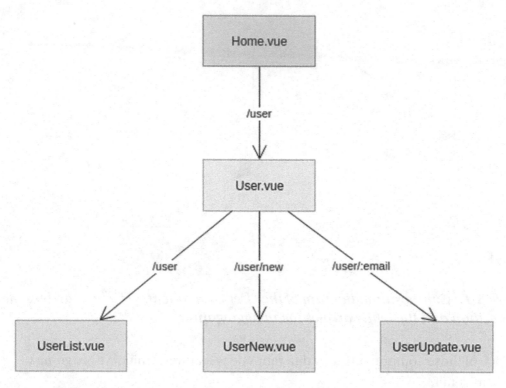

Figure 3-2. *Routing flow though the User components using a URL path*

As you can see in Table 3-1, we have a common path/user over the whole route, so let's override this using a hierarchy.

Table 3-1. *Hierarchical route paths to access the User components. Sometimes one path renders two components.*

Path	Components to Render
/user	User
/	User and UserList
/new	User and UserNew
/:email	User and UserUpdate

Figure 3-3 shows what the navigation structure looks like in a hierarchical way.

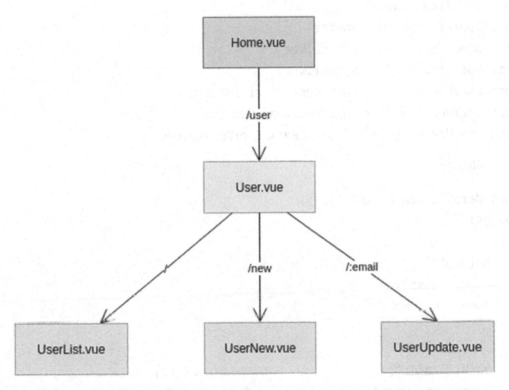

Figure 3-3. *Hierarchical routing flow though the User components using a URL path*

Notice how the components are rendered. As this is a hierarchy, the full path of components from the parent to the child is rendered. In this case, the user component is always rendered and its child is based on the path.

Now, we are going to map this definition using the router plugin for Vue.js in the following section.

Creating a Router Structure: Navigating to New Pages

As we added the router plugin when we created the project, we have a router.js file. We modified it to support our new components. Let's take a look at the code (Listing 3-4).

Listing 3-4. router.js configuration for Router plugin

```
import Vue from 'vue'
import Router from 'vue-router'
import Home from './views/Home.vue'
import User from './views/User.vue'
import UserList from './components/UserList.vue'
import UserNew from './components/UserNew.vue'
import UserUpdate from './components/UserUpdate.vue'

Vue.use(Router)                                    // (1)

export default new Router({
  routes: [
    {
      path: '/',
      name: 'home',
      component: Home
    },
    {
      path: '/user',                               // (2)
      component: User,
      children: [
        {
          path: '/',                               // (3.1)
          name: 'user_list',
          component: UserList
        },
        {
          path: 'new',                             // (3.2)
          name: 'user_new',
          component: UserNew
        },
        {
          path: ':email',                          // (4)
          name: 'user_update',
```

```
      props: (route) => { return { email: route.params.email } },
      component: UserUpdate
    }
  ]
},
{
  path: '/about',
  name: 'about',
  component: () => import(/* webpackChunkName: "about" */ './vicws/
  About.vue')
}
]
})
```

The following is a description of the code sample:

1. First, we add Router as a plugin to our Vue.js application.

2. Now, as we see, we defined a first route, as a root of our User component through the path /user. This means that anytime you link to /user, the User component is going to render.

3. Later, we find the children paths. As they are children from a / user, it means that the full path for routing these components will have /user as the prefix. Let's see in Table 3-2 a full path route configuration.

Table 3-2. *Route paths to access the User creation components. Sometimes one path renders two components.*

Path	Components to Render
/user	User and UserList
/user/new	User and UserNew

75

4. And finally, we have the route for UserUpdate component. This route is special because it requires a param, in this case :email. This means that to access this route, you should have something similar to Table 3-3.

Table 3-3. *Route paths to access the User detail components. Sometimes one path renders two components.*

Path	Components to Render
/user/myemail@email.com	User and UserUpdate
/user/other@email.com	User and UserUpdate
/user/invalidemail	User and UserUpdate

Note   You can see the last example as a wrong email. You shouldn't validate any format in the routes; do it in your component.

And we have the Props configuration:

```
props: (route) => { return { email: route.params.email } }
```

This means we are going to get the param from the URL and send it to our UserUpdate component.

Note   We are going to talk about Props in the following sections.

Now, we just defined how my components are going to route. Next, we will see how to user a router-view to get working on this configuration.

User.vue: Using Router-View for Navigation

As we defined our application routes depending on different paths, we need to define where those components are going to be rendered. The User component is going to handle it as shown in Listing 3-5.

Listing 3-5. HTML template for User component handling the router changes

```
<template>
  <div class="container">
    <h1 class="text-center">Users Management Console</h1>
    <router-view/>
  </div>
</template>
```

There, we only define our module title and router-view. The router-view tag tells Vue.js that part of the template is not defined yet. That part depends on the route you have. Table 3-4 shows an example.

Table 3-4. *Route paths to access the User components for creation and update. Sometimes one path renders two components.*

Path	Components to Render
/user/	UserList
/user/new	UserNew
/user/:email	UserUpdate

Now, the router configuration is ready to link to Vue.js components. In the following sections, you will see UserList, UserNew, and UserUpdate components in detail.

UserList.vue: Using Declarative Rendering, Methods, and Lifecycle Events

Out of the following requirements, the ones marked with * are going to be our focus for this component:

- A user can have an email, name, password, and role *

- The user's role could be ADMIN or USER

- We need to see the whole list of users *

- We need to create a new user

- We need to update an existing user

- We need to remove an existing user *

- The users should persist only for the time the server is up *

Figure 3-4 shows what the UserList.vue component looks like.

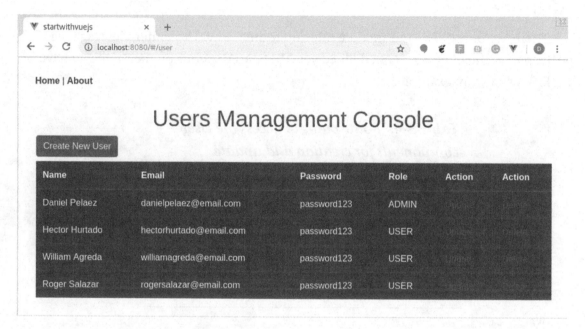

Figure 3-4. *UserList.vue component final view*

Let's discuss it in more detail.

Defining the UserList TypeScript Class

We created the TypeScript component for UserList.ts as follows (Listing 3-6).

Listing 3-6. UserList.ts component

```
<script lang="ts">
import 'bootstrap/dist/css/bootstrap.css'          // (1.1)
import 'bootstrap-vue/dist/bootstrap-vue.css'       // (1.2)
```

```
import { Component, Vue } from 'vue-property-decorator'
import { User } from '../entities/User'

@Component
export default class UserList extends Vue {          // (2)
  users:User[] = []                                  // (3)

  // lifecycle hook
  mounted () {                                        // (6)
    this.getUsers()
  }

  getUsers () {                                       // (4)
    this.users = this.$store.state.users
  }

  remove (userToRemove:User) {                        // (5)
    this.$store.commit('removeUser', userToRemove)
  }
}
</script>
```

The following is a description of the code sample:

1. First, we imported boostrap css to use it in our components. For now, we are going to use boostrap as the default styling.

2. Now, let's define our Vue.js component. @Component tells Vue.js that we want to add this component to your context, and it extends from Vue to get the basic Vue.js component features.

3. As we do in Java, this TypeScript class can have a state and behavior, so, let's discuss them. We created an attribute named users. There, we are going to save the users we are rendering in our table.

4. We added a method named getUsers. It uses Vuex to get the current users' states that we have saved there and assigns them to our users property. $store is the object that handles Vuex and is accessible from any Vue.js component. Remember, we added Vuex to Vue.js to our application in the main.js file.

5. After that, we have the remove method, which receives a User, and it uses Vuex to remove the user from the storage. The commit method in the $store object calls our mutators we defined before in our storage. In this case, we call the removeUser mutator.

6. Finally, we added a lifecycle hook to detect when is the first time Vue.js renders this component. It is named as mounted.

Tip   The mounted hook in Vue.js is like a @PostContruct for EJBs on JEE.

What we do here is call getUsers to initialize our users property when the component is started.

There are more lifecycle hooks like created, updated, and destroy. For more information, you can see `https://vuejs.org/v2/guide/instance.html#Instance-Lifecycle-Hooks`.

Defining the UserList HTML Template

Now, let's use declarative rendering to show our Users list in UserList.ts (Listing 3-7).

Listing 3-7. UserList.ts HTML template

```
<template>
  <div>
    <div class="row">
      <div class="col-sm">
       <router-link to="/user/new" class="btn btn-primary">Create New
       User</router-link>              <!--(1)-->
      </div>
    </div>
    <div class="row mt-2">
      <div class="col-sm">
        <table class="table  table-dark">              <!--(2)-->
          <thead>
            <tr>
              <th>Name</th>
              <th>Email</th>
```

```
      <th>Password</th>
      <th>Role</th>
      <th>Action</th>
      <th>Action</th>
    </tr>
  </thead>
  <tbody>
    <tr v-for="user in users" v-bind:key="user.email">
    <!--(2.a)-->
      <td>{{user.name}}</td>              <!--(2.b)-->
      <td>{{user.email}}</td>
      <td>{{user.password}}</td>
      <td>{{user.role}}</td>
      <td><router-link  :to="{ name: 'user_update', params: {
      email: user.email }}">Update</router-link></td>
      <!--(2.c)  >
      <td><a v-on:click="remove(user)" href="#">Delete</a></td>
                      <!--(2.d)-->
    </tr>
  </tbody>
</table>
</div>
</div>
</div>
</template>
```

The following is a description of the code sample:

1. First, we define a router-link element, which is a Vue.js
    component that renders a link pointing to a specific route. In this
    case, this link points to the /user/new page. We talked about the
    router component in detail in the previous sections.

2. Let's see the declarative rendering part. We are going to render a
    table, one row at a time by the user. There is a lot happening, so
    let's see each step one by one:

a. v-for is a Vue.js directive, and it is like the foreach syntax in Java. You have a user's list and define a variable named user where it saved each element of the list, iterating over it. user's list is our UserList class property. You can access the state and method in your class from the template. v-bind:key is another directive. It is used to differentiate each element from Vue.js by a key. You can find more information at `https://vuejs.org/v2/guide/` list. html#Maintaining-State.

b. That is "Mustache" syntax to access a property and render it. In this case, we access the name of a user and render it in a td tag. For more information about "Mustache" syntax in Vue.js, you can check at `https://vuejs.org/v2/guide/syntax.html`

c. Here, we added a router-link to point to the updated user view. In this case, we send a param named email, with the user's email. How the URL is rendered, is defined in the router configuration with name user_update.

d. And finally, we capture a click event from a link using v-on, to call our remove method in our UserList class. We send the user object that we iterate over the v-for directive. v-on is used to capture any event generated by an HTML component. In this case, we are capturing the click event generated by a User List tag. However, you can capture custom events. We are going to talk about it in the following section.

After defining the UserList component, we should start with the capture of data regarding the users. For this, you will see the UserForm component in the following section.

UserForm.vue: Using Props, Handling User Input, Conditional Rendering, and Emitted Events

Out of the following requirements, the ones marked with * are going to be our focus for this component:

- A user can have an email, name, password, and role *

- The user's role could be ADMIN or USER *

- We need to see the whole list of users

- We need to create a new user *

- We need to update an existing user *

- We need to remove an existing user

- The users should persist only for the time the server is up

Figure 3-5 shows what a UserForm.vue component looks like.

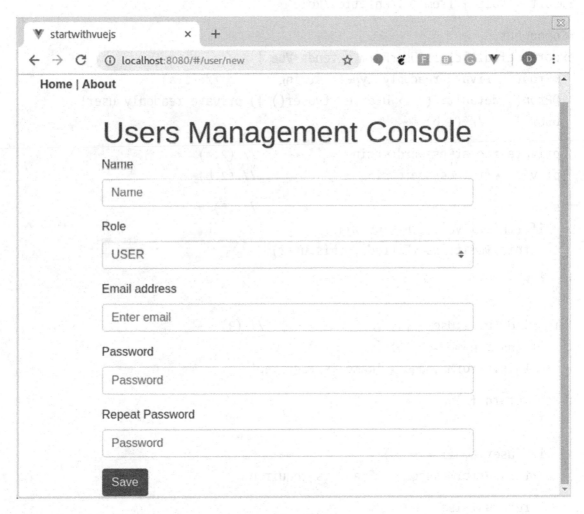

Figure 3-5. *UserForm.vue component final view*

Defining the UserForm.ts TypeScript Class

We created the following component for the UserForm.ts (Listing 3-8).

Listing 3-8. UserForm.ts script

```ts
<script lang="ts">
import { Component, Prop, Vue } from 'vue-property-decorator'
import { User } from '../entities/User'
import { Role } from '../entities/Role'

@Component
export default class UserForm extends Vue {
  @Prop() private readonly type!: string         // (1.a)
  @Prop({ default: () => User.emptyUser() }) private readonly user!:
  User        // (1.b)

  private repeatPassword:string = ''         // (2.a)
  private errorMessage:string = ''           // (2.b)

  save () {                                  // (5)
    if (this.isValid(this.user)) {
      this.$emit('userFilled', this.user)
    }
  }

  isValid (user:User) {                      // (3)
    if (user.name === '') {
      this.errorMessage = 'Name is required'

      return false
    }

    if (user.email === '') {
      this.errorMessage = 'Email is required'

      return false
    }
```

```
    if (user.email === '') {
      this.errorMessage = 'Email is required'

      return false
    }

    if (user.password === '') {
      this.errorMessage = 'Password is required'

      return false
    }

    if (user.password !== this.repeatPassword) {
      this.errorMessage = "Passwords don't match"

      return false
    }

    return true
  }

  get updateMode () {                    // (4)
    return this.type === 'update'
  }
}
</script>
```

The following is a description of the code sample:

1. Here, we declare some attributes in our class as Props:

    In this case, Prop helps parent components to communicate with children and send data. In our User application, we have the following hierarchy as shown in Figure 3-6.

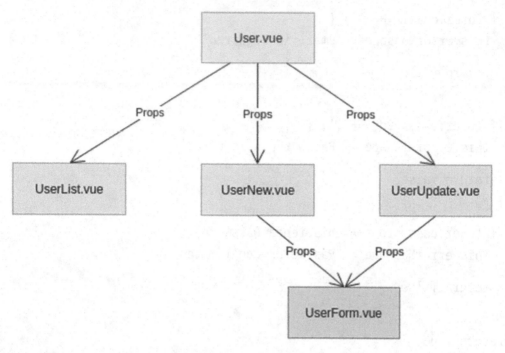

Figure 3-6. *Props flow through the User components, from the root to the leaves of the tree*

This means:

- UserList.vue, UserNew.vue, and UserUpdate.vue are children for User.vue

- UserForm.vue is a child of UserNew.vue and UserUpdate.vue

User type defines the behavior of our UserForm component; in this case, it can be created or update.

User defines a User object we are going to use to populate/update our form. It has a default value of an empty User.

Both are populated by their parent.

Imaging a Prop like a constructor argument in a Java class. The client (parent) who creates the UserForm class needs to send a type and user through its constructor to be able to use a new User object. For more information, you can see `https://vuejs.org/ v2/guide/components-props.html`

Remember, the attributes of our Vue.js components are reactive. It means that type and user attributes are reactive, so if the parent component changes some user's property, UserForm is going to react to that change. The same happens with the type of attribute.

2. Later, we define more of a component's state. There, we save the value of the password where you have another field to validate that it was well typed, and an error message if something wrong happens. Those two attributes are used in the isValid method.

3. This method is used to validate that the data into our User is valid; in this case, its attributes must not be empty, and the two passwords must be the same.

4. Now, we created a get method to know to determine which type of form we want to use.

5. And finally, we create the save method. This first validates if our current User data is valid, and if it is, it emits an event named userFilled, with the user object as data.

Note   If it is not valid, the errorMessage property is filled and the template is going to react to that. We will see this in the following section.

We saw that a Prop helps parents communicate with children, and now an event helps a child communicates with its parent. The events' flow in our application looks like Figure 3-7.

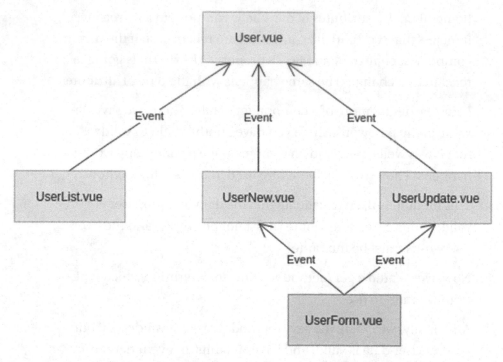

Figure 3-7. *Events flow through the User components, from the leaves to the root*

This means that the UserForm component is only responsible for validating and filling a User object, and its parents (UserNew and UserUpdate components) will be responsible for its persistence.

Note   For more information about events, you can check `https://vuejs.org/v2/guide/components-custom-events.html`.

Defining the UserForm HTML Template

Now, let's use declarative rendering to show our user's form (Listing 3-9).

Listing 3-9. UserForm.ts HTML template

```
<template>
<div>
  <div class="row">
    <div class="col-sm">
```

```
    <div v-if="errorMessage" class="alert alert-danger"
    role="alert">              <!--(1)-->
      {{errorMessage}}
    </div>
  </div>
</div>
<div class="row">
  <div class="col-sm">
    <div class="form-group">
      <label for="name">Name</label>
      <input
        v-model="user.name"
        type="text"
        class="form-control"
        id="name"
        placeholder="Name"
        required
      >
    </div>
    <div class="form-group">
      <label for="role">Role</label>
      <select class="custom-select" id="role" v-model="user.role">
        <option selected value="ADMIN">ADMIN</option>
        <option value="USER">USER</option>
      </select>
    </div>
    <div class="form-group">    <!--(2)-->
      <label for="email">Email address</label>
      <input
        v-model="user.email"
        type="email"
        class="form-control"
        id="email"
        aria-describedby="emailHelp"
```

```
          placeholder="Enter email"
          :readonly="updateMode"
          required
        >
      </div>
      <div class="form-group">
        <label for="password">Password</label>
        <input
          v-model="user.password"
          type="password"
          class="form-control"
          id="password"
          placeholder="Password"
          required
        >
      </div>
      <div class="form-group">        <!--(3)-->
        <label for="password">Repeat Password</label>
        <input
          v-model="repeatPassword"
          type="password"
          class="form-control"
          id="repeatPassword"
          placeholder="Password"
          required
        >
      </div>
      <button class="btn btn-primary" v-on:click="save">{{updateMode ?
      'Update' : 'Save'}}</button>    <!--(4)-->
    </div>
  </div>
</div>
</template>
```

The following is a description of the code sample:

1. First, we have some conditional rendering. v-if validates whether there is any errorMessage. If there is any, this div tag is going to render; otherwise it won't. For conditional rendering, we have v-show too. The difference between v-show and v-if is that v-if removes the element from the DOM, then meanwhile, v-show only hides it through CSS. For more information, you can check `https://vuejs.org/v2/guide/conditional.html`. The errorMessage looks like what is shown in Figure 3-8.

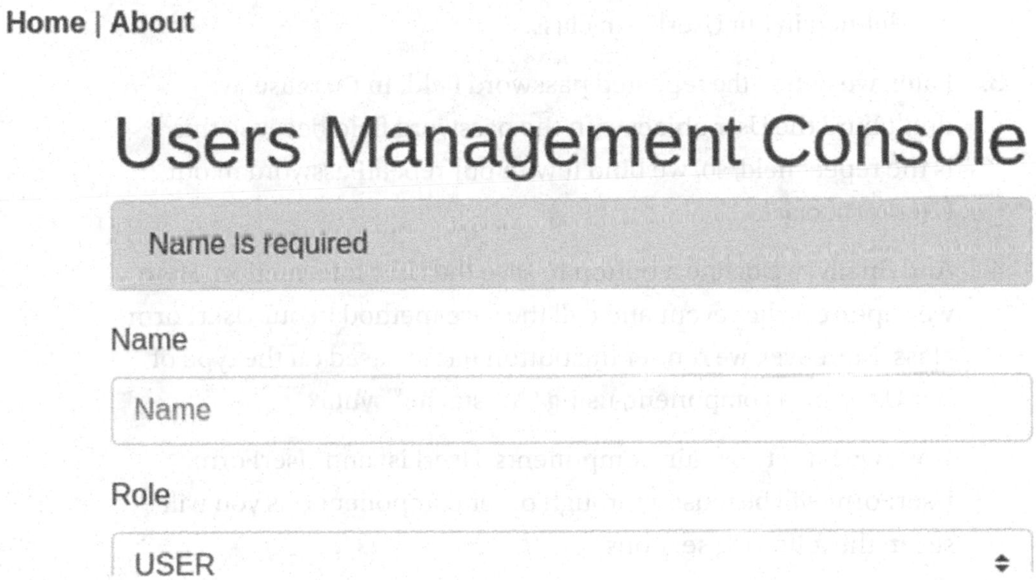

Home | About

Users Management Console

Name is required

Name

```
Name
```

Role

```
USER                                              ⬍
```

Figure 3-8. Error message format for the User Management Console

2. Now we created the form for our user. Let's focus on the interesting input fields. Email address input gets its initial value from user.email, and when you change the input value in your browser, the same field is going to change. This is named Input Binding. You are connecting a User property with your input, and that property is going to react to changes.

> **Tip**   For more information about Input Binding, you can check at `https://vuejs.org/v2/guide/forms.html`.

Now, let's see some interesting way to pass attributes to an HTML element:

- **id="email":** this is the normal way, the static way; nothing weird happens here.

- **:readonly="updateMode":** This is a dynamic way. Here, the readonly value is defined from the updateMode get method we defined in our UserForm class.

3. Later, we define the repeated password field. In this case, we don't bind the User object with the password field because this is the repeat field, so, we bind it with our repeatPassword in our UserForm class.

4. And finally, we define a button to save the User information. Here we capture a click event and call the save method in our UserForm class. Moreover, we render the button name based on the type of our UserForm component, using "Mustache" syntax.

Now, we have two main components, UserList and UserForm. UserForm will be reused through other components, as you will see in the following sections.

UserNew.vue: Reusing the UserForm Component and Router Redirection

Out of the following requirements, the ones marked with * are going to be our focus for this component:

- A user can have an email, name, password, and role

- The user's role could be ADMIN or USER

- We need to see the whole list of users

- We need to create a new user *

- We need to update an existing user

- We need to remove an existing user

- The users should persist only for the time the server is up *

Figure 3-9 shows what the UserNew.vue component looks like.

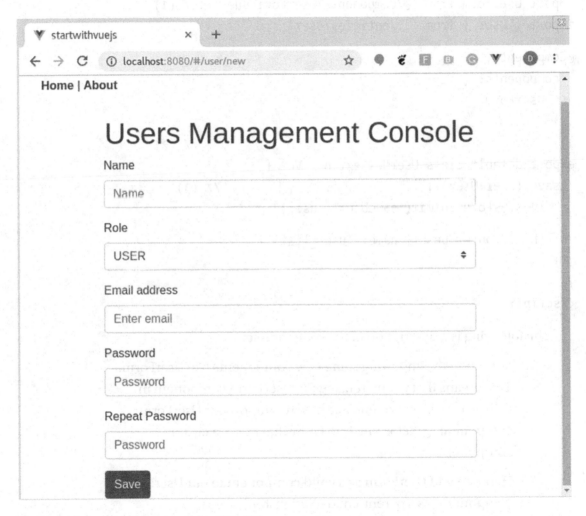

Figure 3-9. *Final view of the UserNew.vue component*

Defining the UserNew TypeScript Class

We created the following TypeScript component in the UserNew.ts (Listing 3-10).

Listing 3-10. UserNew.ts script

```ts
<script lang="ts">
import { Component, Vue } from 'vue-property-decorator'
import UserForm from '@/components/UserForm.vue'    // (1)
import { User } from '../entities/User'

@Component({
  components: {
    UserForm
  }
})                                                  // (2)
export default class UserNew extends Vue {
  save (user:User) {                                // (3)
    this.$store.commit('saveUser', user)

    this.$router.push({ name: 'user_list' })
  }
}
</script>
```

The following is a description of the code sample:

1. We started by importing some new components like UserForm. This means that we are reusing the UserForm component in the UserNew component. See how we import our UserForm component. @ helps Vue.js to know that this is a custom component.

2. Here, we add UserForm as a child component to our UserNew component (as a parent-child relationship).

3. And finally, we create a save method: Here, we use the $store object to call the saveUser mutator, with the User object we want to save. Later, we use $router object to push a new URL, in

this case, we call the route defined with the name user_list. The behavior will be that after adding a new user, you are going to redirect to the UserList component.

Note   This is named Programmatic Navigation. You can find more information at `https://router.vuejs.org/guide/essentials/navigation.html`.

Defining the UserNew HTML Template

Now, let's see what our UserNew component looks like; see Listing 3-11.

Listing 3-11. UserNew.ts HTML template

```
<template>
  <div>
    <UserForm v-on:userFilled="save($event)"></UserForm>
  </div>
</template>
```

Here, we use our UserForm component. See how our custom component is a normal tag in our HTML template.

Remember, we defined Props for the UserForm component (type and user). As we don't send any of those Props here, it means that UserForm is going to behave as default, with type = create and an empty user.

Moreover, we capture an event, in this case a userFilled event. When this event is emitted from UserForm component, UserNew component reacts calling the save method. $event has User information.

UserUpdate.vue: Reusing UserForm Component with Props and Router Redirection

Out of the following requirements, the ones marked with * are going to be our focus for this component:

- A user can have an email, name, password, and role
- The user's role could be ADMIN or USER

- We need to see the whole list of users

- We need to create a new user

- We need to update an existing user *

- We need to remove an existing user

- The users should persist only for the time the server is up *

Figure 3-10 shows what the UserUpdate.vue looks like.

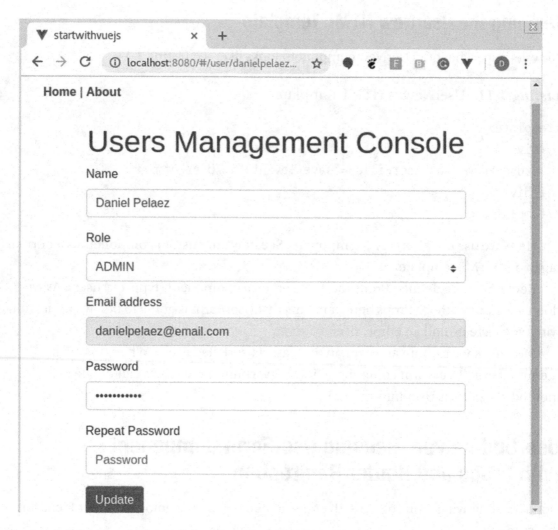

Figure 3-10. *Final view of the UserUpdate.vue component*

Let's see the UserUpdate.vue component in detail.

Defining the UserUpdate.ts TypeScript Class

We created the following TypeScript component in the UserUpdate.ts (Listing 3-12).

Listing 3-12. UserUpdate.ts script

```ts
<script lang="ts">
import { Component, Prop, Vue } from 'vue-property-decorator'
import UserForm from '@/components/UserForm.vue'
import { User } from '../entities/User'

@Component({
  components: {
    UserForm
  }
})                                          // (1)
export default class UserUpdate extends Vue {
  @Prop() private readonly email!: string       // (2)

  private user:User = User.emptyUser()          // (3.1)
  private type:string = 'update'                // (3.2)

  mounted () {                                   // (6)
    this.getUser(this.email)
  }

  getUser (email:string) {                       // (4)
    let userToUpdate:User = this.$store.getters.getUserByEmail(email)

    this.user.copyUser(userToUpdate)
  }

  update (user:User) {                           // (5)
    this.$store.commit('updateUser', user)

    this.$router.push({ name: 'user_list' })
  }
}
</script>
```

The following is a description of the code sample:

1. Here, we define our UserUpdate class: the UserUpdate component uses the UserForm component too.

2. Later, we defined a Prop for the email. This Prop is set by our route. Remember, we defined a route /user/:email for the UserUpdate component, and there we set a Prop for the email variable.

3. Now, we define some state. There, we define an empty User and the type as update. We are going to send those values to our UserForm component.

4. Later, we query the user we want to update. Here, based on the email, we call a getter named getUserByEmail from the $store object, sending the email. It responds to us with a User matching that email. After that, we copy the found User to our component User, using the copyUser method. This step is very important. Remember that Vue.js is reactive. So, if you send the same User object you found in the $store to our UserForm component, any changes you make in your inputs are going to be reflected immediately in the $store because the object is the same. This is not the expected behavior for our use cases. We expect you to click the update button before updating the User information.

5. The following method helps us to update the User information. There we use the $store object to commit a change named updateUser, and we send the User data. After that, we use $router to redirect to the user_list route. The behavior will be that after you update a User, you will see the UserList component.

6. And finally, we add a lifecycle hook. This helps us to get the User we want to update when the UserUpdate component is rendered. We defined the UserUpdate route with an email param.

Tip   We can get that email here using $route.params.email too if you don't use Props and routes to inject it.

Defining the UserUpdate HTML Template

Now, let's see what our UserUpdate component looks like in Listing 3-13.

Listing 3-13. UserUpdate.ts template

```
<template>
  <div>
    <UserForm v-on:userFilled="update($event)"
              :user="user"
              :type="type">
    </UserForm>
  </div>
</template>
```

Here, we use our UserForm component. See how our custom component is a normal tag in our HTML template. Unlike the UserNew component, we send some Props to the UserForm component.

First we send the type; in this case, it is an update. Second, we send the User object to update.

Note   Remember, adding two points (:) at the beginning of an attribute allows you to calculate the value dynamically.

Moreover, we capture an event: in this case, userFilled event. When this event is emitted from the UserForm component, the UserUpdate component reacts by calling the update method - that $event has User information.

Now we are ready with a full Vue.js application.

The Final User Management Application

Finally, we have our full User Management CRUD ready for us.

1. First, we can find the User CRUD button on the home page of our application (Figure 3-11).

Figure 3-11.   *Final view of the home page of User Management Console*

2. After clicking on the User CRUD button, we are redirected to the
    Users list page (Figure 3-12).

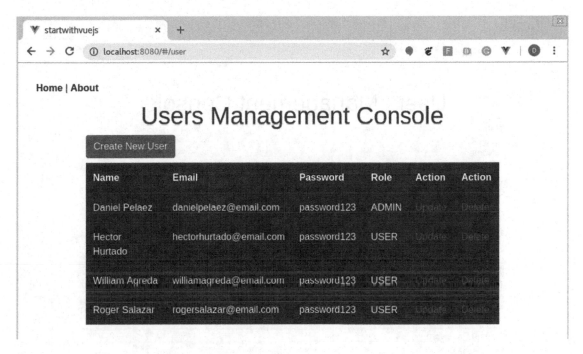

Figure 3-12. *List of created Users in the Users Management Console*

3. Now, let's create a new User clicking on Create New User. We will
    see the User form as shown in Figure 3-13.

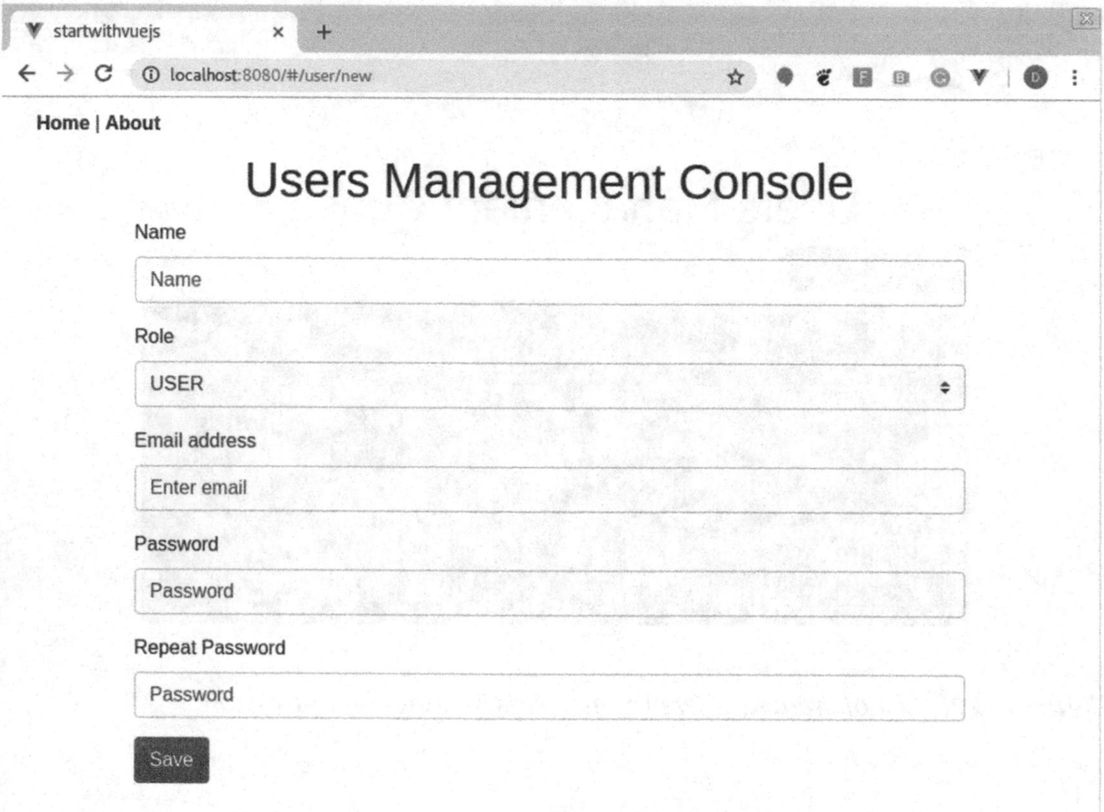

Figure 3-13. *User form in the Users Management Console*

4. Let's fill those fields with some mock data (Figure 3-14).

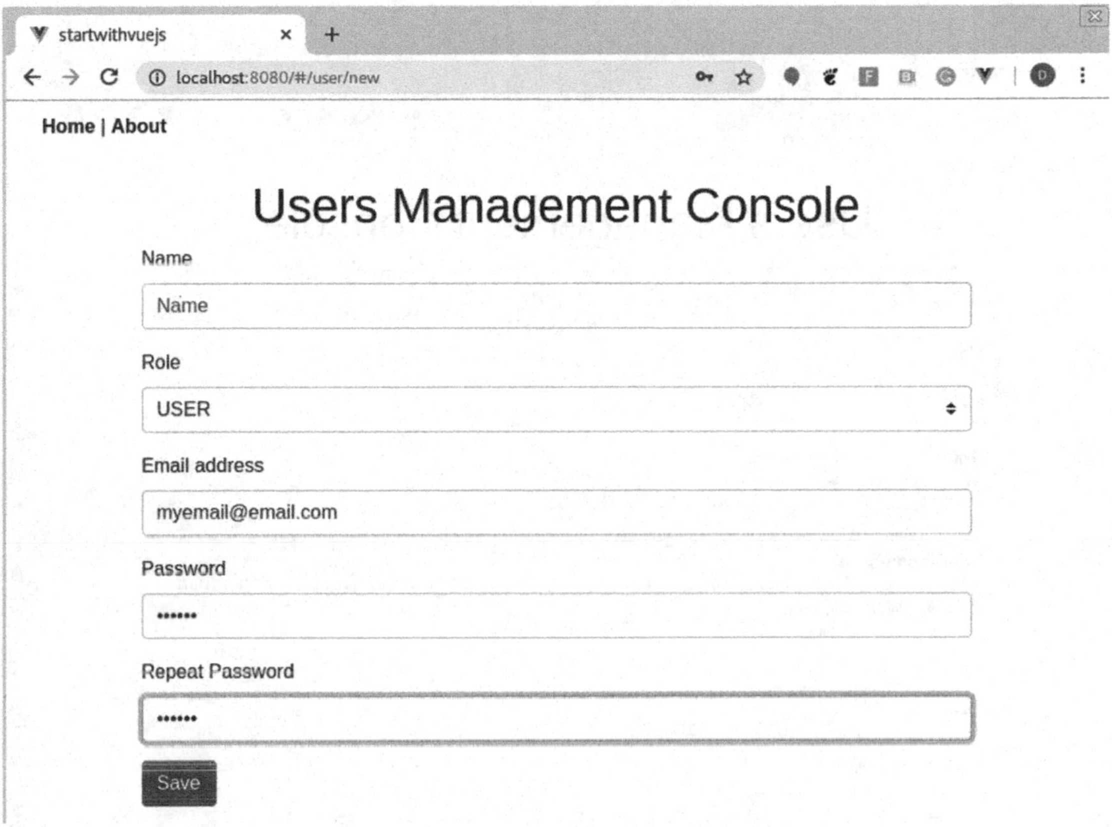

Figure 3-14. *User filled form in the Users Management Console*

5. We missed the name. If we try to save the User, we get a message as shown in Figure 3-15.

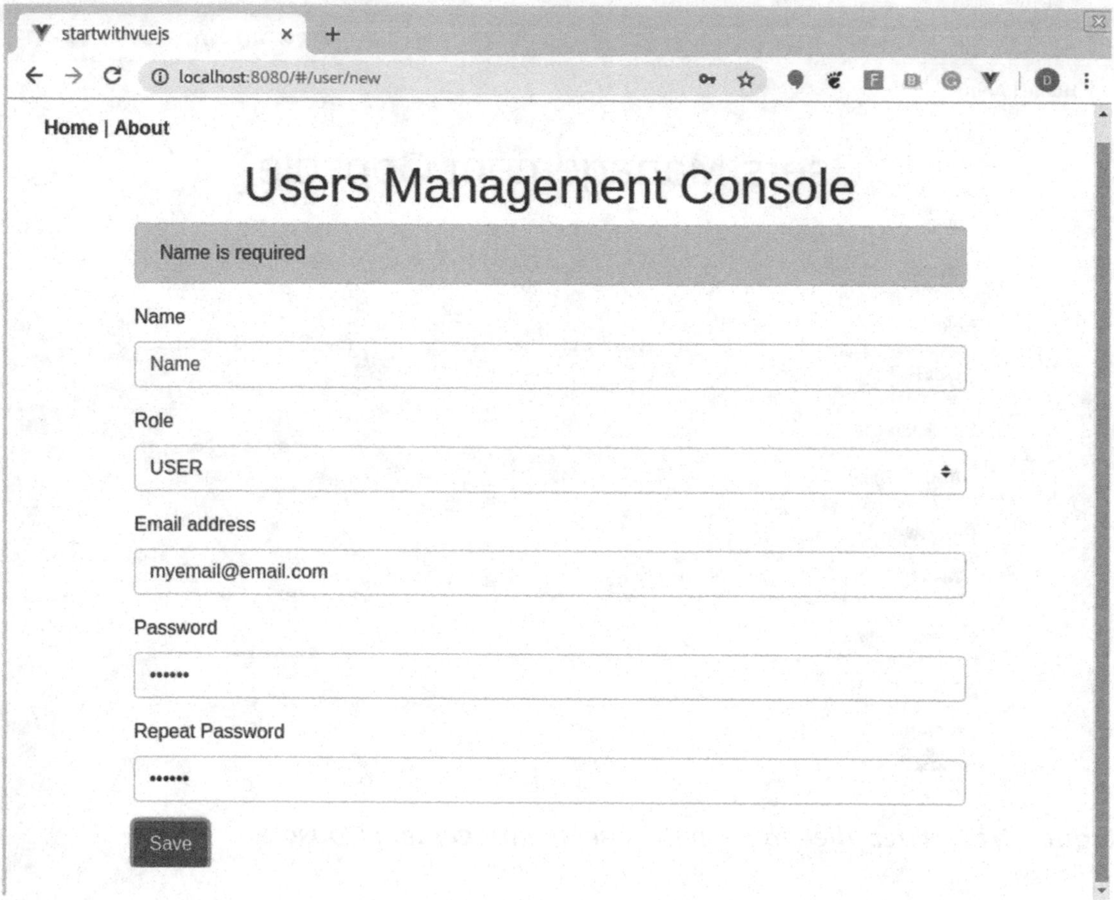

Figure 3-15. User form error message in the Users Management Console

6. Let's fill in the name and click on Save the User. We will be
    redirected to the User list, and we find the new User there
    (Figure 3-16).

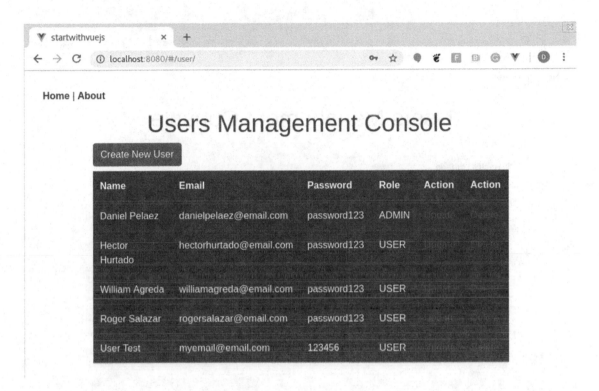

Figure 3-16. *New User added to the Users list in the Users Management Console*

7. Now, let's update the Hector Hurtado user. Click on the Update button, which will bring the following screen (Figure 3-17).

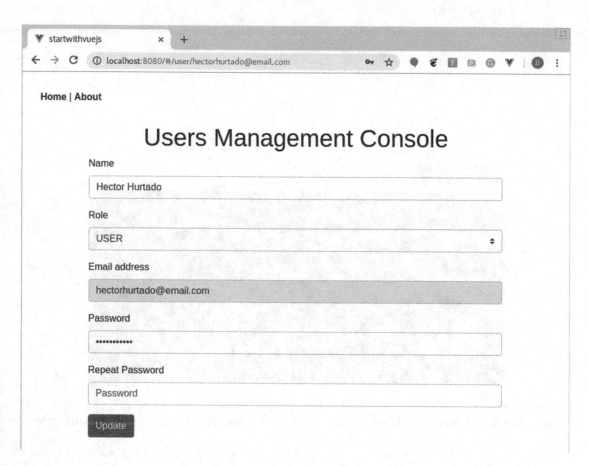

Figure 3-17. *Updating a User in the Users Management Console*

8.   Change the name and click on Update (Figure 3-18).

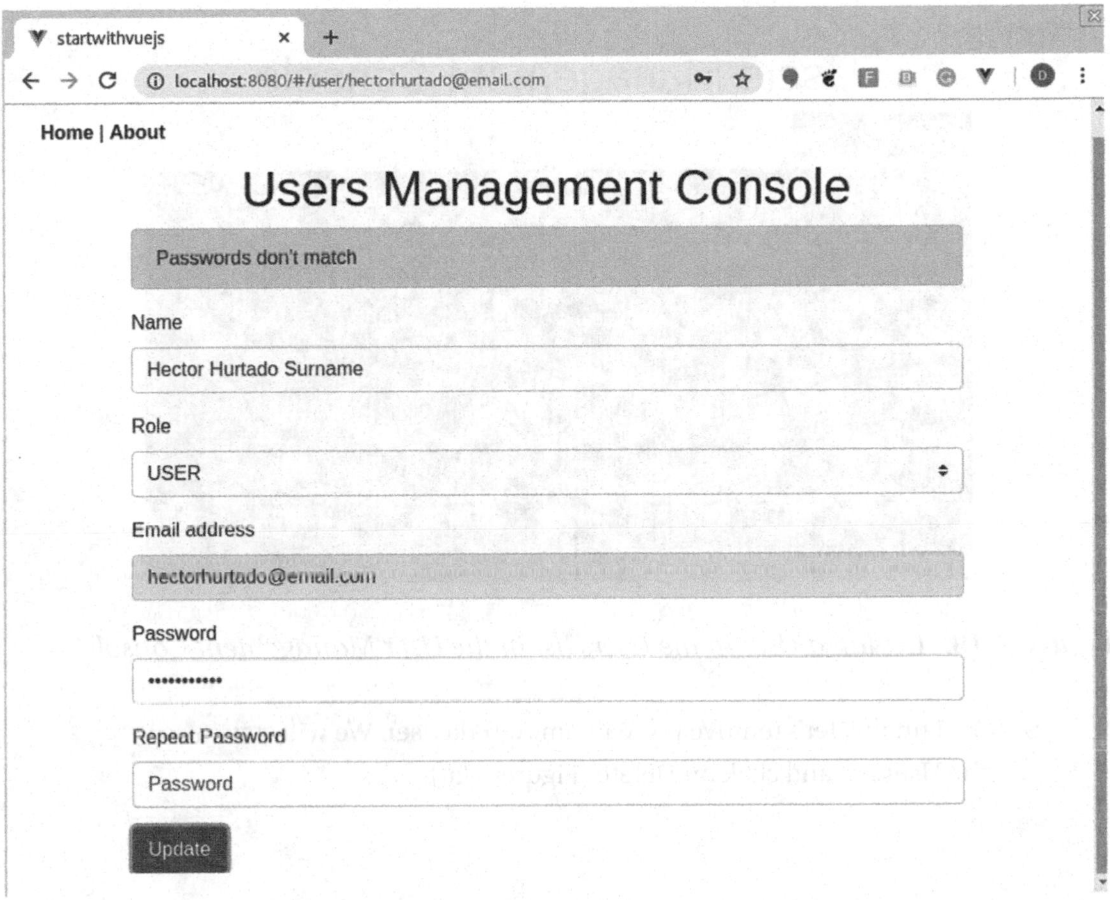

Figure 3-18. *Passwords not matching error in the Users Management Console*

We need to set the password to update a User. So, we do that and we update the User. We will redirect to the User list and there we can see the Hector Hurtado name updated (Figure 3-19).

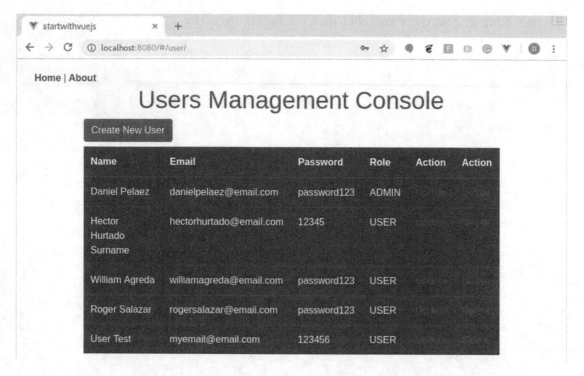

Figure 3-19. *Updated User in the Users list in the User Management Console*

9. And finally, let's remove the William Agreda user. We will stay in
    the User list and click on Delete (Figure 3-20).

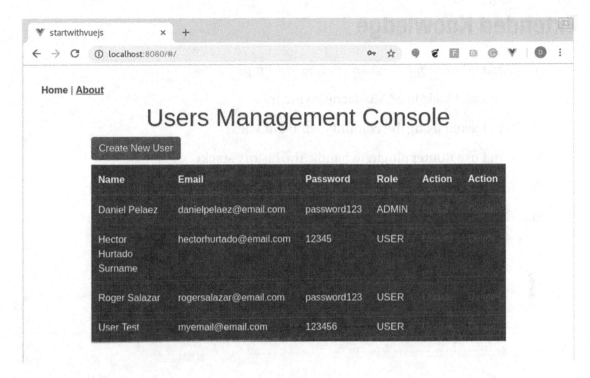

Figure 3-20. *Updated User in the Users list in the User Management Console*

And there it is, our full User Management CRUD.

Summary

Creating an application with Vue.js is pretty straightforward. In this chapter, we just talked about the basic features you need to understand to start a Vue.js application like Props, Methods, Classes, Templates, and Components. We moved forward adding some routers, events, and state management with Vuex. And finally, we created forms to handle data, in a full CRUD application. Now, you have the skills needed to create a full CRUD application using Vue.js.

In the next chapter, we are going to learn how to analyze and design a full-stack application.

Extended Knowledge

1. What other properties can I define in a Prop?

2. Can I add logic in a "Mustache" syntax?

3. Can I avoid using the commit method in Vuex?

4. Can I use Router plugin to handle the history stack?

5. Are the events emitted flowing through the whole hierarchy?

6. Can I send Props through a router-view tag?

## CHAPTER 4

Requirement Analysis for Your Full-Stack Web Application

In this chapter, we are going to talk about requirement analysis: how to understand and write what the client wants, while thinking in an iterative and incremental way. Remember, software development is a challenging task, and clients do not usually know what they actually want.

We are going to define and analyze a business named Daniel's Delivery, a company that enables connecting Food Services with its customers using the Daniel's Delivery web page.

After this chapter, you will be able to create high-level requirements, split them in stories in an incremental and valuable way, and finally, figure out some quality attributes like responsiveness and latency.

The following topics will be covered in this chapter:

- Understanding the current state of Daniel's Delivery company

- Proposing a solution for the current problems of Daniel's Delivery Company

- Writing high-level requirements and estimating them

- Writing stories in an iterative and incremental way

- Finding quality attributes and creating scenarios for testing

© Daniel Andres Pelaez Lopez 2021
D. A. P. Lopez, *Full-Stack Web Development with Jakarta EE and Vue.js*,
https://doi.org/10.1007/978-1-4842-6342-6_4

Daniel's Delivery

Daniel's Delivery is a start-up company with a focus on food delivery. It connects restaurants with customers, allowing them to see a variety of restaurants and its products, in only one place.

Today, on the Daniel's Delivery web page, you can find restaurants and its products. Those products have detailed information about ingredients, combos, and so on. For the restaurants, you can find detailed descriptions and contact information such as email, phone number, and address.

Daniel's Delivery board has noticed a huge opportunity. The company currently handles 20 restaurants and 500 customers in only one city, but they think they can expand to a much larger community across multiple cities and countries. In 2 years, they estimate to be in 8 main cities in its current country with nearly 500,000 customers; and in the next 3 years to be in 2 more nearby countries (in at least 1 major city), with a total of nearly 1 million customers.

However, to reach that goal, they think the Daniel's Delivery website needs to improve. So, they want to add more value to their customers, allowing them to request food directly in the web page, knowing which restaurants are good and ranking them, time of delivery, and online payments.

Moreover, they are concerned about how Daniel's Delivery's website could support those new requirements. So, they hire us to propose a solution.

Technical Details about Daniel's Delivery Web Page

Daniel's Delivery web page was built fast and its time to market was short. So, they made the following architectural choices:

- JSP as a web page rendering

- Custom CSS layout

- Java EE 5 using JDBC directly

- Glassfish as an application server

- MySQL database

- On-premise infrastructure

Moreover, they are concerned about the general maintenance and evolution costs over the last few years. Let's talk about each one in detail.

JSP as a Web Page Rendering

The full web application is built over JSP, mixing with Java code to generate HTML. Figure 4-1 shows where the JSP and HTML components are and how the final user (in this case, the browser) interacts with them.

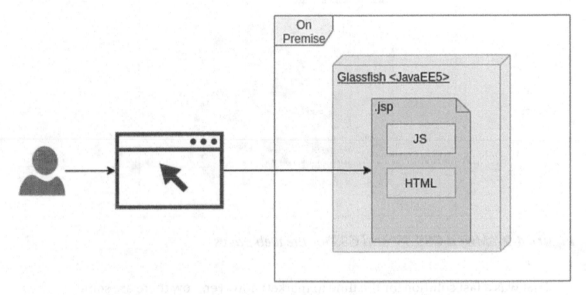

Figure 4-1. *JSP as a main web page rendering in the server side*

This approach carries a lot of troubles:

- The view logic and the rendering are mixed in the JSP.

- There is not a way to maintain only the HTML and CSS code. It means a developer needs to know Java too.

- The performance for light pages is not good. It is all server-side render. It is difficult to create responsive web pages.

- There is some JavaScript logic to do validations and some custom server-side communication. That is plain JavaScript, so some parts fail in some browsers.

Custom CSS Layout

The CSS definitions are mixed in .css files with the same HTML in the JSP pages, as shown in Figure 4-2.

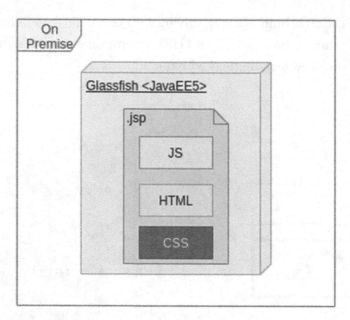

Figure 4-2. *Mixed CSS, JS, and CSS for the web pages*

That was a fast solution for the time to market; however, now there are some problems:

- There is a lot of styling out of the .css files, which means there is not a central point where you can find the whole styling.

- You cannot reuse a lot of styles, because they are in the same HTML definition. It is pretty difficult to have different themes based on the user type.

- There is no support for multiple browsers. This is working only on IE 9.

Java EE 5 Using JDBC Directly

Java EE 5 was the stable version at that time when the Daniel's Delivery website was created. The architects chose it due to its great support and new practices such as Dependency Injection. However, they chose to connect directly to the database using JDBC. Moreover, they used JSP as a server-side HTML rendering, as shown in Figure 4-3.

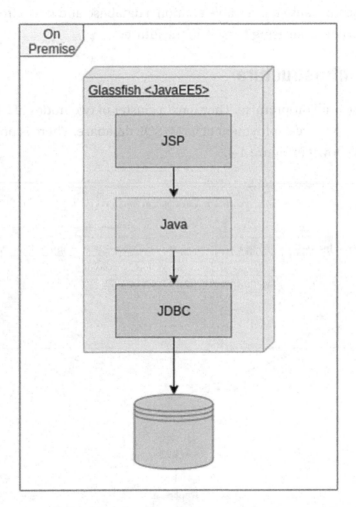

Figure 4-3. *Direct access to the database using JDBC*

For the business, it is pretty important to continue using Java EE; however, using JDBC directly is slowing down the development process, as they need to manage the low-level details for database connection.

GlassFish as an Application Server

GlassFish was chosen since it is the default Java EE server and it is free. The business wants to continue using GlassFish in the future.

MySQL Database

MySQL was chosen because it is a stable relational database and it was free. The business wants to continue using MySQL in the future.

On-Premise Infrastructure

The infrastructure is all on-premise. They have a cluster of two nodes of GlassFish servers and active-passive deployment of its MySQL database. There is no disaster recovery plan, as shown in Figure 4-4.

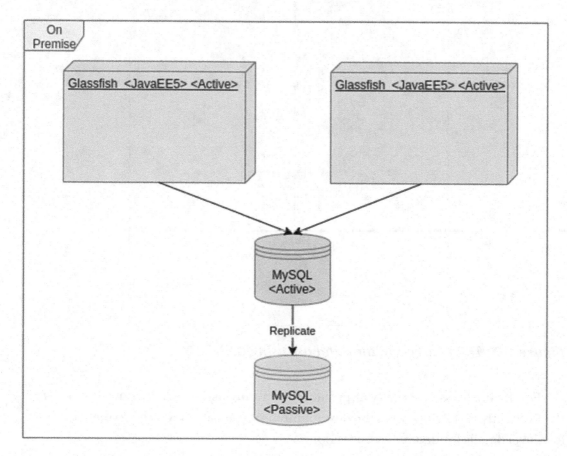

Figure 4-4. *GlassFish cluster on-premise*

Moreover, last month the business got some complaints about the web page's performance. This is more evident at dinner or lunch times and on rainy days, when there is a peak on the users using the web page, as everybody wants to get a delivery.

As we know the current state from the technology point of view, we are going to move to the business side, teams, and costs.

Analyzing the Current Team and Costs

The business is pretty concerned about the high costs the technology area is carrying over the last three years. Let's have a look at some comparison data.

Team vs. Time

Figure 4-5 shows how the technology team has grown throughout the months.

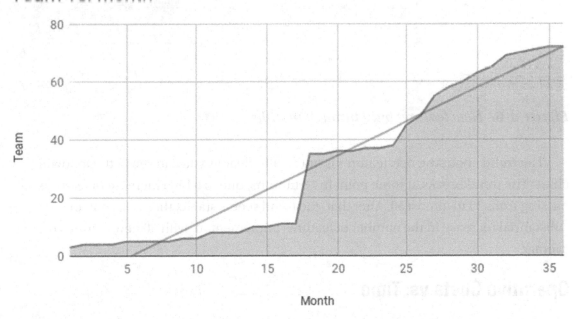

Figure 4-5. *Technology team growth through the months and trend*

Now it is clear that we have a trend here about the team: the team has grown a lot from the beginning. And now the trend is that we are going to continue growing. This takes into account the whole technology area.

117

New Features vs. Time

Figure 4-6 shows how the new number of features has been implemented over the months.

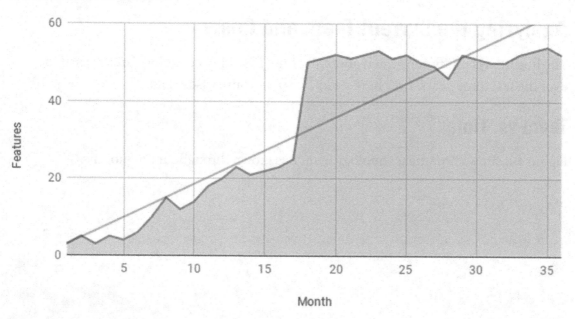

Figure 4-6. *New features built through months*

The trend about the new features is not totally clear as you can see in the following chart. The trend breaks at some point in 18 months, due to a high increase of features passing from 25 to almost 50. After that, the trend seems stable; there was not any substantial increase in the number of features implemented, with 50 new features on average.

Operative Costs vs. Time

Figure 4-7 shows how the operative costs behave over time.

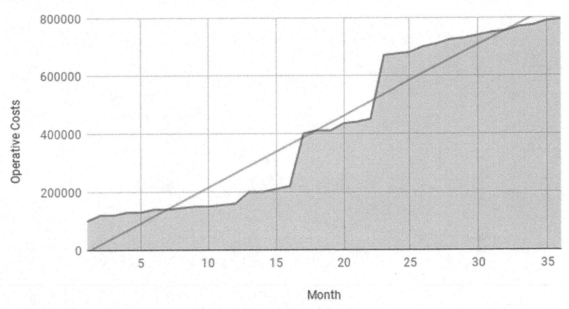

Figure 4-7. *Operative costs through months*

We can see a clear trend about the operative costs here. This means that over time, the operative costs of the technology area have increased a lot, almost 8 times out of the initial amount in 35 months.

Analysis of the Current Situation

Now we are going to analyze the behavior of the team and the features implemented through time, as shown in Figure 4-8.

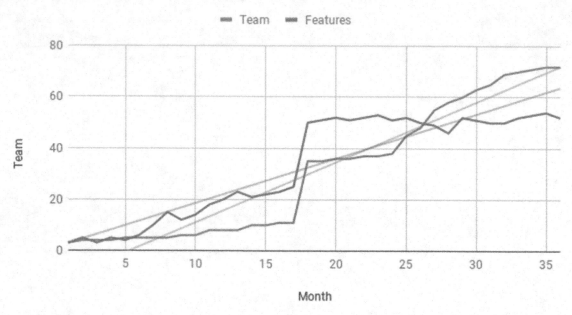

Figure 4-8. *Team and new features through months*

This means that before the 25th month, any time we increased the team capacity, the team implemented more new features. However, after the 25th month, the trend changed. In spite of adding new team members, the number of new features implemented continues to be stable; there is no added value.

Moreover, this moves us to see the behavior of the new features and the operational costs of the technology area through time (Figure 4-9).

Features and Operative Costs

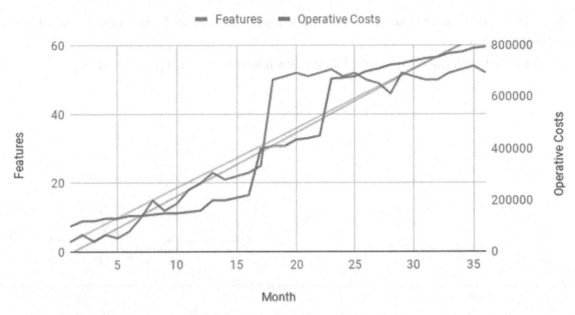

Figure 4-9. *Features and operative costs through months*

This is pretty interesting. In the first 15 months, the new features were implemented and the operative costs were balanced; that means a great trade-off between new features and operative costs. Between the 15th and 23rd months, the company invested in this technology area, gaining a pretty good increase of new features implemented. However, after the 23rd month, the company invested again, but the number of new features implemented continued to be stable. So it seems like the investment didn't help, and now they are paying more for the same added value.

The trend now moves the company to invest more in something that is not adding new value. The current chief technology officer (CTO) is concerned about this analysis. So the business hires us to give them an assessment and a solution for these troubles. We are going to discuss that in the next section.

A Proposal for the New Daniel's Delivery

The current CTO asked us to create a proposal about a new Daniel's Delivery application that will handle the whole new drive of the business. We are going to start analyzing the current state and later we will propose a new architecture.

Possible Causes of the Current Situation

We are now going to analyze the causes of the trends as to what the business found in its technology area.

Let's start with the current trend about new features vs. team (Figure 4-10).

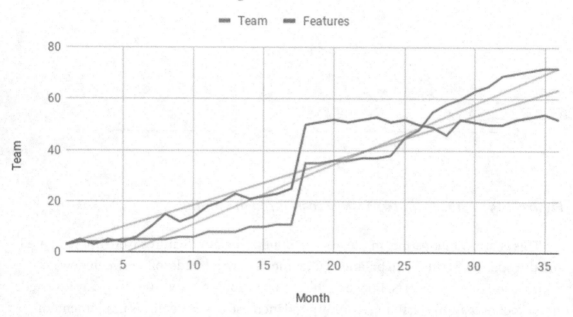

Figure 4-10. Team growth and new features through months

It is not normal to need more people to maintain the technology area. The cause could be an architecture that doesn't fit the business needs, which is difficult to extend and fix.

Figure 4-11 shows how a maintainable system with good architecture definitions behaves.

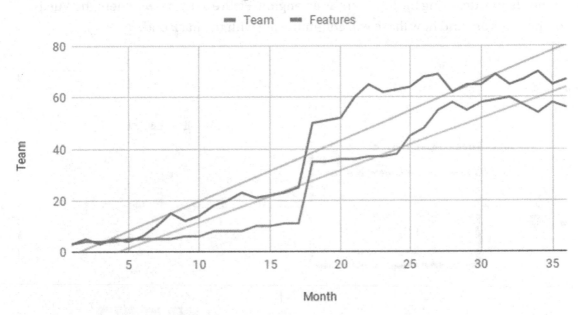

Team and Features Through Time

Figure 4-11. *Team growth and new features through months in a maintainable system*

As we can see, the team can grow, but the new features must grow with them. The chart is stable through time. This means our system needs to be refactored to a more maintainable technology and architecture, modern and stable. We are going to define it in the following sections.

Defining a New Architecture

In the following sections, we are going to define the new architecture step by step, moving from where Daniel's Delivery is today, to the ideal architecture based on its business drivers.

Vue.js as a Front-End Progressive Framework

Well, the current system uses JSP, mixing logic with HTML and CSS to render the page. Moreover, the render is done on the server side, and if we have a high level of transactions, our servers could break.

Vue.js is a single page application framework. That means the application is built on the client side, using the browsers as an engine. Figure 4-12 shows where the Vue.js components are and how those will communicate with the back end.

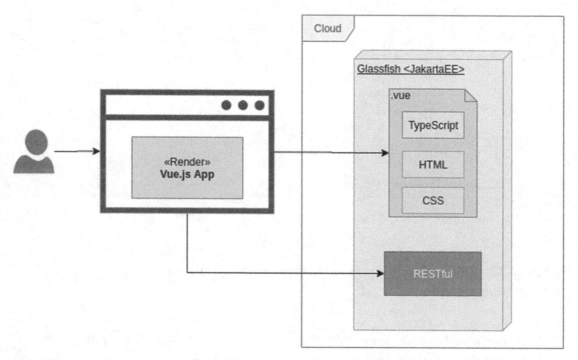

Figure 4-12. *Vue.js as a UI framework using RESTful services*

Vue.js is going to help us separate concerns. It only focuses on front-end rendering. It binds well with TypeScript, HTML, and CSS. Moreover, we let the server only serve the HTML and TypeScript files, but the browser is going to render the page, releasing the server of that responsibility.

Vue.js is progressive, which means we can build an application, component by component, isolated one by other, encapsulated with specific features and finally reusing them through the whole application.

Now, as Vue.js is a single page application framework, we are going to need to expose some services to be consumed by this application. In our case, we will expose some RESTful services. We are going to discuss more about those RESTful services in the following section.

Jakarta EE: Our New Back-End Framework

We currently use Java EE 5 with a GlassFish application server. As our business wants to continue working with it, we are going to upgrade to Jakarta EE.

Now, we are using JDBC to connect directly to our database. The performance of this solution is pretty good; however, maintaining it is hard. The SQL is around everywhere, and there are no business objects clearly defined through the whole application. So, we will move to use JPA as an Object Relationship Mapping framework as shown in Figure 4-13.

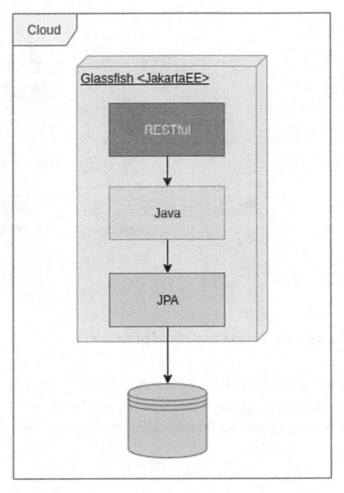

Figure 4-13. *RESTful services using JPA to access the database*

We are going to use RESTful services to expose our logic to the front-end application.

As we have some business constraints regarding the GlassFish application server and MySQL database, we will upgrade those to the latest version.

AWS as an Infrastructure Provider

We identified that the whole infrastructure is on-premise. Maintaining it is costly and hard. Moreover, there is not a disaster recovery plan. We suggest moving the operation to a cloud provider; in this case, we choose AWS, as shown in Figure 4-14.

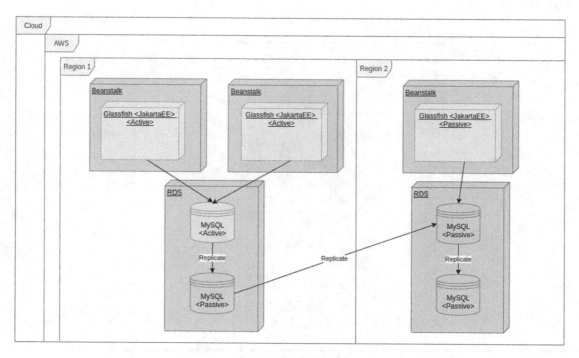

Figure 4-14. *AWS as an infrastructure cloud provider*

Now, we are going to use AWS Elastic Beanstalk as a server. This is a service that quickly allows starting our infrastructure based on application servers such as GlassFish.

Moreover, that is going to manage for the scaling, nodes, resources, and so on, saving us money and time.

The MySQL database is going to be moved to the AWS RDS (Relational Database Service). We defined a passive replica. The copy is handled by RDS itself; we do not need to have a manual process there.

For disaster recovery, we plan in the future to move a copy of the infrastructure to another AWS region. In the case Zone 1 is down, so Zone 2 will start and receive all of the traffic.

With the AWS infrastructure, we are going to save costs in maintenance. Moreover, we can adjust our infrastructure based on the scalability requirements, adding or removing resources as we need them.

Now, we have a complete vision of what our new Daniel's Delivery architecture should look like. Next, we are going to apply an agile approach to define the new Daniel's Delivery requirements.

An Agile Approach for the New Daniel's Delivery

Agile methodologies have been in the market for a long time: from XP to Scrum, they have been used by a lot of organizations around the world.

Note   For more information about Agile, I suggest checking first the Agile Manifesto at `https://agilemanifesto.org/`. Later, you can check the details regarding some implementations such as Scrum (`https://www.scrum.org/resources/what-is-scrum`) and XP (`http://www.extremeprogramming.org/`).

We are going to use some concepts of agile development to define the development process for the new Daniel's Delivery application.

We are going to start with high-level features, named epics. After that we are going to choose the first delivery with some stories, and finally we are going to add some quality attributes to build our solution.

Defining High-Level Features: Epics

An epic is a high-level feature, difficult to estimate, implement, and deliver due to its size. Those are the more generic wishes from the business perspective. Analyzing the expected requirements by the business, we found the following high-level features:

- Delivery flow: The delivery flow epic will handle the whole flow related to the customer's interaction to our application. This will have a user's preferences, user's addresses, Food Services searching, choosing food products and requesting its delivery, showing closest Food Services, rates of the service, and waiting time.

- Food Services management: The Food Services epic will handle the whole administration of the Food Services, like its basic data, the food they offer, prices, and promotions.

- Online payments: The online payments epic will handle the whole process to allow the customer to pay online directly through our web page. It has different payments types like credit cart and handling promotion codes.

- Security: The security epic will handle anything related to security, from log in to services authorization.

- Cloud infrastructure: The cloud infrastructure epic will handle anything related to the delivery and production infrastructure in the AWS cloud, from AWS Beanstalk to a disaster recovery strategy.

Note   We are going to define a customer as any client who wants to request a delivery and Food Services or any restaurant or similar place that wants to offer its products in our application.

Schedule the Plan

The business knows that doing everything at the same time is difficult. So they have the following schedule in mind for delivering the first version of the new Daniel's Delivery application, as shown in Figure 4-15.

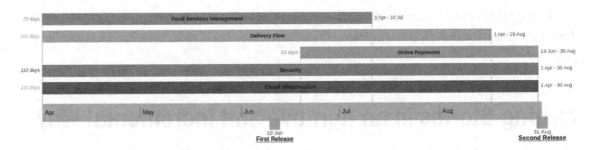

Figure 4-15. *High-level schedule plan*

This estimation was done based on the experiences of the architects, and the business is aware that this could go wrong in the time being. The business understands what an agile project means and expects to see a great job.

The business expects to deliver a first functional version in two months. They understand that it is not possible to have everything they want right now, so they expect us to give them the features that are going to be included in this release.

As we can see, the initial plan is to have two releases for five months. For the purposes of this book, we are going to focus on the first release only, as seen in Figure 4-16.

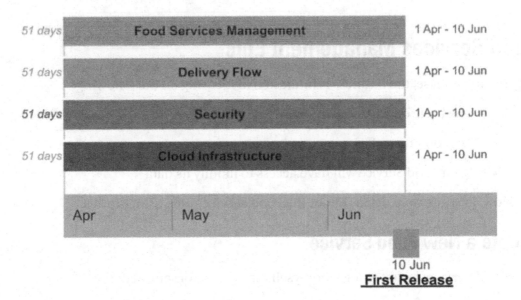

Figure 4-16. *First release plan*

The business made the decision of avoiding the online payment for the first release. Based on this schedule, we are going to build stories by each epic, bounded to the first release.

Writing Stories in an Iterative and Incremental Way

Stories define what the system should do. This is the functional requirements side of our application: what the business needs to see to accept our product. This is the more obvious outcome of the software development process.

We are going to focus on the Food Service management and delivery flow epics, defining stories to build for the first release.

Note   We are not going to use any specific Agile methodology such as Scrum or XP. Our focus here is on moving forward, with some basic requirements. We are also not going to talk about security and infrastructure epics. Those will be handled as quality attributes in the following section.

Food Services Management Epic

For the first release, the business is interested in focusing on the following:

- The basic data about each Food Service

- The food they offer

- Each Food Service will have access to modify its data

Now, let's get more details about the Food Services epic using stories.

Create a New Food Service

As a Food Service, I want to register myself. Conditions of satisfaction:

- Food Service must have a name, address, type of food, password, admin email, and the fee for delivery

- Type of food could be Chinese, pizza, and so on

Update Food Service Information

As a Food Service, I want to update my information. Conditions of satisfaction:

- The Food Service can update its name, address, a fee for delivery, type of food, and password

Deactivate a Food Service

As a Food Service, I want to deactivate my account. Conditions of satisfaction:

- Food Service can deactivate its account using the web page
- The Food Service won't show up in the main Food Service search

Create a Food Product to Offer

As a Food Service, I want to create a food product in my account. Conditions of satisfaction:

- A food product must have its price, name, description, and image.

Update a Food Product to Offer

As a Food Service, I want to update a food product in my account. Conditions of satisfaction:

- The Food Service can update in a food product, its price, name, description, and image.

Deactivate a Food Product to Offer

As a Food Service, I want to deactivate a food product. Conditions of satisfaction:

- Food Service can deactivate a food product.
- The food product won't show up in the main Food Service search.

Delivery Flow Epic

For the first release, the business is interested in focusing on the following:

- Show the whole Food Services list.
- Filter the Food Services list by type of food.

131

- Show the whole products a Food Service offers.

- Add food products to the cart.

- Request the delivery to an address.

Now, let's get more detail about this using stories.

Show the Whole Food Services List

As a customer, I want to see the whole Food Services list. Conditions of satisfaction:

- When you open the list of Food Services, you will see the active Food Services only.

- Each Food Service must show its name, an image, and the charge for delivery.

- The list must load using an infinite scroll.

Filter the Whole Food Services List by Type of Food

As a customer, I want to filter the whole Food Services list by type of food. Conditions of satisfaction:

- When you open the list of Food Services, you will see the active Food Services only.

- Each Food Service must show its name, an image. and the charge for delivery.

- The list must load using an infinite scroll.

- Only Food Services with the same type of food will be shown.

Tip   See how this story increases the features of the [Delivery Flow]. Show the whole Food Services list? Those are incremental stories. You do not to do everything now; you can split the features and increase its capabilities through time.

Show the Whole Food Products a Food Service Offers

As a customer, I want to see the whole food products a Food Service offers. Conditions of satisfaction:

- When you open a Food Service, you will see the list of food products it actively offers.
- Each food product will show its image, name, and price. The list must load using an infinite scroll.

Add Food Products to My Cart

As a customer, I want to add food products to my cart. Conditions of satisfaction:

- You can choose how many products you want.
- You can add those products to your cart.

Request Delivery of the Products in My Cart

As a customer, I want to request a delivery of my food products in my cart. Conditions of satisfaction:

- When you request the delivery, you will see a summary of your cart.
- That summary will have the whole products you chose, the total amount to pay, and the fee for the delivery.
- The customer will add an address, email, and phone number for the delivery.

Remove Food Products in Your Cart

As a customer, I want to remove food products in my cart. Conditions of satisfaction:

- When you request the delivery, you will see a summary of your cart.
- You can update the amount or remove food products from that summary.

Tip   See how this story increases the features of the [Delivery Flow]. Request delivery of the products in my cart? Those are incremental stories. You do not do everything now; you can split the features and increase its capabilities through time.

After we have a clear view of the functional requirements, we move forward to check the nonfunctional, or better named, quality attributes, in the following section.

Finding Quality Attributes

Quality attributes handle how your system should work. Those are properties that won't be so obvious for the business. They are usually named nonfunctional requirements.

Tip   Be careful with the term nonfunctional requirements. In my opinion, they are functional, for instance, if your application doesn't respond in an acceptable time, your final users will be angry and they won't be able to work on your application, and it means the system is not functional. Quality attributes sound more accurate to me.

There are plenty of standards or specifications of quality attributes. For the purposes of this book, we are going to use the ISO/IEC FCD 25010 as shown in Figure 4-17.

Figure 4-17. ISO/IEC FCD 25010

Tip   You can find detailed information at `http://iso25000.com/index.php/en/iso-25000-standards/iso-25010`.

Handling quality attributes is important to accomplish the business's current needs. We are going to talk about some of them, its implications for our new Daniel's Delivery application, and create some scenarios to test and validate them.

A quality attribute scenario is a way to test and validate how that quality attributes behaviors in our system. As this kind of requirement is different, its testing will be different too. They are defined in a flow of Source ➤ Stimulus ➤ Artifact ➤ Response ➤ Response Measure, bounded in an environment.

We are not going to detail each scenario for the purposes of this book.

Security Epic

For the security epic, the security quality attribute is applied

Security is all about data vs. access rights. Here, we find authentication, authorization, roles, and so on. Only Food Services roles can access the Food Services management module, except for the registration form that is going to be public. Let's create some scenarios we think the business will care about.

Remember, the new Daniel's Delivery application is a full-stack application. This means you have two ways to use its services: one through the web page and the other through the API. You must secure both.

Scenario 1: Public Registration Page for Food Services

Let's see how to test the public registration page in Figure 4-18.

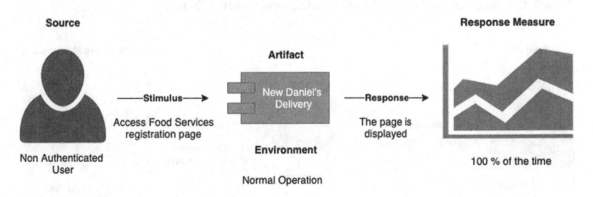

Figure 4-18. *Public registration page scenario*

Here, a non-authenticated user is trying to access the registration page, and the system will allow him to do it 100% of the time.

Scenario 2: Foods Services Management Module Requires Login

In Figure 4-19, we see how to test the login for a Food Service.

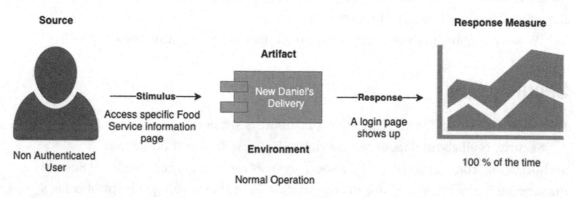

Figure 4-19. *Food Services management module requires login scenario*

Here, a non-authenticated user tries to access the specific information page for a Food Service, and the system shows a login page 100% of the time.

Scenario 3: Foods Services Management API Requires Authorization

We will now see how to test the API authorization (Figure 4-20).

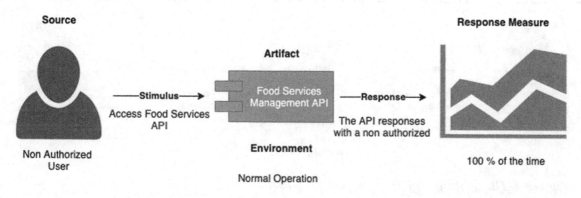

Figure 4-20. *Food Services management API requires authorization scenario*

Here, a non-authorized user tries to access the Food Services management API module through its API, and the system returns a non-authorized response 100% of the time.

Infrastructure Epic

Performance efficiency and reliability quality attributes apply to the infrastructure epic, which means those quality attributes are involved in the infrastructure definition.

Performance efficiency is about resources vs. use. Resources could be the memory, disk, net, and so on. However, reliability defines how a system works under specific conditions over time. Those conditions could be like in a disaster recovery event, normal operation, and so on.

After our analysis of the current situation of Daniel's Delivery, we found that those two quality attributes are not well addressed. So, the following scenarios will address the business concerns on these topics.

Scenario 1: Web Page Latency Should Average to 2 Seconds

Next we see how to test the expected latency for the website in Figure 4-21.

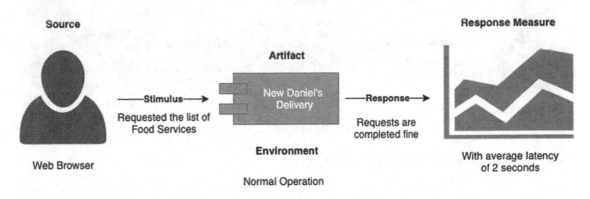

Figure 4-21. *Web page latency should average to 2 seconds scenario*

Here, a web browser requested the list of Food Services. The system processes the requests just fine with an average latency of 2 seconds.

Scenario 2: API Latency Should Average to 1 Second

In Figure 4-22, we see how to test the expected latency for the API.

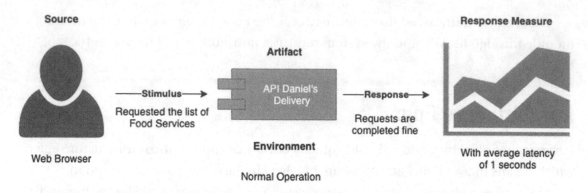

Figure 4-22. *API latency should average to 1 second scenario*

Here, a web browser requested the list of Food Services to the API. The system processes the requests just fine with an average latency of 1 second.

Scenario 3: Disaster Recovery

Let's see how to test the disaster recovery strategy in Figure 4-23.

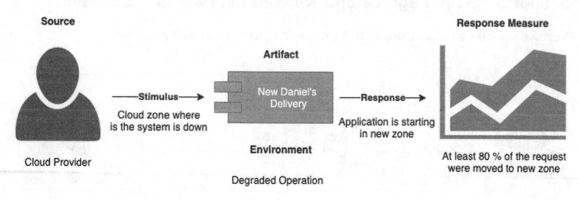

Figure 4-23. *Disaster recovery scenario*

Here, we defined a disaster recovery plan for our application. In this case, if the zone where our application is running is down, the traffic should be moved to a new zone where new infrastructure is starting for our application.

A Traversal Quality Attribute: Maintainability

Maintainability is all about system improvement or modification. For instance, how fast could you add a new feature? How fast could you fix a bug?

As we saw in the evaluation of the current state, the current maintainability degree is pretty low. We need a lot of people to maintain and improve the system by adding a few features. So, we are going to define some scenarios to guarantee the maintainability of our new Daniel's Delivery application.

Tip   You will notice how the scenario's environment changes from normal operation to development. Maintainability is more related to the development process, not to the operational process.

Scenario 1: The System Should Have Good Unit Test Coverage

Figure 4-24 shows how to test the unit tests coverage.

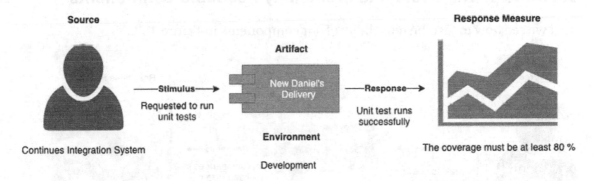

Figure 4-24.   *The system should have good unit tests coverage scenario*

Here, a CI system is going to run the full unit tests in our application and the expected result must be at least 80% of the code coverage.

Scenario 2: The System Should Have Good Integration Test Coverage

In Figure 4-25, we see how to test the integration tests coverage.

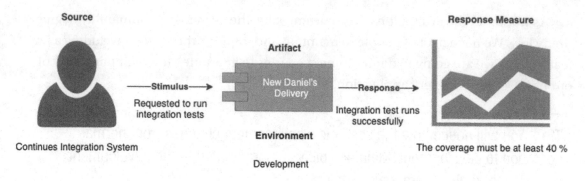

Figure 4-25. *The system should have a good integration tests coverage scenario*

Here, a CI system is going to run the full integration tests in our application and the expected result must be at least 40% of code coverage.

Scenario 3: The System Is Created by Reusable Components

Next we see how to test the reusability of our components in Figure 4-26.

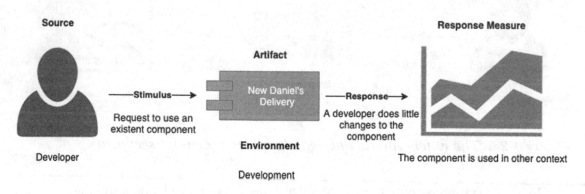

Figure 4-26. *The system is created by reusable components scenario*

Here, a developer wants to reuse an existing component. So he needs to change a little to it to accomplish its new goal, and finally, the component can be used in a new context.

Scenario 4: Any Change into the Code Should Move to a New/Updated Unit Test

Finally, we see how to test the quality of the unit tests in Figure 4-27.

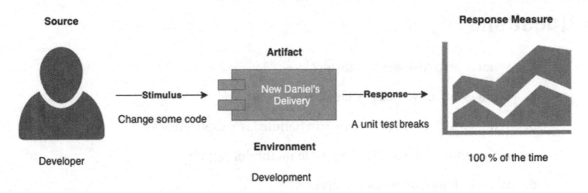

Figure 4-27. *Any change into the code should move to a new/update unit test scenario*

Here, if a developer changes some code in the application and runs the unit tests, they should break, or be updated, 100% of the time.

We have now completed our analysis of the current application status and we defined how we are going to move forward for the new Daniel's Delivery application. In the following chapters, we are going to implement those stories and quality attributes using JEE 8 and Vue.js.

Summary

In this chapter, we introduced you to the Daniel's Delivery company, which has a web application where we can find some information about Food Services and deliveries. We found that the business is not happy with it and they have found some problems. Moreover, they want to move to the next level. So, we analyzed its current state and proposed to them a new Daniel's Delivery application that addresses their needs.

Here, you learned how to analyze the current state of an application and suggest a new architecture with the latest technologies such as Jakarta EE, cloud computing, and Vue.js. Moreover, you know how to define epics and stories to reflect business needs, adding quality attributes that address some hiding behaviors that any business would like to have.

In the following chapter, we are going to start to build our new Daniel's Delivery website, focusing on how to handle the data and data access components on the back-end side.

Questions

1. What is an active-active cluster?

2. What is an active-passive cluster?

3. Which other cloud providers can handle Java applications?

4. Is Scrum better than Kanban Agile methodologies?

5. What is a disaster recovery strategy?

6. What is the difference between a unit test and an integration test?

7. Which estimation strategies can be used?

CHAPTER 5

Modeling Your Entities and Data with JPA

The persistence layer is always a necessity for any real software project in which you need to access and save your data somewhere.

In this chapter, we are going to analyze the new Daniel's Delivery application and define the data access using relational databases and JPA over Jakarta EE. We will discover entities to map our requirements and understand how we can connect to a data source, creating basic CRUDS structures. As you will see in detail with both the entity modeling and implementation process, this chapter is extensive.

The following topics will be covered in this chapter:

- Defining the entity-relationship model using the new Daniel's Delivery website use cases.

- Building JPA entities using Netbeans and a database schema.

- Understanding the basic JPA configuration from entity annotations to persistence.xml.

- Designing the persistence layer from packages to repository interfaces.

- Implementing the persistence layer with its required CRUD structures, using EJB and JPA, through the EntityManager to access the data.

- Testing our persistence layer using JUnit and Arquillian.

After we discuss these topics, you will be able to design and implement a database access layer, using Jakarta EE, with integration testing for high quality.

© Daniel Andres Pelaez Lopez 2021
D. A. P. Lopez, *Full-Stack Web Development with Jakarta EE and Vue.js*,
https://doi.org/10.1007/978-1-4842-6342-6_5

Technical Requirements

To follow the instructions in this chapter, you will need the following:

- Java 1.8

- Netbeans 11

- GlassFish 5.1

- Jakarta Enterprise Edition

- Docker

- MySQL 8.0.16

- DBeaver Community 6.1.1

We are not going to cover the installation of those tools in this chapter.

You can check the whole project and code at `https://github.com/Apress/full-stack-web-development-with-jakartaee-and-vue.js/tree/master/CH5`.

Defining Your Entity-Relationship Model

The entity-relationship model has been used to define how the information should be structured for a defined context. This model relies on two basic concepts: entities and relations. An entity holds properties, and those properties can be constrained by type; and relation is a link between entities, a link that defines a dependency. For instance, in the context of parents and children, parent and child are two entities, and there is a relation between them; a parent can have multiple children.

In this section, we will go through user stories and extract our entities and their relations using the nouns and properties strategy; and finally, we will design a database using the entity-relationship model.

Extracting Business Entities from User Stories

Now we are going to find nouns and properties in the user stories. Nouns will be bolded, and properties will be underlined.

Create a New Food Service

As a **Food Service**, I want to register myself. Conditions of satisfaction:

- **Food Service** must have a <u>name, address, type of food, password, admin email,</u> and the <u>fee</u> for delivery.

- **Type of food** could be Chinese, pizza, and so on.

Update Food Service Information

As a **Food Service**, I want to update my information. Conditions of satisfaction:

- The **Food Service** can update its <u>name</u>, <u>address</u>, a <u>fee</u> for delivery, <u>type of food</u>, and <u>password.</u>

Deactivate a Food Service

As a **Food Service**, I want to deactivate my account. Conditions of satisfaction:

- **Food Service** can <u>deactivate</u> its account using the web page.

- The deactivated **Food Service** won't show up in the main **Food Service** search.

Create a Food Product to Offer

As a **Food Service**, I want to create a **food product** in my account. Conditions of satisfaction:

- A **food product** must have its <u>price,</u> <u>name,</u> <u>description,</u> and an <u>image</u>.

Update a Food Product to Offer

As a **Food Service**, I want to update a **food product** in my account. Conditions of satisfaction:

- The **Food Service** can update a <u>food product</u>, its <u>price</u>, <u>name</u>, <u>description</u>, and <u>image.</u>

Deactivate a Food Product to Offer

As a **Food Service**, I want to <u>deactivate</u> a **food product**. Conditions of satisfaction:

- **Food Service** can <u>deactivate</u> a **food product.**

- The deactivated **food product** won't show up in the main **Food Service** search.

Show the Whole Food Services List

As a **customer**, I want to see the whole **Food Services** list. Conditions of satisfaction:

- When you open the list of **Food Services**, you will see the <u>active</u> **Food Services** only.

- Each **Food Service** must show its <u>name</u>, an <u>image,</u> and the <u>charge for delivery.</u> The list must load using an infinite scroll.

Filter the Whole Food Services List by Type of Food

As a **customer**, I want to filter the whole **Food Services** list by <u>type of food</u>. Conditions of satisfaction:

- When you open the list of **Food Services**, you will see the <u>active</u> **Food Services** only.

- Each **Food Service** must show its <u>name</u>, an <u>image,</u> and the <u>charge for delivery.</u> The list must load using an infinite scroll.

- Only **Food Services** with the same <u>type of food</u> will be shown.

Show the Whole Food Products a Food Service Offers

As a **Customer**, I want to see the whole **food products** a **Food Service** offers. Conditions of satisfaction:

- When you open a **Food Service**, you will see the list of **food products** it actively offers.

- Each **food product** will show its <u>image</u>, <u>name</u>, and <u>price.</u>

- The list must load using an infinite scroll.

Add Food Products to My Cart

As a **Customer**, I want to add **food products** to my **cart**. Conditions of satisfaction:

- You can choose how many **products** you want.

- You can add those **products** to your **cart**.

Request Delivery of the Products in My Cart

As a **Customer**, I want to request a **delivery** of my **food products** in my cart. Conditions of satisfaction:

- When you request the **delivery**, you will see a summary of your **cart**.

- That summary will have the whole **products** you chose, the total amount to pay, and the fee for the delivery.

- The **customer** will add an address, email, and phone number for the **delivery**.

Remove Food Products in Your Cart

As a **Customer**, I want to remove my **food products** in my **cart**. Conditions of satisfaction:

- When you request the **delivery**, you will see a **summary** of your **cart**.

- You can update the amount or remove **food products** from that **summary**.

Choosing Entities and Properties

The following are the nouns we found in the user stories: Food Service, Type of Food, Food Product, Customer, Cart, Delivery, and Request. However, not every noun we found should be taken into account for the first version of the product, for example:

- Delivery and Request seem to be the same.

- Customer is not required in this version, because we don't have any use case for it.

- Customer registration. In the Delivery, we ask about phone, address, and email for the customer for now, and this information is enough.

- Type of food seems to be a property on the Food Service, not an entity.

Besides, we should add new entities that we cannot find clearly in the user stories: a User entity to hold the basic login data for Food Services, and an Item entity to hold, by Food Product, in a Delivery, how many you requested. For instance, you request delivery of 5 pizzas and 2 sodas.

Figure 5-1 shows how those business entities relate to each other.

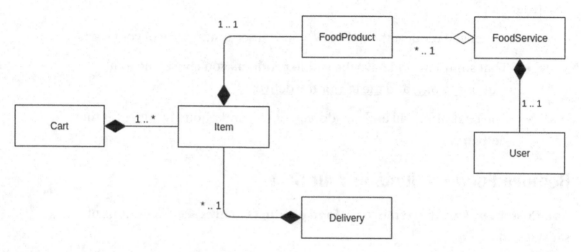

Figure 5-1. *Business entity relationship. The bold arrows mean composition, the white arrows mean aggregation.*

In that diagram, we can see how the business entities connect each other, and that detail plus its properties can be found as follows:

- FoodService properties: email, address, food_type, delivery_fee, active. A FoodService has a relation with only one User, plus has multiple FoodProduct User properties: email, password.

- FoodProductproperties: id, name, price, description, image_url, active Item properties: amount. An Item has only one FoodProduct associated.

- Cart properties: email, address, phone, list of items. A Cart has multiple Items. Delivery properties: address, phone, total, email, fee, state. A Delivery has multiple Items.

Note   Careful, this is not a database relationship model, but a business entity model.

Defining the Database Entity-Relationship Model

Now we can define how those business entities will be persistent in the database as shown in Figure 5-2.

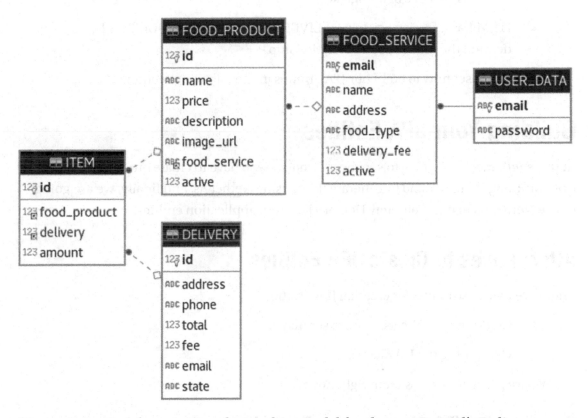

Figure 5-2. *Database entity relationship model for the new Daniel's Delivery*

Tip   We won't persist Cart entity for now, because there is no any requirement talking explicitly about it. That means we are going to let the front end handle the Cart.

When we talk about a relational database model, we won't use the relation concept anymore: we will use the foreign key concept. A foreign key is a link between two entities, where we have an origin property and a destination property.

Now, let's describe what we see in that database entity relationship diagram:

- FOOD_SERVICE has a foreign key to USER_DATA, through their email. FOOD_PRODUCT has a foreign key to FOOD_SERVICE, where a FOOD_SERVICE can have multiple FOOD_PRODUCT.

- DELIVERY is free of foreign keys.

- ITEM has a foreign key to a DELIVERY and FOOD_PRODUCT and defined the amount of this relationship.

Well, we are set now to build our JPA entities in the following section.

Building Your JPA Entities

In this section, we are going to see the alternatives we have to create our JPA entities, from building them at hand to generate them using Netbeans, and finally, we are going to use Netbeans to build our new Daniel's Delivery application entities.

Alternatives to Create JPA Entities

There are two alternatives for creating JPA entities:

1. Creating the JPA classes from scratch.

2. Generating the JPA classes.

We are going to discuss them right now.

Creating the JPA Classes from Scratch

The process to create the JPA classes from scratch is the following:

1. Define the database entity-relationship model. You can use the strategy of nouns and properties we applied to the previous section.

2. By each table, create a JPA entity class. This class should be annotated at least by @Entity.

3. Map any attribute by hand with the right JPA annotations. You can add other annotations like @Column, @Table and so on.

4. Map any relationship by hand between entities like many to one. Those relationships should use annotations like @OneToMany, @ManyToOne, and so on.

5. Use JPA to create the database from the JPA entities. Some JPA providers like Hibernate allow us to generate database tables from the entities.

This approach has the following advantages:

- You have total control on how the classes map to the database.

- You can generate the database from the JPA entities.

And this has some disadvantages:

- You need to understand fairly well how the JPA annotations work.

- You need to understand fairly well how JPA maps relationships.

- If the tables have tons of fields, it will take time to create your entities.

Generating the JPA Classes

Now this is the process to generate JPA entities from a database:

1. Define the database entity-relationship model. Again, you can use the strategy of nouns and properties we applied to the previous section.

2. Create the tables and relations in your database. There are a lot of tools for this, like DBeaver, where you can connect a database and create tables.

3. Choose a tool that generates entities. Netbeans is a good option.

4. Connect the tool to the database. You might need to define a data source. We will see this in the following section.

5. Set up what the tool asks you.

6. Generate the entities.

Note   The details regarding this process will be shown in the following section.

This approach has the following advantages:

- You don't need to worry about the details of basic annotations.

- You don't need to code the entities.

- You will have a JPA entities base.

- You don't need to worry about entities relations.

- You can re-create the database from the new entities.

And this has some disadvantages:

- You need a database with its tables running.

- The tool might generate more code than you need.

- You always change the generated entities to adjust to specific needs.

In the next section, we are going to use the generated entities option, as we can see it has more advantages than disadvantages, for our new Daniel's Delivery website.

Generating JPA Entities Using Netbeans

We are going to use a Netbeans feature to generate JPA entities from the database. This is the process:

1. Run a database in your local machine; in this case, we are going to use a MySQL 8.0.16. We are using Docker to start a MySQL 8.0.16 database locally. You can use the following command:

   ```
   docker run --name deliverymysql -p 3306:3306 -e MYSQL_ROOT_
   PASSWORD=deliverydb -e MYSQL_USER=deliverydb -e MYSQL_
   PASSWORD=deliverydb -d mysql:8.0.16
   ```

2. Open a database client to connect to the database. We are going to use the DBeaver application as shown in Figure 5-3. (You can choose your favorite database client.)

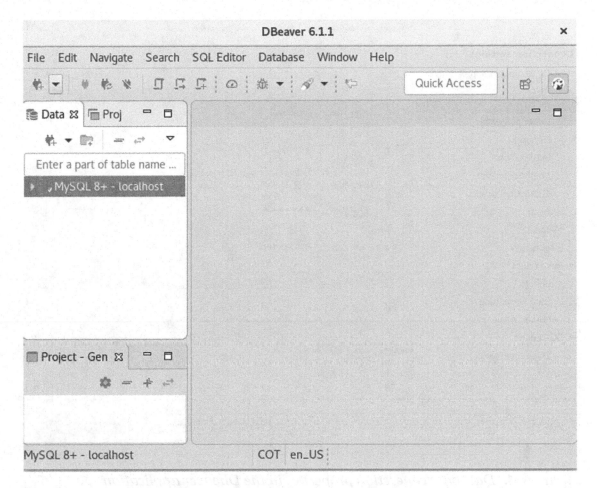

Figure 5-3. *Database connected in the Dbeaver application*

3. Now, create a connection to your database (Figure 5-4).
    The connection data should be something like this:

    Server: localhost
    Port: 3306
    User name: root Password: deliverydb

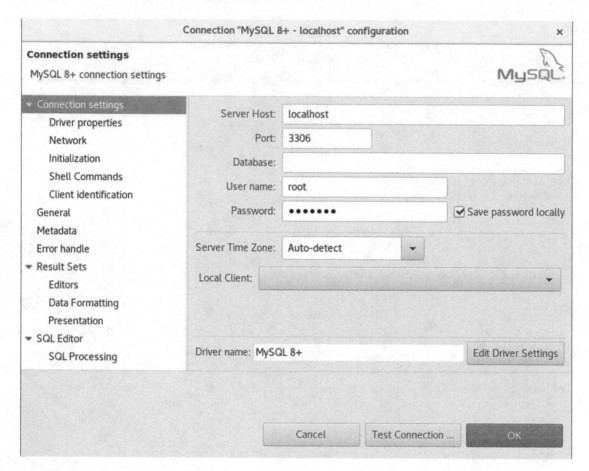

Figure 5-4. *Database conecction properties in the Dbeaver application*

4. Now, create a new database named deliverymysql.

5. Later, create the tables we defined in the section "Defining Your Entity-Relationship Model (Figure 5-5).

Figure 5-5. *Database conecction created in the Dbeaver application*

Note   You can find the full script for the tables here: `https://github.com/` `Apress/full-stack-web-development-with-jakartaee-and-vue.js/` `blob/master/CH5/StartWithJEE/StartWithJEE-ejb/src/main/` `resources/database.sql`.

---

6. Download the MySQL 8.0.16 driver from `https://dev.mysql.` `com/downloads/connector/j/`

7. Unzip your driver.

8. Open Netbeans and move to the Service | Drivers as shown in Figure 5-6.

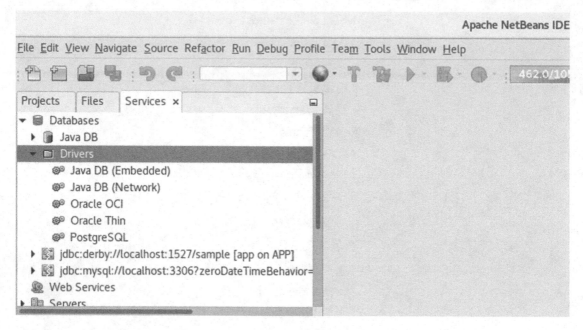

Figure 5-6. *Netbeans driver to connect to a database*

9. Right-click create a New Driver.

10. Choose the driver jar named mysql-connector-java-8.0.16.jar and set the Driver Class to com.mysql.jdbc.Driver.

11. Click OK, and you should see Figure 5-7.

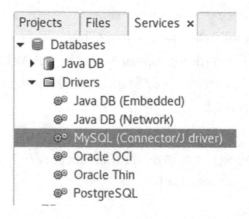

Figure 5-7. *Netbeans MySQL driver to connect to a database*

12. Now, click on Databases | New Connection, and choose MySQL (Connector/Jdriver) Driver.

13. Click Next, set your connection properties, and Test Connection (Figure 5-8).

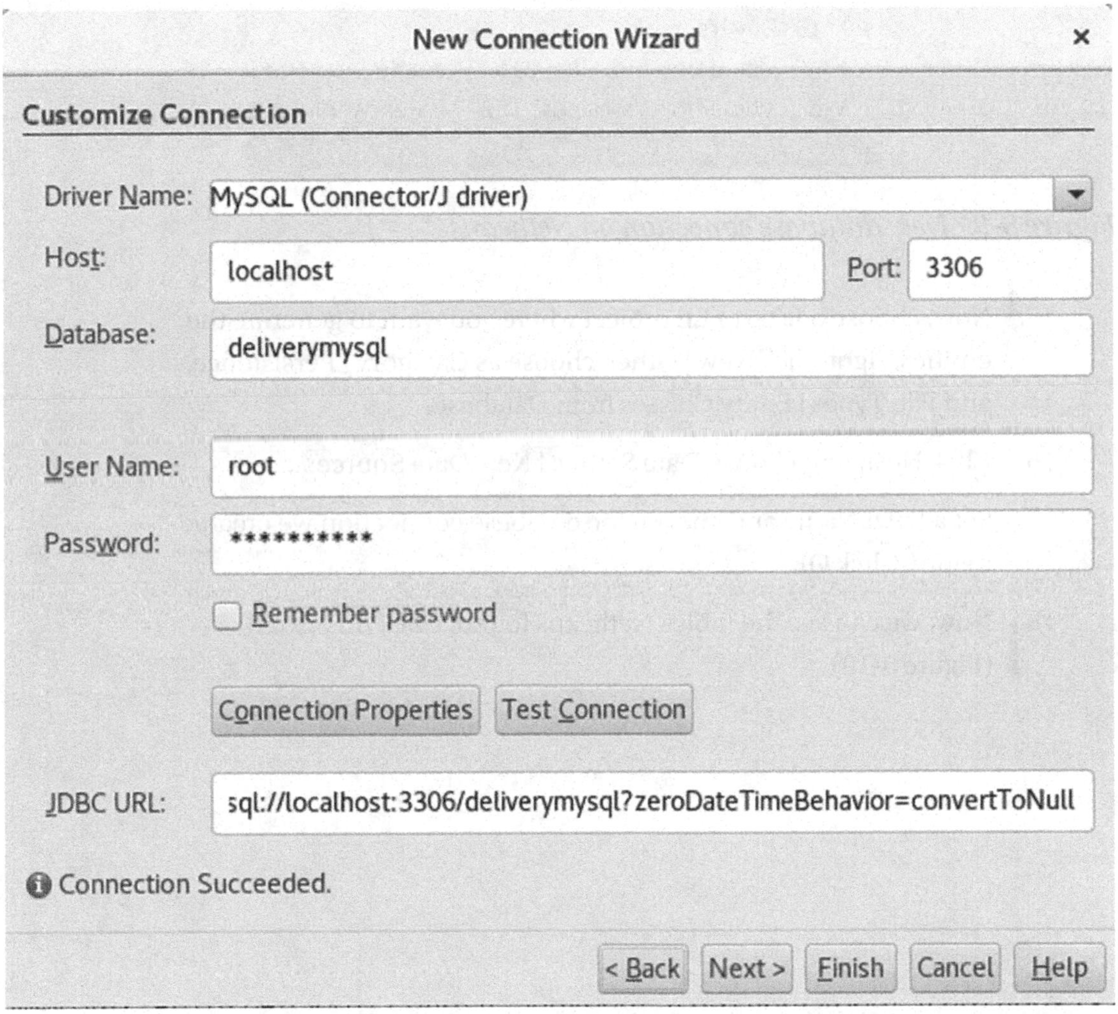

New Connection Wizard   ✕

Customize Connection

Driver Name: MySQL (Connector/J driver)

Host: localhost   Port: 3306

Database: deliverymysql

User Name: root

Password: **********

☐ Remember password

[Connection Properties] [Test Connection]

JDBC URL: sql://localhost:3306/deliverymysql?zeroDateTimeBehavior=convertToNull

ⓘ Connection Succeeded.

[< Back] [Next >] [Finish] [Cancel] [Help]

Figure 5-8. *Setting the database conection properties on Netbeans*

14. Click Finish, and you will see what is shown in Figure 5-9.

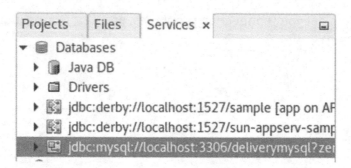

Figure 5-9. *New database conection on Netbeans*

15. Now, choose a Jakarta EE project where you want to generate the entities, right-click New | Other, choose as Category | Persistence, and File Types | Entity Classes from Database.

16. Click Next, and choose Data Source | New Data Source...:

17. Set a JNDI Name and choose the database connection we created before. Click OK.

18. Now, we can see the tables Netbeans found. Click on Add All (Figure 5-10).

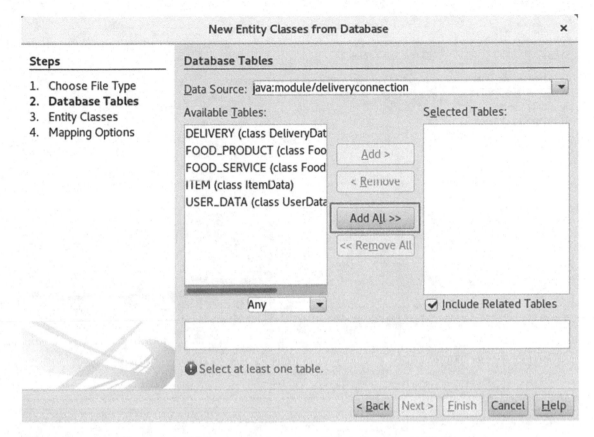

Figure 5-10. *Choosing tables to generate entities classes on Netbeans*

19.   And click on Next (Figure 5-11).

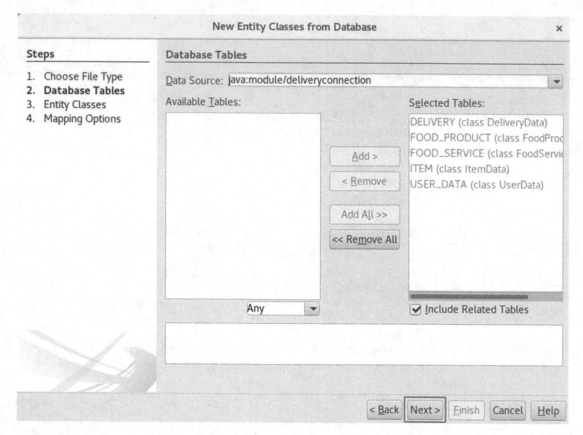

Figure 5-11. *Choosing which tables to generate entities classes on Netbeans*

20. You can see the mapping between tables and classes (Figure 5-12).
     We are going to add the suffix Data to the class names. This
     is for explicitly saying that they are data structures. Set your
     location and package as you wish and click Next. (Remember,
     a data structure has a public state but not behavior, a class has
     a behavior but a hidden state. You can read more about this
     here: `http://blog.cleancoder.com/uncle-bob/2019/06/16/`
     `ObjectsAndDataStructures.html`.)

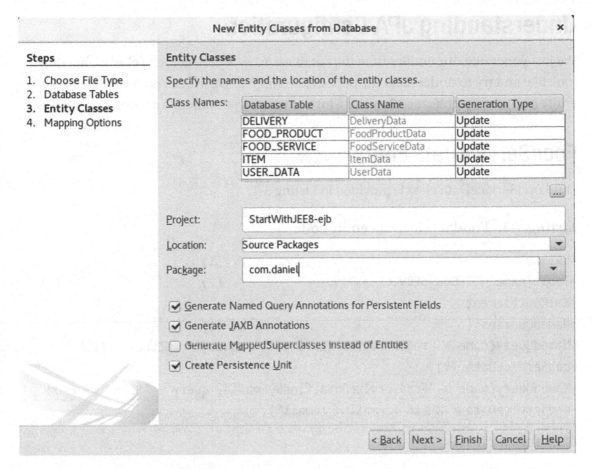

Figure 5-12. *Defining how the tables map to entities classes on Netbeans*

21. Choose as Collection Type java.util.List and click Finish.
    The default value for Collection Type is java.util.Collection. That
    interface is usually not useful in most use cases because it is too
    generic.

22. Now you can see the generated entities.

In the following section, we are going to check in detail what those JPA entities look
like, as well as some JPA basic configuration.

Understanding JPA Configuration

We just generated our entities from the database. Now we are going to check what they look like and try to understand the persistence.xml file. We are not going to detail each entity and property because they use a lot of common annotations and features.

FoodServiceData Entity

Our FoodServiceData class is provided in Listing 5-1.

Listing 5-1. FoodServiceData entity code

```
@Entity                                     // (1)
@Table(name = "FOOD_SERVICE")               // (2)
@XmlRootElement
@NamedQueries({                             // (3)
@NamedQuery(name = "FoodServiceData.findAll", query = "SELECT f FROM
FoodServiceData f"),
@NamedQuery(name = "FoodServiceData.findByEmail", query = "SELECT f FROM
FoodServiceData f WHERE f.email = :email"),

// More queries

@NamedQuery(name = "FoodServiceData.findByDeliveryFee", query = "SELECT f
FROM FoodServiceData f WHERE f.deliveryFee = :deliveryFee"),
@NamedQuery(name = "FoodServiceData.findByActive", query = "SELECT f FROM
FoodServiceData f WHERE f.active = :active")})

public class FoodServiceData implements Serializable {

// More fields

   // @Pattern(regexp="[a-z0-9!#$%&'*+/=?^_`{|}~-]+(?:\\.[a-
z0-9!#$%&'*+/=?^_`{|}~-]+)*@(?:[a-z0-9](?:[a-z0-9-]*[a-z0-9])?\\.)+
[a- z0-9](?:[a-z0-9-]*[a-z0-9])?", message="Invalid email")//if the field
contains email address consider using this annotation to enforce field
validation                  // (7.3)
   @Id                          // (4)
   @Basic(optional = false)     // (5)
```

```java
@NotNull                              // (7.1)
@Size(min = 1, max = 100)             // (7.2)
@Column(name = "email")               // (6)
private String email;

@Basic(optional = false)
@NotNull
@Size(min = 1, max = 100)
@Column(name = "food_type")
private String foodType;

// More fields

@Basic(optional = false)
@NotNull
@Column(name = "delivery_fee")
private int deliveryFee;

@Basic(optional = false)
@NotNull
@Column(name = "active")
private boolean active;

// More fields

@OneToMany(                                       // (8)
  cascade = CascadeType.ALL,                      // (9)
  mappedBy = "foodService")                       // (10)
private List<FoodProductData> foodProductDataList;  // (13)

@JoinColumn(name = "email", referencedColumnName = "email", insertable
= false, updatable = false)                       // (12)
@OneToOne(optional = false)                       // (11)
private UserData userData;

// Constructors, Getters, Setters, Equals, Hashcode

}
```

There, we can find a lot happening:

1. @Entity annotation tells JPA that FoodServiceData class will be used as an entity and will map a database table.

2. @Table tells JPA a specific mapping configuration against the database; in this case, it tells JPA the name of the table is FOOD_ SERVICE.

3. Next, we see some @NamedQuery annotations. Those represent JPA queries. Netbeans generates one query filtering by each table property. Remember, those queries are not SQL queries; they are JPQL queries.

4. @Id tells JPA which property is the primary key of the table. In this case, it will be the email.

5. @Basic tells JPA that that the property is plain, not a relationship with another table. Besides, you can define if the property could be optional or how you want to load it, using lazy or eager.

6. @Column tells JPA how it needs to map this property with a table column, for instance, @Column(name = "email") maps an email Java property with an email table column.

7. @Pattern, @NotNull, and @Size tell JPA how those fields should be validated. For instance, @Size(min = 1, max = 100) means this field length cannot be lower than 1 or greater than 100.

8. Remember, a FoodService can have multiple FoodProduct associated, but FoodService only relates to one User. @OneToMany tells JPA that FoodServiceData entity relates to multiple FoodProductData.

9. CascadeType.ALL means that any operation against this entity will affect the relationship with FoodProductData. For instance, if you are going to save a FoodServiceData with two FoodProductData, you only need to persist FoodServiceData, and JPA is going to take care of persisting the two FoodProductData.

10. mappedBy is the related field of the FoodProductData entity. That means in the FoodProductData class, you will find a property named FoodService. That defines the link between FoodProductData and FoodServiceData, and tells JPA that FoodServiceData owns the relationship, which means the foreign key will be FoodProductData table.

11. @OneToOne tells JPA that the FoodServiceData entity relates only with on User.

12. @JoinColumn tells JPA what the foreign key is. In this case, it tells JPA that FOOD_SERVICE as a foreign key to USER_DATA, through the email column.

13. Why doesn't foodProductDataList doesn't have an @JoinColumn? Well, FOOD_SERVICE doesn't have the foreign key to FOOD_PRODUCT. FOOD_PRODUCT does have the foreign key to FOOD_SERVICE.

DeliveryData Entity

Our DeliveryData class is provided in Listing 5-2.

Listing 5-2. DeliveryData entity code

```
@Entity                          // (1)
@Table(name = "DELIVERY")        // (2)
@XmlRootElement
@NamedQueries({                  // (3)
@NamedQuery(name = "DeliveryData.findAll", query = "SELECT d FROM
DeliveryData d"),
@NamedQuery(name = "DeliveryData.findById", query = "SELECT d FROM
DeliveryData d WHERE d.id = :id"),

// More queries

@NamedQuery(name = "DeliveryData.findByEmail", query = "SELECT d FROM
DeliveryData d WHERE d.email = :email"),
```

```java
@NamedQuery(name = "DeliveryData.findByState", query = "SELECT d FROM
DeliveryData d WHERE d.state = :state")})

public class DeliveryData implements Serializable {

// More fields

  @Id                                        // (4)
  @GeneratedValue(strategy = GenerationType.IDENTITY)  // (5)
  @Basic(optional = false)                             // (6)
  @Column(name = "id")                                 // (7)
  private Integer id;

  @Basic(optional = false)
  @NotNull                                   // (8.1)
  @Size(min = 1, max = 100)                  // (8.1)
  @Column(name = "address")
  private String address;

  // More fields

  @Basic(optional = false)
  @NotNull
  @Size(min = 1, max = 100)
  @Column(name = "state")
  private String state;

  // More fields

  @OneToMany(                         // (9.1)
  cascade = CascadeType.ALL,          // (9.1)
  mappedBy = "delivery")              // (10)
  private List<ItemData> itemDataList;

  // Constructors, Getters, Setters, Equals, Hashcode

}
```

Let's understand the happenings in the preceding code block:

1. @Entity annotation tells JPA that DeliveryData class will be used as an entity and will map a database table.

2. @Table tells JPA a specific mapping configuration against the database; in this case, it tells JPA the name of the table is DELIVERY.

3. Next, we see some @NamedQuery annotations. Those represent JPA queries. Netbeans generates one query filtering by each table property. Again, those queries are not SQL queries, they are JPQL queries.

4. Well, here we map the basic properties of the table FOOD_ SERVICE to our FoodServiceData class: @Id tells JPA which property is the primary key of the table. In this case, it will be an integer.

5. @GeneratedValue(strategy = GenerationType.IDENTITY) tells JPA that id property is autogenerated, which means the database will use the IDENTITY strategy to generate a new id anytime you create a new row in the DELIVERY table.

6. @Basic tells JPA that that property is plain, not a relationship with another table.

7. @Column tells JPA how it needs to map this property with a table column, for instance, @Column(name = "address") maps the address Java property with the address table column.

8. @NotNull and @Size tell JPA how those fields should be validated. For instance, @Size(min = 1, max = 100) means this field length cannot be lower than 1 or greater than 100.

9. @OneToMany(cascade = CascadeType.ALL, mappedBy = "delivery") private List<ItemData> itemDataList.

    As we can see, a Delivery can have multiple Items associated: @OneToMany tells JPA that a DeliveryData entity relates with multiple ItemData. CascadeType.ALL means that any operation against this entity will affect the relationship with

FoodProductData. For instance, if you are going to save a DeliveryData with two Items, you only need to persist DeliveryData entity, and JPA is going to take care of persisting the two Items.

10. mappedBy is the related field of the Item entity. That means you will find a field named delivery in the Item entity.

11. Why doesn't itemDataList have an @JoinColumn? Well, DELIVERY doesn't have the foreign key to ITEM. ITEM does have the foreign key to DELIVERY.

ItemData Entity

Our ItemData class is provided in Listing 5-3.

Listing 5-3. ItemData entity code

```
@Entity                                         // (1)
@Table(name = "ITEM")                           // (2)
@XmlRootElement
@NamedQueries({                                 // (3)
@NamedQuery(name = "ItemData.findAll", query = "SELECT i FROM ItemData i"),
@NamedQuery(name = "ItemData.findById", query = "SELECT i FROM ItemData i
WHERE i.id = :id"),
@NamedQuery(name = "ItemData.findByAmount", query = "SELECT i FROM ItemData
i WHERE i.amount = :amount")})

public class ItemData implements Serializable {

@Id                                 // (4)
@GeneratedValue(strategy = GenerationType.IDENTITY)  // (5)
@Basic(optional = false)                        // (6)
@Column(name = "id")                            // (7)
private Integer id;

@Basic(optional = false)
@NotNull                                        // (8)
@Column(name = "amount")
```

```
private int amount;

@JoinColumn(name = "delivery", referencedColumnName = "id")    // (10)
@ManyToOne(optional = false)                    // (9)
private DeliveryData delivery;

@JoinColumn(name = "food_product", referencedColumnName = "id")    // (10)
@ManyToOne(optional = false)                    // (9)
private FoodProductData foodProduct;

  // Constructors, Getters, Setters, Equals, Hashcode

}
```

There, we can find a lot happening:

1.   @Entity annotation tells JPA that ItemData class will be used as an entity and will map a database table.

2.   @Table tells JPA a specific mapping configuration against the database; in this case, it tells JPA the name of the table is ITEM.

3.   Next, we see some @NamedQuery annotations. Those represent JPA queries. Netbeans generates one query filtering by each table property. Remember, those queries are not SQL queries; they are JPQL queries.

4.   Here we map the basic properties of the table ITEM to our ItemData class: @Id tells JPA which property is the primary key of the table. In this case, it will be an integer.

5.   @GeneratedValue(strategy = GenerationType.IDENTITY) tells JPA that the id property is autogenerated, which means the database will use the IDENTITY strategy to generate a new id anytime you create a new row in the ITEM table.

6.   @Basic tells JPA that that property is plain, not a relationship with another table, and it is required.

7.   @Column tells JPA how it needs to map this property with a table column, for instance, @Column(name = "amount") maps the amount Java property with amount table column.

8.   @NotNull tells JPA how those fields should be validated.

9.   As we can see, a Delivery can have multiple Items associated: @ManyToOne tells JPA that DeliveryData and FoodProductData entities relate with multiple ItemData.

10.   @JoinColumn tells JPA what the foreign key is. In this case, we have two foreign keys:

First from ITEM table, column delivery, to the DELIVERY table, column id.

Second from ITEM table, column food_product, to the FOOD_PRODUCT table, column id.

Now we have the bases on how JPA maps entities classes against database tables. In the following section, we are going to see the basic JPA configuration using the persistence.xml file.

Understanding the persistence.xml File Basics

When we generate the entities using Netbeans from the database, Netbeans generates a file named persistence.xml with the content provided in Listing 5-4. The persistence.xml file is where we tell JPA how to behave; where the database is; and which are the entities, specific JPA provider properties, and other amounts.

Listing 5-4.   Default persistence.xml file

```
<?xml version="1.0" encoding="UTF-8"?>
<persistence version="2.1" xmlns="http://xmlns.jcp.org/xml/ns/
persistence" xmlns:xsi="http://www.w3.org/2001/XMLSchema-instance"
xsi:schemaLocation="http://xmlns.jcp.org/xml/ns/persistence http://xmlns.
jcp.org/xml/ns/persistence/persistence_2_1.xsd">

<persistence-unit
  name="com.daniel_StartWithJEE8-ejb_ejb_1.0-SNAPSHOTPU"
  transaction-type="JTA">  <!--(1)-->
  <jta-data-source>java:module/deliveryconnection</jta-data-
  source>                    <!--(2)-->
```

```
<exclude-unlisted-classes>false</exclude-unlisted-classes>      <!--(3)-->
<properties/>
</persistence-unit>

</persistence>
```

Let's detail its content:

1. persistence-unit represents a set of related entities and specific connection properties.

   For instance, a MySQL connection with a specific configuration. You can have multiple persistence-unit tags in your persistence. xml file. That means you can have one unit pointing to a MySQL database and another pointing to a PostgreSQL database.

   The name of the persistence-unit is used to inject EntityManager objects using the @PersistenceContext annotation.

   And finally, a persistence-unit has an EntityManagerFactory with many EntityManager objects, which we use to connect to the database. We are going to talk about this in the following section.

   transaction-type="JTA" means that the JEE container is going to handle the transactions. So, you won't need to take care of starting and committing transactions. We are going to talk about this more in the following section.

2. jta-data-source sets which data source this persistence unit is going to use.

   A data source is a set of connection properties to a specific database, and it is handled by the application server.

3. exclude-unlisted-classes defines that any unlisted entity classes out of the current persistence unit won't be loaded to the persistence context.

   Now we know the basic configuration of the persistence.xml file and the JPA entities. In the following section, we are going to create CRUDs of these entities, defining unit tests; and finally, we are going to create integration tests using an H2 in-memory database.

Designing the Persistence Layer

We saw how to create our JPA entities and the basic configuration for a JPA project. Now we are going to design our persistence layer using the Main and Abstraction strategy.

Understanding the Packages

We are going to split our persistence layer in two parts, the Main and the Abstraction, as shown in Figure 5-13.

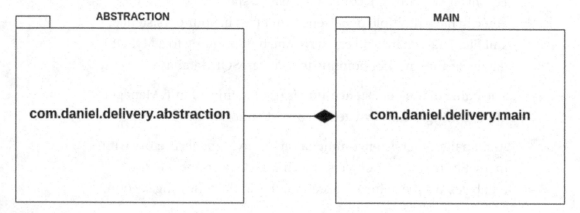

Figure 5-13. *Package structure, spliting the application between the abstraction and main*

Abstraction is our business core, which includes business entities, use cases, interfaces, definitions, and so on.

Main is everything else, like frameworks, data access like JPA entities, transactions, queues, containers, and so on.

As you can see, Main needs the Abstraction to exist; however, Abstraction can live without knowing about Main. This is the Dependency Inversion Principle.

Note   You can read more about the Main and the Abstraction here: `https://coderstower.com/2019/04/02/main-and-abstraction-the-decoupled-peers/` and Dependency Inversion here `https://coderstower.com/2019/03/26/dependency-inversion-why-you-shouldnt-avoid-it/`.

Now we are going to define some internal packages. The com.daniel.delivery. abstraction package is going to hold anything related to our business logic, and the com. daniel.delivery.main.repository package is going to hold the data access framework, in this case, JPA, as we can see in Figure 5-14.

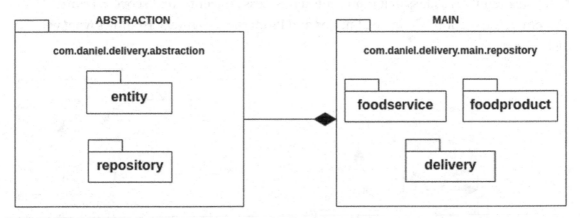

Figure 5-14. *Detail package structure, splitting the application between the abstraction and main*

In the following sections, we are going to focus on the design of our persistence layer, which means we are going to focus on our abstractions definitions, not Main.

We can see how they look like in our JEE project (Figure 5-15).

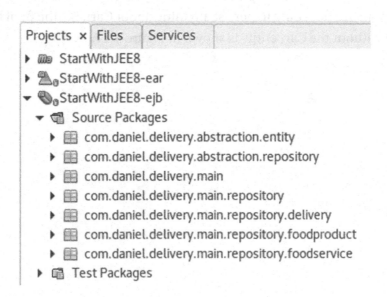

Figure 5-15. *Detail package structure into the project*

Well, let's see what we have on each of those packages.

Defining our Business Entities

A business entity is a class that represents a business concept. We discovered some of them in the section "Choosing Entities and Properties." Figure 5-16 shows what we discovered.

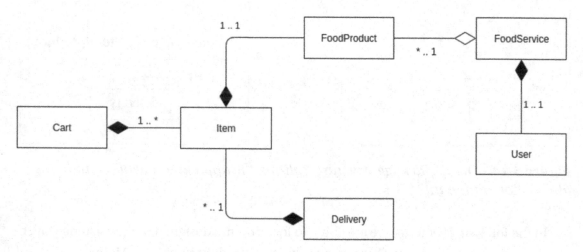

Figure 5-16. *Full business entitiy relationship model of Daniel's Delivery*

Remember, we are not going to persist anything about Cart. So, the final business entity diagram without the Cart entity is shown in Figure 5-17.

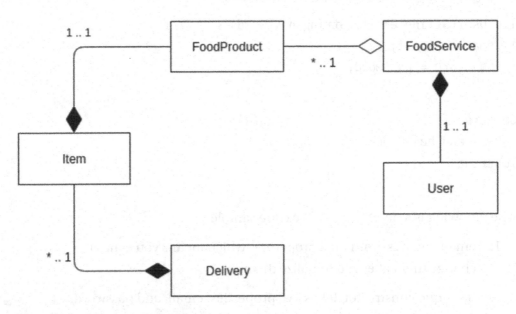

Figure 5-17. *Cart business entities is removed from the business entitiy relationship model of Daniel's Delivery*

We are now going to create our business entities.

Note   Our business entities will look pretty similar to the JPA entities we defined before. However, the business entities are classes (they will have behavior); meanwhile, the JPA entities are data structures (they do not have behavior). For more information, you can see `http://blog.cleancoder.com/uncle-bob/2019/06/16/ObjectsAndDataStructures.html`.

User Entity

The User entity is provided in Listing 5-5.

Listing 5-5. *User business entity*

```
public class User implements Serializable {
 private final String email;     // (1)
 private final String password;
```

```java
public User(String email, String password) {    // (2)
 this.email = email;
 this.password = password;
}

// Getters                         // (3)
// Equals and hashcode
// ToString
}
```

The following is a description of the code sample:

1. email and password final properties, which means you cannot change them after you initialize them.

2. A unique constructor, it has two properties: email, and password. Getters methods return the properties values.

3. equals and hashcode is when you must override equals and hashCode, and it is a good practice to add toString to debug our business entity.

FoodService Entity

The FoodService entity is provided in Listing 5-6.

Listing 5-6. FoodService business entity

```java
public class FoodService implements Serializable {
 private final String email;       // (1)
 private final String name;
 private final String address;
 private final String foodType;
 private final int deliveryFee;
 private final boolean active;
 private final User user;
 private final List<FoodProduct> foodProductList;
```

```
public FoodService(String email, String name, String address, String
foodType, int deliveryFee, boolean active, User user, List<FoodProduct>
foodProductList) {          // (2)
 this.email = email;
 this.name = name;
 this.address = address;
 this.foodType = foodType;
 this.active = active;
 this.foodProductList = foodProductList;
 this.deliveryFee = deliveryFee; this.user = user;
}
// Getters                              // (3)
// Equals and hashcode
// ToString
}
```

The following is a description of the code sample:

1. email, name, address, foodType, foodProductList, deliveryFee,
   and user final properties, which means you cannot change them
   after you initialize them.

2. A unique constructor, it has the whole properties. Getters methods
   return the properties values.

3. equals and hashcode is when you must override equals and
   hashCode, and it is a good practice.

FoodProduct Entity

The FoodProduct entity is provided in Listing 5-7.

Listing 5-7. FoodProduct business entity

```
public class FoodProduct implements Serializable {
 private final Integer id;          // (1)
 private final String name;
 private final int price;
```

```
private final String description;
private final boolean active;
private final String imageUrl;
private final String foodService;    // (2)

public FoodProduct(Integer id, String name, int price, String description,
boolean active, String imageUrl, String foodService) {              // (3)
 this.id = id;
 this.name = name; this.price = price;
 this.description = description; this.active = active;  this.imageUrl =
imageUrl; this.foodService = foodService;
}

// Getters                        // (4)
// Equals and hashcode
// ToString
}
```

The following is a description of the code sample:

1. id, name, price, description, active, imageUrl, and foodService
    final properties, which means you cannot change them after you
    initialize them.

2. See the foodService property. That seems to be a reference to the
    FoodService entity, and what it does. Why is that property a String
    but not a FoodService type? Well, remember that FoodProduct is a
    business entity, so we don't need to map exactly how the database
    or the JPA entities look like. For our current use cases, we only
    need the email for that FoodService.

3. A unique constructor, it has the whole properties.

4. Getters methods to return the properties values, equals,
    hashCode, and toString.

Item Entity

The item entity is provided in Listing 5-8.

Listing 5-8. Item business entity

```
public class Item implements Serializable {
 private final Integer id;                 // (1)
 private final int amount;
 private final FoodProduct foodProduct;

public Item(Integer id, int amount, FoodProduct foodProduct) {    // (2)
 this.id = id;
 this.amount = amount;
 this.foodProduct = foodProduct;
}

// Getters                          // (3)
// Equals and hashcode
// ToString
}
```

The following is a description of the code sample:

1. id, amount, and foodProduct final properties, which means you cannot change them after you initialize them.

   Remember, ItemData has a reference to DeliveryData and FoodProductData as foreign keys, so why don't we reference in the Item entity the Delivery entity? Well, for our use cases, it is not necessary.

2. A unique constructor, it has the whole properties.

3. Getters methods to return the properties values, equals, hashCode, and toString.

Delivery Entity

The FoodService entity is provided in Listing 5-9.

Listing 5-9. Delivery business entity

```
public class Delivery implements Serializable {

  private final Integer id;        // (1)
  private final String address;
  private final String phone;
  private final int total;
  private final int fee;
  private final String email;
  private final String state;
  private final List<Item> itemList;

public Delivery(Integer id, String address, String phone, int total, int
fee, String email, String state, List<Item> itemList) {          // (2)
  this.id = id;
  this.address = address;
  this.phone = phone;
  this.total = total;
  this.fee = fee;
  this.email = email;
  this.state = state;
  this.itemList = itemList;
}

// Getters                      // (3)
// Equals and hashcode
// ToString
}
```

The following is a description of the code sample:

1.   id, address, phone, total, fee, email, state, and itemList final
     properties, which means you cannot change them after you
     initialize them.

2.   A unique constructor, it has the whole properties.

3.   Getters methods to return the properties values, equals, hashCode, and toString.

Now, we have just see how our business entities are. Let's now define some repositories.

Defining Aggregates

An aggregate is a special business entity. They are root entities, which means they have children entities or value objects. That root creates a graph of entities and value objects, and those are related to each other.

An aggregate cluster is bound together, which means they are usually created, updated, or deleted together.

For our new Daniel's Delivery website, we will define the following aggregates shown in Figure 5-18.

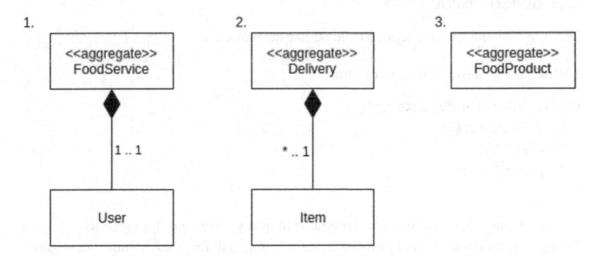

Figure 5-18. *Defining aggregates for Daniel's Delivery*

1.   FoodService aggregate is composed by the FoodService entity as a root and User entity as a child.

2.   Delivery aggregate is composed by the Delivery entity as a root and Item entity as a child.

181

3. And finally, FoodProduct aggregate is composed by FoodProduct entity as root and there are no children.

As we defined our aggregates, let's create our repositories.

Designing Repositories

A repository is a module that handles our business aggregates and entities. The main responsibilities are Query business aggregates and entities, Save business aggregates and entities, Update business aggregates and entities, and Delete business aggregates and entities.

Remember that our business aggregates and entities are different than JPA entities. That means, the repositories are logic storage for aggregates and entities, but they are not any database, disk, memory, or so on.

We are going to define a generic repository for our aggregates and entities, and we are going to create some extensions by each aggregate.

The Generic Repository

Let's see what our generic Repository looks like in Listing 5-10.

Listing 5-10. Repository abstraction

```
public interface Repository<T> {
  List<T> getAll();
  T save(T t);
  T update(T t);
}
```

As we can see, we have generic methods to query, save, and update. Each implementation/extension of this interface is going to define which entity/aggregate will map.

FoodServiceRepository Interface

Now we start to define the specific repositories: in this case, the FoodServiceRepository interface is showing in Listing 5-11.

Listing 5-11. FoodServiceRepository interface

```
public interface FoodServiceRepository extends Repository
<FoodService>{              // (1)
    List<FoodService>   getByFoodType(String foodType);  // (2)
}
```

We can observe the following features:

1. It extends from Repository, using FoodService aggregate as our generic definition.

2. We add a new method named getByFoodType. This is going to be used to query FoodService aggregates by its food type.

DeliveryRepository Interface

Of course, we need to handle the data regarding deliveries, so, we define our DeliveryRepository interface in Listing 5-12.

Listing 5-12. DeliveryRepository interface

```
public interface DeliveryRepository extends Repository<Delivery>{     // (1)
    List<Delivery> getByEmailAndState(String email, String state);    // (2)
}
```

We can observe the following features:

1. It extends from Repository, using Delivery aggregate as our generic definition.

2. We add a new method named getByEmailAndState. This is going to be used to query Delivery aggregates by its email and state.

FoodProductRepository Interface

Finally, we define how to access the FoodProduct entities with the FoodProductRepository interface as shown in Listing 5-13.

Listing 5-13. FoodProductRepository interface

```
public interface FoodProductRepository extends
Repository<FoodProduct>{          // (1)
  List<FoodProduct>    getByFoodService(String email);  // (2)
}
```

We can observe the following features:

1. It extends from Repository, using FoodProduct aggregate as our generic definition.

2. We add a new method named getByFoodService. This is going to be used to query FoodProduct aggregates by its food service owner.

Well, we just defined our design for the Abstraction of our persistence layer. In the following section, we are going to focus on how to implement the Main.

Implementing the Persistence Layer

We saw in the previous chapter how we defined our Abstraction for the persistence layer. In this section, we are going to focus on the implementation of our Main. Figure 5-19 shows our focus.

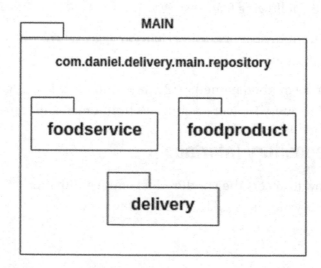

Figure 5-19. *Defining packages into the repository parent*

As we can see, we define the main packages (com.daniel.delivery.main.repository. foodservice, com.daniel.delivery.main.repository.foodservice, and com.daniel.delivery. main.repository.delivery) where we will save anything related to the JPA framework, by each entity type, in this case, FoodService, FoodProduct, and Delivery.

Remember, the Main is everything else, like frameworks, data access like JPA entities, transactions, queues, containers, and so on.

Defining the Structure and Responsibilities

Our Main is going to have repository implementations. Figure 5-20 shows what the Main packages will have.

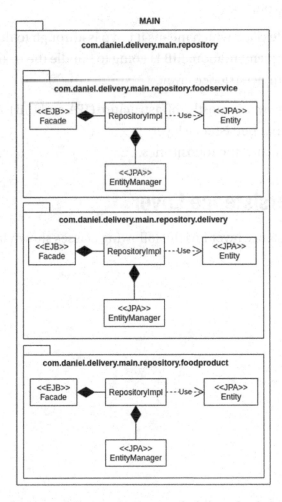

Figure 5-20. *General view of the packages and classes by business entity*

Let's discuss what those mean:

- They are grouped by aggregate.

- RepositoryImpl is the implementation of each repository interface. They will have any transformation from JPA entities to business entities, and any access to the database.

- JPA entity is the specific JPA class for each aggregate. They could be more than one, for instance, the Delivery aggregate has the DeliveryData JPA entity and the ItemData entity.

- The EntityManager is the main JPA class. It handles anything related to the persistence context, like save, delete, update, entities cache, and so on.

- EJB is a facade class, which means it is a passthrough to the repository implementation. EJB is going to handle the transactional context for our persistence layer.

As you can see, this layer is mostly infrastructure (JPA and EJB); that is why this belongs to the Main of our persistence layer.

Now, let's discuss each of the repositories.

FoodService Persistence Layer

The FoodService persistence layer has the following classes shown in Figure 5-21.

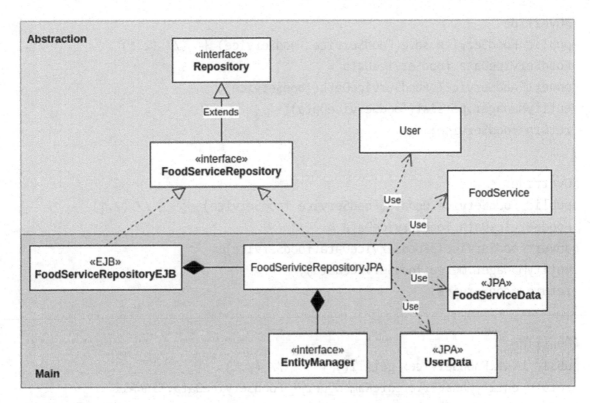

Figure 5-21. *Detailed view of classes and relationships of FoodService business entity*

Let's talk about them in detail.

FoodServiceRepositoryJPA Class

The FoodServiceRepositoryJPA class has the logic related to access the database, using the EntityManager, and transforms them from JPA entities to business entities and vice versa.

Let's see the code in Listing 5-14.

Listing 5-14. FoodServiceRepositoryJPA class

```
public class FoodServiceRepositoryJPA implements FoodServiceRepository {

  private final EntityManager entityManager;  // (1)

  public FoodServiceRepositoryJPA(EntityManager entityManager)  {
  this.entityManager = entityManager;
  }
```

```
 @Override
 public FoodService save(FoodService foodService) {   // (2.1)
 FoodServiceData foodServiceData =
convertFoodServiceToFoodServiceData(foodService);
 entityManager.persist(foodServiceData);
 return foodService;
}

@Override
 public FoodService update(FoodService foodService) {    // (2.1)
 FoodServiceData foodServiceData =
convertFoodServiceToFoodServiceData(foodService);
 entityManager.merge(foodServiceData);
 return foodService;
}

@Override
public List<FoodService> getAll() {      // (3.1)
 return entityManager.createNamedQuery("FoodServiceData.findAll",
FoodServiceData.class)
  .getResultList()
  .stream()
  .map(this::convertFoodServiceDataToFoodService)
  .collect(Collectors.toList());
}

@Override
public List<FoodService> getByFoodType(String foodType) {     // (3.2)
  return
entityManager.createNamedQuery("FoodServiceData.findByFoodType",
FoodServiceData.class)
  .setParameter("foodType", foodType)
  .getResultList()
  .stream()
  .map(this::convertFoodServiceDataToFoodService)
  .collect(Collectors.toList());
 }
```

```
// Converter methods
}
```

The following is a description of the code sample:

1. First, we require the EntityManager to build the FoodServiceRepositoryJPA class.

2. Now, we have the save and update methods for FoodService business entity. However, we need to transform FoodService in the FoodServiceData to use the EntityManager.

   You might ask, where do we persist the UserData entity? Well, we don't do it manually. We defined in the FoodServiceData the attribute userData, as a cascade = CascadeType.ALL. That means, any operation we do, using the EntityManager over FoodServiceData is going to affect the UserData child. In this case, if we persist the FoodServiceData, JPA is going to persist UserData automatically.

3. After this, we have two queries. We use the named queries defined in our JPA entities.

FoodServiceRepositoryEJB Class

This class is going to be a facade for our FoodServiceRepositoryJPA class. We are going to let the EJB container handle our transactions for us. Let's see this class step by step in Listing 5-15.

Listing 5-15. FoodServiceRepositoryEJB class

```
@Stateless              // (1)
@Local
@Infrastructure         // (2)
public class FoodServiceRepositoryEJB implements FoodServiceRepository{

 @Inject
 private FoodServiceRepositoryJPA foodServiceRepositoryJPA;    // (3)
```

```java
@Override
public List<FoodService> getAll() {     // (4.1)
 return foodServiceRepositoryJPA.getAll();
}

@Override
public FoodService save(FoodService foodService) {  // (4.2)
 return     foodServiceRepositoryJPA.save(foodService);
}

@Override
public FoodService update(FoodService foodService) {  // 3(4.1)
 return foodServiceRepositoryJPA.update(foodService);
}

@Override
public List<FoodService> getByFoodType(String foodType) {  // (4.4)
 return foodServiceRepositoryJPA.getByFoodType(foodType);
}
}
```

The following is a description of the code sample:

1. First, we have an EJB definition. This is @Stateless @Local bean.

2. @Infrastructure, which means this is an infrastructure implementation of the interface FoodServiceRepository. We added the custom infrastructure annotation to differentiate the FoodServiceRepository implementations. We have two - a JPA and EJB implementations - and if we upload those implementations to the CDI context, we need a way to identify them.

3. We inject the FoodServiceRepositoryJPA class into our EJB. We are going to see later where we tell the CDI container this class is and how it should be injected in other components.

4. Finally, we have the passthrough methods. By default, each EJB method is the transaction required. That means any database access using the entity manager will be in a transaction, starting when the EJB method starts and committing when the EJB method ends, or rollbacking when the EJB method throws a Runtime Exception.

Delivery Persistence Layer

The Delivery persistence layer has the following classes shown in Figure 5-22.

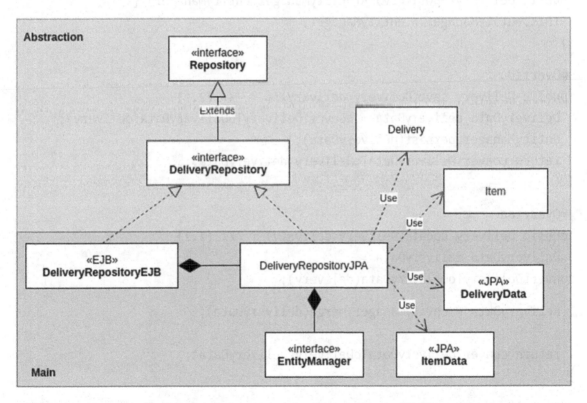

Figure 5-22. *Detailed view of classes and relationships of Delivery business entity*

Let's talk about them in detail.

DeliveryRepositoryJPA Class

DeliveryRepositoryJPA class has the logic related to access the database, using the EntityManager, and transforming from JPA entities to business entities and vice versa.

Let's see the code in Listing 5-16.

Listing 5-16. DeliveryRepositoryJPA class

```
public class DeliveryRepositoryJPA implements DeliveryRepository {

  private final EntityManager entityManager;     // (1)

  public DeliveryRepositoryJPA(EntityManager entityManager) {
    this.entityManager = entityManager;
  }

  @Override
  public Delivery save(Delivery delivery) {     // (2.1)
    DeliveryData deliveryData = convertDeliveryToDeliveryData(delivery);
    entityManager.persist(deliveryData);
    return convertDeliveryDataToDelivery(deliveryData);
  }

  @Override
  public Delivery update(Delivery delivery) {  // (2.2)
    DeliveryData deliveryData =
convertDeliveryToDeliveryData(delivery);

    deliveryData = entityManager.merge(deliveryData);

    return convertDeliveryDataToDelivery(deliveryData);
  }

  @Override
  public List<Delivery> getAll() {     // (3.1)
    return entityManager.createNamedQuery("DeliveryData.findAll",
    DeliveryData.class)
    .getResultList()
    .stream()
```

```
  .map(this::convertDeliveryDataToDelivery)
  .collect(Collectors.toList());
}

@Override
public List<Delivery> getByEmailAndState(String email, String state)
{                      // (3.2)
  return
entityManager.createNamedQuery("DeliveryData.findByEmailAndState",
DeliveryData.class)
    .setParameter("state", state)
    .setParameter("email", email)
    .getResultList()
    .stream()
    .map(this::convertDeliveryDataToDelivery)
    .collect(Collectors.toList());
}

// Converter methods
}
```

The following is a description of the code sample:

1. First, we require the EntityManager to build the
   DeliveryRepositoryJPA class.

2. Now, we have the save and update methods for the Delivery
   business entity. However, we need to transform Delivery in the
   DeliveryData to use the EntityManager.

   You might ask, where do we persist the ItemData list? Well, we
   don't do it manually. We defined in the DeliveryData the attribute
   itemDataList, as a cascade = CascadeType.ALL. That means, any
   operation we do, using the EntityManager over DeliveryData is
   going to affect the ItemData children. In this case, if we persist
   the DeliveryData, JPA is going to persist the ItemData list
   automatically.

3. After this, we have two queries. We use the named queries defined
    in our JPA entities.

We updated the DeliveryData entity, adding to the itemDataList attribute, the fetch =
FetchType.EAGER property. This means that any time we query a DeliveryData, we are
going to get the whole ItemData list ready to use. As Delivery is an aggregate, and the size
of the ItemData list is not huge, we can allow that.

Be careful to use fetch = FetchType.EAGER wisely. If the list/object you want to
EAGER is huge, this could give you performance issues.

DeliveryRepositoryEJB Class

This class is going to be a facade for our DeliveryRepositoryJPA class. We are going to let
the EJB container handle our transactions for us; and it will be like Listing 5-17.

Listing 5-17. DeliveryRepositoryEJB class

```
@Stateless                   // (1)
@Local
@Infrastructure              // (2)
public class DeliveryRepositoryEJB implements DeliveryRepository{

 @Inject
 private DeliveryRepositoryJPA deliveryRepositoryJPA; // (3)

 @Override
 public List<Delivery> getAll() {          // (4.4)
  return deliveryRepositoryJPA.getAll();
 }

 @Override
 public Delivery save(Delivery delivery) {       // (4.4)
  return deliveryRepositoryJPA.save(delivery);
 }

 @Override
 public Delivery update(Delivery delivery) {       // (4.4)
  return deliveryRepositoryJPA.update(delivery);
 }
```

```
@Override
public List<Delivery> getByEmailAndState(String email, String state)
{        // (4.4)
  return deliveryRepositoryJPA.getByEmailAndState(email, state);
 }

}
```

The following is a description of the code sample:

1. First, we have an EJB definition. This is @Stateless @Local bean.

2. @Infrastructure, which means, this is an infrastructure
   implementation of the interface DeliveryRepository.

   We added the infrastructure annotation to differentiate the
   DeliveryRepository implementations. We have two, a JPA and EJB
   implementations, and if we upload those implementations to the
   CDI context, we need a way to identify them.

3. We inject the DeliveryRepositoryJPA class into our EJB. We are
   going to see later where this class lives into the CDI container and
   how it should be injected into other components.

4. Finally, we have the passthrough methods.

As we defined the Delivery persistence layer, let's move to the FoodProduct.

FoodProduct Persistence Layer

The FoodProduct persistence layer has the following classes shown in Figure 5-23.

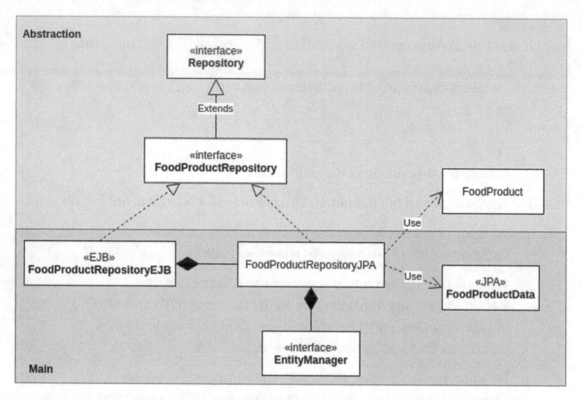

Figure 5-23. *Detailed view of classes and relationships of FoodProduct business entity*

Let's talk about them in detail.

FoodProductRepositoryJPA Class

The FoodProductRepositoryJPA class has the logic related to access the database, using the EntityManager, and transforming from JPA entities to business entities and vice versa.

Let's see the code in Listing 5-18.

Listing 5-18. FoodProductRepositoryJPA class

```
public class FoodProductRepositoryJPA implements FoodProductRepository {

 private final EntityManager entityManager;     // (1)

 public FoodProductRepositoryJPA(EntityManager entityManager)    {
  this.entityManager = entityManager;
 }
```

```java
@Override
public FoodProduct save(FoodProduct foodProduct) {   // (2.1)
  FoodProductData foodProductData =
convertFoodProductToFoodProductData(foodProduct);
  entityManager.persist(foodProductData);
  return convertFoodProductDataToFoodProduct(foodProductData);
}

@Override
public FoodProduct update(FoodProduct delivery) {   // (2.2)
  FoodProductData foodProductData =
convertFoodProductToFoodProductData(delivery);

  foodProductData = entityManager.merge(foodProductData);

  return convertFoodProductDataToFoodProduct(foodProductData);
}

@Override
public List<FoodProduct> getAll() {     // (3.1)
  return entityManager.createNamedQuery("FoodProductData.findAll",
  FoodProductData.class)
   .getResultList()
   .stream()
   .map(this::convertFoodProductDataToFoodProduct)
   .collect(Collectors.toList());
}

@Override
public List<FoodProduct> getByFoodService(String email)  {   // (3.2)
  return
entityManager.createNamedQuery("FoodProductData.findByFoodService",
FoodProductData.class)
   .setParameter("email", email)
   .getResultList()
   .stream()
```

```
    .map(this::convertFoodProductDataToFoodProduct)
    .collect(Collectors.toList());
  }
}
```

The following is a description of the code sample:

1. First, we require the EntityManager to build the
   FoodProductRepositoryJPA class.

2. Now we have the save and update methods for the FoodProduct
   business entity. However, we need to transform FoodProduct in
   the FoodProductData, to use the EntityManager.

3. And finally, we have two queries. We use the named queries
   defined in our JPA entities.

   getAll method queries the whole bunch of FoodProducts, and
   meanwhile, getByFoodService just queries the FoodProducts
   related to an email. Those methods use Java Functional
   programming to be more readable as this process is a flow of steps.

FoodProductRepositoryEJB Class

This class is going to be a facade for our FoodProductRepositoryJPA class. We are going
to let the EJB container handle our transactions for us. The EJB looks like Listing 5-19.

Listing 5-19. FoodProductRepositoryEJB class

```
@Stateless           // (1)
@Local
@Infrastructure      // (2)
public class FoodProductRepositoryEJB implements FoodProductRepository{

  @Inject
  private FoodProductRepositoryJPA foodProductRepositoryJPA;    // (3)

  @Override
  public List<FoodProduct> getAll() {       // (4.1)
    return foodProductRepositoryJPA.getAll();
  }
```

```
@Override
public FoodProduct save(FoodProduct foodProduct) {  // (4.2)
  return   foodProductRepositoryJPA.save(foodProduct);
}

@Override
public FoodProduct update(FoodProduct foodProduct) {   // (4.3)
  return   foodProductRepositoryJPA.update(foodProduct);
}

@Override
public List<FoodProduct> getByFoodService(String email) {    // (4.4)
  return foodProductRepositoryJPA.getByFoodService(email);
}
}
```

The following is a description of the code sample:

1. First, we have an EJB definition. This is @Stateless @Local bean.

2. @Infrastructure, which means this is an infrastructure implementation of the interface FoodProductRepository.

   We added the infrastructure annotation to differentiate the FoodProductRepository implementations. We have two, a JPA and EJB implementations, and if we upload those implementations to the CDI context, we need a way to identify them.

3. We inject the FoodProductRepositoryJPA class into our EJB. We are going to see later where we tell the CDI container what this class is and how it should be injected in other components.

4. Finally, we have the passthrough methods.

Now, as we defined the persistence layer, we can move to see how the CDI service helps us to initialize it.

Defining the Provider for the CDI

We defined some JPA classes with dependencies to the EntityManager, but, where do we put all of this together? We use a Provider.

A Provider is a class that creates components with its dependencies and saves them in the CDI context. This helps us to separate the Main and the Abstraction, where the Provider is responsible for putting both together.

We defined the following RepositoryProvider for our persistence layer in Listing 5-20.

Listing 5-20. RepositoryProvider class

```
@Stateless
@LocalBean
public class RepositoryProvider {

 @PersistenceContext private EntityManager em;

 @Produces
 public EntityManager getEntityManager() {
   return em;
 }

 @Produces
 public FoodServiceRepositoryJPA    getFoodServiceRepositoryJPA(Entity
Manager entityManager) {
  return new FoodServiceRepositoryJPA(entityManager);
 }

 @Produces
 public DeliveryRepositoryJPA getDeliveryRepositoryJPA(EntityManager
entityManager) {
  return new DeliveryRepositoryJPA(entityManager);
 }

 @Produces
 public FoodProductRepositoryJPA getFoodProductRepositoryJPA(EntityManager
entityManager) {
  return new FoodProductRepositoryJPA(entityManager);
 }
}
```

The following is a description of the code sample:

1. The Provider is a stateless local bean.

2. We inject the EntityManager and expose it into the CDI context.

3. Finally, we create our repository classes, injecting the EntityManager dependency.

We just finished implementing our Persistence layer; however, how do we test it? We are going to see that in the next section.

Testing the Persistence Layer

Well, we created a pretty good persistence layer for our new Daniel's Delivery website; however, we haven't tested it.

In this section, we are going to create unit tests using JUnit and Mockito, and integration tests using Arquillian.

Remember, we have quality attributes related to coverage and unit testing.

Note   We are going to focus on the DeliveryRepositoryJPA implementation tests and only some methods; however, you can find the whole code in our GitHub repository.

Unit Tests with JUnit and Mockito

We created a test class by each productive class and used Mockito and JUnit to test its behavior.

We are going to show the DeliveryRepositoryJPATest as an example. You can find the whole unit tests class in our GitHub repository.

DeliveryRepositoryJPATest Class Example

This class is going to test everything about the DeliveryRepositoryJPA class. Let's see how it does that in Listing 5-21.

Listing 5-21. DeliveryRepositoryJPATest class

```
@RunWith(MockitoJUnitRunner.class)           // (1)
public class DeliveryRepositoryJPATest {

 @Mock
 private EntityManager entityManager;       // (1.1)
 @Mock
 private TypedQuery typedQuery;             // (1.2)
 @InjectMocks
 private DeliveryRepositoryJPA deliveryRepositoryJPA;

 @Test
 public void save() {                  // (2)
// (3)
  FoodProduct foodProduct = new FoodProduct(1, "Pizza", 23500, "Pinaple
  Pizza", true, "imageUrl", "email1@email.com");

Item item = new Item(1, 1, foodProduct);

Delivery delivery = new Delivery(1, "Street 50", "555233564", 23600, 100,
"email5@email.com", "PENDING", Arrays.asList(item));

// (4)

  FoodServiceData foodServiceData = new FoodServiceData();   foodServiceData.
  setEmail("email1@email.com");
  FoodProductData foodProductData = new FoodProductData();
  foodProductData.setId(foodProduct.getId());
  foodProductData.setActive(true);
  foodProductData.setDescription(foodProduct.getDescription());
  foodProductData.setImageUrl(foodProduct.getImageUrl());
  foodProductData.setName(foodProduct.getName());
  foodProductData.setPrice(foodProduct.getPrice());
  foodProductData.setFoodService(foodServiceData);

  ItemData itemData = new ItemData();
  itemData.setAmount(item.getAmount());
  itemData.setId(item.getId());
  itemData.setFoodProduct(foodProductData);
```

```
DeliveryData deliveryData = new DeliveryData();
deliveryData.setId(delivery.getId());
deliveryData.setFee(delivery.getFee());
deliveryData.setPhone(delivery.getPhone());
deliveryData.setAddress(delivery.getAddress());
deliveryData.setTotal(delivery.getTotal());
deliveryData.setEmail(delivery.getEmail());
deliveryData.setState(delivery.getState());
deliveryData.setItemList(Arrays.asList(itemData));

// (5)
when(entityManager.find(FoodProductData.class, 1)).thenReturn
(foodProductData);

deliveryRepositoryJPA.save(delivery);

verify(entityManager).persist(deliveryData);
}
// More tests
}
```

The following is a description of the code sample:

1. We define the Mockito initialization and some mocks for our test, like the EntityManager.

2. Next, we create a test for the save method.

3. Here, we start with preparing the test data.

4. Later, we prepare the expected data.

5. And finally, we mock the behavior we need, execute the test, and verify some results.

Now, let's move to the integration tests using Arquillian.

Integration Tests Using Arquillian and Derby

Arquillian is a framework that helps us to test Jakarta EE applications. The main features it has is that you can start an embedded application server and deploy into it your application, and then later, you can inject some components and run some tests.

As we want to test our persistence layer, Figure 5-24 shows the strategy we are going to follow.

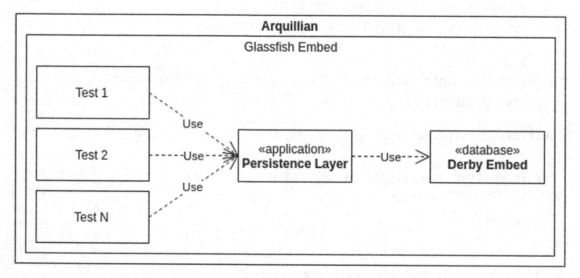

Figure 5-24. *Arquillian tests structure*

As we can see, we are going to use an embedded GlassFish Application Server and a Derby embedded database.

This is a white box test. That means we need to know the internal components we are going to test, in this case, DeliveryRepositoryEJB, and ask the Jakarta EE container to inject that component in our test to use it.

A Derby embedded database is included in GlassFish and is started when you start the server and stopped when the server stops.

Next we are going to define a special persistence.xml, some SQL files for initial data, and finally, how to use Arquillian to test the DeliveryRepositoryEJB.

We are going to show only the integration test over DeliveryRepositoryEJB; however, you can find the whole test for the other repositories in our GitHub.

Adding Maven Dependencies for Arquillian

We need to add some of the management dependency for Arquillian to StartWithJEE/
pom.xml as shown in Listing 5-22.

Listing 5-22. Maven Dependency management configuration for Arquillian

```
<dependencyManagement>
 <dependencies>
  <dependency>
   <groupId>org.jboss.arquillian</groupId>
   <artifactId>arquillian-bom</artifactId>
   <version>1.4.1.Final</version>
   <scope>import</scope>
   <type>pom</type>
  </dependency>
 </dependencies>
</dependencyManagement>
```

After this, we add the Maven dependencies to StartWithJEE/StartWithJEE-ejb/pom.
xml shown in Listing 5-23.

Listing 5-23. Maven dependencies configuration for Arquillian

```
<dependency>
 <groupId>org.jboss.arquillian.junit</groupId>
 <artifactId>arquillian-junit-container</artifactId>
 <scope>test</scope>
</dependency>

<dependency>
 <groupId>org.glassfish.main.extras</groupId>
 <artifactId>glassfish-embedded-all</artifactId>
 <version>5.1.0</version>
 <scope>test</scope>
</dependency>
```

```
<dependency>
 <groupId>org.jboss.arquillian.container</groupId>
 <artifactId>arquillian-glassfish-embedded-3.1</artifactId>
 <version>1.0.2</version>
 <scope>test</scope>
</dependency>
```

Add the arquillian-junit-container, glassfish-embedded- all, and arquillian-glassfish-embedded-3.1 dependencies to the StartWithJEE/StartWithJEE-ejb/pom.xml file.

glassfish-embedded-all and arquillian-glassfish-embedded-3.1 dependencies are required as we want to test using the GlassFish application server.

After this, we will be able to access Arquillian classes to create our integration test. We will detail that in the following section.

Creating Data Initialization

We now need to fill the Derby database somehow for our tests. So we are going to create some SQL files with basic data to insert into our in-memory database.

The following SQL files were created:

- deliverydata.sql: It has the data related to test the Delivery repository.

- foodservicedata.sql: It has the data related to test the FoodService repository.

- foodproductdata.sql: It has the data related to test the FoodProduct repository.

For instance, deliverydata.sql looks like Listing 5-24.

Listing 5-24. deliverydata.sql inserts

```
INSERT INTO "USER_DATA" (EMAIL, PASSWORD) VALUES ('email1@email.com',
'pass1'),('email2@email.com', 'pass2')

INSERT INTO "FOOD_SERVICE" (email, name, address, food_type, delivery_fee,
active) VALUES('email1@email.com', 'Pizzas 25', 'Street 89', 'PIZZA', 100, 1)
```

```
INSERT INTO "FOOD_PRODUCT" (name, price, description, image_url, food_
service, active) VALUES('Pizza', 23500, 'Pinaple Pizza', 'imageUrl',
'email1@email.com', 1)

INSERT INTO "DELIVERY" (address, phone, total, fee, email, state)
VALUES('Street 50', '555233564', 23600, 100, 'email5@email.com', 'PENDING')

INSERT INTO "ITEM" (food_product, delivery, amount) VALUES(1, 1, 1)
```

As you can see, we insert enough data to create a Delivery.

Defining a Persistence.xml for Testing

We need to connect to our Derby database somehow. In this case, we are going to create a new persistence.xml configuration into StartWithJEE/StartWithJEE-ejb/src/test/resources/META-INF/ just for testing purposes.

Listing 5-25 shows a basic persistence.xml file to connect to a Derby database.

Listing 5-25. persistence.xml setup to use some preload scripts and the entity classes

```
<?xml version="1.0" encoding="UTF-8"?>
<persistence version="2.1" xmlns="http://xmlns.jcp.org/xml/ns/
persistence" xmlns:xsi="http://www.w3.org/2001/XMLSchema-instance"
xsi:schemaLocation="http://xmlns.jcp.org/xml/ns/persistence http://xmlns.
jcp.org/xml/ns/persistence/persistence_2_1.xsd">
  <persistence-unit name="deliverymysql" transaction-type="JTA">
    <!--(1)-->
    <class>com.daniel.delivery.main.repository.delivery.DeliveryData
    </class>
    <class>com.daniel.delivery.main.repository.delivery.ItemData</class>
    <class>com.daniel.delivery.main.repository.foodservice.
FoodServiceData</class>
    <class>com.daniel.delivery.main.repository.foodservice.UserData</class>
    <class>com.daniel.delivery.main.repository.foodproduct.
FoodProductData</class>

    <!--(2)-->
```

```
    <property name="javax.persistence.schema- generation.database.action"
    value="drop-and-create"/>
    <property name="javax.persistence.schema-generation.create-source"
    value="metadata"/>

    <!--(3)-->
    <property name="javax.persistence.sql-load-script-source"
    value="META-INF/data.sql" />
</persistence>
```

The following is a description of the code sample:

1. First, we tell JPA which entities belong to this persistence unit
    using the class tag.

2. Next, we define the tables creation strategy; in this case, it is
    create-drop and using the annotations we have in our JPA entities.

    As we don't define an <jta-data-source> element, when the
    application starts, GlassFish is going to use a default data source it
    has to connect to the embedded Derby database.

    What that means is when the persistence context is started, JPA is
    going to create the tables in Derby, using the table definitions we
    have in our JPA entities

3. And finally, we tell JPA which SQL script to run after the tables
    were created.

This script is going to help us to add default data into the database for testing
purposes. The script is executed after the creation of the tables is done.

Creating an Integration Test for DeliveryRepositoryEJB

Let's see how to use Arquillian to create an integration test. First, Listing 5-26 shows the
DeliveryRepositoryEJB test.

Listing 5-26. DeliveryRepositoryEJBIT class

```
@RunWith(Arquillian.class)                        // (1)
public class DeliveryRepositoryEJBIT {

  @Inject
  @Infrastructure
  private DeliveryRepository deliveryRepository;    // (2)

  @Deployment
  public static JavaArchive createDeployment() {    // (3)
    return   ShrinkWrap.create(JavaArchive.class)
                  .addPackages(true, "com.daniel.delivery")
                  .addAsResource("META-INF/persistence.xml")
                  .addAsResource("META-INF/deliverydata.sql", "META-
INF/data.sql")  // (4)

.addAsManifestResource(EmptyAsset.INSTANCE, "beans.xml");

  }

  @Test
  @InSequence(1)
  public void getAll_basicData_same() {           // (5)
      FoodProduct foodProduct = new FoodProduct(1, "Pizza", 23500,
      "Pinaple Pizza", true, "imageUrl", "email1@email.com");

    Item item = new Item(1, 1, foodProduct);

    Delivery delivery = new Delivery(1, "Street 50", "555233564", 23600,
    100, "email5@email.com", "PENDING", Arrays.asList(item));

    List<Delivery> deliveries = deliveryRepository.getAll();

    assertThat(deliveries).isEqualTo(Arrays.asList(delivery));
  }

  @Test
  @InSequence(2)
  public void save_new_getAll() {             // (6)
```

```
    FoodProduct foodProduct = new FoodProduct(1, "Pizza", 23500, "Pinaple
    Pizza", true, "imageUrl", "email1@email.com");

    Item item1 = new Item(1, 1, foodProduct);

     Delivery delivery1 = new Delivery(1, "Street 50", "555233564", 23600,
     100, "email5@email.com", "PENDING", Arrays.asList(item1));

   Item newItem = new Item(null, 2, foodProduct);

   Delivery newDelivery = new Delivery(null, "Street 89", "55587412", 20100,
   100, "email10@email.com", "PENDING", Arrays.asList(newItem));

   Item expectedItem = new Item(2, 2, foodProduct); Delivery
   expectedDelivery = new Delivery(2, "Street 89",
"55587412", 20100, 100, "email10@email.com", "PENDING",
Arrays.asList(expectedItem));

    newDelivery = deliveryRepository.save(newDelivery); List<Delivery>
    deliveries = deliveryRepository.getAll();

    assertThat(deliveries).isEqualTo(Arrays.asList(delivery1,
    expectedDelivery));
  }
// More tests
}
```

The following is a description of the code sample:

1. We tell JUnit to use the Arquillian runner.

2. We inject our DeliveryRepository interface into our test.

   We have two implementations for the DeliveryRepository
   interface, DeliveryRepositoryJPA, and DeliveryRepositoryEJB. As
   we are creating integration tests, we want to test from the EJB, so,
   @Infrastructure tells the CDI container which implementation it
   must inject; in this case, it will be the DeliveryRepositoryEJB as we
   annotated it with @Infrastructure too.

3. Define which components of our project we want to test. In this case, we tell Arquillian to load any class in the package com. daniel.delivery, use the persistence.xml for testing, adding the data.sql file and using an empty beans.xml.

4. We are mapping the deliverydata.sql file to data.sql file because we have hard-coded data.sql in our persistence.xml for testing. beans.xml is a file where you can define the CDI container, its beans, and its relations. We don't care about it for now.

5. We create a test for the getAll method. There, we prepare the data for testing, execute the test, and assert the results.

    As this is the first test, the current data in the Derby database is the data we insert using the deliverydata.sql file. This means the data we prepared in this test is exactly the same as the data we have in a deliverydata.sql file.

6. And finally, we create a test for the save method. Here, we prepare more data, save it, and assert the result.

    @InSequence(2) means that this test will run in second place. So, as our Derby database is online in the whole tests, the order in which the tests run is important. In this case, you can see that the database has our init data, so the assert validates the new data we are saving plus the old data that was there before. You can find the whole integration tests in our GitHub.

We just created a full persistence layer, from the design to the integration tests.

Summary

In this chapter, we learned how to create a persistence layer using Jakarta EE, from the entities' discovery to the integration tests.

We learned how to discover business entities and relationships from the use cases; create a database entity-relationship model; translate them into a database schema; generate some JPA entities in a fast way; implementing the persistence layer with its transactions and basic JPA configuration; and finally, we learned how to create and test a CRUD using a Derby database.

In the following chapters, we are going to move to the front end for our new Packet Delivery website, designing the Vue.js components.

Questions

1. Can I generate JPA entities from Eclipse?

2. Can I run my integration tests against a non in-memory database?

3. If you already generated the entities, but you change your database tables, can you regenerate them?

4. Can I use JPA outside the JEE container?

5. Can I use a different configuration than JTA for my transactional context?

6. What kind of transaction attributes can I define in an EJB method?

7. Can I define EJBs different than @Stateless?

## CHAPTER 6

Designing Your Front-End UI with Vue.Js Components

In previous chapters, we defined the persistence layer of our application using JPA and JakartaEE 8 for our new Delivery Daniel's website. Now, we are going to move to the front-end side of our new application, designing its requirements and interfaces using wireframes, relating them to Vue.js components and reusing those in a composed way, and finally, implementing those components using different features like inputs, conditionals, plugins, and navigation using routes in Vue.js.

The following topics will be covered in this chapter:

- Defining the basic wireframes for new Daniel's Delivery Splitting of your wireframes into Vue.js pages and components

- Creating reusable components and composing them in a hierarchy

- Using the CartItems component as an example for iterators, functions, lifecycle events, user inputs, user events, conditionals, and executing business rules

- And finally, routing through the URL to components and to send the data

© Daniel Andres Pelaez Lopez 2021
D. A. P. Lopez, *Full-Stack Web Development with Jakarta EE and Vue.js*,
https://doi.org/10.1007/978-1-4842-6342-6_6

Technical Requirements

To follow the instructions in this chapter, you will need the following:

- Node.js 10.13.0

- Npm 6.7.0

- Nvm 0.34.0

- Visual Studio Code 1.33.1

You can check the whole project and code at `https://github.com/Apress/`
`full-stack-web-development-with-jakartaee-and-vue.js/tree/master/CH6`.

Defining the Basic Wireframes for New Daniel's Delivery

Designing a user interface is a challenge; you need to take the business requirements
and translate them to views and interaction.

In this section, we are going to cross the requirements from the new Daniel's
Delivery to the wireframes.

Note   You can check the detailed requirements for the new Daniel's Delivery in
Chapter 4, "Requirement Analysis for Your Full-Stack Web."

Home Page Wireframe

Any application needs a home page. There is no explicit requirement, however, but we
think it should look like Figure 6-1.

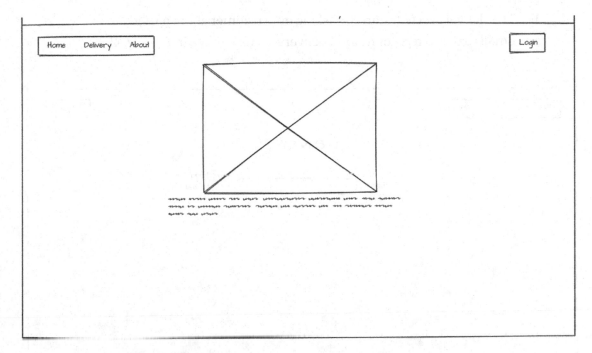

Figure 6-1. *Wireframe for the Daniel's Delivery home*

As we see, we have the right menu with the following sections:

- Home: this is the home page, with space to add images or text.

- Delivery: this is where the customers are going to find the food services and its products; moreover, they will be able to request food.

- About: this is a simple page where we talk about our new Delivery Daniel's website.

On the left side we have another option:

- Login: There, a Food Service admin will be able to log in into the system to update its information about Food Products and so on.

Delivery Flow

The delivery flow of our Daniel's Delivery website is pretty important; there, the customers will be able to see the registered Food Services and its Food Products; moreover, they will be able to create a food request and follow it.

1. The delivery section starts by asking our customer about a valid email to use to register its food delivery, as we can see in Figure 6-2.

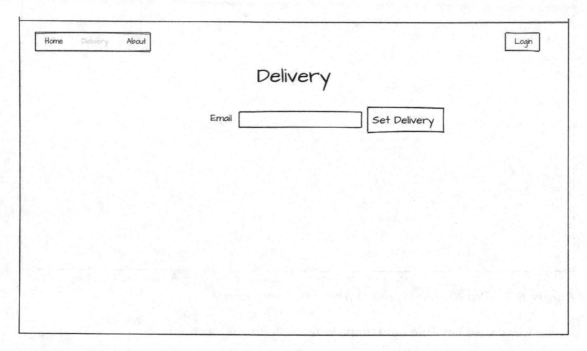

Figure 6-2. *Wireframe for the Daniel's Delivery page to request a delivery by email*

2. After you set the email, you will be redirected to the Food Services list that looks like Figure 6-3.

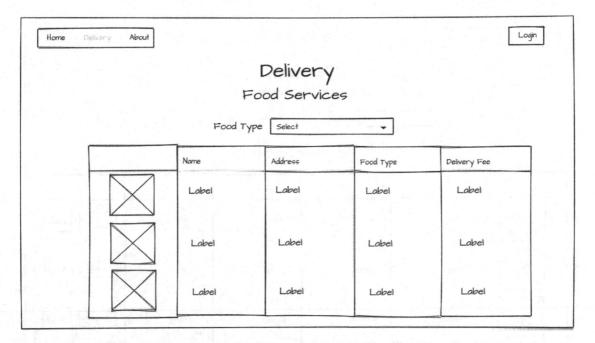

Figure 6-3. *Wireframe for the Food Services available*

We have a drop-down to filter the data by Food Type, and the list is going to be loaded using an infinite scroll.

We usually see a pagination menu when the results are more than we can see into the page. In this case, we use an infinite scroll, which means we do not have a menu to move between the whole data; we just scroll down and the data is going to show up until there is no more data. You can find a good discussion here: `https://uxplanet.org/ux-infinite-scrolling-` vs-pagination-1030d29376f1

3. After they choose a Food Service, the customer will see the Food Service detail with its Food Products, as shown in Figure 6-4.

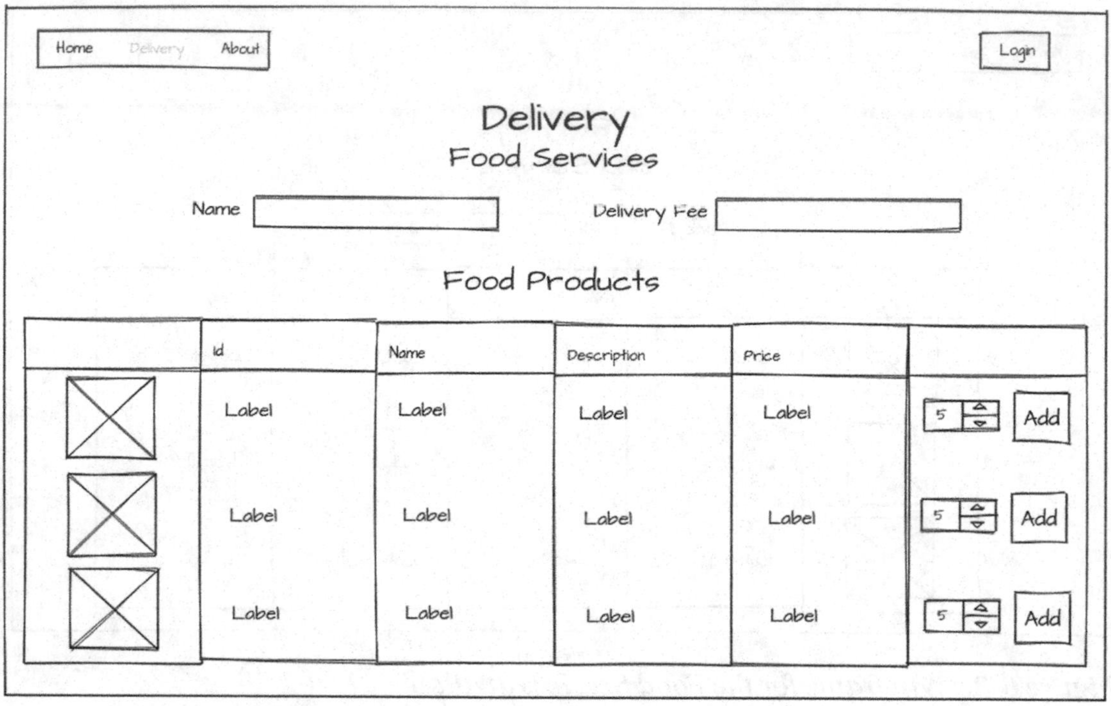

Figure 6-4. *Wireframe for the Food Products on specific Food Service offers*

Moreover, they will be able to choose the number of Food Products they want to add to the order.

The product list is going to be loaded using an infinite scroll.

4. Now, when they add some Food Products to their order, they will see a cart as shown in Figure 6-5.

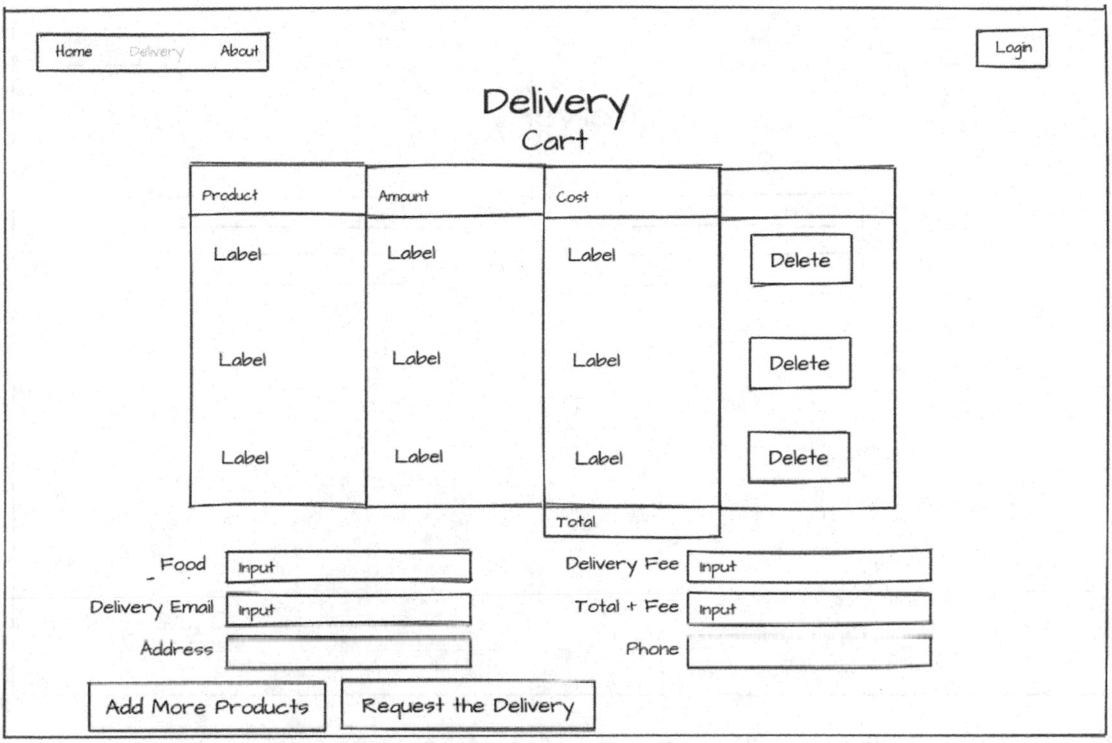

Figure 6-5. *Wireframe for the Delivery Cart*

In the cart, they will find the Food Products they added, the total cost of the products, and some information about the Food Service.

The customer will need to fill in the delivery address and the phone to confirm the request.

5. After the customer requests the delivery, they will see a summary as shown in Figure 6-6.

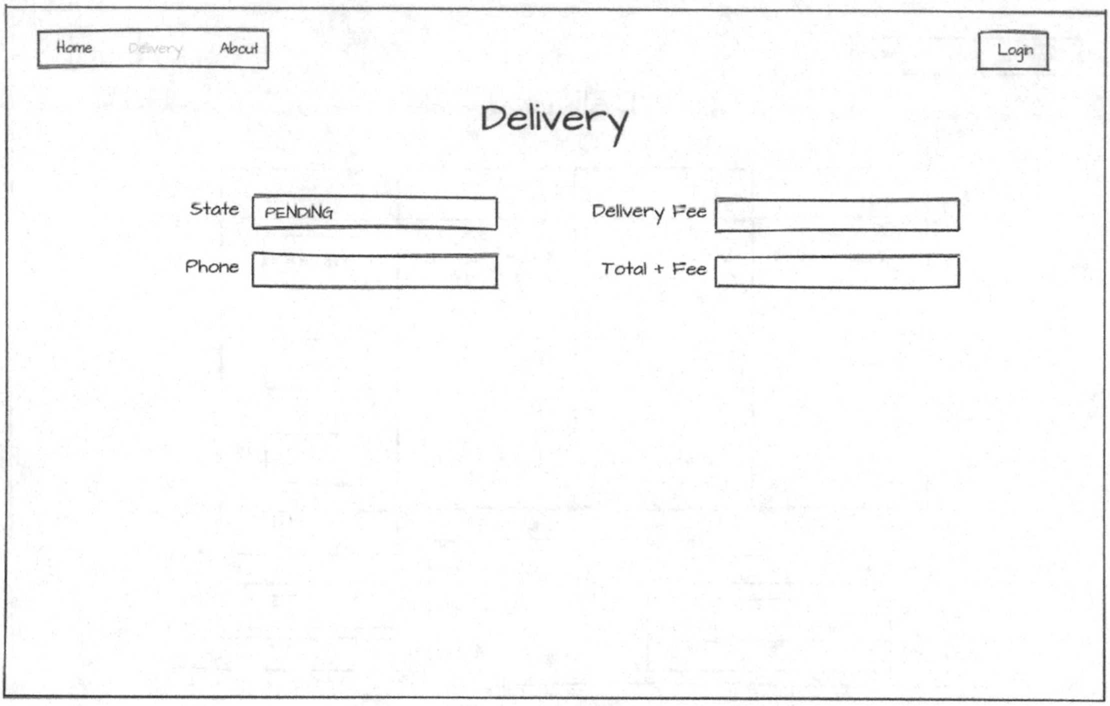

Figure 6-6. *Wireframe for the summary of the delivery request*

Now, we have completed the flow to request delivery in our new Daniel's Delivery website.

Food Service Settings Flow

The Food Service settings flow is responsible for creating and updating a Food Service in the new Daniel's Delivery website. This is going to handle the Food Service and its Food Products information. We see the defined flow next:

1. First, when a Food Service admin clicks on the Login menu, they will see what is displayed in Figure 6-7.

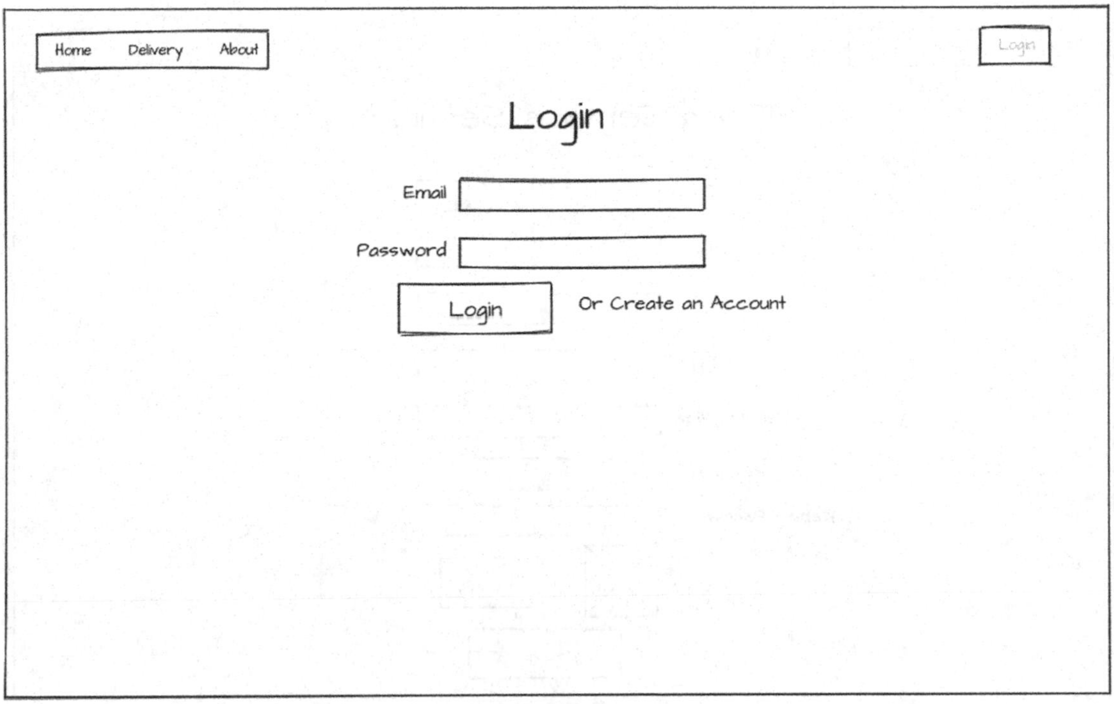

Figure 6-7. Wireframe for the Food Service login

There, a Food Service admin can log in using its email and password or create a new account if they don't have one.

2. If the Food Service admin chooses to create a new account, they will see what is shown in Figure 6-8.

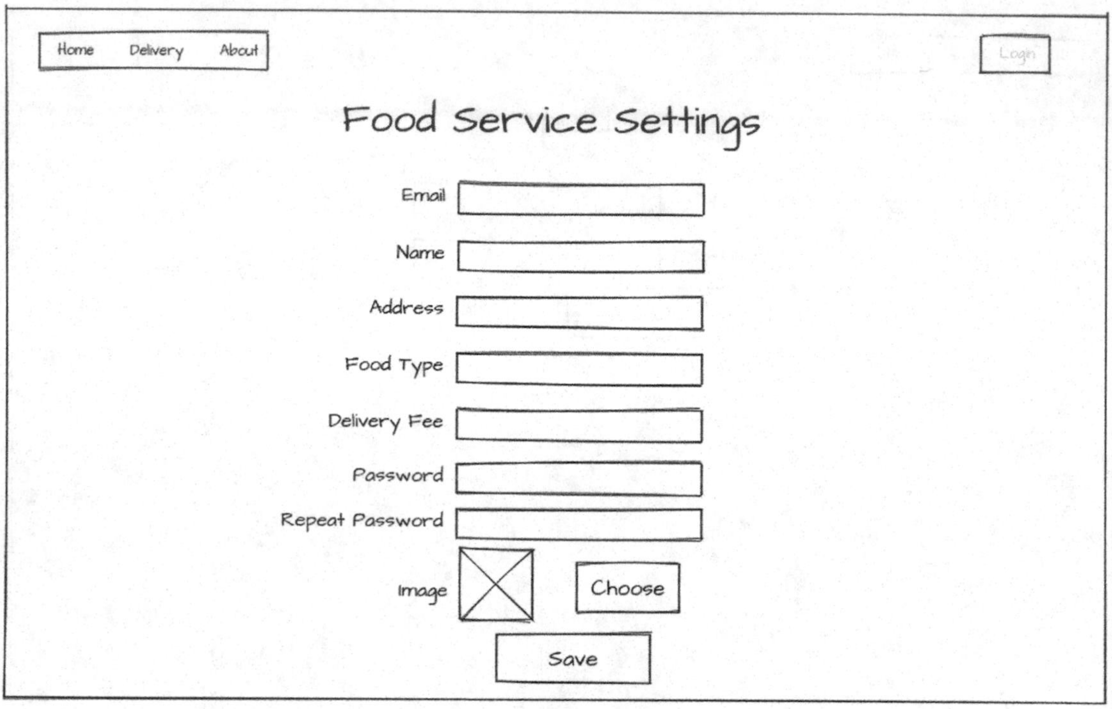

Figure 6-8. *Wireframe for the Food Service settings to create a new account*

When the Food Service admin saves the data, they will be redirected to log in again.

3. When the Food Service admin logs in into the application, they will see Figure 6-9.

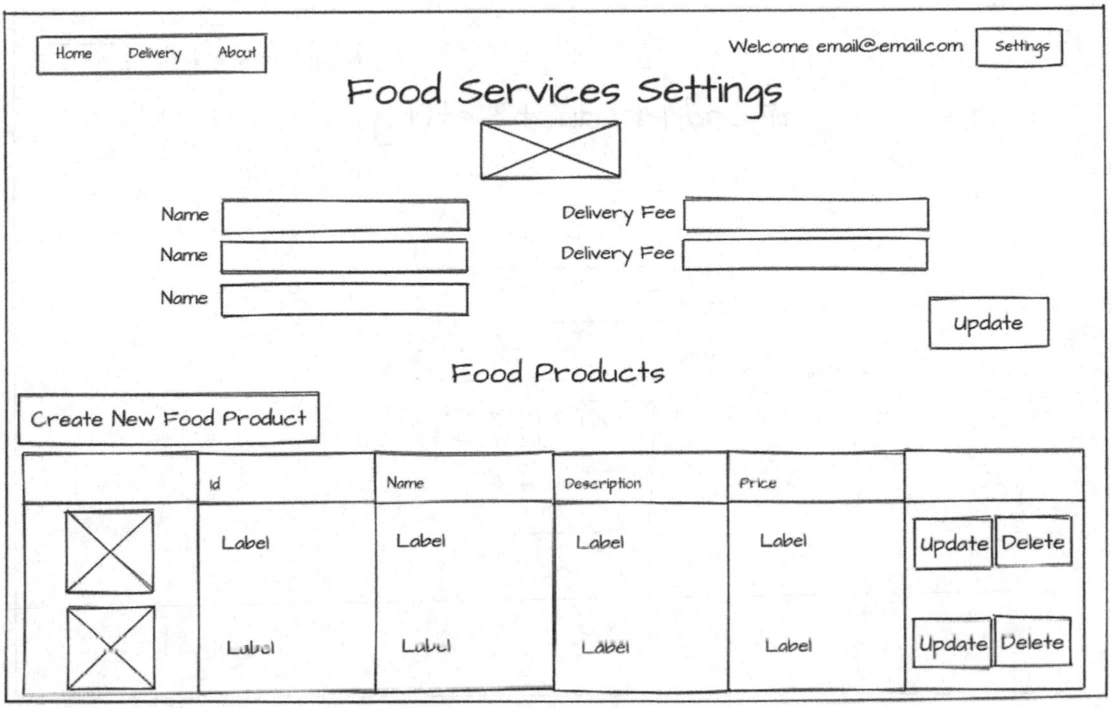

Figure 6-9. *Wireframe for the Food Service settings with its products*

A Food Service admin can update its information, add more Food Products, or update or delete them.

4. When a Food Service admin clicks on update, they will see a similar form like the registration.

5. When a Food Service admin clicks on Create New Food Product, they will see Figure 6-10.

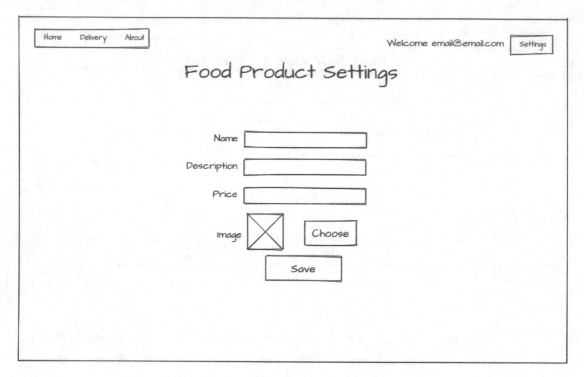

Figure 6-10. *Wireframe for the Food Product settings*

6. When a Food Service admin clicks on delete a Food Product, the
    product will no longer be available.

7. When a Food Service admin clicks on update a Food Product, they
    will see a similar form like the creation of Food Product.

With these wireframes, we completed the whole process for the Food Service settings
flow in our new Daniel's Delivery website.

Splitting Your Wireframes into Vue.js Pages and Components

We defined what our new Daniel's Delivery website should look like, but now we need to
split those wireframes into Vue.js pages and components.

A page in Vue.js is a component that has a specific URL into the application. That
URL can have children; however, any other children component is rendered into the
same page. That means a page is built of components, and those components are built of
more components.

In the following sections, we are going to talk about each page and what components we need there.

Delivery Page

The delivery page is going to have everything related to the delivery process, from choosing a Food Service and Food Product, to requesting the delivery. Let's see the components we are going to use:

- Delivery Email component: This component will have the email for delivery (Figure 6-11).

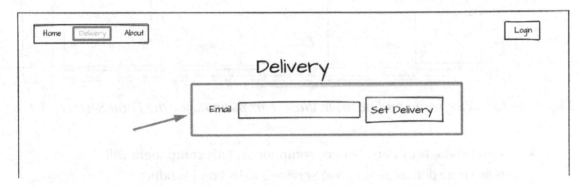

Figure 6-11. *Wireframe and possible Vue.js components for the delivery page by email*

- Food Services list component: This will show the whole list of Food Services available and you can filter using the Food Type drop-down (Figure 6-12).

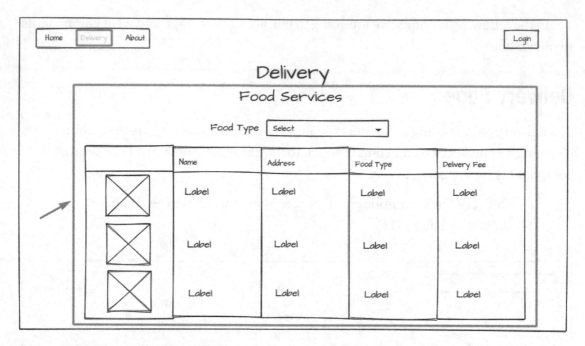

Figure 6-12. *Wireframe and possible Vue.js components for the Food Services list*

- Food Products by Food Service component: This component will show some details about Food Service and its Food Products; moreover, you will be able to add Food Products to your cart (Figure 6-13).

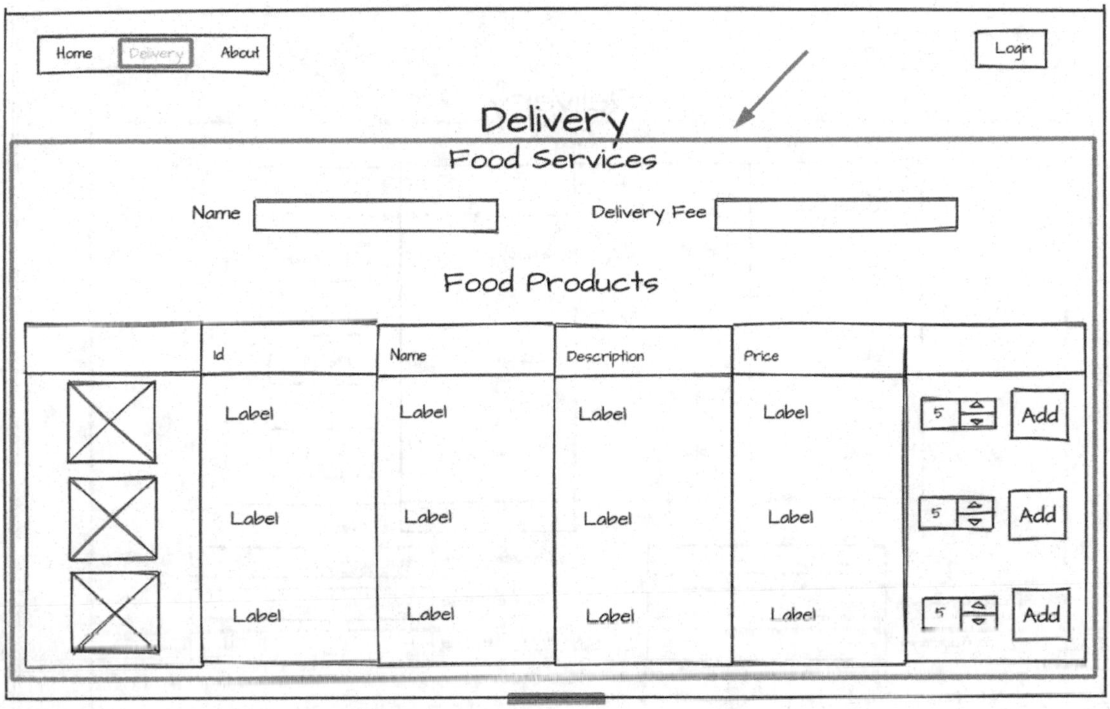

Figure 6-13. Wireframe and possible Vue.js components for the Food Services detail

- Cart component: This component is the customer cart. There, they will find the products, costs, and can request the delivery (Figure 6-14).

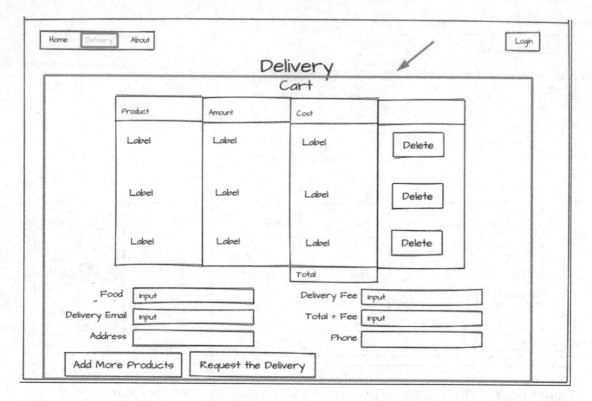

Figure 6-14. *Wireframe and possible Vue.js components for the Cart detail*

- Delivery Summary component: There, we will find the delivery
  summary of your request (Figure 6-15).

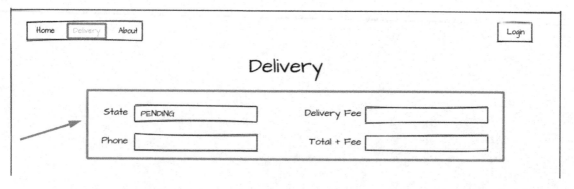

Figure 6-15. *Wireframe and possible Vue.js components for the Delivery summary*

Now, we just defined the components for our Delivery page. We will move to the Food Services Settings page.

Food Services Settings Page

The Food Service settings page is going to handle everything about Food Service, its data, and its Food Products. Let's see the components we are going to use:

- Food Service Form component: This component is the form to create/update a Food Service. This component is going to be reused to create and update Food Services (Figure 6-16).

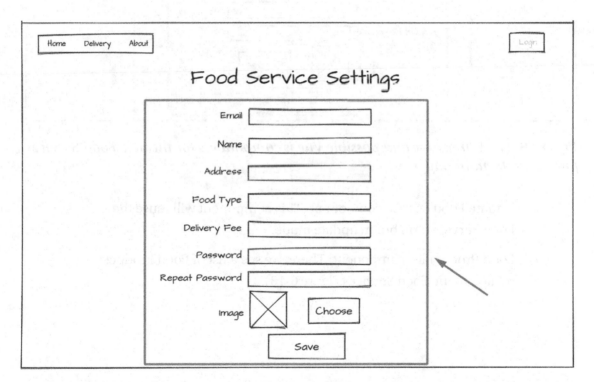

Figure 6-16. *Wireframe and possible Vue.js components for the new Food Service form*

- New Food Service component: This component is going to use the Food Service (Figure 6-17).

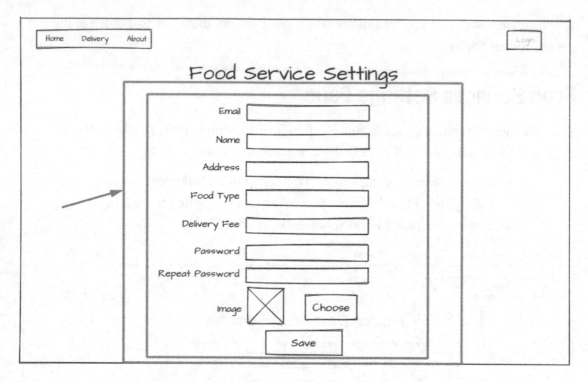

Figure 6-17. *Wireframe and possible Vue.js components for the new Food Service form and its main page*

- Update Food Service component: This component will reuse the Food Service form but in update mode.

- Food Product list component: There, we see a list of Food Products related to the Food Service (Figure 6-18).

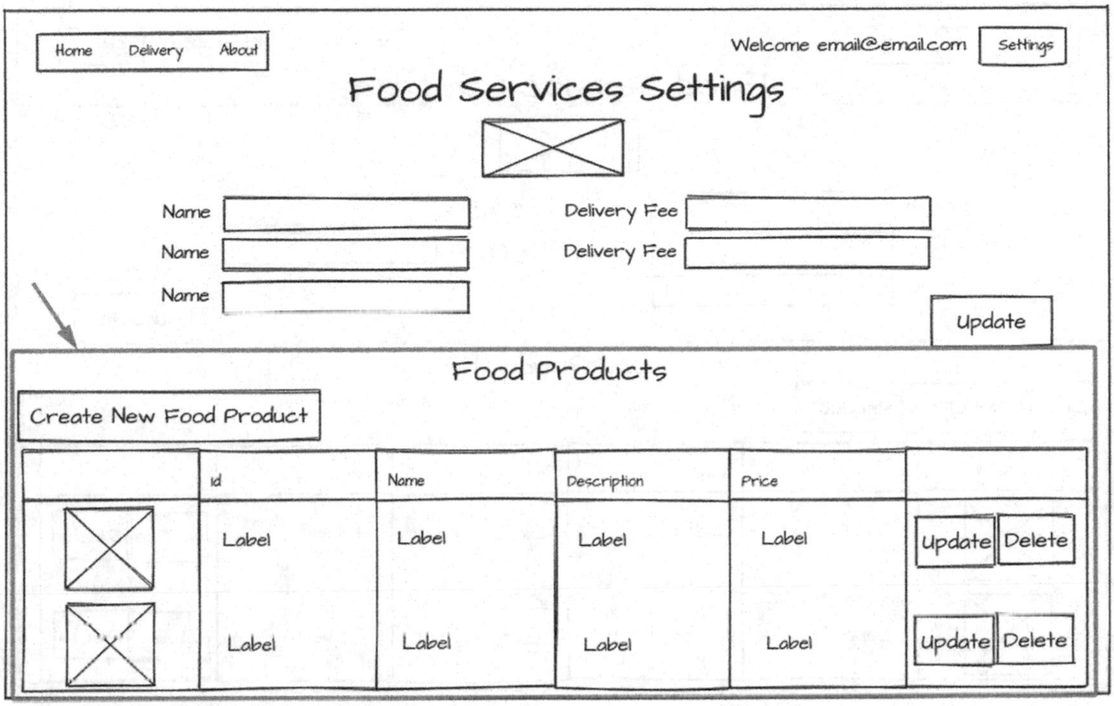

Figure 6-18. *Wireframe and possible Vue.js components for the new Food Services details*

- Food Service View component: This component will show the Food Service details and its Food Products (Figure 6-19).

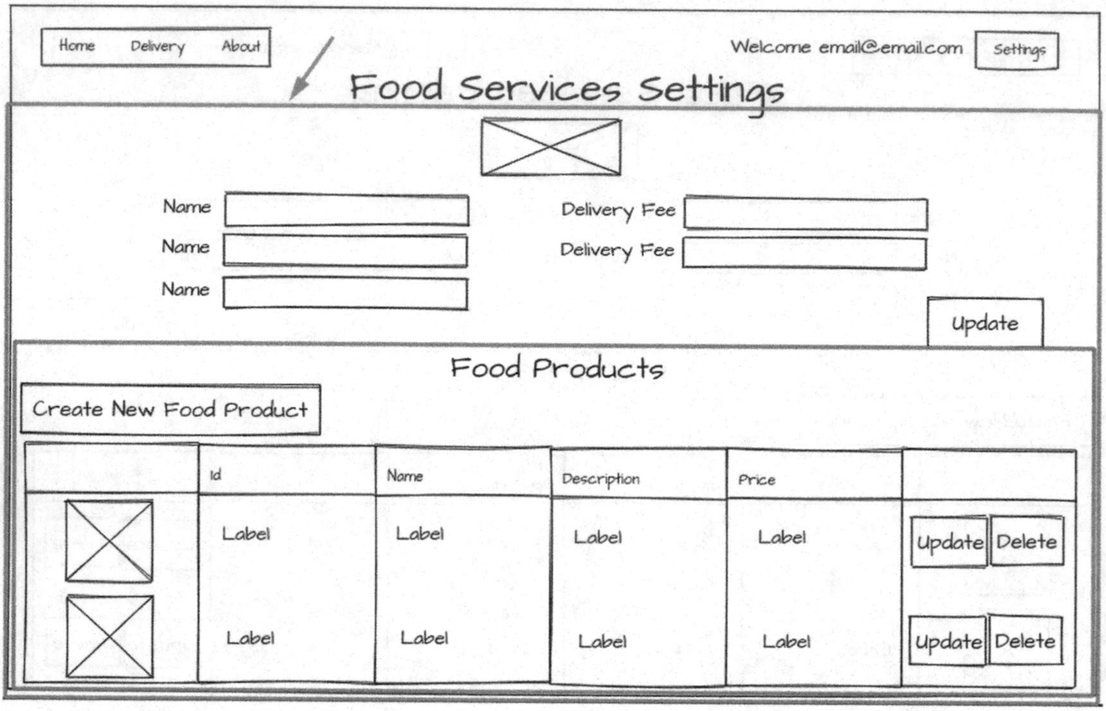

Figure 6-19. *Wireframe and possible Vue.js components for the new Food Services details and the main page*

- Food Product form component: This is the form to create/update a Food Product (Figure 6-20).

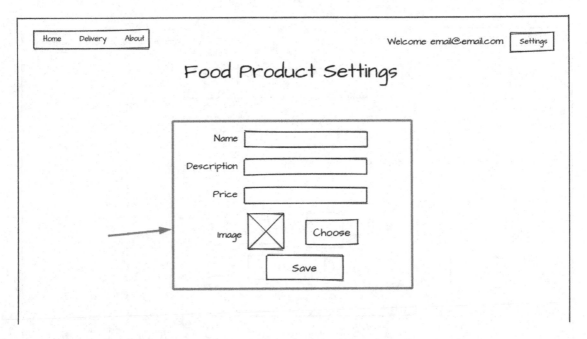

Figure 6-20. *Wireframe and possible Vue.js components for the new Food Product form*

- Update Food Product component: This component will reuse the Food Product form but in update mode.

- New Food Product component: This component will reuse the Food Product form but in creation mode (Figure 6-21).

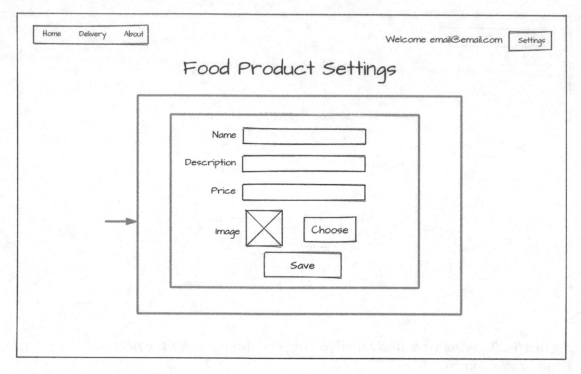

Figure 6-21. Wireframe and possible Vue.js components for the new Food Product form and its page

Now that we have defined the components for our Food Services Settings page, we will move to other pages.

Other Pages

We defined other pages that handle basic information about our website:

- Home page: This page is going to have some landing information for our final users.

- Login page: This page is going to have the login form.

- About page: This page is going to have a description of our application and how our customers can contact us.

We just defined the whole Vue.js components by page, using our wireframes. In the following sections, we are going to create the Vue.js components for our new Daniel's Delivery website.

Creating Reusable Components and Compose Them in a Hierarchy

As we saw in the previous section, we took our wireframes and defined which components we are going to need to build our new Daniel's Delivery website.

For our new Daniel's Delivery website, we defined the following pages.

Delivery.vue

Delivery.vue holds the whole delivery flow. We defined which components we need to meet those requirements. Figure 6-22 shows how the delivery components and pages are related to each other:

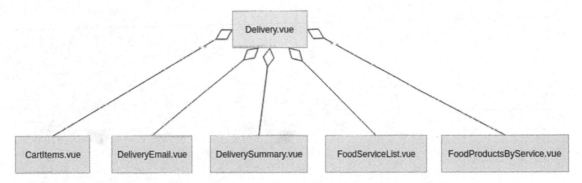

Figure 6-22. *Delivery Vue.js components and its relationship in the new Daniel's Delivery app. The arrow means aggregation.*

- CartItems.vue is the customer cart. There, he will find his products, costs and he can request the delivery.

- DeliveryEmail.vue will have the customer email to notify updartes about the delivery.

- DeliverySummary.vue will show the delivery summary of your request.

- FoodProductsByService.vue will show some details about Food Service and its Food Products, moreover, you will be able to add Food Products to your cart.

- FoodServiceList.vue will show the whole list of Food Services available and you can filter using the Food Type dropdown.

As we can see, those components belong to the Delivery.vue page, who is going to render each of them depending on the URL.

FoodProduct.vue

FoodProduct.vue handles the Food Product settings. Besides, we defined which components we need to meet those requirements. Figure 6-23 shows how the Food Products components and pages are related to each other.

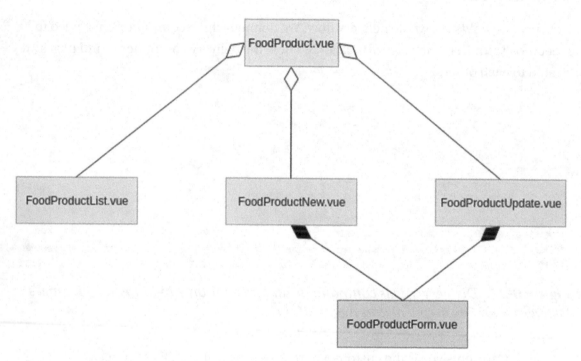

Figure 6-23. *FoodProduct Vue.js components and its relationship in the new Daniel's Delivery app. The white arrow means aggregation and the bold means composition.*

- FoodProductForm.vue is the form used to create or update a Food Product.

- FoodProductList.vue is the form used to create or update a user.

- FoodProductNew.vue uses the FoodProductForm.vue in update mode.

- FoodProductUpdate.vue uses the FoodProductForm.vue in update mode. See how we reuse the FoodProductForm.vue? This is to avoid replicating code.

FoodService.vue

FoodService.vue handles the Food Service settings. We defined which components we need to meet those requirements. Figure 6-24 shows how the Food Services components and pages are related to each other.

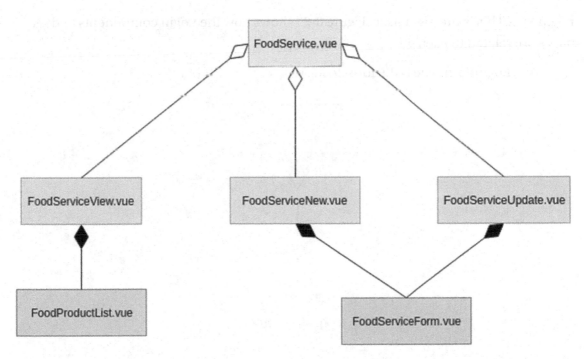

Figure 6-24. *FoodService Vue.js components and its relationship in the new Daniel's Delivery app. The white white means aggregation and the bold means composition.*

- FoodServiceForm.vue is the form used to create or update a Food Service.

- FoodServiceNew.vue uses the FoodServiceForm.vue in update mode.

- FoodServiceUpdate.vue uses the FoodServiceForm.vue in update mode. See how we reuse the FoodProductForm.vue? This is to avoid replicating code.

- FoodServiceView.vue shows the Food Service detail and uses the FoodProductList.vue for its products.

Login.vue

Login.vue: This is the login page. Figure 6-25 shows how the Login components and pages are related to each other.

- LoginForm.vue is the form to log in.

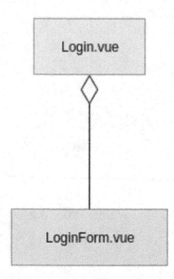

Figure 6-25. *Login Vue.js components and its relationship in the new Daniel's Delivery app. The white arrow means aggregation and the bold means composition.*

Each of those components needs to be redirected based on a path. We are going to discuss the routing structure in the following section.

Routing through URL to Components and Sending the Data

Routing components and pages are essential in any application. In this section, we are going to define how to route our new Daniel's Delivery components and which data we are going to receive.

We are going to focus the following sections on the Delivery flow.

Defining the Navigation Structure for the Delivery Flow

Let's define the navigation structure for each component – whether it is routable and how we are going to access it:

- Delivery.vue: We are going to access it through /delivery path. This is our root path for the Delivery module.

- DeliveryEmail.vue: We are going to access it through the /delivery path.

- FoodServiceList.vue: We are going to access it through the /delivery/food_service path.

- FoodProductsByService.vue: We are going to access it through the /delivery/food_service/:foodservice path. The last part of the path is a param named foodservice. There, we must add the email of the Food Service we are going to view.

- CartItems.vue: We are going to access it through the /delivery/cart/:foodservice path. The last part of the path is a param named foodservice. There, we must add the email of the Food Service cart we are going to view.

- DeliverySummary.vue: We are going to access it through the /summary/:email path. The last part of the path is a param named email. There, we must add the email of the Customer delivery we are going to view.

Here's how the navigation structure looks (Figure 6-26).

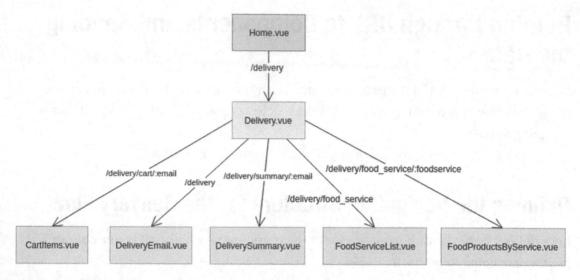

Figure 6-26. *Flow of routing of the Vue.js components with its paths*

Now, as you can see, we have a common path /delivery over the whole routes, so let's override this using a hierarchy, as shown in Table 6-1.

Table 6-1. *Hierarchical paths and the components to render*

Path	Components to Render
/delivery	Delivery
/	Delivery and DeliveryEmail
/cart	N/A
/:email	Delivery and CartItems
/summary	N/A
/:email	Delivery and DeliverySummary
/food_service	Delivery and FoodServiceList
/:foodservice	Delivery and FoodProductsByService

There are empty routes (N/A). That means some paths don't render any component.

Figure 6-27 shows how the navigation structure looks in a hierarchical way.

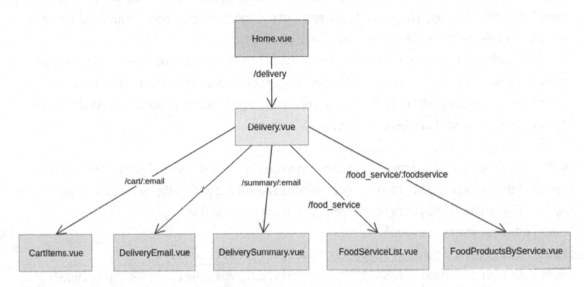

Figure 6-27. *Flow of routing of the Vue.js components with its paths in a hierarchical manner*

Notice how the components are rendered. As this is a hierarchy, the full path of components from parent to the child is rendered. In this case, Delivery component is always rendered and its child is based on the path.

Now, we are going to map this definition using the Router plugin for Vue.js in the following section.

Creating a Router Structure: Navigating to New Pages

As we added the Router plugin when we created the project, we have a router.js file. We modified it to support our new components. Let's take a look at the code in Listing 6-1.

Listing 6-1. router.js configuration for the new Daniel's Delivery app

```
import Vue from 'vue'
import Router from 'vue-router'
import Home from './views/Home.vue'

// (1)
import FoodProduct from './views/FoodProduct.vue'
```

```
import FoodProductList from './components/foodProduct/FoodProductList.vue'
import FoodProductNew from './components/foodProduct/FoodProductNew.vue'
import FoodProductUpdate from './components/foodProduct/FoodProductUpdate.vue'
import FoodService from './views/FoodService.vue'
import FoodServiceView from './components/foodService/FoodServiceView.vue'
import FoodServiceNew from './components/foodService/FoodServiceNew.vue'
import FoodServiceUpdate from './components/foodService/FoodServiceUpdate.vue'
import Login from './views/Login.vue'
import Delivery from './views/Delivery.vue'
import DeliveryEmail from './components/delivery/DeliveryEmail.vue'
import FoodServiceList from './components/delivery/FoodServiceList.vue'
import FoodProductsByService from './components/delivery/
FoodProductsByService.vue'
import CartItems from './components/delivery/CartItems.vue'
import DeliverySummary from './components/delivery/DeliverySummary.vue'

Vue.use(Router)          // (2)

export default new Router({     // (3)
  routes: [
    // More routes

    {
      path: '/delivery',          // (4)
      component: Delivery,
      children: [                 // (5)
        {
          path: '',
          name: 'delivery_email',      // (6)
          component: DeliveryEmail
        },
        {
          path: 'food_service',
          name: 'food_service_list',
          component: FoodServiceList
        },
```

```
        {
          path: 'food_service/:foodService',
          name: 'food_products_by_service',
          props: (route) => { return { foodService: route.params.
          foodService } },
          component: FoodProductsByService
        },
        {
          path: 'cart/:foodService',
          name: 'cart',
          props: (route) => { return { foodService: route.params.
          foodService } },    // (7.1)
          component: CartItems
        },
        {
          path: 'summary/:email',
          name: 'delivery_summary',
          props: (route) => { return { email: route.params.email }
          },              // (7.2)
          component: DeliverySummary
        }
      ]
    },

  // More routes
  ]
})
```

The following is a description of the code sample.

1. We import our components.

2. Later, we add Router as a plugin to our Vue.js application.

3. After that, we define the Router object and export it.

4. Now, let's see what the routes for Delivery flow look like. As we see, we defined a root of our Delivery component through the path /delivery. This means that anytime you link to /delivery, the Delivery component is going to render.

5. Later, we find the children paths. As they are children from /delivery, it means, the full path for routing these components will have /delivery as the prefix. In this case, the full paths and components to render are the follwoing:

    •   /delivery/: Delivery and DeliveryEmail

    •   /delivery/food_service: Delivery and FoodServiceList

6. The name attribute helps us to link to these routers by name using the $router object or router-link tag.

7. And finally, we have some routes that require params to be passed. Those routes are special because they require a param, for instance, DeliverySummary requires :email. This means we are going to get the param from the URL and send it to our DeliverySummary component.

    In this case, the full paths and components to render are the following:

    •   /delivery/summary/myemail@email.com: Delivery and DeliverySummay

    •   /delivery/summary/other@email.com: Delivery and DeliverySummay

    •   /delivery/summary/invalidemail: Delivery nad DeliverySummay

We have just defined how my components are going to route. Next, we will see how to get the Delivery router-view working in this configuration.

Delivery.vue: Using Router-View for Navigation

Since we defined how our application routes depending on different paths, we need to define where those components are going to be rendered.

A Delivery component is going to handle it as shown in Listing 6-2.

Listing 6-2. Delivery.vue component to route to components

```
<template>
  <div class="container">
    <h1 class="text-center">Delivery</h1>
    <div class="row">
    <div class="col-sm">
      <router-view/>
    </div>
    </div>
  </div>
</template>
```

There, we only define our module title and router-view. router-view tag tells Vue.js that that part of the template is not defined yet. That part depends on the route you have. Regarding the routes we defined in the previous section, the router-view will render the following components based on a path, as shown in Table 6-2.

Table 6-2. *Plain paths and the components to render*

Path	Components to Render
/delivery/	DeliveryEmail
/delivery/summary/	DeliverySummary
/delivery/food_service	FoodServiceList
/delivery/food_service/:email	FoodProductsByService
/delivery/cart/:email	CartItems

CartItems Component: A Vue.js Approach

CartItems component is an essential element in our new Daniel's Delivery website. We are going to use this component to explain some Vue.js features like conditionals, iterators, functions, lifecycle events, and input handling.

This is what the CartItems component looks like (Figure 6-28).

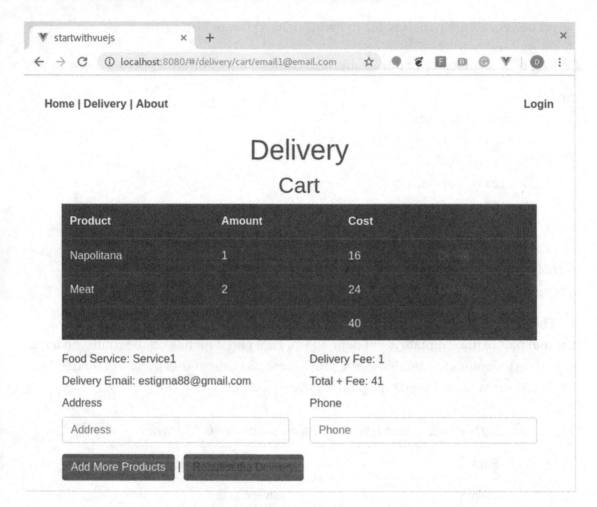

Figure 6-28. *Cart page for the new Daniel's Delivery app*

As we can see, the CartItems component shows your food request, which food service you have, and asks about some data needed to deliver your food. This is the summary of your delivery request.

Component Logic

Our CartItems component needs a lot of Vue.js features to work well. Let's see them.

Let's start with the CartItems properties we need, as shown in Listing 6-3.

Listing 6-3. Script for the CartItems.vue component

```ts
<script lang="ts">
// Imports

@Component
export default class CartItems extends Vue {
  @Prop() private readonly foodService!: string
  private items:Item[] = []              // (1.1)
  private deliveryEmail: string = ''        // (1.2)
  private foodServiceData: FoodService = FoodService.
  emptyFoodService()              // (1.3)
  private address: string = ''            // (2.1)
  private phone: string = ''              // (2.2)
  private errorMessage:string = ''         // (2.3)

  // lifecycle hook
  mounted () {                             // (3)
    this.getCart()
  }

  getCart () {                             // (4)
    this.items = this.$store.state.cart.items
    this.deliveryEmail = this.$store.getters.getCurrentDeliveryEmail()
    this.foodServiceData = this.$store.getters.getFoodServiceByEmail(
      this.foodService
    )
  }

  remove (itemToRemove:Item) {           // (5)
    this.$store.commit('removeItemFromCart', itemToRemove)
  }

  requestDelivery () {            // (6)
    if (this.address === '') {
      this.errorMessage = 'Address is required'

      return false
    }
```

```
    if (this.phone === '') {
      this.errorMessage = 'Phone is required'

      return false
    }

    this.$store.commit('addDelivery', Delivery.newDelivery(this.$store.
    state.cart, this.address, this.deliveryEmail, this.phone, 'PENDING',
    this.total + this.foodServiceData.deliveryFee))

    this.$router.push({ name: 'delivery_summary', params: { email: this.
    deliveryEmail } })      // (7)
  }

  get total () {                          // (8)
    return this.items.length !== 0 ? this.items.map((item: Item) => item.
amount * item.foodProduct.price).reduce((previous: number, current: number)
=> current + previous) : 0
  }
}
</script>
```

The following is a description of the code sample:

1. There, we defined the items we want to request for delivery, the delivery email, and the basic Food Service data we want to show to our customer.

2. Here, we see the property's address and phone. Additionally, we have an errorMessage property for validation purposes.

3. mounted is a lifecycle hook that is executed the first time the component is rendered. There are more lifecycle events. You can find them here: https://vuejs.org/v2/guide/ nstance. html#Instance-Lifecycle-Hooks

   mounted is like the Java main method for the component or a @PostConstruct for an EJB.

4. mounted calls getCart function to get some data from our store.
    We fill the items we have in our cart plus other information. $store
    is a Vuex plugin for sharing states between components. You can
    see more information about Vuex in Chapter 2.

5. Removes an item from the cart.

6. This requests a delivery. The method validates the input fields for
    non-empty values; if there is an error, it sets an errorMessage; and
    the message is going to show in the page. If the validation is ok, it
    creates a delivery request using Vuex.

7. We can see how we redirect to DeliverySummary after the request
    for delivery is a success: we use the $router property to push
    a redirect to a new route, named delivery_summary with the
    deliveryEmail as a param.

8. We get the computed total property, which sums the value of each
    requested item in the delivery. A computed property is a property
    calculated each time we need to render it. This is pretty useful
    with logic but we need to refresh any time we render.

HTML Structure

We have the following HTML for Cart.vue component, as shown in Listing 6-4.

Listing 6-4. Template for the CartItems.vue component

```
<template>
<div>
  <h2 class="text-center">Cart</h2>
    <div class="row">
      <div class="col-sm">
        <table class="table  table-dark">
          <thead>
            <tr>
              <th>Product</th>
              <th>Amount</th>
              <th>Cost</th>
```

```
              <th></th>
            </tr>
          </thead>
          <tbody>
            <tr v-for="item in items" v-bind:key="item.foodProduct.id">
            <!--(1)-->
              <td>{{item.foodProduct.name}}</td>
              <td>{{item.amount}}</td>
              <td>{{item.amount * item.foodProduct.price}}</td>
              <td><a v-on:click="remove(item)" href="#">Delete</a></td>
              <!--(3)-->
            </tr>
          </tbody>
          <tfoot>
            <tr>
              <td></td>
              <td></td>
              <td>{{total}}</td>
              <td></td>
            </tr>
          </tfoot>
        </table>
      </div>
    </div>
  <div class="row">
    <div class="col-sm">
        <label>Food Service: {{foodServiceData.name}}</label>    <!--(2)-->
    </div>
    <div class="col-sm">
        <label>Delivery Fee: {{foodServiceData.deliveryFee}}</label>
    </div>
  </div>
  <div class="row">
    <div class="col-sm">
        <label>Delivery Email: {{deliveryEmail}}</label>
    </div>
```

```
  <div class="col-sm">
      <label>Total + Fee: {{foodServiceData.deliveryFee + total}}</label>
  </div>
</div>
<div class="row" v-if="errorMessage">
  <div class="col-sm">
    <div class="alert alert-danger" role="alert">
      {{errorMessage}}
    </div>
  </div>
</div>
<div class="row">
  <div class="col-sm">
      <div class="form-group">
        <label for="address">Address</label>
        <input
          v-model="address"
          type="text"
          class="form-control"
          id="address"
          placeholder="Address"
          required
        >
      </div>
    </div>
    <div class="col-sm">
      <div class="form-group">
        <label for="phone">Phone</label>
        <input
          v-model="phone"
          type="text"
          class="form-control"
          id="phone"
          placeholder="Phone"
          required
        >
```

```
        </div>
      </div>
    </div>
  <div class="row">
    <div class="col-sm">         <!--(4)-->
      <router-link :to="{ name: 'food_products_by_service', params:
      {foodService: foodService} }" class="btn btn-primary">Add More
      Products</router-link>
      |
      <a class="btn btn-primary" v-on:click="requestDelivery">Request the
      Delivery</a>
    </div>
  </div>
</div>
</template>
```

The following is a description of the code sample:

1. You can find there how we iterate over the items to render a table.

2. Remember, {{property}} is a mustache syntax, and it is used to
    access properties of Vue.js handled objects.

3. Moreover, the following code is a link to a function. That means
    when a customer clicks to delete an item from the Cart, the
    remove(item) function is going to be called.

4. CartItems needs to route to the DeliverySummary after you
    request the delivery, and back to the FoodProductsByService if
    you want to add more products to your cart. We defined a router-
    link to a route name food_products_by_service, and sent a data
    called foodService, with the foodservice email.

With this, we finish our front-end definition for our new Daniel's Delivery website.
In the following chapter, we are going to talk about the back-end structure using JEE.

Summary

We just learned how to define a front-end application using wireframes, based on business requirements. Later, we split those definitions into Vue.js components and then defined how to reuse and compound them. And finally, we created components with a bunch of Vue.js features like iterators, functions, lifecycle events, user inputs, user events, conditionals, and routes.

At this moment, we are ready with our persistent layer and front-end layer. In the following chapter, we are going to focus on finishing our back-end layer using JEE, creating RESTFul services, and connecting it with the previously defined persistent layer. That will be the final step before connecting our Vue.js layer with our JEE layer.

Extended Knowledge

1. Which plugin do we use for an infinite scroll?

2. How do we upload images to Vue.js?

3. Do we use TypeScript entities?

4. Which application do we use to create the wireframes?

5. How do we pass the routing properties to the component?

6. What does the project structure look like?

7. Can I add CSS styling by component?

CHAPTER 7

Creating Your Back End with Jakarta EE

In any application, we need business logic, and we need to expose that logic somehow to be consumed by external clients.

In this chapter, we are going to analyze business requirements and define the business logic we need to create. We are also going to design a RESTful API using JAX-RS to expose that logic to the external world.

The following topics will be covered in this chapter:

- Designing and implementing the business layer using use cases. See how the business layer connects to the persistence layer.

- Designing the RESTful API for the use cases implementing the RESTful API using the JAX-RS framework.

- Understand how to use the Context and Dependency Injection framework to connect the new Daniel's Delivery application layers.

- Use Arquillian to do a black-box test over our application.

Technical Requirements

To follow the instructions in this chapter, you will need the following:

- Java 1.8

- Netbeans 11

- GlassFish 5.1

- Jakarta Enterprise Edition

© Daniel Andres Pelaez Lopez 2021
D. A. P. Lopez, *Full-Stack Web Development with Jakarta EE and Vue.js*,
https://doi.org/10.1007/978-1-4842-6342-6_7

You can check the whole project and code at `https://github.com/Apress/full-stack-web-development-with-jakartaee-and-vue.js/tree/master/CH7`.

Designing and Implementing the Business Layer

A business layer is where your business rules are. Those business rules are the main goal of your application: what the business does.

In this chapter, we are going to design and implement the business layer for our new Daniel's Delivery website.

Packages for the Business Layer

For our new Daniel's Delivery website, we defined a new package for our business rules (Figure 7-1).

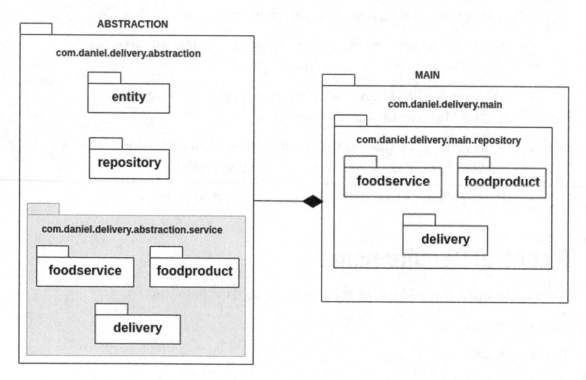

Figure 7-1. *Abstraction packages for the business entities logic*

That package is going to hold our services' interfaces and implementations. See how those business rules are in the Abstraction package? Remember, those are the core of our application, and they should be decoupled by any framework/technology.

Let's see how our business rules should connect in a generic way with the repositories.

FoodService Business Layer

The FoodService business layer has the following classes as shown in Figure 7-2.

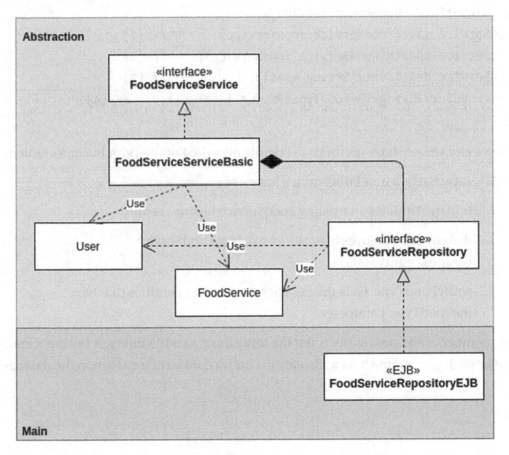

Figure 7-2. *FoodServiceService dependencies with lower layers*

As we can see, our FoodServiceServiceBasic class has a dependency on the FoodServiceRepository interface.

Note that our dependencies in the abstraction layer are only against the abstraction layer. This is decoupling the Main and the Abstraction.

Let's talk about our new classes in more detail in the subsequent sections.

FoodServiceService Interface

FoodServiceService interface has the API defined to access the FoodService business rules (Listing 7-1).

Listing 7-1. FoodServiceService interface

```
public interface FoodServiceService {
  FoodService save(FoodService foodService);        // (1)
  FoodService update(FoodService foodService);      // (2)
  FoodService deActivate(String email);             // (3)
  List<FoodService> getByFoodType(String foodType);    // (4)
}
```

As we can see, we have methods to operate over the FoodService business entity:

1. save: Saves a new FoodService business entity.

2. update: Updates an existing FoodService business entity.

3. deActivate: Removes logically an existing FoodService business entity.

4. getByFoodType: Gets the FoodService business entities that have the foodType parameter.

Remember, a business entity is not the same thing as a JPA entity. A business entity has business logic; meanwhile, a JPA entity is only a data structure to map the database.

FoodServiceServiceBasic Class

The FoodServiceServiceBasic class implements the FoodServiceService interface and uses the FoodServiceRepository to access the persistence layer.

Let's see the code in detail (Listing 7-2).

Listing 7-2. FoodServiceService implementation

```
public class FoodServiceServiceBasic implements
FoodServiceService{        // (1)
    private final FoodServiceRepository foodServiceRepository;

    public FoodServiceServiceBasic(FoodServiceRepository
    foodServiceRepository){              // (2)
        this.foodServiceRepository = foodServiceRepository;
    }

    @Override
    public FoodService save(FoodService foodService) {  // (3.1)
        return foodServiceRepository.save(foodService);
    }

    @Override
    public FoodService update(FoodService foodService) {   // (3.2)
        return foodServiceRepository.update(foodService);
    }

    @Override
    public FoodService deActivate(String email) {   // (4)
        FoodService foodService = foodServiceRepository.getById(email)
                .orElseThrow(IllegalArgumentException::new);

        foodService.deActivate();

        return foodServiceRepository.update(foodService);
    }

    @Override
    public List<FoodService> getByFoodType(String foodType) {    // (5)
        List<FoodService> foodServices = Collections.emptyList();
```

```
    if("ALL".equals(foodType)){
        foodServices = foodServiceRepository.getAll();
    }else{
        foodServices = foodServiceRepository.getByFoodType(foodType);
    }

    return foodServices.stream()
            .filter(FoodService::getActive)
            .collect(Collectors.toList());
    }
}
```

The following is a description of the code sample:

1. First, we implement the FoodServiceService interface.

2. Here, it receives the FoodServiceRepository in the constructor.

3. Next, we have the save and update methods. We do not need any specific business logic there, so it works as a passthrough.

4. Now, we have the deActivate method. There, we first query the business entity, deactivate it, and update that new state.

5. And finally, we have the getByFoodType method. If we want ALL, we need to receive ALL as an argument. See that we only return the FoodService business entities as active.

FoodProduct Business Layer

The FoodProduct business layer has the following classes as shown in Figure 7-3.

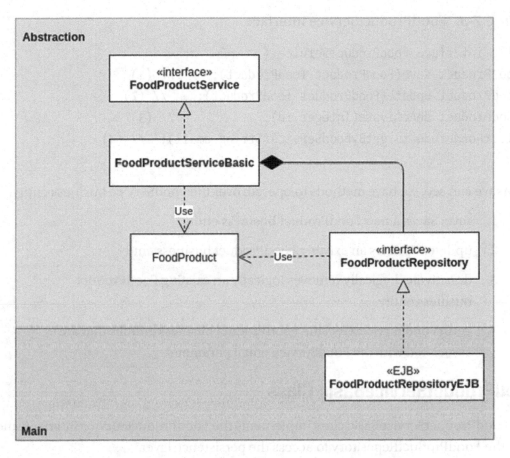

Figure 7-3. *FoodProductService dependencies with lower layers*

As we can see, our FoodProductServiceBasic class has a dependency on the FoodProductRepository interface.

Let's talk about our new classes in more detail.

FoodProductService Interface

The FoodProductService interface has the API defined to access the FoodProduct business rules (Listing 7-3).

Listing 7-3. FoodProductService interface

```
public interface FoodProductService {
  FoodProduct save(FoodProduct foodProduct);      // (1)
  FoodProduct update(FoodProduct foodProduct);     // (2)
  FoodProduct deActivate(Integer id);              // (3)
  List<FoodProduct> getByFoodService(String email);  // (4)
}
```

As we can see, we have methods to operate over the FoodService business entity:

1. save: Saves a new FoodProduct business entity.

2. update: Updates an existing FoodProduct business entity.

3. deActivate: Logically removes logically an existing FoodProduct business entity.

4. getByFoodService: Gets the FoodProduct business entities that are associated with the FoodService email parameter.

FoodProductServiceBasic Class

The FoodProductServiceBasic class implements the FoodProductService interface and uses the FoodProductRepository to access the persistence layer.

Let's see the code in detail (Listing 7-4).

Listing 7-4. FoodProductService implementation

```
public class FoodProductServiceBasic implements
FoodProductService{                                 // (1)
    private final FoodProductRepository foodProductRepository;

    public FoodProductServiceBasic(FoodProductRepository
    foodProductRepository) {                        // (2)
        this.foodProductRepository = foodProductRepository;
    }

    @Override
    public FoodProduct save(FoodProduct foodProduct) {   // (3.1)
        return foodProductRepository.save(foodProduct);
    }
```

```
@Override
public FoodProduct update(FoodProduct foodProduct) {    // (3.2)
    return foodProductRepository.update(foodProduct);
}

@Override
public FoodProduct deActivate(Integer id) {      // (4)
    FoodProduct foodProduct = foodProductRepository.getById(id)
            .orElseThrow(IllegalArgumentException::new);

    foodProduct.deActivate();

    return foodProductRepository.update(foodProduct);
}

@Override
public List<FoodProduct> getByFoodService(String email) {     // (5)
    return foodProductRepository.getByFoodService(email)
            .stream()
            .filter(FoodProduct::isActive)
            .collect(Collectors.toList());
}
```
}

The following is a description of the code sample:

1. First, we implement the FoodProductService interface.

2. Here, we receive the FoodProductRepository in the constructor.

3. Next, we have the save and update methods. We do not need any specific business logic there, so it works as a passthrough.

4. Now, we have the deActivate method. First it queries the business entity, deactivates it, and updates it.

5. And finally, we have the getByFoodService method. That receives the email of a FoodService and returns the FoodProduct entities associated with it. See that we only return the FoodProduct business entities that are active.

Delivery Business Layer

The Delivery business layer has the following classes as shown in Figure 7-4.

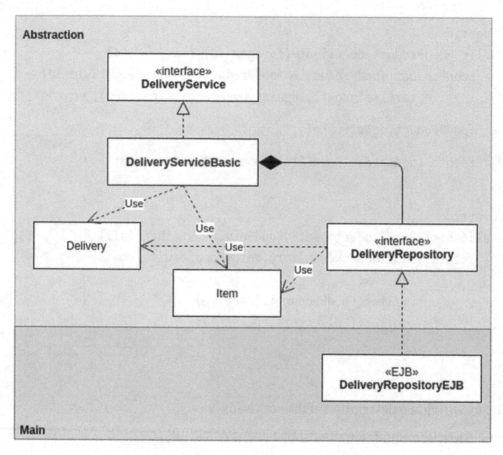

Figure 7-4. *DeliveryService dependencies with lower layers*

As we can see, our DeliveryServiceBasic class has a dependency on the DeliveryRepository interface.

Let's talk about our new classes in more detail.

DeliveryService Interface

The DeliveryService interface has the API defined to access the Delivery business rules (Listing 7-5).

Listing 7-5. DeliveryService interface

```
public interface DeliveryService {
  Delivery request(Delivery delivery);    // (1)
  List<Delivery> getByEmailAndState(String email, String state);      // (2)
}
```

As we can see, we have methods to operate over the Delivery business entity:

1. request: Create a new Delivery with its items.

2. getByEmailAndState: Get the Delivery business entities that are associated with the email and state parameter.

DeliveryServiceBasic Class

The DeliveryServiceBasic class implements the DeliveryService interface and uses the DeliveryRepository to access the persistence layer.

Let's see the code in detail (Listing 7-6).

Listing 7-6. DeliveryService implementation

```
public class DeliveryServiceBasic implements DeliveryService {   // (1)

    private final DeliveryRepository deliveryRepository;

    public DeliveryServiceBasic(DeliveryRepository deliveryRepository)
{                       // (2)
        this.deliveryRepository = deliveryRepository;
    }

    @Override
    public Delivery request(Delivery delivery) {   // (3)
        return deliveryRepository.save(delivery);
    }

    @Override
    public List<Delivery> getByEmailAndState(String email, String state)
{                       // (4)
        return deliveryRepository.getByEmailAndState(email, state);
    }

}
```

The following is a description of the code sample:

1. First, we implement the DeliveryService interface and receive the DeliveryRepository.

2. Next, we have the request method to request a new Delivery.

3. And finally, we have the getByEmailAndState method to get deliveries associated with a delivery email and in a defined state.

We have just defined our business layer. In the following section, we are going to define our RESTful JAX-RS layer for our new Daniel's Delivery website, using the Context and Dependency Injection (CDI) from Jakarta EE to put everything together.

Defining Your RESTful JAX-RS Services

In this section, we are going to define our RESTful JAX-RS layer for our new Daniel's Delivery website, using the Context and Dependency Injection (CDI) from Jakarta EE to put everything together.

Designing the RESTful API

In the previous section we defined our business services, and now we need to define how we are going to access them from external clients, like our Vue.js front end.

It is common to use RESTful services to access resources in our back-end server from a front-end layer.

Representational State Transfer (REST) is an architecture style in which we use the HTTP protocol to communicate to services. REST uses the HTTP methods with URLs to define a unique resource on the web.

For our new Daniel's Delivery website, we defined the following RESTful resources: Delivery resource, FoodProduct resource, and FoodService resource. Let's see the resources and their implementations in detail in the subsequent sections.

The Delivery resource is defined as /deliveries. For this resource, we defined the following operations in Listing 7-7 and 7-8.

Listing 7-7. RESTful API for get deliveries by delivery email and state

```
API

---REQUEST---
GET /api/deliveries/{email}?state={state}

---RESPONSE---
HTTP Status OK
{
....Delivery data.....
}

###### EXAMPLE ######

---REQUEST---
GET /api/deliveries/email5@email.com?state=PENDING

---RESPONSE---
HTTP Status OK [
{
  "address": "Street 50",
  "email": "email5@email.com",
  "fee": 100,
  "id": 1,
  "itemList": [
              {
                "amount": 1,
                "foodProduct": {
                                "active": true,
                                "description": "Pinaple Pizza",
                                "foodService": "email1@email.com",
                                 "id": 1,
                                    "imageUrl": "imageUrl",
                                    "name": "Pizza",
                                    "price": 23500
                                },
```

```
                    "id": 1
                }
            ],
    "phone": "555233564",
    "state": "PENDING",
    "total": 23600
    }
]
```

Listing 7-8. RESTful API for request a delivery

```
API

---REQUEST---
POST /api/deliveries
{
....Delivery data.....
}

---RESPONSE---
HTTP Status OK
###### EXAMPLE ######

---REQUEST---
POST /api/deliveries
{
  "address": "Street 89",
  "email": "email10@email.com",
  "fee": 100,
  "id": 2,
  "itemList": [
                {
                  "amount": 2,
                  "foodProduct": {
                            "active": true,
                            "description": "Pinaple Pizza",
                        "foodService": "email1@email.com",
```

```
                                "id": 1,
                                "imageUrl": "imageUrl",
                                "name": "Pizza",
                                "price": 23500
                        },
                    "id": 2
                }
            ],
    "phone": "55587412",
    "state": "PENDING",
    "total": 20100
}

---RESPONSE---
HTTP Status OK
```

The FoodProduct resource is defined as /foodproducts. For this resource, we defined the following operations in Listing 7-9, 7-10, 7-11 and 7-12.

Listing 7-9. RESTful API for save a new FoodProduct

```
API

---REQUEST---
POST /api/foodproducts
{
....FoodProduct data.....
}
---RESPONSE---
HTTP Status OK

###### EXAMPLE ######

---REQUEST---
POST /api/foodproducts
{
  "active": true,
  "description": "Cheese Pizza",
  "foodService": "email1@email.com", "id": 2,
```

```
  "imageUrl": "imageUrl2",
  "name": "Pizza",
  "price": 23500
}

---RESPONSE---
HTTP Status OK
```

Listing 7-10.   RESTful API for update a new FoodProduct

```
API

---REQUEST---
PUT /api/foodproducts
{
....FoodProduct data.....
}

---RESPONSE---
HTTP Status OK

###### EXAMPLE ######

---REQUEST---
PUT /api/foodproducts
{
  "active": true,
  "description": "Cheese Pizza",
  "foodService": "email1@email.com",
  "id": 2,
  "imageUrl": "imageUrl2",
  "name": "Pizza",
  "price": 23500
}

---RESPONSE---
HTTP Status OK
```

Listing 7-11. RESTful API for deactivate a FoodProduct

```
API

---REQUEST---
DELETE /api/foodproducts/{id}

---RESPONSE---
HTTP Status OK
{
....FoodProduct data.....
}

###### EXAMPLE ######

---REQUEST---
DELETE /api/foodproducts/2

---RESPONSE---
HTTP Status OK
{
  "active": false,
  "description": "Cheese Pizza Old",
  "foodService": "email1@email.com",
  "id": 2,
  "imageUrl": "imageUrl2",
  "name": "Pizza",
  "price": 23500
}
```

Listing 7-12. RESTful API for get FoodProducts by FoodService

```
API

---REQUEST---
GET /api/foodproducts?foodService={foodService}

---RESPONSE---
HTTP Status OK [
{
....FoodProduct data.....
}
]
###### EXAMPLE ######

---REQUEST---
GET /api/foodproducts?foodService=email1@email.com

---RESPONSE---
HTTP Status OK
[
 {
    "active": true,
    "description": "Pinaple Pizza",
    "foodService": "email1@email.com",
    "id": 1,
    "imageUrl": "imageUrl",
    "name": "Pizza",
    "price": 23500
 }
]
```

The FoodService resource is defined as /foodservices. For this resource, we defined the following operations in Listing 7-13, 7-14, 7-15 and 7-16.

Listing 7-13. RESTful API for save a new FoodService

```
API

---REQUEST---
POST /api/foodservices
{
....FoodService data.....
}

---RESPONSE---
HTTP Status OK

###### EXAMPLE ######

---REQUEST---
POST /api/foodserices
{
  "active": true,
  "address": "Street 898",
  "deliveryFee": 120,
  "email": "chicken@email.com",
  "foodProductList": [],
  "foodType": "CHICKEN",
  "name": "Chicken Cool",
  "user": {
     "email": "chicken@email.com",
     "password": "pass2"
  }
}

---RESPONSE---
HTTP Status OK
```

Listing 7-14. RESTful API for update a new FoodService

```
API

---REQUEST---
PUT /api/foodservices
{
....FoodService data.....
}

---RESPONSE---
HTTP Status OK

###### EXAMPLE ######

---REQUEST---
PUT /api/foodservices
{
  "active": true,
  "address": "Street 898",
  "deliveryFee": 120,
  "email": "chicken@email.com",
  "foodProductList": [],
  "foodType": "CHICKEN",
  "name": "Chicken Cool Other",
  "user": {
            "email": "chicken@email.com",
            "password": "pass2"
          }
}

---RESPONSE---
HTTP Status OK
```

Listing 7-15. RESTful API for deactivate a FoodService

```
API

---REQUEST---
DELETE /api/foodservices/{email}

---RESPONSE---
HTTP Status OK
{
....FoodService data.....
}

###### EXAMPLE ######

---REQUEST---
DELETE /api/foodservices/chicken@email.com

---RESPONSE---
HTTP Status OK
{
  "active": false,
  "address": "Street 898",
  "deliveryFee": 120,
  "email": "chicken@email.com",
  "foodProductList": [],
  "foodType": "CHICKEN",
  "name": "Chicken Cool Other",
  "user": {
          "email": "chicken@email.com",
          "password": "pass2"
      }
}
```

Listing 7-16. RESTful API for get FoodServices by food type

API

```
---REQUEST---
GET /api/foodservices?foodType={foodType}

---RESPONSE---
HTTP Status OK [
{
....FoodServices data.....
}
]
###### EXAMPLE ######

---REQUEST---
GET /api/foodservices?foodType=PIZZA

---RESPONSE---
HTTP Status OK
[
  {
    "active": true,
    "address": "Street 89",
    "deliveryFee": 100,
     "email": "email1@email.com",
     "foodProductList": [],
     "foodType": "PIZZA",
    "name": "Pizzas 25",
    "user": {
        "email": "email1@email.com",
        "password": "pass1"
    }
  }
]
```

Using JAX-RS as a RESTful Framework

We just defined how our API is, and now we are going to implement that API using JAX-RS.

JAX-RS is one of the Jakarta EE specifications; in this case, it defines how RESTful services must be created.

In the following sections, we are going to see the implementation of each resource.

Delivery Resource Implementation

The Delivery resource is implemented by the DeliveryController class as shown in Figure 7-5.

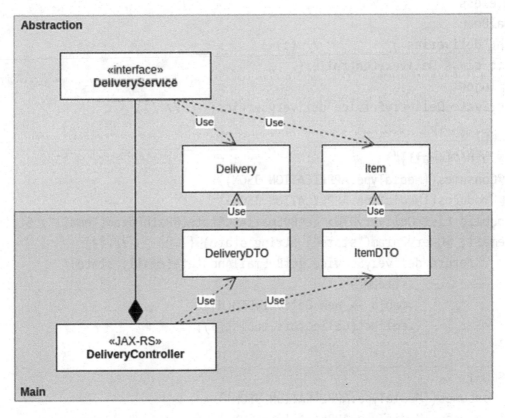

Figure 7-5. *DeliveryController dependencies with the abstraction layer*

As we can see, the DeliveryController is going to use the DeliveryService from the abstraction layer to apply the business rules, and there are some DTOs it uses to respond to the client.

277

See the DTO classes? Those help us to decouple the business entities from the controller. This is an additional transformation between business entities and DTOs, but it is better to decouple here; otherwise you will have problems later.

Now, let's see the code in detail.

DeliveryController Class

DeliveryController uses JAX-RS to expose the Delivery resources as a RESTful service. Let's see the code in detail (Listing 7-17).

Listing 7-17. DeliveryController class

```
@Stateless
@LocalBean
@Path("deliveries")              // (1)
public class DeliveryController{
    @Inject
    private DeliveryService deliveryService;     // (2)

    @GET
    @Path("{email}")
    @Consumes({MediaType.APPLICATION_JSON})
    @Produces({MediaType.APPLICATION_JSON})
    public List<DeliveryDTO> getByEmailAndState(@PathParam("email") String
    email, @QueryParam("state") String state) {         // (3)
        return deliveryService.getByEmailAndState(email, state)
                .stream()
                .map(d -> new DeliveryDTO(d))
                .collect(Collectors.toList());
    }

    @POST
    @Consumes({MediaType.APPLICATION_JSON})
    @Produces({MediaType.APPLICATION_JSON})
    public DeliveryDTO request(DeliveryDTO delivery) {    // (4)
        return new DeliveryDTO(deliveryService.request(delivery.
        toDelivery()));
    }
}
```

The following is a description of the code sample:

1. First, we define our resource path, in this case, /deliveries.

2. Next, we inject the DeliveryService in the controller. We are going to talk about @Inject in more detail in the following sections.

3. Now, we define the resource to get deliveries by email and state. See the new @Path here? JAX-RS adds a path's hierarchy; that means it puts together the class level @Path with the method level @Path, so, the final path will be /deliveries/[email].

4. And finally, there is the resource to request a new delivery.

FoodProduct Resource Implementation

The FoodProduct resource is implemented by the FoodProductController class as shown in Figure 7-6.

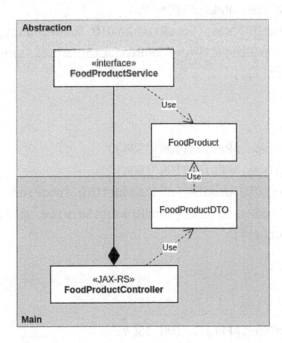

Figure 7-6. *FoodProductController dependencies with the abstraction layer*

Now, let's see the code in detail.

FoodProductController Class

The FoodProductController uses JAX-RS to expose the FoodProduct resources as a RESTful service.

Let's see the code in detail (Listing 7-18).

Listing 7-18. FoodProductController class

```
@Stateless
@LocalBean
@Path("foodproducts")                    // (1)
public class FoodProductController{
    @Inject
    private FoodProductService foodProductService;  // (2)

    @POST
    @Consumes({MediaType.APPLICATION_JSON})
    @Produces({MediaType.APPLICATION_JSON})
    public FoodProductDTO save(FoodProductDTO foodProduct) {  // (3.1)
        return new FoodProductDTO(foodProductService.save(foodProduct.
        toFoodProduct()));
    }

    @PUT
    @Consumes({MediaType.APPLICATION_JSON})
    @Produces({MediaType.APPLICATION_JSON})
    public FoodProductDTO update(FoodProductDTO foodProduct) {  // (3.2)
        return new FoodProductDTO(foodProductService.update(foodProduct.
        toFoodProduct()));
    }

    @Path("{id}")
    @DELETE
    @Consumes({MediaType.APPLICATION_JSON})
    @Produces({MediaType.APPLICATION_JSON})
    public FoodProductDTO deActivate(@PathParam("id") Integer id) {  // (4)
        return new FoodProductDTO(foodProductService.deActivate(id));
    }
```

```
@GET
@Consumes({MediaType.APPLICATION_JSON})
@Produces({MediaType.APPLICATION_JSON})
public List<FoodProductDTO> getByFoodService(@QueryParam("foodService")
String foodService) {          // (5)
    return foodProductService.getByFoodService(foodService)
            .stream()
            .map(f -> new FoodProductDTO(f))
            .collect(Collectors.toList());
  }
}
```

The following is a description of the code sample:

1. First, we define our resource path, in this case, /foodproducts.

2. Next, we inject the FoodProductService in the controller.

3. Now, we define the resources to save and update a food product.

4. Following this, there is the resource to deactivate a food product.

5. And finally, there is the resource to get the food products by
    food service. Note how the only logic we have in the controller is
    regarding transformation between DTO and business entities.

FoodService Resource Implementation

The FoodService resource is implemented by the FoodServiceController class as shown
in Figure 7-7.

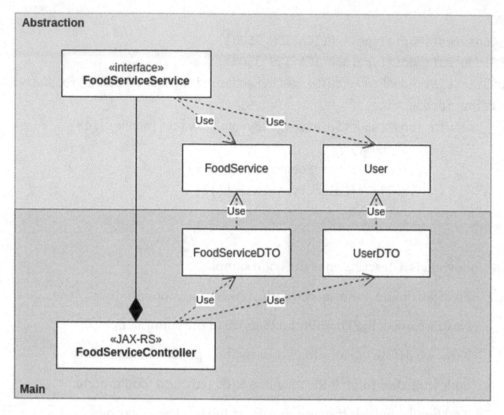

Figure 7-7. *FoodServiceController dependencies with the abstraction layer*

As we can see, the FoodServiceController is going to use the FoodServiceService from the abstraction layer to apply the business rules, and there are some DTOs it uses to respond to the client.

Now, let's see the code in detail.

FoodServiceController Class

The FoodServiceController uses JAX-RS to expose FoodService resources as a RESTful service. Let's see the code in detail (Listing 7-19).

Listing 7-19. FoodServiceController class

```java
@Stateless
@LocalBean
@Path("foodservices")                        // (1)
public class FoodServiceController{
```

```
@Inject
private FoodServiceService foodServiceService;   // (2)

@POST
@Consumes({MediaType.APPLICATION_JSON})
@Produces({MediaType.APPLICATION_JSON})
public FoodServiceDTO save(FoodServiceDTO foodService) {   // (3.1)
    return new FoodServiceDTO(foodServiceService.save(foodService.
    toFoodService()));
}

@PUT
@Consumes({MediaType.APPLICATION_JSON})
@Produces({MediaType.APPLICATION_JSON})
public FoodServiceDTO update(FoodServiceDTO foodService) {   // (3.2)
    return new FoodServiceDTO(foodServiceService.update(foodService.
    toFoodService()));
}

@Path("{email}")
@DELETE
@Consumes({MediaType.APPLICATION_JSON})
@Produces({MediaType.APPLICATION_JSON})
public FoodServiceDTO deActivate(@PathParam("email") String email)
{         // (4)
    return new FoodServiceDTO(foodServiceService.deActivate(email));
}

@GET
@Consumes({MediaType.APPLICATION_JSON})
@Produces({MediaType.APPLICATION_JSON})
public List<FoodServiceDTO> getByFoodType(@QueryParam("foodType")
String foodType) {    // (5)
    return foodServiceService.getByFoodType(foodType)
            .stream()
            .map(f -> new FoodServiceDTO(f))
            .collect(Collectors.toList());
}
}
```

The following is a description of the code sample:

1. First, we define our resource path, in this case, /foodservices.

2. Next, we inject the FoodServiceService in the controller.

3. Now, we define the resources to save and update a food service.

4. Following is the resource to deactivate a food service.

5. And finally, there is the resource to get food services by food type.

Resource Load

We need to tell Jakarta EE that there are JAX-RS services to load into the context, so, we need to add this class (Listing 7-20).

Listing 7-20. RESTfulApplication class to set up the JAX-RS framework

```
import javax.ws.rs.ApplicationPath;
import javax.ws.rs.core.Application;

@ApplicationPath("api")
public class RestfulApplication extends Application {

}
```

This class tells JAX-RS that the context over the resources will be /api. Jakarta EE is going to search into the classpath for classes with the @Path annotation to upload to the context as a RESTful service.

And finally, as we defined our RESTful services, now we need to check how to put our application layers together.

Putting It All Together Using Jakarta EE

We just created our business and JAX-RS layers; however, there is a missing piece: How do we put those layers together?

Well, that's the main goal of the Context and Dependency Injection (CDI) in Jakarta EE. We are going to discuss in this section on how to use CDI to put all of our application together.

Contexts and Dependency Injection for Jakarta EE

Jakarta EE is a specification for application containers, which means it defines how the objects are handled by a container, and it doesn't matter in which server you deploy them if that server is certified as Jakarta EE compliant.

In this chapter, we are going to focus on the context and dependency injection feature (CDI) as shown in Figure 7-8.

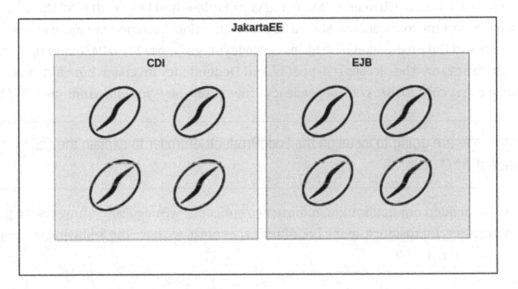

Figure 7-8. *Jakarta EE main components*

The CDI is composed of the following:

- Contexts: This helps us to have objects handled by the container, allowing it to be extended by the container features and with a defined life cycle.

- Dependency Injection: The ability to decouple the object creation from its clients. Dependency injection is a concept related to Inversion of Control and Dependency Inversion. You can find more information here: https://coderstower.com/2019/04/09/inversion-of-control-putting-all-together/ and here https://coderstower.com/2019/03/26/dependency-inversion-why-you-shouldnt-avoid-it/

> **Note** Enterprise Java Beans (EJB) uses some CDI features, too; however, they are a different type of bean that needs a different treatment.

Joining Our New Daniel's Delivery Website Layers

As we talked about in Chapter 5, "Modeling your Entities and Data with JPA," there are two important concepts, the Main and the Abstraction. You can read more about the Main and the Abstraction here https://coderstower.com/2019/04/02/main-and-abstraction-the-decoupled-peers/ and Dependency Inversion here https://coderstower.com/2019/03/26/dependency-inversion-why-you-shouldnt-avoid-it/

> **Note** We are going to focus on the FoodProductController to explain the CDI concept.

As we divided our application in those two concepts, we need something else to put them together; for instance, in the FoodProduct context, we have the following structure as shown in Figure 7-9.

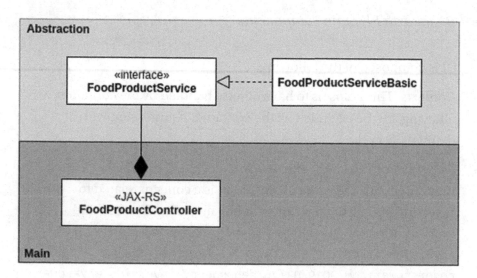

***Figure 7-9.** FoodProductController depends on FoodProductService interface but not the other way around, so the abstraction doesn't depend on the main*

That structure leaves us with some questions:

- Who is going to create the FoodProductServiceBasic object and inject it in the FoodProductController?

- Which implementations of FoodProductService should be injected?

Well, the CDI is going to help us with those questions. For that, we need to add a new class named RESTfulProvider (Figure 7-10).

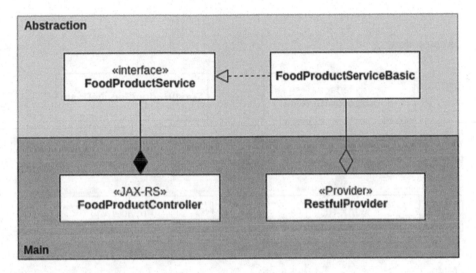

Figure 7-10. *FoodProductServiceBasic is created by the RESTfulProvider, who lives in the Main layer*

The following code shows us part of the provider code (Listing 7-21).

Listing 7-21. Factory method on RestfulProvider to create a FoodProductService class

```
@Stateless
@LocalBean
public class RestfulProvider {
  @Produces
  public FoodProductService getFoodProductService(
                    @Infrastructure FoodProductRepository
                    foodProductRepository) {
```

```
    return new FoodProductServiceBasic(foodProductRepository);
}

// More factory methods
}
```

As we can see, the provider has a factory method annotated by @Produces, which creates a new instance of FoodProductServiceBasic and returns it as a FoodProductService interface. What it means is described in Figure 7-11.

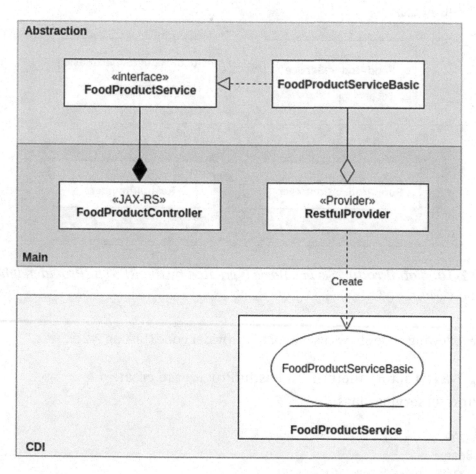

Figure 7-11. *FoodProductServiceBasic is created by the RESTfulProvider, and pushed to the CDI layer, being available for injection into other beans*

In that way, that instance is available for Dependency Injection (Listing 7-22).

Listing 7-22. FoodProductController and dependency injection with FoodProductService

```
@Stateless
@LocalBean
@Path("foodproducts")
public class FoodProductController{

  @Inject
  private FoodProductService foodProductService;
  // More code
}
```

The @Inject tells the CDI to find an implementation of the FoodProductService interface and use it as a dependency in the FoodProductController. That looks like Figure 7-12.

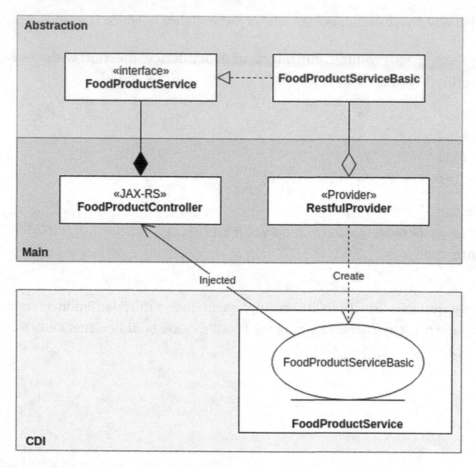

Figure 7-12. *FoodProductServiceBasic is injected by the CDI layer to the FoodProductController. The FoodProductController doesn't know the FoodProductService implementation.*

Okay, but, what about the argument the factory method has? (Listing 7-23)

Listing 7-23. Factory method to create a FoodProductService object depending on a FoodProductRepository instance of type @Infrastructure

```
@Produces
public FoodProductService getFoodProductService(
                        @Infrastructure FoodProductRepository
foodProductRepository) {
        return new FoodProductServiceBasic(foodProductRepository);
}
```

FoodProductServiceBasic has a dependency on the FoodProductRepository. Well, we defined those implementations in Chapter 5, "Modeling Your Entities and Data with JPA," as shown in Figure 7-13.

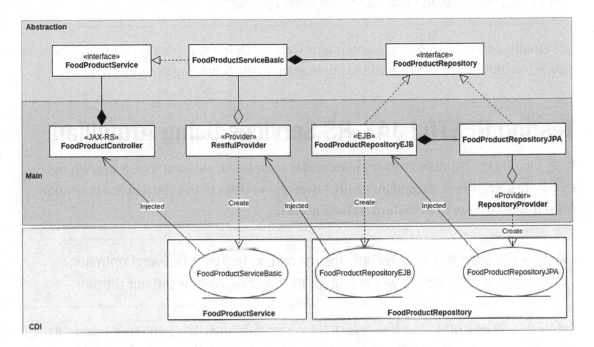

Figure 7-13. *Full dependencies and injections through the layer, from JAX-RS to JPA*

As we can see, the FoodProductRepository has two different implementations, one pushed by the EJB container into the CDI container, and another pushed to the CDI container by the RepositoryProvider, with its factory methods.

The getFoodProductService factory method is injected into the FoodProductRepositoryEJB implementation because we are telling the CDI container to search for the implementation with the stereotype @Infrastructure, as we can see in the FoodProductRepositoryEJB code (Listing 7-24).

Listing 7-24. FoodProductRepositoryEJB annotated by @Infrastructure

```
@Stateless
@Local
@Infrastructure
public class FoodProductRepositoryEJB implements FoodProductRepository{
```

291

Note   Everything related to the CDI container and Jakarta EE technology is on the Main side. Our business rules are on the Abstraction side. The CDI container allows us to decouple how the Main and Abstraction interact.

Finally, as we understand how our new Daniel's Delivery is put together, we can create integration tests for the whole application in the following section.

Testing RESTful JAX-RS Services Using Arquillian

Well, as our new Daniel's Delivery back end is completed, we want to test everything, so we are going to use Arquillian again; however, we want to test the whole application, from the JAX-RS services to the database access.

Note   We are going to show only the integration test over DeliveryController; however, you can find the whole test for the other repositories in our GitHub.

Our tests will be a black-box test, which means we won't use any container resources directly, so we are going to simulate an external user connecting to our RESTful services as shown in Figure 7-14.

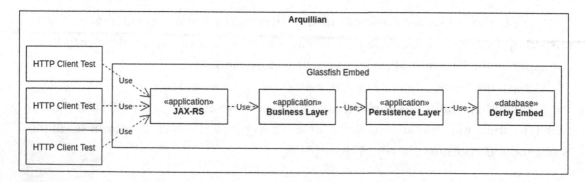

Figure 7-14. *Full Arquillian tests over the application layers*

Now let's see how we use Arquillian to create those tests.

Adding New Maven Dependencies for Arquillian

To support the JAX-RS black-box tests, we need to add new Maven dependencies (Listing 7-25).

Listing 7-25. Arquillian depedencies to support RESTful tests

```xml
<!--1-->
<dependency>
  <groupId>org.jboss.arquillian.extension</groupId>
  <artifactId>arquillian-rest-client-api</artifactId>
  <version>1.0.0.Alpha4</version>
  <scope>test</scope>
</dependency>
<dependency>
  <groupId>org.jboss.arquillian.extension</groupId>
  <artifactId>arquillian-rest-client-impl-3x</artifactId>
  <version>1.0.0.Alpha4</version>
  <scope>test</scope>
</dependency>

<!--2-->
<dependency>
  <groupId>org.jboss.resteasy</groupId>
  <artifactId>resteasy-jackson2-provider</artifactId>
  <version>3.0.9.Final</version>
</dependency>
<dependency>
  <groupId>com.fasterxml.jackson.jaxrs</groupId>
  <artifactId>jackson-jaxrs-json-provider</artifactId>
  <version>2.4.1</version>
</dependency>
<dependency>
  <groupId>com.fasterxml.jackson.core</groupId>
  <artifactId>jackson-databind</artifactId>
  <version>2.4.1</version>
</dependency>
```

The following is a description of the code sample:

1. Add the RESTful extensions for Arquillian.

2. Add RestEasy and Jackson dependencies for marshaling and unmarshaling. See the jackson-databind dependency to map Java classes to JSON format and vice versa.

Now, let's see the code of our integration test.

Creating an Integration Test for DeliveryController

Now, let's see how to use Arquillian to create an integration test for JAX-RS services (Listing 7-26).

Listing 7-26. Arquillian tests for DeliveryController

```
@RunWith(Arquillian.class)                    // (1)
public class DeliveryControllerIT {

    @Deployment(testable = false)        // (2)
    public static WebArchive createDeployment() {
        Path persistence = Paths.get("../StartWithJEE8-ejb/src/test/
        resources/META-INF/persistence.xml");
        Path deliveryData = Paths.get("../StartWithJEE8-ejb/src/test/
        resources/META-INF/deliverydata.sql");

        return ShrinkWrap.create(WebArchive.class)
                .addPackages(true, "com.daniel.delivery")
                .addAsResource(persistence.toFile(), "META-INF/
                persistence.xml")
                .addAsResource(deliveryData.toFile(), "META-INF/data.
                sql");                    // (3)
    }

    @Test
    @RunAsClient                          // (4)
    @InSequence(1)
```

```java
public void getDeliveriesByEmailAndState_emailAndState_list(@Arquillian
ResteasyResource("api") WebTarget webTarget) {        // (5)(6)
    FoodProductDTO foodProduct = new FoodProductDTO(1, "Pizza", 23500,
    "Pinaple Pizza", true, "imageUrl", "email1@email.com");
    ItemDTO item = new ItemDTO(1, 1, foodProduct);
    DeliveryDTO delivery = new DeliveryDTO(1, "Street 50", "555233564",
    23600, 100, "email5@email.com", "PENDING", Arrays.asList(item));

    Response response = webTarget
            .path("deliveries")
            .path("email5@email.com")
            .queryParam("state", "PENDING")
            .request(MediaType.APPLICATION_JSON)
            .get();

    List<DeliveryDTO> deliveries = response.readEntity(new GenericType<
    List<DeliveryDTO>>() { });

    assertThat(deliveries).isEqualTo(Arrays.asList(delivery));
}

@Test
@RunAsClient
@InSequence(2)
public void request(@ArquillianResteasyResource("api") WebTarget
webTarget) {                     // (7)
    FoodProductDTO foodProduct = new FoodProductDTO(1, "Pizza", 23500,
    "Pinaple Pizza", true, "imageUrl", "email1@email.com");

    ItemDTO newItem = new ItemDTO(null, 2, foodProduct);
    DeliveryDTO newDelivery = new DeliveryDTO(null, "Street 89",
    "55587412", 20100, 100, "email10@email.com", "PENDING", Arrays.
    asList(newItem));

    ItemDTO expectedItem = new ItemDTO(2, 2, foodProduct);
    DeliveryDTO expectedDelivery = new DeliveryDTO(2, "Street 89",
    "55587412", 20100, 100, "email10@email.com", "PENDING", Arrays.
    asList(expectedItem));
```

```
Response response = webTarget
        .path("deliveries")
        .request(MediaType.APPLICATION_JSON)
        .post(Entity.entity(newDelivery, MediaType.APPLICATION_
        JSON));

newDelivery = response.readEntity(DeliveryDTO.class);

assertThat(newDelivery).isEqualTo(expectedDelivery);
    }
}
```

The following is a description of the code sample:

1. We tell JUnit to use the Arquillian runner.

2. Note the testable=false property. That tells Arquillian to run
    these integration tests outside of the GlassFish container.
    Remember, this is a black-box test, simulating an external client
    communication with our JAX-RS services.

3. Define which components of our project we want to test. In this
    case, we tell Arquillian to load any class in the package com.
    daniel.delivery, use the persistence.xml for testing, and add the
    data.sql file.

    See we are adding the persistence.xml and its data to the
    deployable. Remember, we want to test everything, from JAX-RS
    services to database access.

4. Note the @RunAsClient; that annotation tells Arquillian to execute
    this test outside of the JEE container.

5. See @ArquillianResteasyResource("api"); that annotation allows
    injecting a WebTarget with path root as /api. Moreover, as
    Arquillian starts the GlassFish container in a random hostname
    and port number, the WebTarget injected is ready with that
    information, so you don't need to worry about it.

6. Now, we create the test for getting the deliveries by the delivery email and state. There, we are using the WebTarget object to create an HTTP request to /api/deliveries/email5@email. com?state=PENDING. And later, we validate that the response is what we expected.

7. Finally, we create a test to request a new Delivery.

The output of this integration test is shown in Figure 7-15.

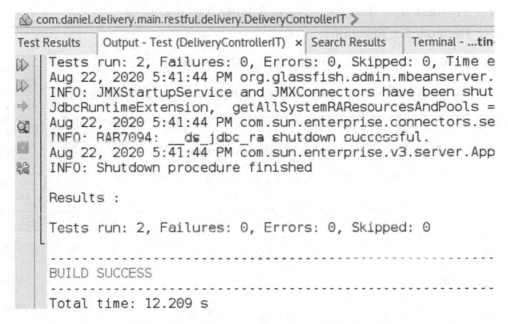

Figure 7-15. *Output of running the new DeliveryControllerIT integration tests*

Now, we are ready with our back-end layer for the new Daniel's Delivery website.

Summary

In this chapter, we saw how to create a business layer and RESTful layer and put them together.

We learned how to create business logic based on use cases and expose them through RESTful services using JAX-RS. Besides that, we learned how the CDI and Jakarta EE container works to put together a whole application; and finally, we created black-box tests using Arquillian to test from the RESTful services to the database.

As we have our back end and front end ready, in the following chapters, we are going to integrate both sides of our new Daniel's Delivery application.

Extended Knowledge

1. Are there other options than a WebTarget to consume JAX-RS services using Arquillian?

2. Are there other Java frameworks that use the concept of Dependency Injection?

3. How can I handle exceptions in my JAX-RS services?

4. Can a JAX-RS service only consume/produce JSON format?

5. Why are the EJB classes pushed to the CDI context automatically?

6. Can I use JAX-RS services without a Web project?

## CHAPTER 8

Connecting Your UI with Your Back End

In previous chapters we created the front-end and back-end layers of our new Daniel's Delivery website. However, we are missing one part: How we are going to put those two together?

In this chapter, we are going to integrate our Vue.js application with our Jakarta EE application, taking into account what we missed in the back-end and new plugins on the Vue.js side that helps us to integrate.

The following topics will be covered in the chapter:

- Checking what we missed in the back-end layer about APIs and images handlers using different configuration properties depending on the environment we deploy our application.

- Defining reusable RESTful client components to call our back-end services using Axios.

- Integration the Axios components to our new Daniel's Delivery pages exception handling in our JAX-RS services and Axios components.

Technical Requirements

To follow the instructions in this chapter, you will need the following:

- Java 1.8

- Netbeans 11

- GlassFish 5.1

© Daniel Andres Pelaez Lopez 2021
D. A. P. Lopez, *Full-Stack Web Development with Jakarta EE and Vue.js*,
https://doi.org/10.1007/978-1-4842-6342-6_8

- Jakarta Enterprise Edition

- Node.js 10.13.0

- Npm 6.7.0

- Nvm 0.34.0

- Visual Studio Code 1.33.1

- Axios 2.1.4

- vue-toasted 1.1.27

We are going to cover the installation of Axios and vue-toasted in this chapter. You can check the whole project and code at `https://github.com/Apress/full-stack-web-development-with-jakartaee-and-vue.js/tree/master/CH8`.

Preparing the Back End for Integration

We built a back-end layer for our new Daniel's Delivery website in previous chapters. However, when you start to integrate it with your front end, you always realize there are some features missing.

In these sections, we are going to complete those features to start integration with the Vue.js layer.

Adding New Endpoints to Our Back End

Integrating our front end and back end for the new Daniel's Delivery website requires us to add new endpoints to support the following use cases:

- FoodService resource:

  - Login

  - Get FoodService by email

  - Get FoodService by FoodType with pagination

- FoodProduct resource:

  - Get FoodProduct by id

  - Get FoodProduct by FoodService with pagination

- Upload and download files

In the following sections, we are going to define the API for those endpoints and see in detail how we implemented the upload and download of images.

Adding New Operations to FoodService Resource

We added a new resources path to /foodservices, and the definitions look like those shown in Listings 8-1 through 8-3.

Login for a FoodService

Listing 8-1. API and example for login for a FoodService

```
API

---REQUEST---
POST /api/foodservices/login
{
"email": <email>, "password": <password>
}

---RESPONSE---
HTTP Status OK
{
....FoodService data.....
}

###### EXAMPLE ######

---REQUEST---
POST /api/foodservices/login
{
"email": "chicken@email.com", "password": "pass2"
}

---RESPONSE---
HTTP Status OK
{
  "active": true,
  "address": "Street 898",
```

```
  "deliveryFee": 120,
  "email": "chicken@email.com",
  "foodProductList": [],
  "foodType": "CHICKEN",
  "name": "Chicken Cool",
  "user": {
     "email": "chicken@email.com",
     "password": "pass2"
  }
}
```

Get FoodService by Email

Listing 8-2. API and example for get FoodService by email

```
API

---REQUEST---
GET /api/foodservices/{email}

---RESPONSE---
HTTP Status OK
{
....FoodService data.....
}

###### EXAMPLE ######

---REQUEST---
GET /api/foodservices/chicken@email.com

---RESPONSE---
HTTP Status OK
{
"active": true,
"address": "Street 898",
"deliveryFee": 120,
"email": "chicken@email.com",
```

```
"foodProductList": [],
"foodType": "CHICKEN",
"name": "Chicken Cool",
"user": {
        "email": "chicken@email.com",
        "password": "pass2"
    }
}
```

Get FoodService by FoodType with Pagination

Listing 8-3. API and example for get FoodService by FoodType with Pagination

```
API

---REQUEST---
GET    /api/foodservices?foodType={foodType}&page={page}&pageSize={pageSize}
---RESPONSE---
HTTP Status OK [
{
....FoodServices data.....
}
]

###### EXAMPLE ######

---REQUEST---
GET /api/foodservices?foodType=PIZZA&page=1&pageSize=10

---RESPONSE---
HTTP Status OK [
    {
      "active": true,
      "address": "Street 89",
      "deliveryFee": 100,
      "email": "email1@email.com",
      "foodProductList": [],
      "foodType": "PIZZA",
```

```
    "name": "Pizzas 25",
    "user": {
            "email": "email1@email.com",
            "password": "pass1"
    }
 }
]
```

Adding New Operations to FoodProduct Resource

We added new resources paths to /foodproducts, and the definitions look like those shown in Listings 8-4 and 8-5.

Get FoodProduct by Id

Listing 8-4. API and example for get FoodProduct by id

```
API

---REQUEST---
GET /api/foodproducts/{id}

---RESPONSE---
HTTP Status OK
{
....FoodProduct data.....
}

###### EXAMPLE ######

---REQUEST---
GET /api/foodproduct/2

---RESPONSE---
HTTP Status OK
{
  "active": true,
  "description": "Cheese Pizza",
  "foodService": "email1@email.com",
  "id": 2,
```

```
    "imageUrl": "imageUrl2",
    "name": "Pizza",
    "price": 23500
}
```

Get FoodProduct by FoodService with Pagination

Listing 8-5. API and example for get FoodProduct by FoodService with Pagination

```
API

---REQUEST--- GET
/api/foodproducts?foodService={foodService}&page={page}&pageSize={pageSize}

---RESPONSE---
HTTP Status OK [
{
....FoodProduct data.....
}
]

###### EXAMPLE ######

---REQUEST---
GET    /api/foodproducts?foodService=email1@email.com&page=1&pageSize=10

---RESPONSE---
HTTP Status OK [
    {
        "active": true,
        "description": "Pinaple Pizza",
        "foodService": "email1@email.com",
        "id": 1,
        "imageUrl": "imageUrl",
        "name": "Pizza",
        "price": 23500
    }
]
```

Files Resource

Files resource is created to handle the upload and download of images we need. The path is /files and we are going to see how we defined the API and some of its implementation.

Designing the Upload and Download of Files

Now we are going to see how we structure some classes to handle the upload and download of files. Figure 8-1 illustrates how this is done.

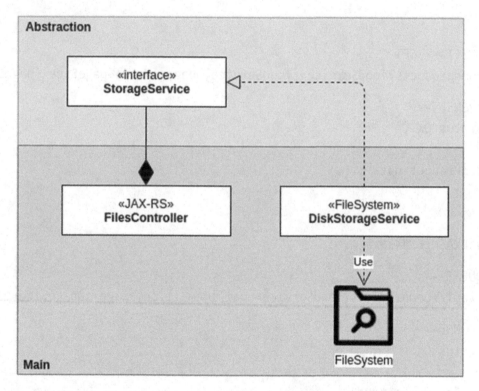

Figure 8-1. *FilesController class depends on StorageService, and DiskStorageService implements StorageService to access the file system*

As we can see, we just have one implementation named DiskStorageService that is going to save files in the filesystem. Also, we created a StorageService interface and an implementation that writes and reads files from disk.

Let's see what the DiskStorageService class looks like (Listing 8-6).

Listing 8-6. DiskStorageService class implementation

```java
public class DiskStorageService implements StorageService{
    private final String rootPath;     // (1)

    public DiskStorageService(String rootPath) {
        this.rootPath = rootPath;
    }

    @Override
    public String save(String fileName, InputStream inputStream) throws
    IOException{          // (2)
        String fileKey = UUID.randomUUID().toString() + "-" + fileName;

        Path pathLocation = Paths.get(this.rootPath, fileKey);

        Files.copy(inputStream, pathLocation);

        return fileKey;
    }

    @Override
    public InputStream load(String fileName) throws IOException
{                          // (3)
        Path pathLocation = Paths.get(this.rootPath, fileName);

        return Files.newInputStream(pathLocation);
    }
}
```

The following is a description of the code sample:

1. First, we need a root path where we are going to save our files.

2. Now we have the save method. This method gets a fileName and an inputStream, creates a UUID to add to the fileName to avoid conflicts, and saves the inputStream into the file system.

3. Finally, we have a load method. We just receive the fileName and return an inputStream.

Now we are going to define the API for those new services and see how to implement them.

So, we have two methods: upload, and load. In the following section, we define how that RESTful API looks.

Upload resource:

This RESTful API is going to receive a file from the client (FoodService image for instance) and save it into the file system (Listing 8-7).

Listing 8-7. API and example for Upload resource images

```
API

---REQUEST---
Content-Type: multipart/form-data; boundary=    XXXXXXXXXXXXXXXXXXXXX
POST /api/files

------XXXXXXXXXXXXXXXXXXXXX
Content-Disposition: form-data; name="file"; filename="<fileName>" Content-
Type: <contentType>

------XXXXXXXXXXXXXXXXXXXXX

---RESPONSE---
HTTP Status OK
{
"imageUrl":"<imageUrl>"
}
###### EXAMPLE ######
---REQUEST---
Content-Type: multipart/form-data; boundary=-----
WebKitFormBoundaryyqWLkBShjOs56onT
POST /api/files
------WebKitFormBoundaryyqWLkBShjOs56onT
Content-Disposition: form-data; name="file"; filename="Chapter7.png"
Content-Type: image/png
------WebKitFormBoundaryyqWLkBShjOs56onT
---RESPONSE---
HTTP Status OK
```

```
{
  "imageUrl":"http://localhost:8080/StartWithJEE8-web/api/files/d696de4a-
2b6c-4d25-abd6-67df1c88d4f1-Chapter7.png"
}
```

Note that the response is an image URL.

Load resource:

This RESTful API is going to receive a file key from the client and return a URL where the image is (Listing 8-8).

Listing 8-8. API and example for load resource images

```
API
---REQUEST---
GET /api/files/{fileKey}
---RESPONSE---
HTTP Status OK
Content-Type: image/webp
###### EXAMPLE ######
---REQUEST---
GET /api/files/d696de4a-2b6c-4d25-abd6-67df1c88d4f1-Chapter7.png

---RESPONSE---
HTTP Status OK
Content-Type: image/webp
```

Now we need a controller to receive the file and download the file. Let's see what we did for it.

First, we need to add some new dependency to our pom.xml into the web project (Listing 8-9).

Listing 8-9. Maven dependencies for image upload using Jersey

```
<dependency>
  <groupId>org.glassfish.jersey.core</groupId>
  <artifactId>jersey-server</artifactId>
  <version>2.28</version>
  <scope>provided</scope>
</dependency>
```

```xml
<dependency>
  <groupId>org.glassfish.jersey.media</groupId>
  <artifactId>jersey-media-multipart</artifactId>
  <version>2.28</version>
  <scope>provided</scope>
</dependency>
```

Those two dependencies help us to handle multipart media, in this case, files. We also need to update our RESTfulApplication class (Listing 8-10).

Listing 8-10. Maven dependencies for image upload using Jersey

```java
import javax.ws.rs.ApplicationPath;
import org.glassfish.jersey.media.multipart.MultiPartFeature;
import org.glassfish.jersey.server.ResourceConfig;

@ApplicationPath("api")
public class RestfulApplication extends ResourceConfig { // (1)

  public RestfulApplication(){
    packages("com.daniel.delivery.main.restful")
                .register(MultiPartFeature.class);  // (2)
  }
}
```

The following is a description of the code sample:

1. There, we extend from a ResouceConfig class from Jersey.

2. We register where our controllers are and a new module named MultiPartFeature.

Now we define our FileController class (Listing 8-11).

Listing 8-11. FileController class to define JAX-RS resources to upload and download images

```java
@Stateless
@LocalBean
@Path("files")
public class FileController {
```

```java
@Context
private UriInfo uriInfo;     // (1)
@Inject
private StorageService storageService;

@Path("{fileKey}")
@GET
@Consumes({MediaType.APPLICATION_JSON})
public InputStream loadFile(@PathParam("fileKey") String fileKey)
throws IOException {        // (2)
    return storageService.load(fileKey);
}

@POST
@Consumes(MediaType.MULTIPART_FORM_DATA)
@Produces(MediaType.APPLICATION_JSON)
public ImageDTO uploadFile(
        @FormDataParam("file") InputStream uploadedInputStream,
        @FormDataParam("file") FormDataContentDisposition fileDetail)
        throws IOException {      // (3)

    String fileKey = storageService.save(fileDetail.getFileName(),
    uploadedInputStream);              // (4)

    return new ImageDTO(uriInfo.getBaseUri() + "files/" + fileKey);
}
}
```

The following is a description of the code sample:

1. There we inject the UriInfo and StorageService class. UriInfo is a JAX-RS class that gives us information about the current controller, like URL and host.

2. Next, we define a resource to load an image: There is nothing weird there; we just delegate that search to the StorageService and return the inputStream.

3. Here, we have the upload method: @FormDataParam("file") helps us to get the data we need from the multipart form data. We get the InputStream and some file information like the name.

4. Later, we delegate the save operation to the StorageService, and finally, we return a new URL pointing to the new created file.

Tip   We created integration tests using Arquillian for this controller. You can check them here: `https://github.com/Apress/full-stack-web-development-with-jakartaee-and-vue.js/blob/master/CH8/StartWithJEE/StartWithJEE-web/src/test/java/com/daniel/delivery/main/restful/files/FileControllerIT.java`.

Allowing Cross Origin Resource Sharing Calls to Our Back End

Cross Origin Resource Sharing (CORS) is a pretty important concept in the web. In general, we need to be sure WHO is calling our services and give them explicit rights to do it.

For now, we are going to allow any client to call our services using the following filter (Listing 8-12).

Listing 8-12. CorsFilter class to allow cross site conections.

```
@Provider
@PreMatching
public class CorsFilter implements ContainerResponseFilter {

  @Override
  public void filter(ContainerRequestContext requestContext,
  ContainerResponseContext responseContext) throws IOException {
  responseContext.getHeaders()
        .add("Access-Control-Allow-Origin", "*"); responseContext.
        getHeaders()
        .add("Access-Control-Allow-Credentials", "true");
        responseContext.getHeaders()
```

```
        .add("Access-Control-Allow-Headers", "origin, content-type,
        accept, authorization"); responseContext.getHeaders()
        .add("Access-Control-Allow-Methods",
"GET, POST, PUT, DELETE, OPTIONS, HEAD");
  }
}
```

For now, we have just set some headers in the response, telling the client to allow everything about any call.

Tip   We are going to talk in more detail about CORS in the chapter about security.

Handling Environment Properties for Jakarta EE

Our new Daniel's Delivery back end is going to need multiple environments where to run, at least, local and production environments.

As we could have different configurations between environments, we need to have a way to use different properties depending on the environment. For instance, in the root path where we save the files that we upload in the application, that path could change from a local and production environment.

As the production environment is going to be on AWS, we could use S3 services to save our images. Currently, we are using the file system where the GlassFish Server is deployed.

Using Properties Files

We are going to use a properties file to save our environment properties. The main idea is to have one properties file by the environment with the following name pattern:

- application.properties for unknow environment,

- application-<ENV>.properties for the ENV environment.

The ENV variable is going to be defined as a system property when we start our server. For instance, we currently have two environments, local and IT (integration tests). This is the application.properties we have:

```
STORAGE_PATH=/home/daniel/Downloads/
```

As we can see, the STORAGE_PATH (where we are going to save our uploaded files) is pointing to a specific local folder on my machine. However, for the IT environment, that should be more generic, as we see in the application-it.properties file:

```
STORAGE_PATH=target/
```

For our IT tests, we save the uploaded files into the target folder that Maven creates, so that it is going to work in any machine; it doesn't matter what the operative system is.

Now those properties files are located in our EJB project (Figure 8-2).

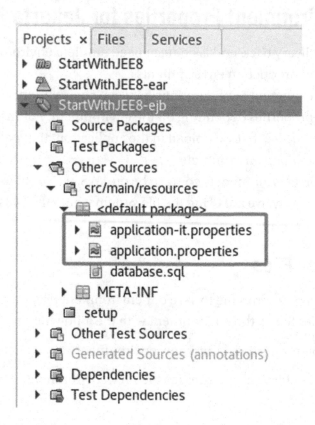

Figure 8-2. *Propertie files into the project to save environment variables*

In the following section, we are going to see how we load those properties files and use them in our application.

The GenericProvider for Environment Properties

We created a new @Provider to push into the CDI properties object. Let's see how we do that (Listing 8-13).

Listing 8-13. GeneralProvider class to load environment properties

```
@Stateless
@LocalBean
public class GeneralProvider {

@Produces
  public Properties getProperties() throws IOException {

    Properties properties = new Properties();
  InputStream inputStream =
 GeneralProvider.class.getResourceAsStream(Optional.ofNullable( System.
 getPro perty("ENV"))
    .map(env -> "/application-" + env + ".properties")
    .orElse("/application.properties"));

  properties.load(inputStream);
  return properties;
 }
}
```

As we can see, we search for a system property named ENV, and if there is that property, we load the application-<ENV>.properties properties file; otherwise, we load the default application.properties. And finally, we push that properties object into the CDI.

Now, our DiskStorage class requires a root path where to save the uploaded files, so this is how we create that object (Listing 8-14).

Listing 8-14. RESTfulProvider class using the environment variables from properties files

```
@Stateless
@LocalBean
public class RestfulProvider {

// More factories

@Produces
  public StorageService getStorageService(Properties properties) {
  return new
DiskStorageService(properties.getProperty("STORAGE_PATH"));
  }
}
```

As we can see, we inject the properties file into our factory method, get the STORAGE_PATH property, and create a new DiskStorageService.

Exception Handling in JAX-RS

Exception handling is pretty important in any application. For our controllers, we are going to define a general catcher for any possible exception. Let's see what it looks like.

First, we create a DTO to save exception data (Listing 8-15).

Listing 8-15. ExceptionResponse class to map a default error information

```
public class ExceptionResponse {
  private final String message;
  private final String stackTrace;

  public ExceptionResponse (String message, String stackTrace){
  this.message = message;
  this.stackTrace = stackTrace;
  }

  public String getMessage() {
  return message;
  }
```

```
public String getStackTrace() {
 return stackTrace;
 }
}
```

And we defined an ExceptionMapper (Listing 8-16).

Listing 8-16. GeneralExceptionHandler class to handle how the exceptions behave

```
@Provider
public class GeneralExceptionHandler implements ExceptionMapper<Exception>
{

  private final Logger logger = Logger.getLogger(GeneralExceptionHandler.
  class.getName());

  @Override
  public Response toResponse(Exception e) {
  logger.log(Level.SEVERE, e.getMessage(), e);

  StringWriter stringWriter = new StringWriter();

  e.printStackTrace(new PrintWriter(stringWriter));

return Response.status(500)
              .entity(new ExceptionResponse(e.getMessage(), stringWriter.
               toString()))
              .type(MediaType.APPLICATION_JSON)
              .build();
  }
}
```

That ExceptionMapper captures any exception in our controllers and processes it to create a readable response for our Vue.js application.

You must always have this kind of last-defense point. There, you can log the exception and allow your client to have something useful in the front-end side.

Integrating Vue.js and the Back End

We now have our back end ready to be used by our Vue.js application. So, in this section, we are going to change some Vuex services previously defined for a network call to our back end using Axios, and we will define some exception handlers and a new way to show error messages to our user.

Note   We won't change how CartItems work. It is using Vuex to save the cart and that's fine because we are not going to save the cart in the back-end; it is only on the front-end side.

Handling Environment Properties in Vue.js

As we did with our back-end, we now need to have different properties in our Vue.js application depending on which environment is deployed.

Which property do we need in Vue.js that changes between environments? Well, we need to know where the back-end services are.

As we are going to call our RESTful services in the back-end side from our Vue.js application, we need the URL, and that URL can change between environments, for instance:

- Local environment: http://localhost:8080/StartWithJEE8-web/api

- Production environment: `https://mynewpack.com/StartWithJEE8-web/api`

So, Vue.js allows us to create properties files (.env) in the root of our application. Those files could be named as follows:

- .env: loaded always,

- .env.[mode]: loaded when the specific mode is set.

Take into account that if you set mode=production, Vue.js is going to load .env and .env.production files, where the production file is going to override any duplicated key in the default file.

For now, we just defined an .env file that looks like this:

```
VUE_APP_RESTFUL_BASE_URL=http://localhost:8080/StartWithJEE8-web/api
```

The prefix VUE_APP_ is required to be loaded by Vue.js. To access the environment variable from Vue.js components, we just need to use process.env.VUE_APP_RESTFUL_BASE_URL.

We just avoided having to hard-code the URL for our back end in the code.

Creating Axios Components to Handle API Calls

Axios is a web library that allows us to call RESTful services.

Installing Axios

To install Axios, we do the following:

1. First, you just need to execute the command:

   ```
   npm install --save axios vue-axios
   ```

   Note that thes command installs Axios and vue-axios. The second one helps us to integrate Axios as a plugin into Vue.js, which means we can access Axios using Vue.axios, this.axios, or this.$http.

2. And finally, in the main.js, we need to add that plugin to our Vue.js context (Listing 8-17).

Listing 8-17. Updated main.js file adding VueAxios plugin

```
// More imports
import axios from 'axios'
import VueAxios from 'vue-axios'

const axiosInstance = axios.create({
    baseURL: process.env.VUE_APP_RESTFUL_BASE_URL
})

// More code
```

```
Vue.use(VueAxios, axiosInstance)
```

```
// More code
```

> We imported the Axios plugin, created an instance, and set it to
> the Vue.js context using the Vue.use method with the VueAxios
> plugin. Note how we create the Axios instance, sending the VUE_
> APP_RESTFUL_BASE_URL property we defined in our .env file.

DeliveryService Using Axios

Now, let's see our DeliveryService component that handles the Delivery calls to our back end using Axios. The DeliveryService class looks like Listing 8-18.

Listing 8-18. Updated DeliveryService.vue component to use Axios

```
import Vue from 'vue'
import { Delivery } from '../entities/Delivery'     // (1)

export class DeliveryService {
  static getDeliveriesByEmailAndState (email:string, state:string)
{                    // (2)
    return Vue.axios.get<Array<Delivery>>(`/deliveries/${email}?state=$
    {state}`)
  }

  static request (delivery: Delivery) {     // (3)
    return Vue.axios.post<Delivery>(`/deliveries`, delivery)
  }
}
```

The following is a description of the code sample:

1. First, we import the Vue and Delivery entity.

2. Now, we define the method to get the deliveries by email and
   state: Note how we don't define the whole URL for the call
   because we set a base URL when we created the Axios instance.

3. And finally, we define the request by a delivery method.

As you can see, we are using the Delivery resource API we defined in previous sections.

FoodProductService Using Axios

Now, let's see our FoodProductService component that handles the FoodProductService calls to our back end using Axios. The FoodProductService class looks like Listing 8-19.

Listing 8-19. Updated FoodProductService.vue component to use Axios

```
import Vue from 'vue'
import { FoodProduct } from '../entities/FoodProduct'    // (1.1)
import { Image } from '../entities/Image'                // (1.2)

export class FoodProductService {

  static getById (id: number) {        // (2.1)
    return Vue.axios.get<FoodProduct>(`/foodproducts/${id}`)
  }

  static deActivate (foodProduct: FoodProduct) {    // (2.2)
    return Vue.axios.delete<FoodProduct>(`/foodproducts/${foodProduct.id}`)
  }

  static getByFoodService (foodService: string, page:number,
  pageSize:number) {                // (2.3)
    return Vue.axios.get<Array<FoodProduct>>(`/foodproducts?foodService=$
    {foodService}&page=${page}&pageSize=${pageSize}`)
  }

  static create (foodProduct: FoodProduct) {    // (3)
    let formData = new FormData()

    formData.append('file', foodProduct.image)

    return Vue.axios.post<Image>(`/files`, formData,
      {
        headers: {
          'Content-Type': 'multipart/form-data'
        }
```

```
        })
        .then(response => {
          foodProduct.imageUrl = response.data.imageUrl

          return Vue.axios.post<FoodProduct>(`/foodproducts`, foodProduct)
        })
  }

  static update (foodProduct: FoodProduct) {      // (4)
    let formData = new FormData()

    formData.append('file', foodProduct.image)

    return Vue.axios.post<Image>(`/files`, formData,
      {
        headers: {
          'Content-Type': 'multipart/form-data'
        }
      })
      .then(response => {
        foodProduct.imageUrl = response.data.imageUrl

        return Vue.axios.put<FoodProduct>(`/foodproducts`, foodProduct)
      })
  }
}
```

The following is a description of the code sample:

1. First, we import Vue, FoodProduct, and Image entity.

2. We defined methods to get a food product by id, food service, and to deactivate a food product.

3. Now, we define the create food product method: note how we push the image of the food product first, and if that is successful, we create the food product. We are going to talk about the .then() method in detail in the following section

4. And finally, we update the food product method. Note that we create a new image in the server; we don't replace it.

FoodServiceService Using Axios

Now let's see our FoodServiceService component that handles the FoodServiceService calls to our back end using Axios. The FoodServiceService class looks like Listing 8-20.

Listing 8-20. Updated FoodServiceService.vue component to use Axios

```
import Vue from 'vue'        // (1.1)
import { FoodService } from '../entities/FoodService'  // (1.2)
import { User } from '../entities/User'       // (1.3)
import { Image } from '../entities/Image'     // (1.4)

export class FoodServiceService {

  static getById (email: string) {          // (2.1)
    return Vue.axios.get<FoodService>(`/foodservices/${email}`)
  }

  static login (user: User) {               // (2.2)
    return Vue.axios.post<FoodService>(`/foodservices/login`, user)
  }

  static getByFoodType (foodType:string, page:number, pageSize:number)
{                 // (2.3)
    return Vue.axios.get<Array<FoodService>>(`/foodservices?foodType=$
    {foodType}&page=${page}&pageSize=${pageSize}`)
  }

  static create (foodService: FoodService) {    // (3)
    let formData = new FormData()

    formData.append('file', foodService.image)

    return Vue.axios.post<Image>(`/files`, formData,
      {
        headers: {
          'Content-Type': 'multipart/form-data'
        }
      })
```

```
      .then(response => {
        foodService.imageUrl = response.data.imageUrl

        return Vue.axios.post<FoodService>(`/foodservices`, foodService)
      })
  }

  static update (foodService: FoodService) {     // (4)
    let formData = new FormData()

    formData.append('file', foodService.image)

    return Vue.axios.post<Image>(`/files`, formData,
      {
        headers: {
          'Content-Type': 'multipart/form-data'
        }
      })
      .then(response => {
        foodService.imageUrl = response.data.imageUrl

        return Vue.axios.put<FoodService>(`/foodservices`, foodService)
      })
  }
}
```

The following is a description of the code sample:

1. First, we import Vue, FoodService, User, and Image entity.

2. We defined methods to get a food service by email, food type, and to log in.

3. Now, we define the create food service method: again, note how we push the image of the food service first, and if that is successful, we create the food service.

4. And finally, the update food service method. Note that we create a new image in the server; we don't replace it.

Well, we have our Axios components ready, but how do we use them? Let's see in the following section.

Using Axios Components from the Vue.js Components

Now we are going to change how we get and push data from our Vue.js components to use the new Axios components.

Note   We are going to focus on LoginForm, FoodProductNew, and FoodServiceList components.

LoginForm.vue and Axios

This is how our new LoginForm.vue looks after integrating Axios components (Listing 8-21).

Listing 8-21. Updated LoginForm.vue component to use Axios through FoodServiceService component

```ts
<template>
......
</template>

<script lang="ts">
import { Component, Prop, Vue } from 'vue-property-decorator'
import { FoodService } from '../../entities/FoodService'
import { FoodServiceService } from '../../services/
FoodServiceService'        // (1)
import { User } from '../../entities/User'

@Component
export default class LoginForm extends Vue {
  private email:string = ''
  private password:string = ''

  login () {            // (2)
    FoodServiceService.login(User.newUser(this.email, this.password))
      .then(response => {
        if (response.status === 204) {     // (3)
          this.$toasted.error('Email or Password are wrong')
```

```
      } else {
        let foodService: FoodService = response.data

        this.$toasted.info(`Welcome ${foodService.name}`)

        this.$store.commit('setCurrentFoodServiceLoggedIn', foodService)
        this.$router.push({ name: 'food_service_view', params: { email:
        this.email } })
      }
    })
  }
}
</script>
```

The following is a description of the code sample:

1. Importing the FoodServiceService component.

2. Updating the login method to use our Axios component: there, we
    call the login method from our Axios component. After that, from
    the response, we can call methods and chain them to process our
    result. The following methods are allowed:

    -   .then(): This method is invoked by Axios when the response of the
        network call has a 2xx status.

    -   .catch(): This method is invoked by Axios when the response has
        a different status code than 2xx.

    -   .finally(): This method is always invoked by Axios.

3. In the login method, we validate that if the response is 204 (login
    invalid), we just show a message; otherwise, we confirm the Food
    Service is valid and continue to move to the settings page.

    Why do not we define a .catch() method? Well, the idea is to
    handle those kinds of errors in a generic way. We will talk about it
    in the following sections.

FoodProductNew.vue and Axios

This is how our new FoodProductNew.vue looks after integrating Axios components (Listing 8-22).

Listing 8-22. Updated FoodProductNew.vue component to use Axios through FoodServiceService component

```ts
<template>
.....
</template>

<script lang="ts">
import { Component, Vue, Prop } from 'vue-property-decorator'
import FoodProductForm from '@/components/foodProduct/FoodProductForm.vue'
import { FoodProduct } from '../../entities/FoodProduct'
import { FoodProductService } from '../../services/
FoodProductService'          // (1)

@Component({
  components: {
    FoodProductForm
  }
})
export default class FoodProductNew extends Vue {
  @Prop() private readonly foodService!: string

  save (foodProduct:FoodProduct) {    // (2)
    foodProduct.active = true

    FoodProductService.create(foodProduct)
      .then(response => {
        this.$toasted.info(`Save successfully`)

        this.$router.push({ name: 'food_service_view', params:
        { email: this.foodService } })
      })
  }
}
</script>
```

The following is a description of the code sample:

1. Importing the FoodProductService component.

2. Updating the save method to use the Axios component: There, if the call was successful, we just redirect to the food service view.

FoodServiceList.vue and Axios

This is what our new FoodServiceList.vue looks like after integrating Axios components (Listing 8-23).

Listing 8-23. Updated FoodServiceList.vue component to use Axios through FoodServiceService component

```ts
<template>
.....
</template>

<script lang="ts">
import 'bootstrap/dist/css/bootstrap.css'
import 'bootstrap-vue/dist/bootstrap-vue.css'
import InfiniteLoading from 'vue-infinite-loading'
import { Component, Vue, Prop } from 'vue-property-decorator'
import { FoodService } from '../../entities/FoodService'
import { FoodServiceService } from '../../services/
FoodServiceService'         // (1)

@Component({
  components: {
    InfiniteLoading
  }
})
export default class FoodServiceList extends Vue {
  private foodServices:FoodService[] = []
  private foodType:string = 'ALL'
  private infiniteId:string = this.foodType
```

```
  private page:number = 1
  private pageSize:number = 4

  resetFilter () {
    this.foodServices = []
    this.page = 1
    this.infiniteId = this.foodType
  }

  getFoodServices (foodType:string, page:number, pageSize:number) {
    return this.$store.getters.getFoodServiceByFoodType(foodType, page,
    pageSize)
  }

  populateFoodProducts (state:any) {        // (2)
    FoodServiceService.getByFoodType(this.foodType, this.page, this.
    pageSize)
      .then(response => {
        let foodServicesLoaded:FoodService[] = response.data

        if (foodServicesLoaded.length) {
          this.foodServices.push(...foodServicesLoaded)
          state.loaded()
          this.page += 1
        } else {
          state.complete()
        }
      })
  }
}
</script>

<style scoped>
....
</style>
```

The following is a description of the code sample:

1. Importing the FoodServiceService component.

2. Updating the populateFoodProducts method to use the Axios component: there, if the call was successful, we add the new page to the current list of food products. Remember, the populateFoodProducts method is called by an infinite scroll plugin.

Now, as we just integrated our components to use Axios, we can move to define how to handle exceptions.

Handling Exceptions from Our Back-End Services

We saw that in Axios we can chain .catch() methods to the response; however, that means we need to do that by each call we do.

A better approach is to have a last handler exception point to avoid showing it to the users, an error they don't care about, so Axios allows us to add a generic exception handler, as we can see in the following main.js code (Listing 8-24).

Listing 8-24. Adding exception handler to Axios in the main.js file

```
// More imports

import axios from 'axios'
import VueAxios from 'vue-axios'

const axiosInstance = axios.create({
baseURL: process.env.VUE_APP_RESTFUL_BASE_URL
})

axiosInstance.interceptors.response.use(response => { return response
}, error => {
Vue.toasted.error('Ops, an unexpected error occurred') return Promise.
reject(error)
})

// More code

Vue.use(VueAxios, axiosInstance)
```

There, we add to interceptors.response.use, a generic error handler. That handler shows a friendly message to the user and rejects the promise, logging the exception in the console.

Figure 8-3 shows an example of error handling.

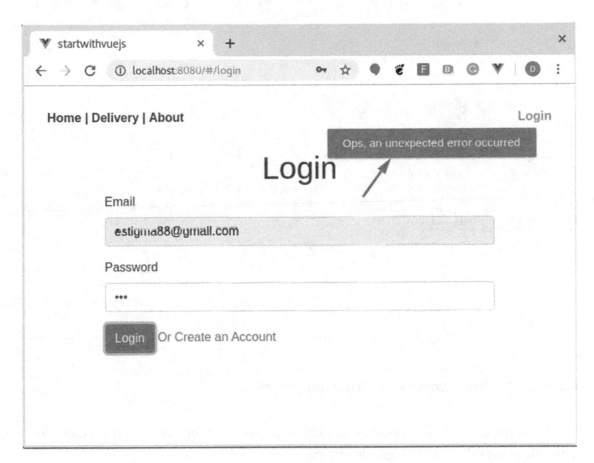

Figure 8-3. *Error example using toasted plugin*

And Figure 8-4 shows the error is logged in the console.

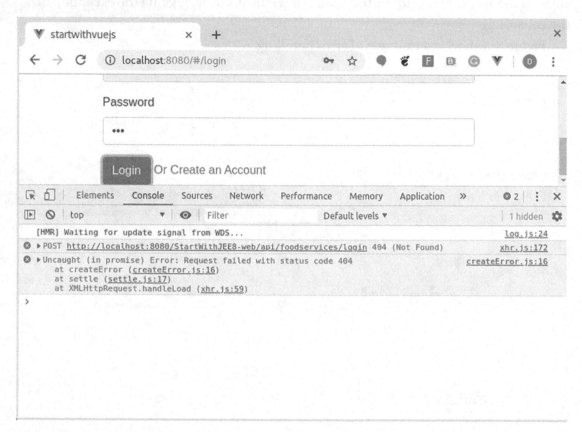

Figure 8-4. *Error example printed in the console*

Remember, it is pretty important to trace your error; it doesn't matter if the console gets ugly - that is better than ignoring them.

We just completed our front-end and back-end integration, using RESTful communication through Axios and JAX-RS.

Summary

In this chapter, we saw how to integrate our front-end layer with the back-end layer.

We learned how to upload files using JAX-RS, create Axios components to handle APIs calls to RESTful services from Vue.js, and define actions to take when handling exceptions in both layers.

We are missing a pretty important part: What about security? Well, in the following chapters, we are going to talk about it.

Extended Knowledge

1. How do you set the ENV variable for the integration tests?

2. Can I map specific exceptions using the ExceptionMapper?

3. How can I install the vue-toasted plugin?

4. I am getting this error javax.ejb.AccessLocalException: Client not authorized for this invocation. How can I fix it?

5. Why did we need to add other libraries to handle the multipart uploads?

6. Can I perform multiple concurrent requests using Axios?

7. Can I use Vuex and Axios in the same Vue.js project?

CHAPTER 9

Securing Your Full-Stack Application

In previous chapters, we created a full-stack application using Vue.js and JEE. However, we have not yet covered security, which is a must in any application.

Consequently, in this chapter, we will focus on securing your full-stack application.

Here, we are going to focus on basic security concepts like authentication and authorization, as well as talking about the most commonly used security protocols. Finally, we will cover how to set up a security provider.

The following topics will be covered in this chapter:

- What are authentication and authorization?

- Understanding the OpenID Connect protocol

- Installing an Open Source OpenID Connect Identity Provider to secure a full-stack application

After this chapter, you will have knowledge regarding the security bases and OpenID Connect protocol, how they work, and why they are important; and finally, you will be able to use one Identity Provider, from installation to configuration.

Technical Requirements

To follow the instructions in this chapter, you will need Keycloak 7.0.0. We are going to cover the installation of Keycloak in this chapter.

© Daniel Andres Pelaez Lopez 2021
D. A. P. Lopez, *Full-Stack Web Development with Jakarta EE and Vue.js*,
https://doi.org/10.1007/978-1-4842-6342-6_9

Security Basics: Authentication and Authorization

The application's security is pretty important for any business. As an example, we are going to use the new Daniel's Delivery website, which will need to start receiving online payments and saving more of the clients' private information. For this, we need to guarantee our data (and money) is protected. Therefore, we will apply two main aspects of security basics, authentication and authorization.

In this section, we are going to define those concepts and how they will apply to our new Daniel's Delivery website.

Authentication: Who Are You?

Authentication addresses the question of who are you? In other words, we want to know if you are who you say you are. For instance, you meet a new friend who says he is Albert Einstein; however, you want to see if that is true (you want to authenticate him). So, you do a little research and find out that he is not Albert Einstein, as he died decades ago. Therefore, the authentication failed.

In the case of the new Daniel's Delivery website, any time a user tries to access information in our application, it is going to ask an external Identity Provider if he knows that user.

An Identity Provider is an external application that handles anything security related, usually the basics like authentication and authorization. So, we can register users into the provider, and define which users have the rights to access which applications.

We created a login page in previous chapters where we didn't have an Identity Provider, so we handled the authentication by ourselves.

However, security is usually hard to do and the problem is already solved in a pretty good way by providers, so we suggest you use an external Identity Provider when that's possible

In Figure 9-1, we will see how the new Daniel's Delivery website is going to interact with the identity provider.

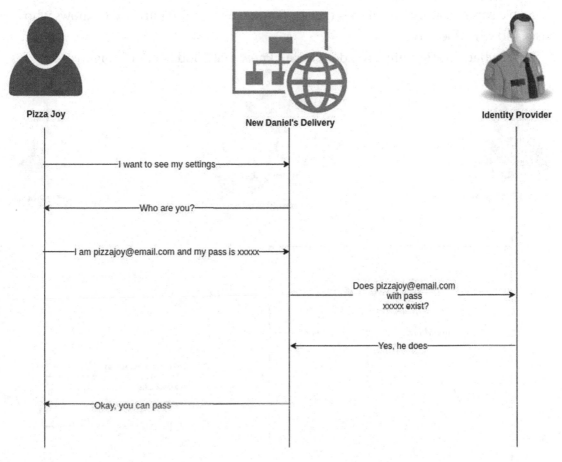

Figure 9-1. *Authentication flow using an identity provider with successful result*

As we can see, the Pizza Joy user is trying to access the settings page in the website, but the website needs to authenticate them against the identity provider before giving them any access; in this case, the identity provider knows that user, so he lets them pass.

Note   As we saw in previous chapters, the new Daniel's Delivery website has Food Services (restaurants that want to offer their products on the website) and Customers (users that want to request a food delivery on the website). Customers don't need to log in to the website to request a delivery; however, Food Services needs to log in to access its settings, like basic information and related products they offer.

As we can see, authentication is usually federated to a third party, who knows who exists and who does not.

Now, what if the identity provider doesn't know that Food Service? (Figure 9-2)

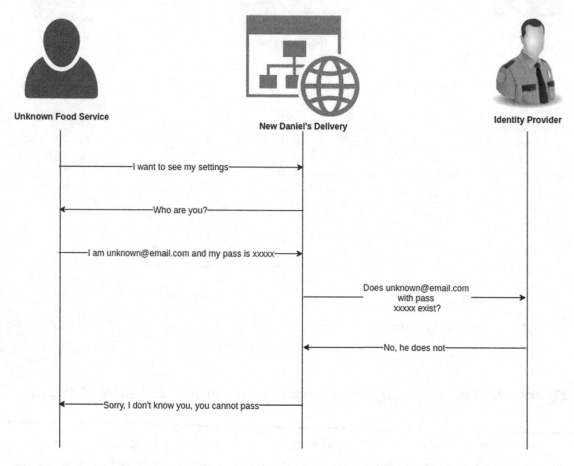

Figure 9-2. *Authentication flow using an identity provider with failed result*

Well, in this case, as the identity provider doesn't know that Food Service, our new Daniel's Delivery website won't allow them to access it.

However, we are missing a part here. What if I am a valid Food Service but I try to access data in the application in which I am not allowed to access? Authorization helps us to validate what you can access and what you cannot.

Authorization: What Can You Do?

We saw how authentication tells us who you are, so now authorization is going to tell us what you can do: that means what operations or information you can access after you are in the new Daniel's Delivery website.

To handle the authorization, we add a new module in our application. Why don't we use an external provider as we did for the authentication? Well, authorization is pretty particular to each application. I mean that each application knows what operation has been done and what else can be done there, so it feels natural to let the authorization into the application.

Note   The RESTful API module has authorization too, as that is an API and can be invoked outside of our Vue.js page, so we should secure it.

Figure 9-3 illustrates how the authorization flow works.

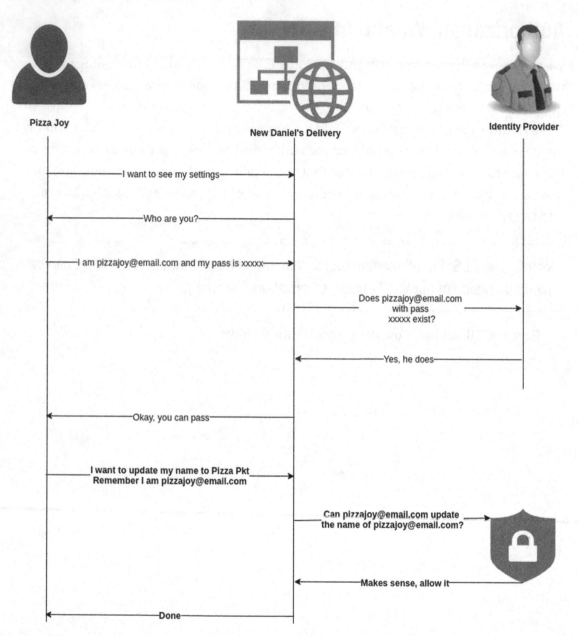

Figure 9-3. *Authorization flow using an identity provider with successful result*

There we can see how the identity provider (authentication flow) and the authorization module interact to allow Pizza Joy's user to access operations on the website. In this case, Pizza Joy's user wants to update his name on the website and the authorization module allows him.

Now, what if a Food Service tries to do something that he doesn't have rights to do? (Figure 9-4)

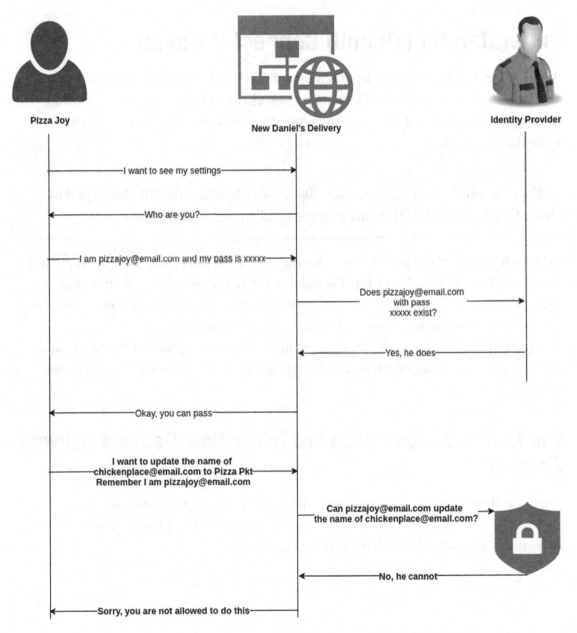

Figure 9-4. *Authorization flow using an identity provider with failed result*

As we can see, the Pizza Joy user is a valid user; however, when it tries to update the name that belongs to Chicken Place, the authorization module must not allow it.

Now, as we defined the basis for authentication and authorization, let's talk about how we can implement those securities concerns.

Understanding OpenID Connect Protocol

OpenID Connect is an authentication protocol, based on OAuth 2.0 specification, which allows delegating the authentication process to an identity provider, allowing our applications to forget about maintaining passwords, as those are handled by the authorization server.

Note   OAuth 2.0 is a set of specifications that handles different message flows based on JSON and HTTP to allow authentication and authorization.

As OpenID Connect is a protocol, which means it can be implemented in multiple ways and technologies, so it offers a lot of possibilities and interoperability with multiple applications. Have you ever used your Google account to log in into an application? Well, it is probably that you are using the OpenID Connect protocol there

OpenID Connect protocol has different flows. For the purposes of this book, we are going to focus on the authorization code flow as it is the most used and offers better security.

The Authorization Code Flow in the New Daniel's Delivery Website

The authorization code flow uses a code delivered by the identity provider to get the necessary tokens to secure our access to the new Daniel's Delivery website. The following steps are performed in this flow (Figure 9-5).

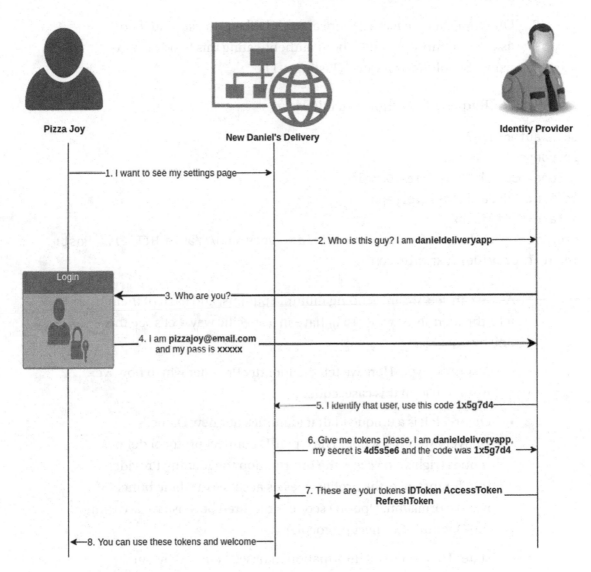

Figure 9-5. *Authorization flow in the Daniel's Delivery app using an identity provider with successful result*

Now, let's discuss those steps one by one:

1. The Food Service tries to access through the browser the URL
   `www.mynewdanieldelivery.com/food_service/pizzadaniel`
   `@email.com` (this represents the settings page).

2. Our application checks if there are valid tokens to use, and if not, asks the identity provider about authenticating this Food Service, using the following request (Listing 9-1).

Listing 9-1. Request to authorize a client

```
GET /authorize?
response_type=code
&scope=openid%20profile%20email
&client_id=danieldeliveryapp
&state=af0ifjsldkj
&redirect_uri=https://www.mynewdanieldelivery.com/#/auth HTTP/1.1 Host:
identityprovider.example.com
```

As we can see, we are sending multiple params, and each of them tells the identity provider to behave in a specific way. Let's see this one by one:

- response_type: Here we tell the Identity Provider which flow we want to use: in this case, code.

- client_id: It is a unique id that identifies our new Daniel's Delivery website. scope: The OpenID connect protocol defines scopes (rights) to access the information the Identity Provider has, for instance, the profile gives us access to a whole bunch of user information. OpenID scope is required because we are using the OpendID Connect protocol.

- state: This is general information in base64 created by our application. This information flows back to us after the Identity Provider responds, so, it allows us to handle states between requests. A typical use case for a state is the URL of the page the user tried to access before being asked to log in. When the Identity Provider responds back, we can use that URL to redirect the user where they wanted to go.

- redirect_url: This is the URL where the Identity Provider must respond back to us with the authentication code. Be careful, as we are sending a URL as a param in another URL, so we must escape the unallowed characters.

3. After calling the Identity Provider with the params we want, the Identity Provider redirects the user to its own login page. The login page is handled by the Identity Provider. That is pretty good because the Identity Provider can add other security filters like Multifactor Authentication. Look for more information here: https://www.cyber.gov.au/publications/multi-factor-authentication

4. The Food Service fills the required login data and submits it to the Identity Provider.

5. If the Identity Provider identifies that Food Service, it responds back to our application using the redirect_url and adds a unique authentication code for that flow (Listing 9-2).

Listing 9-2. Response from an authorized client

```
HTTP/1.1 302 Found
Location: https://www.mynewdanieldelivery.com/#/auth? code=1x5g7d4
&state=af0ifjsldkj
```

When the Location header is sent in the response of an HTTP request with the 302 Found status code, the browser is going to redirect to that Location. Note that the state param is the same we sent in step 3.

6. Our application asks the Identity Provider about delivering some tokens (Listing 9-3).

Listing 9-3. Request for getting a valid token

```
POST /token HTTP/1.1
Host: identityprovider.example.com
Content-Type: application/x-www-form-urlencoded Authorization: Basic
czZCaGRSa3F0MzpnWDFmQmF0M2JW

grant_type=authorization_code&code=1x5g7d4
&redirect_uri=https://www.mynewdanieldelivery.com/#/auth
```

Remember to escape the redirect_uri.

The Authorization header is required if you didn't define the client authentication type in step 2. There, we use the client id and client secret to authenticate. To keep them safe, we might need to create some endpoints in our RESTful API to keep them safe. For instance, you can use client_id=danieldeliveryapp&client_secret=some_secret12345 instead of the Authorization header.

7. The Identity Provider returns the tokens. The following is a possible response (Listing 9-4).

Listing 9-4. Response with token from the identity provider

```
HTTP/1.1 200 OK
Content-Type: application/json Cache-Control: no-store Pragma: no-cache

{
"access_token": "SlAV32hkKG",
"token_type": "Bearer",
"refresh_token": "8xLOxBtZp8", "expires_in": 3600,
"id_token": "eyJhbGciOiJSUzI1NiIsImtpZCI6IjFlOWdkazcifQ.ewogImlzc
yI6ICJodHRwOi8vc2VydmVyLmV4YW1wbGUuY29tIiwKICJzdWIiOiAiMjQ4Mjg5
NzYxMDAxIiwKICJhdWQiOiAiczZCaGRSa3F0MyIsCiAibm9uY2UiOiAibi0wUzZ
fV3pBMk1qIiwKICJleHAiOiAxMzExMjgxOTcwLAogImlhdCI6IDEzMTEyODA5Nz
AKfQ.ggW8hZ1EuVLuxNuuIJKX_V8a_OMXzROEHR9R6jgdqrOOF4daGU96Sr_P6q
Jp6IcmD3HP99Obi1PRs-cwh3LO-p146waJ8IhehcwL7F09JdijmBqkvPeB2T9
CJ NqeGpe-gccMg4vfKjkM8FcGvnzZUN4_KSPOaAp1tOJ1zZwgjxqGByKHiOtX7Tpd
QyHE5lcMiKPXfEIQILVq0pc_E2DzL7emopWoaoZTF_mO_NOYzFC6g6EJbOEoRoS
K5hoDalrcvRYLSrQAZZKflyuVCyixEoV9GfNQC3_osjzw2PAithfubEEBLuVVk4
XUVrWOLrLlOnx7RkKU8NXNHq-rvKMzqg"
}
```

As we can see, the Identity Provider offers us the following parameters:

- access_token: It is a credential to allow access to a specific resource, in this case, to our new Daniel's Delivery website. The access token might expire or become invalid with time.

- token_type: By default it is Bearer unless the client asked the Identity Provider for another kind.

- refresh_token: It is a credential to allow us to get access tokens when it expires or becomes invalid. This token is optional and might not be delivered by the Identity Server.

- expires_in: Time in seconds when the access token is going to expire.

- id_token: This is an extension OpendID Connect does over OAuth 2.0. The ID Token contains security information about the client, named claims. Claims can have data about the authenticated user like name, email, groups, and other. Also, this token could be encrypted and signed.

  We are going to discuss that the format of the ID token is a JSON Web Token (JWT) in the following sections.

8. The new Daniel's Delivery website must save these tokens in a secure way.

Using the Access and Refresh Tokens

Now, as we have our access and refresh tokens, we can use them to access our resources: in this case, our RESTful back-end. Figure 9-6 illustrates how we use those tokens.

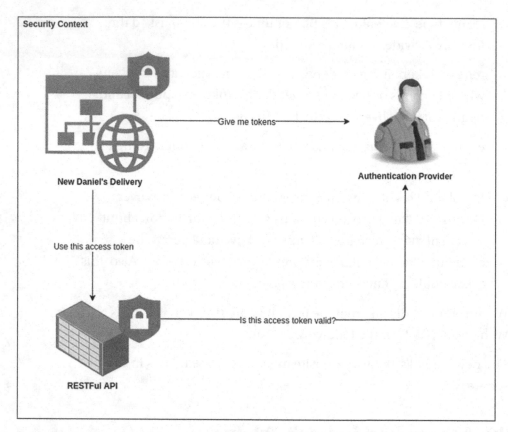

Figure 9-6. *Using access and refresh tokens*

As we can see, we are going to use the access token to communicate against our RESTful API. The back end is going to validate if the access token is OK to allow the operation; otherwise, the back end won't allow it.

Validating a token means checking a set of features a token must comply with, for instance:

- The token is well-formed? Its structure is what the standard defines.

- Its date of expiration is not reached yet? Any token has an expiration time, and if this time passes, the token becomes invalid.

- The digital signature is valid? A token has a digital signature signed by the Identity Provider. The RESTful API can use the Identity Provider public key to check that the signature is valid.

- If the token is encrypted, can I decrypt it? The token can be encrypted, so to see the information, the RESTful API must decrypt it.

This validation could be done in situ (your back-end or front-end application) using public keys downloaded from the Identity Provider or remotely, using an Identity Provider endpoint named introspect.

In the case of the front end, we can use different JavaScript security libraries regarding encryption and signatures validation; however, it is costly in performance to do it onto the client-side (browser), so, try to use it only if you must.

Tip   It is not necessary for the RESTful API to communicate with the Identity Provider each time to validate an access token. There are other alternatives like caching a public key. You can find a lot of frameworks that handle that validation for you, and you can check them here: `https://openid.net/developers/certified/`.

So, let's see how the access and refresh token flow works (Figure 9-7).

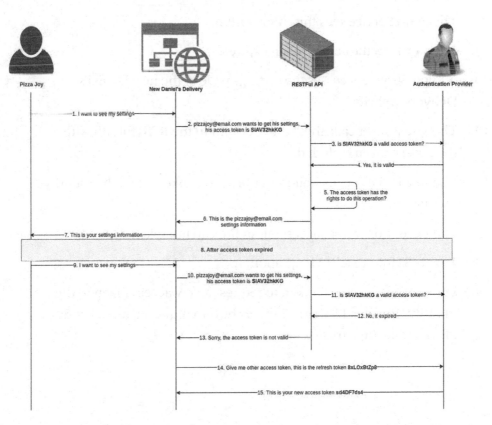

Figure 9-7.   *Using refresh token to update the expired access token*

Let's discuss these steps one by one:

1. A Food Service accesses the settings page of the new Daniel's Delivery website.

2. The Vue.js layer calls the right endpoint in the RESTful API with the access token included.

3. The RESTful API calls/validates the access token using the Identity Provider.

4. The validation is successful.

5. The RESTful API checks the claims into the token and validates if the Food Service has the rights to access this resource. To check the claims, we need to process the access token. We are going to talk about this in the JSON Web Tokens (JWT) section.

6. The RESTful API responds with the settings data.

7. The Food Service sees this information.

8. After a while, the access token expires.

9. A Food Service accesses the settings page of the new Daniel's Delivery website.

10. The Vue.js layer calls the right endpoint in the RESTful API with the access token included.

11. The RESTful API calls/validates the access token using the Identity Provider.

12. The validation is not successful, so the GitHub token expired.

13. The RESTful API tells Vue.js about it.

14. Vue.js uses the refresh token to request a new access token to the Identity Provider. Listing 9-5 shows how to request a new access token using the refresh token.

Listing 9-5. Request to refresh access tokens

```
POST /token HTTP/1.1
Host: identityprovider.example.com
Content-Type: application/x-www-form-urlencoded

client_id=danieldeliveryapp
&client_secret=some_secret12345
&grant_type=refresh_token
&refresh_token=8xLOxBtZp8
&scope=openid%20profile
```

> In the preceding code snippet, client_id is a unique id for the new
> Daniel's Delivery app in the Identity Provider and client_secret
> is a secret to authenticate the client against the Identity Provider.
> grant_type tells the Identity Server that we are using a refresh
> token to request a new access token. scope defines which rights
> we want for this new access token.

15. The Identity Provider responds with a new access token
    (Listing 9-6).

Listing 9-6. Response with a new access token from a refresh token

```
HTTP/1.1 200 OK
Content-Type: application/json Cache-Control: no-store Pragma: no-cache

{
"access_token": "TlBN45jURg",
"token_type": "Bearer",
"refresh_token": "9yNOxJtZa5",
"expires_in": 3600
}
```

> Here, access_token is a new valid access token, token_type is the
> token type, refresh_token is a new refresh token, and expires_in is
> the time in seconds when the new access token expires.

We have defined how our new Daniel's Delivery website is going to interact with the Identity Provider. In the following section, we are going to talk about JSON Web Tokens.

JSON Web Tokens (JWT)

JWT is a standard defined in RFC 7519 for representing claims securely between two parties in a JSON format. This information is digitally signed, so, it can be verified by the client.

Besides the signature, JWT could be encrypted to guarantee secrecy between parties; this is important if you have confidential information in your JWT like passwords, credit card numbers. or something similar. Remember that a digital signature just tells you if who delivers the JWT is who says he is, but the information is plain text; encryption helps us to opaque the information into the JWT so only the right people can see it.

As we saw in the previous section, the ID token is a JWT (Listing 9-7).

Listing 9-7. ID Token from OpenId connect protocol

```
"id_token": "eyJhbGciOiJSUzI1NiIsImtpZCI6IjFlOWdkazcifQ.ewogImlzc
yI6ICJodHRwOi8vc2VydmVyLmV4YW1wbGUuY29tIiwKICJzdWIiOiAiMjQ4Mjg5
NzYxMDAxIiwKICJhdWQiOiAiczZCaGRSa3F0MyIsCiAibm9uY2UiOiAibiOwUzZ
fV3pBMk1qIiwKICJleHAiOiAxMzExMjgxOTcwLAogImlhdCI6IDEzMTEyODA5Nz
AKfQ.ggW8hZ1EuVLuxNuuIJKX_V8a_OMXzROEHR9R6jgdqrOOF4daGU96Sr_P6q
Jp6IcmD3HP99Obi1PRs-cwh3LO-p146waJ8IhehcwL7F09JdijmBqkvPeB2T9
CJ NqeGpe-gccMg4vfKjkM8FcGvnzZUN4_KSPOaAp1tOJ1zZwgjxqGByKHiOtX7Tpd
QyHE5lcMiKPXfEIQILVqOpc_E2DzL7emopWoaoZTF_mO_NOYzFC6g6EJbOEoRoS
K5hoDalrcvRYLSrQAZZKflyuVCyixEoV9GfNQC3_osjzw2PAithfubEEBLuVVk4
XUVrWOLrLlOnx7RkKU8NXNHq-rvKMzqg"
```

JWT structure is defined in three parts split by dots. This structure consists of the following: header payload signature.

Each part is coded in Base64. Let's start with the header.

JWT Header

The JWT header usually contains basic information about the JWT. For instance, the following is an encoded token:

```
eyJhbGciOiJIUzI1NiIsInR5cCI6IkpXVCJ9
```

And it is decoded to the following JWT header (Listing 9-8).

Listing 9-8. Basic JWT headers

```
{
  "alg": "HS256",
  "typ": "JWT"
}
```

We can see there the following properties:

- alg: The algorithm used to sign this JWT

- typ: The type of token

The Identity Provider might require you to add some additional information to the header. This information depends on the implementation, for instance, the OpenID Connect protocol because the ID token requires other headers you can find here: https://openid.net/specs/openid-connect-core-1_0.html#CodeIDToken

JWT Payload

The payload contains the claims, and those claims are information about the entity/user related with this token. Let's see an example:

eyJzdWIiOiI3ODQ1NTIxIiwibmFtZSI6IkRhbmllbCBQZWxhZXoiLCJhZG1pbiI6dHJlZXO

Here is the payload information there (Listing 9-9).

Listing 9-9. Basic JWT payload

```
{
  "sub": "7845521",
  "name": "Daniel Pelaez",
  "admin": true
}
```

We have here the following elements:

- sub: An identifier for this client

- name: The user name for this JWT

- admin: If the logged person is an admin or not

The OpenID Connect protocol might require you to add some additional information to the payload; and remember, if you sign the token but you do not encrypt it, this information is readable by anyone, so do not put sensitive information here.

JWT Signature

The signature is used to validate that the information in the token hasn't changed in the way from its origin to its destination.

For instance, in a man of the middle attack, someone can capture the JWT in the network and replace some information there before reaching its destination. If you check the signature of this JWT, you will realize the JWT was changed and it's corrupted, so you can avoid using it.

To sign the token, you should do the following:

1. Encode the header

2. Encode the payload

3. Define a secret (could be a password or a private key)

4. Define the algorithm

5. And finally, generate the signature

This process is done by the Identity Provider. The final JWT looks like the following:

eyJhbGciOiJIUzI1NiIsInR5cCI6IkpXVCJ9.eyJzdWIiOiI3ODQ1NTIxIiwibmFtZSI6IkRhbm
llbCBQZWxhZXoiLCJhZG1pbiI6dHJ1ZX0.nv- bBX3bjIxz7bEIWvn6OA4CUaw1SYgzqb_
jE9ypyGQ

Now that we understand how the OpenID Connect protocol and JWT work, let's see an open source Identity Provider.

Keycloak: An Open Source Identity Provider

Keycloak is an Identity and Access management provider, and it is open source. It complies with OpendID Connect protocol, so we are going to use it as our initial Identity Provider in the local environment.

In this section, we will set up Keycloak and navigate through its interface to understand how the OpendID Connect protocol is implemented.

Installing Keycloak

Now, let's install Keycloak:

1. Download the installer from `https://www.keycloak.org/downloads.html`. Use the Server option, the Stand-alone server distribution.

2. Unzip your installer.

3. Go to the bin folder and run the right executable for your Operative System. For instance, for Linux:

    ```
    $ ./standalone.sh -Djboss.http.port=8082
    ```

    -Djboss.http.port=8082 allows us to change the port of our application. As 8080 is usually used in the GlassFish server, it is better to use the other one here.

    You should see something like that shown in Figure 9-8.

```
daniel@daniel-Inspiron-5566: ~/Documents/DevelopmentTools/Book/keycloak-7.0.0/bin        ✕

 File   Edit   View   Search   Terminal   Help
$ ./standalone.sh -Djboss.http.port=8082
==================================================================================

  JBoss Bootstrap Environment

  JBOSS_HOME: /home/daniel/Documents/DevelopmentTools/Book/keycloak-7.0.0

  JAVA: java

  JAVA_OPTS:  -server -Xms64m -Xmx512m -XX:MetaspaceSize=96M -XX:MaxMetaspaceSiz
e=256m -Djava.net.preferIPv4Stack=true -Djboss.modules.system.pkgs=org.jboss.byt
eman -Djava.awt.headless=true

==================================================================================

15:36:54,433 INFO  [org.jboss.modules] (main) JBoss Modules version 1.9.1.Final
15:36:54,772 INFO  [org.jboss.msc] (main) JBoss MSC version 1.4.8.Final
15:36:54,782 INFO  [org.jboss.threads] (main) JBoss Threads version 2.3.3.Final
15:36:54,890 INFO  [org.jboss.as] (MSC service thread 1-2) WFLYSRV0049: Keycloak
 7.0.0 (WildFly Core 9.0.2.Final) starting
15:36:55,573 INFO  [org.wildfly.security] (ServerService Thread Pool -- 17) ELY0
0001: WildFly Elytron version 1.9.1.Final
15:36:56,080 INFO  [org.jboss.as.controller.management-deprecated] (Controller B
oot Thread) WFLYCTL0028: Attribute 'security-realm' in the resource at address '
```

Figure 9-8. *Output console when Keycloak is started*

4. You can now access the Identity Server at http://localhost:8082/
    auth, and you will see something like Figure 9-9.

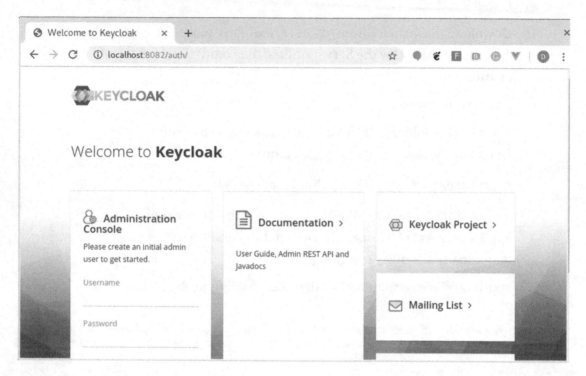

Figure 9-9. Keycloak home page

5. Create an admin account where you define your username and
    password.

6. Now click on Admin Console; you will need to log in to be
    presented to the Keycloak console.

Now that we just installed our Keycloak Identity Provider, let's move to create our
first OpenID Connect application there.

Creating a Realm

A realm is a set of users that share some features. In this case, we are going to create one
realm to handle the users for the new Daniel's Delivery website.

1. After you log in, you will see the Keycloak console as shown in the following screen. First, click on the drop-down where you see the Master and click on Add realm (Figure 9-10).

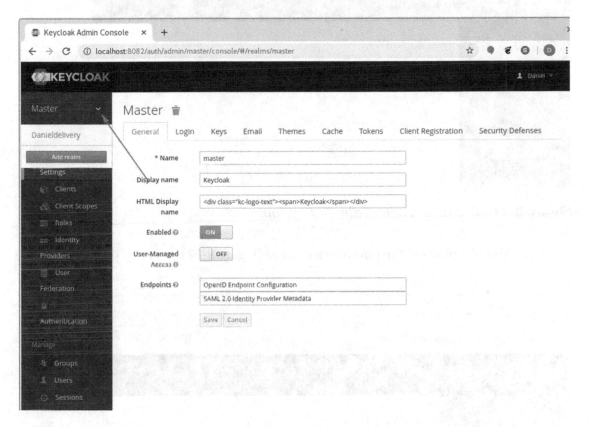

Figure 9-10. *Master realm in Keycloak*

2. Type the name of the new realm and click on Create (Figure 9-11).

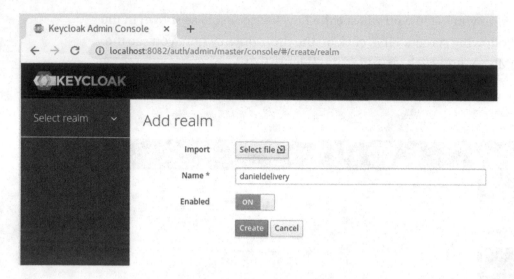

Figure 9-11. *Creating a new realm in Keycloak*

3. You can now see the new realm created (Figure 9-12).

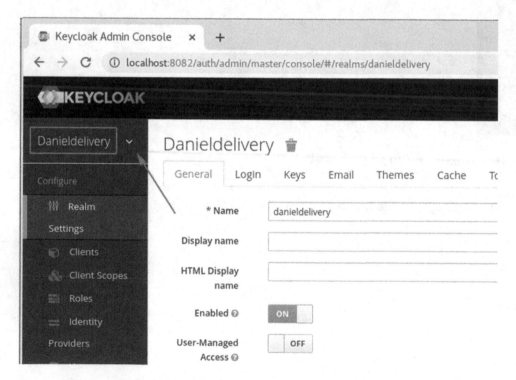

Figure 9-12. *New realm in Keycloak*

After creating a realm, let's now create a basic user.

Creating a New User

In order to create a new user, let's follow these steps:

1. First, we create a group, so, you click on Groups and New button
   (Figure 9-13).

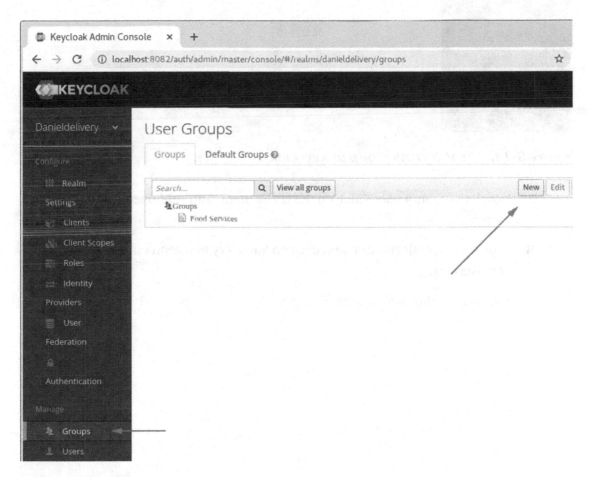

Figure 9-13. *Current groups in Keycloak*

2. We see a form to create the group, so we type the group name and
   click Save (Figure 9-14).

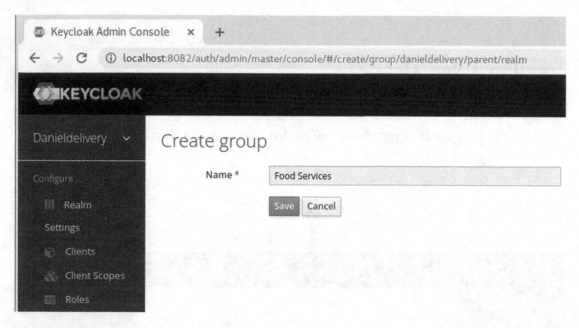

Figure 9-14. *Creating new group in Keycloak*

3. Now let's create a user. Click on the Users menu and Add user button.

4. Type the user information and click on Save. Try to use an email as a username.

5. You will see the user created (Figure 9-15).

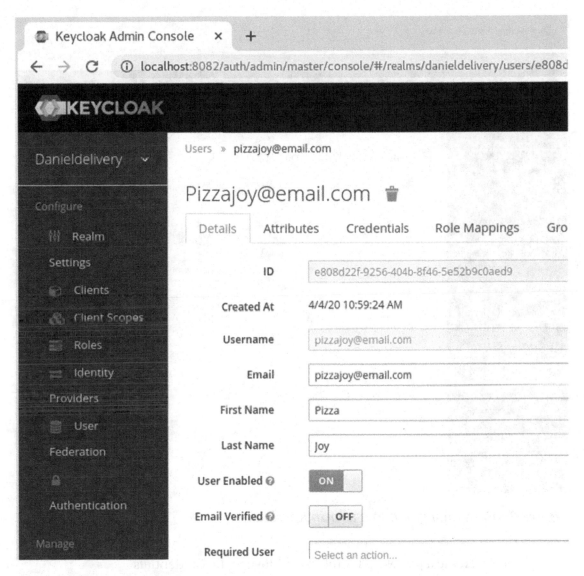

Figure 9-15. *New user in Keycloak*

6. Now, let's associate him with the previous group we created. Move
    to the tab Groups, choose the Food Services group, and click on
    Join (Figure 9-16).

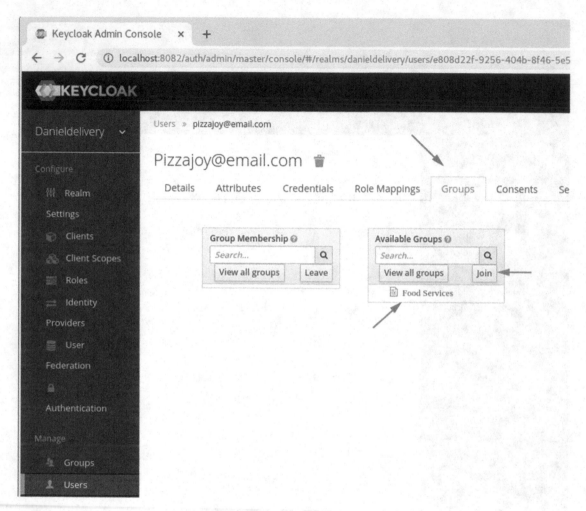

Figure 9-16. *Assign group to a user in Keycloak*

7. Let's create a password for this user. Move to the Credentials
    tab and type a password, and next click on Reset password
    (Figure 9-17).

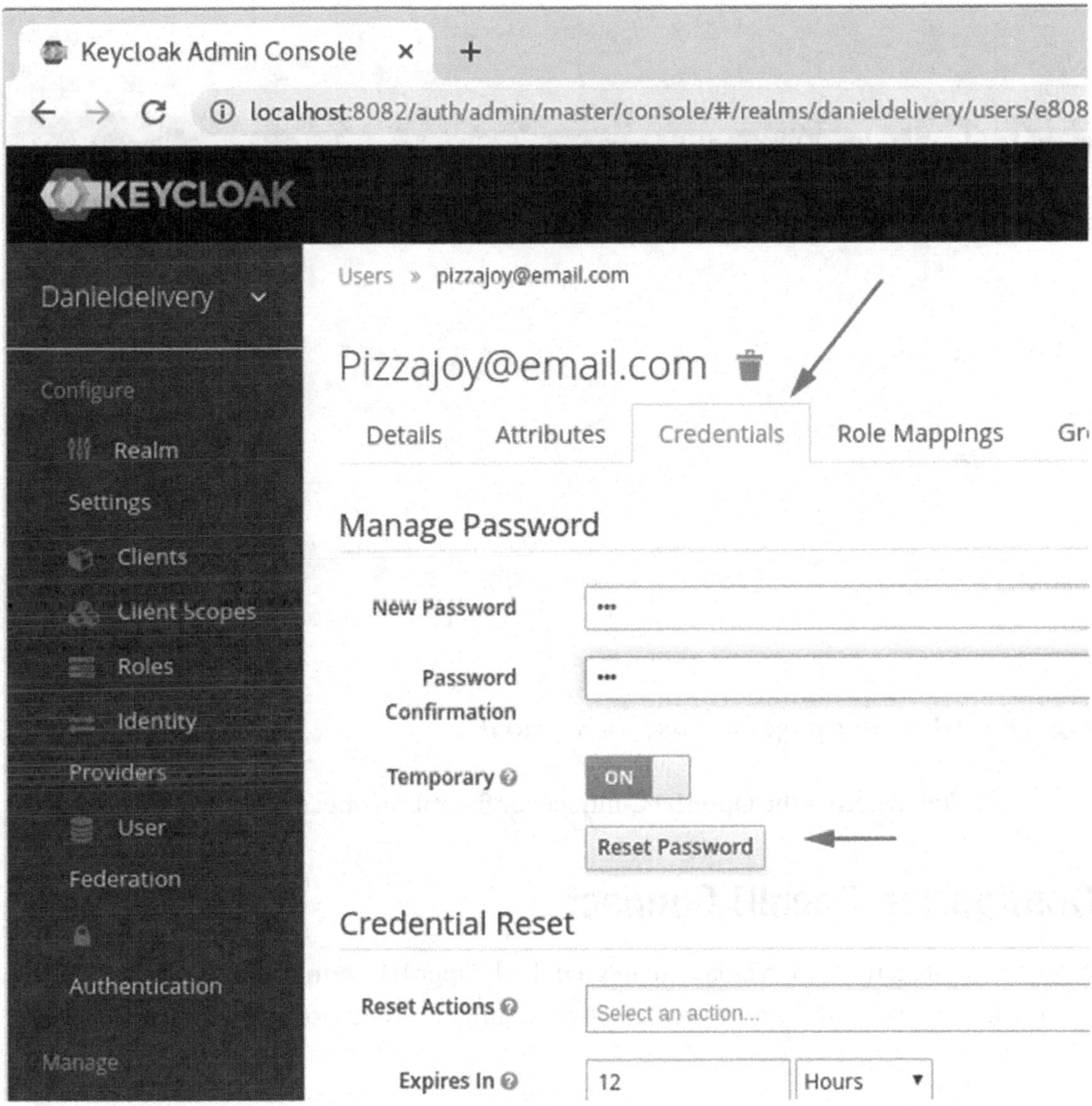

Figure 9-17. *Setting a user password in Keycloak*

8. Well, we can now try to log in to the default Keycloak page at
   http://localhost:8082/auth/realms/danieldelivery/account.

   We will see a home page for our user (Figure 9-18).

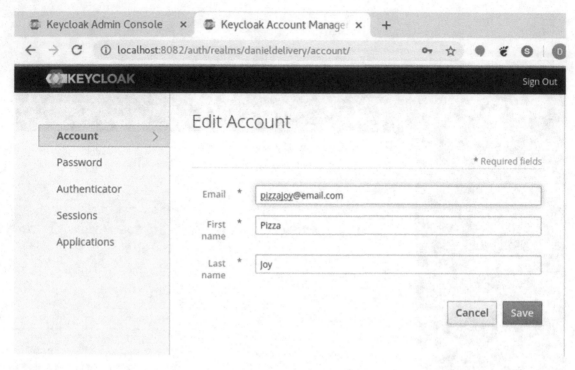

Figure 9-18. *Home page for a user in Keycloak*

9.   Now where is the OpenID Connect configuration? Let's see.

Configuring OpenID Connect

After we create a realm, Keycloak creates a default OpenID Connect configuration. You can click on Clients, and we will see the list of configuration as follows (Figure 9-19).

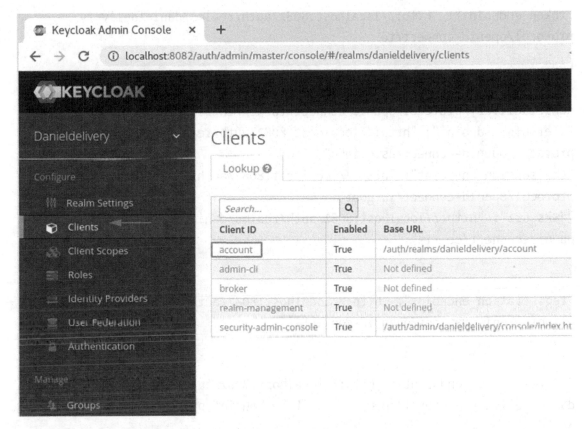

Figure 9-19. *OpenID Connect configuration in Keycloak*

account is the default OpenID Connect application created by default. We will see more details about this configuration in Chapter 10.

Now, there is a special URL where you can find the OpendID Connect configuration, for instance, if you click http://localhost:8082/auth/realms/danieldelivery/.well-known/ openid-configuration, you will see the following JSON (Listing 9-10).

Listing 9-10. Well-known endpoint from Keycloak

```
{
"issuer": "http://localhost:8082/auth/realms/danieldelivery",
"authorization_endpoint":
"http://localhost:8082/auth/realms/danieldelivery/protocol/openid-connect/
au th",
```

```
"token_endpoint": "http://localhost:8082/auth/realms/danieldelivery/
protocol/openid-connect/to

ken",
"token_introspection_endpoint": "http://localhost:8082/auth/realms/
danieldelivery/protocol/openid-connect/to ken/introspect",
"userinfo_endpoint": "http://localhost:8082/auth/realms/danieldelivery/
protocol/openid-connect/us erinfo",
"end_session_endpoint": "http://localhost:8082/auth/realms/danieldelivery/
protocol/openid-connect/lo gout",
"jwks_uri": "http://localhost:8082/auth/realms/danieldelivery/protocol/
openid-connect/ce rts"

...

"registration_endpoint": "http://localhost:8082/auth/realms/danieldelivery/
clients-registrations/open id-connect"

...

"introspection_endpoint": "http://localhost:8082/auth/realms/
danieldelivery/protocol/openid-connect/to ken/introspect"
}
```

As we can see, there we find the URLs for our OpenID Connect protocol, from authorization to token. The JSON was trimmed to allow readability, but there is more information this endpoint offers, like claims_supported, grant_types_supported, and so on.

Note   Remember, the OpenID Connect protocol in the authorization code flow uses the authorization_endpoint and the token_endpoint. There will be others involved when we implement the security in Chapter 10.

Now, we are ready with our Keycloak configuration. In the following chapter, we are going to use Keycloak to secure our new Daniel's Delivery website.

Summary

In this chapter, we learned the security basics, understanding that authentication answers the question of who are you? and authorization answers of what can you do?

We learned the OpenId Connect protocol and how it helps us to authorize users into an application, plus, we implemented that protocol using an Open Source SSO Identity Provider like Keycloak.

Now you will be able to understand your security requirements and use the OpenId Connect protocol to solve them using an Identity Provider like Keycloak.

In the following chapter, we are ready to secure our full-stack application.

Extended Knowledge

1.   What kinds of claims in a JWT exist?

2.   Which algorithms can I use to sign a JWT?

3.   Which claims does the OpenID Connect protocol require in the ID token?

4.   Is there something to help me to create JWTs, decode, and encode them?

5.   Are there other flows I can use instead of authorization code?

6.   Where can I find which Identity Providers are valid for OpenId Connect Protocol?

CHAPTER 10

Authentication and Authorization

In this chapter, we are going to focus on implementing the Authentication and Authorization flow using the OpenID Connect protocol for our new Daniel's Delivery website. We are going to use Keycloak as the Identity Provider and the Authorization Flow Code.

The following topics will be covered in this chapter:

- Using Keycloak as a new Users datastore

- Applying authorization via JWT in the JAX-RS layer

- Handling authentication in the Vue.js layer with Vuex

Technical Requirements

To follow the instructions in this chapter, you will need the following:

- Java 1.8

- Netbeans 11

- GlassFish 5.1

- Jakarta Enterprise Edition

- Node.js 10.13.0

- Npm 6.7.0

- Visual Studio Code 1.33.1

369

© Daniel Andres Pelaez Lopez 2021
D. A. P. Lopez, *Full-Stack Web Development with Jakarta EE and Vue.js*,
https://doi.org/10.1007/978-1-4842-6342-6_10

- Axios 2.1.4

- vue-toasted 1.1.27

You can check the whole project and code at `https://github.com/Apress/full-stack-web-development-with-jakartaee-and-vue.js/tree/master/CH10`.

Using Keycloak as the Source of Users

We saw in the last chapter how we can use Keycloak as an Authorization Provider with multiple features, like the whole OpenId Connect and Users management.

Currently, our new Daniel's Delivery site is using a database to save the User information, in this case, the Food Service information (Figure 10-1).

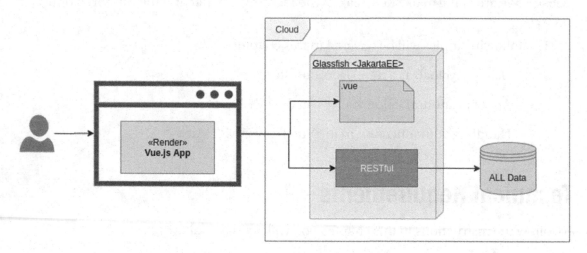

Figure 10-1. *Current architecture where the user information is stored in the database*

Now that we have an Authorization Provider, we should move that responsibility to him (Figure 10-2).

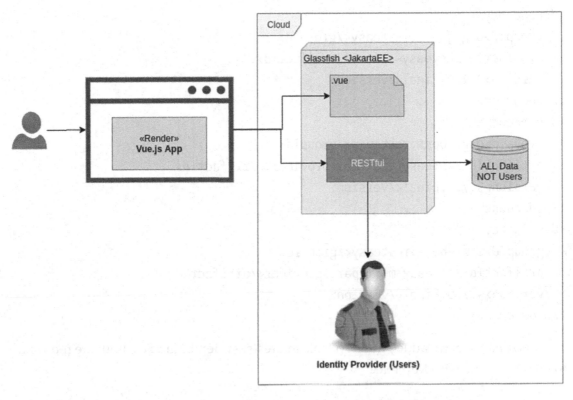

Figure 10-2. *Moving the users data from the database to an Identity Provider*

In the following sections, we are going to see how the Keycloak API for Users management works and how we implement it in our back end.

Keycloak Client

Keycloak has a Java client that allows us to do operations over it. So we need to add this dependency to our Jakarta EE project (Listing 10-1).

Listing 10-1. Keycloak Maven dependencies

```
<dependency>
  <groupId>org.keycloak</groupId>
  <artifactId>keycloak-admin-client</artifactId>
  <version>7.0.0</version>
</dependency>
```

```
<dependency>
  <groupId>org.jboss.resteasy</groupId>
  <artifactId>resteasy-client</artifactId>
  <version>3.7.0.Final</version>
</dependency>
<dependency>
  <groupId>org.jboss.resteasy</groupId>
  <artifactId>resteasy-jackson2-provider</artifactId>
  <version>3.7.0.Final</version>
</dependency>
<dependency>
  <groupId>org.jboss.resteasy</groupId>
  <artifactId>resteasy-multipart-provider</artifactId>
  <version>3.7.0.Final</version>
</dependency>
```

As we can see, we added the Keycloak and resteasy dependencies. Both are required to communicate with Keycloak.

New UserRepository Implementation

Now we need to create a new implementation regarding the UserRepository. Remember, we have a UserRepository implementation named FoodServiceRepositoryJPA to connect to the database. We will deprecate this in favor of Keycloak, as we can see here (Listing 10-2).

Listing 10-2. KeyCloakFoodServiceRepository implementation

```
public class KeyCloakFoodServiceRepository implements FoodServiceRepository
{          // (1)

    private final Keycloak keycloak;
    private final String realm;

    public KeyCloakFoodServiceRepository(Keycloak keycloak, String realm)
    {          // (2)
        this.keycloak = keycloak;
        this.realm = realm;
    }
```

```java
@Override
public FoodService save(FoodService foodService) {    // (3.1)
    Response response = keycloak
            .realm(realm)
            .users()
            .create(convertFoodServiceToUserRepresentation
            (foodService));

    if (response.getStatus() != 200) {
        throw new IllegalArgumentException("Food service " +
        foodService.getEmail() + " couldn't be saved in KeyCloak: " +
        response.readEntity(String.class));
    }

    return foodService;
}

@Override
public FoodService update(FoodService foodService) {    // (3.2)
    UserResource userResource = keycloak
            .realm(realm)
            .users()
            .get(foodService.getId());

    userResource.update(convertFoodServiceToUserRepresentation
    (foodService));

    return foodService;
}

@Override
public List<FoodService> getAll() {    // (4.1)
    return keycloak
            .realm(realm)
            .users()
            .list()
            .stream()
```

```java
                .map(this::convertUserRepresentationToFoodService)
                .collect(Collectors.toList());
    }

    @Override
    public List<FoodService> getAll(Integer page, Integer pageSize)
{       // (4.2)
        return keycloak
                .realm(realm)
                .users()
                .list((page - 1) * pageSize, pageSize)
                .stream()
                .map(this::convertUserRepresentationToFoodService)
                .collect(Collectors.toList());
    }

    @Override
    public List<FoodService> getByFoodType(String foodType, Integer page,
    Integer pageSize) {       // (5.1)
        return keycloak
                .realm(realm)
                .users()
                .list()
                .stream()
                .map(this::convertUserRepresentationToFoodService)
                .filter(foodService -> foodService.getFoodType().
                equals(foodType))
                .limit(pageSize)
                .skip((page - 1) * pageSize)
                .collect(Collectors.toList());
    }

    @Override
    public Optional<FoodService> getById(String id) {    // (5.2)
        return Optional.ofNullable(keycloak
                .realm(realm)
                .users()
```

```
            .get(id))
            .map(userResource -> userResource.toRepresentation())
            .map(this::convertUserRepresentationToFoodService);
}

@Override
public Optional<FoodService> getByEmailAndPassword(String email, String
password) {       // (6)
    throw new UnsupportedOperationException();
}

private UserRepresentation convertFoodServiceToUserRepresentation(FoodS
ervice foodService) {                  // (7.1)
    UserRepresentation userRepresentation = new UserRepresentation();
    userRepresentation.setId(foodService.getId());
    userRepresentation.setEmail(foodService.getEmail());
    userRepresentation.setUsername(foodService.getEmail());
    userRepresentation.setFirstName(foodService.getName());
    userRepresentation.setEnabled(foodService.getActive());

    Map<String, List<String>> attributes = new HashMap<>();
    attributes.put("foodType", Arrays.asList(foodService.
    getFoodType()));
    attributes.put("deliveryFee", Arrays.asList(String.
    valueOf(foodService.getDeliveryFee())));
    attributes.put("imageUrl", Arrays.asList(foodService.
    getImageUrl()));
    attributes.put("address", Arrays.asList(foodService.getAddress()));

    userRepresentation.setAttributes(attributes);

    return userRepresentation;
}

private FoodService convertUserRepresentationToFoodService
(UserRepresentation userRepresentation) {                  // (7.2)
    User user = new User(userRepresentation.getEmail(),
    userRepresentation.getEmail());
```

```java
    return new FoodService(userRepresentation.getId(),
    userRepresentation.getEmail(), userRepresentation.getFirstName(),
    getAttribute(userRepresentation.getAttributes(), "address"),
    getAttribute(userRepresentation.getAttributes(), "imageUrl"),
    getAttribute(userRepresentation.getAttributes(), "foodType"),
    Integer.parseInt(Optional.ofNullable(getAttribute(userRepresentat
    ion.getAttributes(), "deliveryFee")).filter(s -> !s.equals("")).
    orElse("0")), userRepresentation.isEnabled(), user, Collections.
    emptyList());
}

private String getAttribute(Map<String, List<String>> attributes,
String name) {
    return Optional.ofNullable(attributes)
            .map(att -> att.get(name))
            .orElse(Collections.emptyList())
            .stream()
            .findFirst()
            .orElse("");
}
}
```

The following is a description of the code sample:

1. We implement the UserRepository interface.

2. Define the constructor, injecting the Keycloak client and realm.

3. Now, we define the save and update methods using the Keycloak API.

4. Later, we define the new getAll methods: note how the Keycloak API has, by default, the pagination features through list (skip, pageSize) method.

5. Next, we have some query methods. Note that Keycloak API doesn't have support for querying through the attributes field, so we needed to filter and paginating after the API call is done using normal Streams. If you have tons of users, you should evaluate this option carefully.

6. See the getByEmailAndPassword method; that one was used to log in the User. However, as we are going to use the OpendId Connect protocol, this method doesn't make sense now.

7. And finally, we have some methods to transform the Keycloak User representation to our Food Service.

Now, we create a new UserRepository using properties from the environment:

1. We define in our environment properties file the basic parameter that we need to connect to Keycloak.

   ```
   SSO_AUTH_URL=http://localhost:8082/auth/ SSO_AUTH_
   USER=danieldelivery
   SSO_AUTH_PASSWORD=danieldelivery
   SSO_REALM=danieldelivery
   ```

   SSO_AUTH_USER and SSO_AUTH_PASSWORD are the credentials for an admin user in Keycloak

2. And finally, we add the Keycloak client to our CDI context using the properties previously defined (Listing 10-3).

Listing 10-3. RepositoryProvider class updated to use the new KeyCloak repository

```
@Stateless
@LocalBean
public class RepositoryProvider {

  // More factories

  @Produces
  public KeyCloakFoodServiceRepository getKeyCloakFoodServiceRepository(Pro
  perties properties) {
  Keycloak keycloak = Keycloak.getInstance( properties.getProperty("SSO_
  AUTH_URL"), "master", properties.getProperty("SSO_AUTH_USER"),
  properties.getProperty("SSO_AUTH_PASSWORD"), "admin-cli");
```

```
return new KeyCloakFoodServiceRepository(keycloak, properties.
getProperty("SSO_REALM"));
}

  // More factories
}
```

As our application is decoupled using the main and the abstraction strategies, we don't need to change anything more.

Authorization in JAX-RS

Our new Daniel's Delivery website relies upon RESTful services through JAX-RS. As those services can be accessed through the network, we need to guarantee that who is calling is authorized to call.

In this section, we are going to see how to secure our JAX-RS endpoints using Keycloak and JWT.

We are going to implement the Authorization Code flow from OpenId Connect, without the refresh token process.

Validating the Token

As we saw in Chapter 9, "Securing Your Full-Stack Application," a JSON Web Token (JWT) usually is signed by an Identity Provider. This is done to guarantee the source of the token, but how can you validate that? Well, we need to use a JSON Web Key (JWK) to validate the signature.

Note   The signature is named JSON Web Signature (JWS) and you can find more information here: `https://tools.ietf.org/html/rfc7515`

The Identity Provider offers a JWK URL where you can find the keys used to sign JWTs. In the case of Keycloak, it is the following one: http://localhost:8082/auth/realms/danieldelivery/ protocol/openid-connect/certs

Note   Remember, you can check the whole URLs available in Keycloak using http://localhost:8082/auth/realms/danieldelivery/.well-known/openid-configuration

Our endpoints are going to receive an authorization token, which should be validated to guarantee that it has access. Figure 10-3 shows how the token flows from the client to the back-end layer.

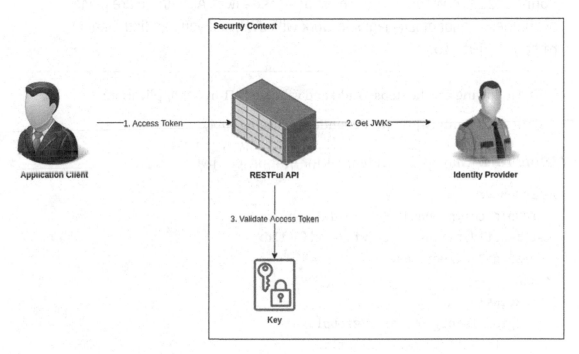

Figure 10-3.   *Access token flow through the Client and Provider*

As we can see, we use the JWK URL to get the keys, caching them, and using them to check if the sign of the access token is right.

The validation is not just if the sign is right or not; it usually checks the expiration time, token issuer, and so on.

Let's see how we can now implement this.

Using Nimbus JOSE + JWT to Validate JWT Tokens

As OpenId Connect and JWT are standards, you can find multiple Java libraries to abstract that standard behavior in your own application. For this book, we are going to use Nimbus JOSE + JWT as a JWT library.

Note   You can find more information regarding Nimbus JOSE + JWT at `https://connect2id.com/products/nimbus-jose-jwt`. Also, there are plenty of libraries in a lot of languages to work with JWT, and you can find them at `https://jwt.io`.

The following are the steps to add and validate JWT in our application:

1.   Add nimbus-jose-jwt dependency (Listing 10-4).

Listing 10-4.   Maven dependencies for ninbus jose jwt

```
<dependency>
  <groupId>com.nimbusds</groupId>
  <artifactId>nimbus-jose-jwt</artifactId>
  <version>7.8</version>
  <exclusions>
    <exclusion>
      <groupId>org.ow2.asm</groupId>
      <artifactId>asm</artifactId>
    </exclusion>
  </exclusions>
</dependency>
```

We exclude org.ow2.asm dependency because we had conflicts with some GlassFish libraries.

2.   We created a new Security Provider to define and reuse our JWT validation. We start with the basic setup for Nimbus JOSE + JWT (Listing 10-5).

Listing 10-5. SecurityProvider class to create the JWTProcessor

```java
@Stateless
@LocalBean
public class SecurityProvider {

    @Produces
    public JWTProcessor getJWTProcessor(Properties properties) throws
    MalformedURLException {

        ConfigurableJWTProcessor jwtProcessor = new DefaultJWTProcessor();

        JWKSource keySource = new RemoteJWKSet(new URL(properties.
        getProperty("SSO_JWK_URL")));

        JWSAlgorithm expectedJWSAlg = JWSAlgorithm.RS256;

        JWSKeySelector keySelector = new JWSVerificationKeySelector
        (expectedJWSAlg, keySource);
        jwtProcessor.setJWSKeySelector(keySelector);

        return jwtProcessor;
    }

    @Produces
    public TokenValidationService getTokenValidationService(JWTProcessor
    jwtProcessor) {
        return new TokenValidationJWK(jwtProcessor);
    }

    @Produces
    @Testing
    public TokenValidationService getNullObjectTokenValidation() {
        return new NullObjectTokenValidation();
    }
}
```

Here, there is a lot of important code. First, we created a default
JWT processor. Next, we defined a JWK source; the source in
this case is the Keycloak JWK URL (http://localhost:8082/auth/

realms/danieldelivery/protocol/openid- connect/certs). This source helps us to retrieve the keys, cache them, and gracefully handle key rollover. Now, we define the algorithm the signature is using and finally, we create a key selector, which is going to help us find the right key to validate our access token.

The JWK URL can return more than one key, so the JWSKeySelector checks the data available in the JWT and chooses the right key to process it; moreover, the key in the Security Provider could be configured to rotate and expire, so RemoteJWKSet abstracts that complexity for us.

3. And finally, we abstract this validation to a new class (Listing 10-6).

Listing 10-6. TokenValidationJWT class to validate a JWT token

```
public class TokenValidationJWK implements TokenValidationService {

    private final JWTProcessor jwtProcessor;

    public TokenValidationJWK(JWTProcessor jwtProcessor) {
        this.jwtProcessor = jwtProcessor;
    }

    @Override
    public Map<String, Object> validate(String jwt) {
        try {
            return jwtProcessor.process(jwt, null).getClaims();
        } catch (Exception ex) {
            throw new AuthorizationException("Token validation fails", ex);
        }
    }
}
```

This class just uses the JWTProcessor we defined before to process the JWT and get a map of claims.

Securing the RESTful Endpoints with Filters

We defined how to validate the token, but now we need to define where and when we are going to do that. As we have RESTful endpoints, those should be the first line of defense, so we are going to define a filter that is going to be invoked each time a request arrives.

First, we defined a stereotype named RequiredAuthorization (Listing 10-7).

Listing 10-7. RequiredAuthorization annotation

```
@NameBinding
@Retention(RUNTIME)
@Target({TYPE, METHOD})
public @interface RequiredAuthorization {
}
```

This annotation is going to help us to mark what needs to be secured.

Now, we define the filter (Listing 10-8).

Listing 10-8. AuthorizationFilter class to validate if a token in the request is valid or not

```
@Provider
@Stateless
@LocalBean
@RequiredAuthorization
public class AuthorizationFilter implements ContainerRequestFilter {
    @Inject
    private TokenValidationService tokenValidationService;

    @Override
    public void filter(ContainerRequestContext requestContext) throws
    IOException {
        String authorizationHeader = Optional.ofNullable(requestContext.
        getHeaderString(HttpHeaders.AUTHORIZATION))
                .orElseThrow(() -> new NotAuthorizedException("Authorizati
                on header not found"));
```

```
    String token = authorizationHeader.substring("Bearer".length()).
    trim();

    tokenValidationService.validate(token);
  }
}
```

This filter gets the Authorization header from the request, extracts the JWT, and validates it with the previous TokenValidationService that we defined. If something goes wrong, the validate(token) is going to throw an exception.

See the @RequiredAuthorization annotation. This tells Jakarta EE to use this filter only if that annotation is present in the current code execution.

Next, we mark the RESTful endpoints we want to secure. We show only some as an example (Listing 10-9).

Listing 10-9. RequiredAuthorization annotation added to the uploadFile resource in the FileController

```
@POST
@Consumes(MediaType.MULTIPART_FORM_DATA)
@Produces(MediaType.APPLICATION_JSON)
@RequiredAuthorization
public ImageDTO uploadFile(
        @FormDataParam("file") InputStream uploadedInputStream,
        @FormDataParam("file") FormDataContentDisposition fileDetail)
        throws IOException {
    String fileKey = storageService.save(fileDetail.getFileName(),
    uploadedInputStream);

    return new ImageDTO(uriInfo.getBaseUri() + "files/" + fileKey);
}
```

As we can see, we added the @RequiredAuthorization on the uploadFile method. That means, any time a client calls this endpoint, we are going to validate if there is a valid JWT there. However, as loadFile doesn't have the annotation, the validation is not going to happen.

Finally, we defined a new ExceptionHandler for the new NotAuthorizedException class (Listing 10-10).

Listing 10-10. NotAuthorizedExceptionHandler class to handle the unauthorized exception

```
@Provider
public class NotAuthorizedExceptionHandler implements ExceptionMapper<NotAu
thorizedException> {

    private final Logger logger = Logger.getLogger(NotAuthorizedException
    Handler.class.getName());

    @Override
    public Response toResponse(NotAuthorizedException e) {
        logger.log(Level.SEVERE, e.getMessage(), e);

        StringWriter stringWriter = new StringWriter();

        e.printStackTrace(new PrintWriter(stringWriter));

        return Response.status(401)
                .entity(new ExceptionResponse(e.getMessage(),
                e.getMessage()))
                .type(MediaType.APPLICATION_JSON)
                .build();
    }
}
```

This ExceptionHandler helps us to customize the response when unauthorized access was done. In this case, we return a 401 HTTP error.

Requesting the Token

We just saw how to validate a JWT, but how can we request one to the Security Provider? We are going to create a new RESTful endpoint to abstract that complexity.

First, we created a new class named OpenIdConnectServiceBasic (Listing 10-11).

Listing 10-11. OpenIdConnectServiceBasic class to handle the token request to the identity provider

```java
public class OpenIdConnectServiceBasic implements OpenIdConnectService {

    private final TokenValidationService tokenValidationService;
    private final Client client;
    private final String identityProviderUrl;
    private final String clientId;
    private final String clientSecret;

    public OpenIdConnectServiceBasic(TokenValidationService
    tokenValidationService, Client client, String identityProviderUrl,
    String clientId, String clientSecret) {
        this.tokenValidationService = tokenValidationService;
        this.client = client;
        this.identityProviderUrl = identityProviderUrl;
        this.clientId = clientId;
        this.clientSecret = clientSecret;
    }

    @Override
    public Token requestToken(String grantType, String code, String
    redirectUrl) {
        Form form = new Form()
                .param("grant_type", grantType)
                .param("code", code)
                .param("redirect_uri", redirectUrl)
                .param("client_id", clientId)
                .param("client_secret", clientSecret);

        Response response = client.target(identityProviderUrl)
                .request(MediaType.APPLICATION_FORM_URLENCODED_TYPE)
                .accept(MediaType.APPLICATION_JSON_TYPE)
                .post(Entity.form(form));
```

```
    if (response.getStatus() != 200) {
        throw new IllegalStateException("The tokens couldn't be gotten
        " + response.readEntity(String.class));
    }

    Map<String, String> map = response.readEntity(new
    GenericType<HashMap<String, String>>() {
    });

    Map<String, Object> claims = tokenValidationService.validate(map.
    get("id_token"));

    Token token = new Token(getClaim(claims, "sub"), getClaim(claims,
    "given_name") + " " + getClaim(claims, "family_name"),
    getClaim(claims, "email"), map.get("access_token"), map.
    get("refresh_token"), map.get("expires_in"));

    return token;
}

private String getClaim(Map<String, Object> claims, String name){
    return Optional.ofNullable(claims.get(name))
            .map(String.class::cast)
            .orElseThrow(() -> new IllegalStateException("Claim " +
            name + " was expected"));
}

}
```

Here, we send a request to the Identity Provider token endpoint, with the clientId and secretId, besides the code for this authentication process.

For more information about how the token endpoint works in the Identity Provider, you can check Chapter 9, "Securing Your Full-Stack Application."

After the token is retrieved, we validate it using the TokenValidationService, getting the claims, and creating a Token object with this information.

There, we have the TokenValidationService for JWT validation purposes, a JAX-RS client, and some important properties:

- identityProviderUrl: This is the token request endpoint of the Identity Provider, in this case, http://localhost:8082/auth/realms/danieldelivery/protocol/ openid-connect/token

- clientId: This is the defined client Id in the Identity Provider, in this case, account.

- clientSecret: This is a secret the Identity Provider gives us of that specific clientId.

That information can be found in the Keycloak, for the clientId here (Figure 10-4).

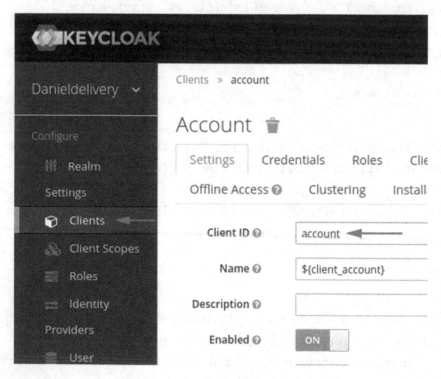

Figure 10-4. *Client ID in the Keycloak console*

And it can be found for the clientSecret here (Figure 10-5).

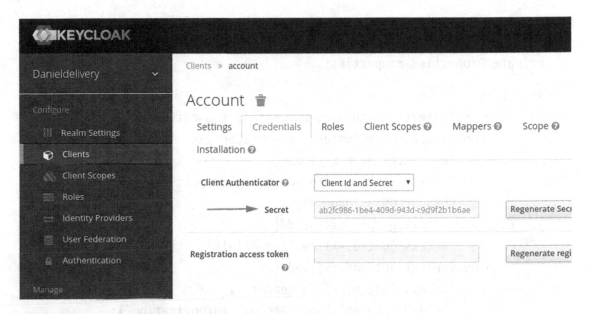

Figure 10 5. Client Secret in the Keycloak console

Note   Remember, the clientId and clientSecret should be confidential, as if this data is open, a hacker can request access token to get in your application.

Now, we have the necessary structure in our back end to work with. In the following section, we are going to see how to secure the Vue.js layer with those new services.

Using CORS to Add Security

We saw in previous chapters how CORS can help to add another security layer, allowing only the right hosts to access our application. To allow our Vue.js application to access the RESTful API, we just need to add its URL in the Access-Control-Allow-Origin, as we can see in the following piece of code (Listing 10-12).

Listing 10-12. CorsFilter class to setup the cross site policy

```
@Provider
@Stateless
@LocalBean
@PreMatching
```

```java
public class CorsFilter implements ContainerResponseFilter {
    @Inject
    private Properties properties;

    @Override
    public void filter(ContainerRequestContext requestContext,
            ContainerResponseContext responseContext) throws IOException {
        responseContext.getHeaders().add(
                "Access-Control-Allow-Origin", properties.getProperty("SSO_
                CORS_ALLOW", "none"));
        responseContext.getHeaders().add(
                "Access-Control-Allow-Credentials", "true");
        responseContext.getHeaders().add(
                "Access-Control-Allow-Headers",
                "origin, content-type, accept, authorization");
        responseContext.getHeaders().add(
                "Access-Control-Allow-Methods",
                "GET, POST, PUT, DELETE, OPTIONS, HEAD");
    }
}
```

There, the value of SSO_CORS_ALLOW is http://localhost:8081, meaning that this is the only host allowed to access our RESTful API. We let a condition in where if there is not SSO_CORS_ALLOW defined, no application can access it. This is called the principle of least privilege, which means, you should have only the bare minimum privileges necessary to perform its function.

Authentication in Vue.js

We just saw how to validate and request JWT tokens using our Identity Provider. Now, we need to authenticate the user somehow in our Vue.js application and send the access token back to the RESTful services so we can access those endpoints (Figure 10-6).

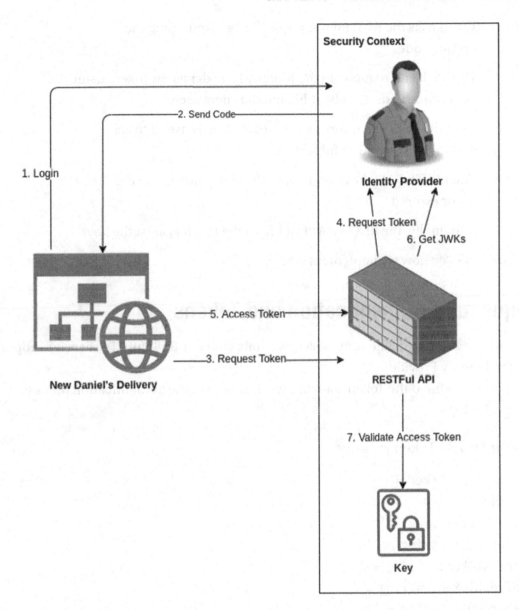

Figure 10-6. *Security flow in the new Daniel's Delivery app*

There, we enhance the back end with the Vue.js flow, in the following way:

1.   Vue.js asks the Identity Provider to log in a User that is asking for access.

2.   After login is successful, the Identity Provider sent back a unique code for that authorization process.

3. Vue.js asks the RESTful API requesting a token, using the unique code.

4. The back end requests to the Identity Provider a new token, using the unique code, the client Id, and the client secret.

5. After the back end returns a new token, Vue.js uses it to call endpoints in the RESTful API.

6. The RESTful API downloads the JWKs if they are not in the cache yet or expired.

7. And finally, the RESTful API validates the token against the key.

Now, let's see how we implement that.

Requesting Authentication and Tokens

First, we are going to define some services to talk with our RESTful API security endpoint and the Identity Provider.

Now, we defined the Token class to save the result of the authentication process (Listing 10-13).

Listing 10-13. Token.js entity

```
export class Token {
  userId: string = ''
  userName: string = ''
  userEmail: string = ''
  accessToken: string = ''
  refreshToken: string = ''
  expiresOn: string = ''

//More code
}
```

Second, we create the AuthorizationService to handle the security requests. In this case, we started with the requestToken method (Listing 10-14).

Listing 10-14. AuthorizationService.ts component to handle the token request and redirect of authorization

```
import Vue from 'vue'
import { Token } from '../entities/Token'

export class AuthorizationService {
  static getToken (grantType: string, code: string, redirectUrl: string)
{          // (1)
    const params = new URLSearchParams()
    params.append('grant_type', grantType)
    params.append('code', code)
    params.append('redirect_uri', redirectUrl)

    return Vue.axios.post<Token>(`/openidconnect/token`, params)
  }

  static authorize () {          // (2)
    window.location.href = `${process.env.VUE_APP_SSO_
AUTHORIZATION}?response_type=code&scope=openid%20profile%20email&client_
id=${process.env.VUE_APP_SSO_CLIENT_ID}&redirect_uri=${process.env.VUE_APP_
SSO_REDIRECT_URL}`
  }
}
```

The following is a description of the code sample:

1. This method just calls the RESTful API we defined in the previous section, with the unique code provided by the Identity Provider.

2. And we defined the redirect operation, to use it when the User is not logged in yet. This is just a redirect to the authorization URL for the Identity Provider. The value of the environment variables in this case is the following:

    ```
    VUE_APP_SSO_AUTHORIZATION: http://localhost:8082/auth/realms/
    danieldeli very/protocol/openid-connect/auth
    VUE_APP_SSO_CLIENT_ID: account
    VUE_APP_SSO_REDIRECT_URL: http://localhost:8081/auth/
    ```

Remember, the VUE_APP_SSO_REDIRECT_URL is where the Identity Provider is going to send the authorization code to continue with the authentication process. You need to tell Keycloak about that URL here (Figure 10-7).

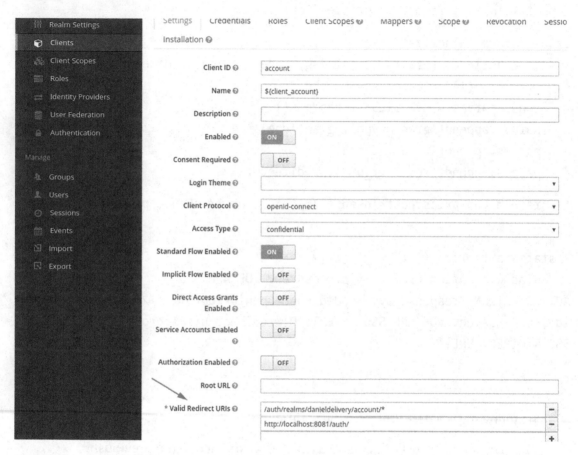

Figure 10-7. *Valid redirect URLs in the Keycloak console*

This allows having stronger security, as Keycloak will only generate and send valid codes to that URL.

Now, after we get the token, where should I save it? We are going to discuss that in the following section.

Using Vuex to Keep the Token

We are going to use Vuex to save the Token object we get from the authentication process.

First, we update the State class to support the Token object (Listing 10-15).

Listing 10-15. Updated State.ts entity to add a token

```
export class State {
    cart: Cart = Cart.emptyCart()
    currentDeliveryEmail: string = '';
    token: Token = Token.emptyToken()
}
```

Now, we update the store.ts file, adding some mutations and queries (Listing 10-16).

Listing 10-16. Updated store.ts file to add the token configuration

```
import Vue from 'vue'
import Vuex from 'vuex'
import { Item } from './entities/Item'
import { State } from './entities/State'
import { Cart } from './entities/Cart'
import { Token } from './entities/Token'

Vue.use(Vuex)

const stateBase: State = {
  cart: Cart.emptyCart(),
  currentDeliveryEmail: '',
  token: localStorage.getItem('token') ? JSON.parse(localStorage.
  getItem('token')!) : Token.emptyToken()                        // (1)
}

export default new Vuex.Store<State>({
  state: stateBase,
  mutations: {
    setCurrentDeliveryEmail (state:State, currentDeliveryEmail:string) {
      state.currentDeliveryEmail = currentDeliveryEmail
    },
    saveItemToCart (state:State, item:Item) {
      state.cart.items.push(item)
    },
```

```
  removeItemFromCart (state:State, itemToRemove:Item) {
    const index = state.cart.items.findIndex(item => item.foodProduct.id
    === itemToRemove.foodProduct.id)

    Vue.delete(state.cart.items, index)
  },
  setToken (state:State, token:Token) {    // (2)
    const parsed = JSON.stringify(token)

    localStorage.setItem('token', parsed)

    state.token = token
  }
},
actions: {

},
getters: {
  getCurrentDeliveryEmail: (state) => () => {
    return state.currentDeliveryEmail
  },
  getToken: (state) => () => {                // (3)
    return state.token
  }
 }
})
```

The following is a description of the code sample:

1. As we can see, we get the Token object from the localStorage; if the Token is not present, we just set an empty one. Saving the token in the localStorage helps us to maintain the stage into the browser, so, if you reload the page, you will still have access to the token.

    If you want to know more about localStorage, you can learn about it here: https://developer.mozilla.org/es/docs/Web/API/Window/localStorage

> **Caution**   Careful, saving confidential information in localStorage is not the best choice. You can be hacked using XSS and CSRF attacks.

2.   After that, we create a mutation to save the Token. There, we save the Token in the localStorage.

3.   And finally, we defined a getter for the Token.

Login: Putting the Whole Process Together

We just defined how the back-end and front-end are going to handle the authorization process. We are missing how and when we use this new security feature.

Let's see how we implement this. First, we start with the main.js setup and Axios (10-17).

Listing 10-17. Add in an Axios interceptor to check the 401 status of unauthorized and use a default header for the Authorization header

```
const axiosInstance = axios.create({
  baseURL: process.env.VUE_APP_RESTFUL_BASE_URL
})

axiosInstance.interceptors.response.use(response => {
  return response
}, error => {
  if (error.response.status === 401) {       // (1)
    AuthorizationService.authorize()
  } else {
    Vue.toasted.error('Ops, an unexpected error occurred')
  }

  return Promise.reject(error)
})

const token = store.getters.getToken()

axiosInstance.defaults.headers.common['Authorization'] = `Bearer ${token.accessToken}`                 // (2)
```

```
Vue.config.productionTip = false
Vue.use(BootstrapVue)
Vue.use(Toasted, { duration: 2000 })
Vue.use(VueAxios, axiosInstance)

new Vue({
  router,
  store,
  render: h => h(App)
}).$mount('#app')
```

The following is a description of the code sample:

1. First, in the main.ts file, we defined what to do when there is
    unauthorized access to a RESTful API. There, if any 401 error occurs in
    an Axios call, we just use the redirect method in the AuthorizationService
    to authenticate the User against the Identity Provider.

2. Next, we get the current Token and set the default Authorization
    header in the Axios defaults.

Now, we create a new AuthorizationCallback Vue.js component (Listing 10-18).

Listing 10-18. AuthorizationCallback.vue component to handle the
authorization code and request a JWT

```
<template>
  <div>Authorization</div>
</template>

<script lang="ts">
import { Component, Prop, Vue } from 'vue-property-decorator'
import { Token } from '../../entities/Token'
import { AuthorizationService } from '../../services/AuthorizationService'
import { User } from '../../entities/User'

@Component
export default class AuthorizationCallback extends Vue {
  mounted () {
    let code:string = this.$route.query.code as string
```

```
AuthorizationService.getToken('authorization_code', code, process.env.
VUE_APP_SSO_REDIRECT_URL)
  .then(response => {
    let token:Token = response.data

    this.$store.commit('setToken', token)

    Vue.axios.defaults.headers.common['Authorization'] = `Bcarer $
    {token.accessToken}`

    this.$toasted.info(`Welcome ${token.userName}`)

    this.$router.push({ name: 'food_service_view', params: { id: token.
    userId } })
  })
  }
}
</script>
```

This component is going to receive the redirect from the Identity Provider with the authorization code. After a successful login, request a new Token, save the Token into our Vuex storage, set the Authorization header by default, and route to the Food Service view.

Of course, we need to define a router for it in the route.js file (Listing 10-19),

Listing 10-19. Updated route.js file adding the authorization path

```
export default new Router({ mode: 'history',
routes: [
// More routes

{
  path: '/auth',
  name: 'auth',
  component: AuthorizationCallback
}

// More routes
]
})
```

See the mode: 'history' property. This helps us to remove the # from our Vue.js URLs.

This is important as Keycloak doesn't accept the redirect URL as http://localhost:8081/#/auth/, just as http://localhost:8081/auth/. You need to take this into account when you are going to deploy the Vue.js application into a server, as that server needs to be aware of the path to correctly redirect. For more information, you can find it here: `https://router.vuejs.org/guide/essentials/history-mode.html#example-server-configurations`.

Summary

In this chapter, we saw how to implement an authorization and authentication flow using OpendID Connect protocol with Keycloak Identity Provider, using features from JAX-RS like filters and from Vue.js like services and Vuex.

Now, we are ready to check the best practices we should apply and later, we will be deploying our new Daniel's Delivery website to the cloud.

Extended Knowledge

1. What are XSS and CSRF attacks?

2. How can I modify the integration tests to avoid the new security layer?

3. Where can I control how long my access token is valid?

4. What is a digital signature?

5. What is a key?

6. Which Java libraries can help me to abstract the OpenID Connect process?

7. Which libraries can help me to abstract the JW* validation and process?

## CHAPTER 11

Design Patterns and Best Practices

In the previous chapter, we talked about security, adding authentication and authorization to our Daniel's Delivery website, from the back-end to the front-end. We know that building quality software is not an easy task. There are plenty of frameworks and practices that we should take into account to transform business requirements into software systems. Best practices and design patterns are two of the main topics we should add to any system to improve its quality.

In software building, there are plenty of ways of doing things; however, some of them are the most useful ones, and those are named best practices.

In those best practices, we can find design patterns. A design pattern is a common solution to a common problem in software design. We can find plenty of design patterns, with different structures and scopes, from an architecture level to a component level. Of course, these patterns are a common solution, but that doesn't mean we must use them as they are; we can modify them to apply on our context.

Those design patterns and good practices are traversals to any software project and are pretty important for building quality software.

In this chapter, we are going to focus on some good practices for a web project, focusing on the following:

- Decoupling software using good Object Oriented Programming practices.

- Analyzing why stateless servers are the best option for today's software challenges.

- Defining what kind of security we should use based on business requirements.

D. A. P. Lopez, *Full-Stack Web Development with Jakarta EE and Vue.js*,
https://doi.org/10.1007/978-1-4842-6342-6_11

- Comparing server-side web pages vs. single page applications.

- Understanding which types of databases exist and why it is important to address them using business cases.

- Designing a good RESTful API using resources and not operations.

These will help you to apply some of the best practices in the market in your own projects, increasing the quality of your solution.

Technical Requirements

None

Decoupling the View and Database from Your Business Rules

Software is complex by nature. Handling that complexity is difficult when you are in a hurry and need to show results soon. However, quality is pretty important, and being fast doesn't mean doing a good job.

As complexity moves us to create huge systems with lots of frameworks, how do you know which is really important or not? We should keep in mind that the business rules are why we build the software in the first place, so they are the more important thing in our software.

Decoupling the important (business rules) from the non-important (everything else) is crucial to create maintainable and extendible software.

In this section, we are going to talk about how to build decoupled software, thinking about what is really important, and leaving what is not open for change.

Main and Abstraction

Any software product has two concepts, the Main and the Abstraction. The Abstraction is our business rules, and the Main is everything else. Both are peers: they need each other to create useful software. In the following sections, we are going to expand those ideas.

The Abstraction Concept

The Abstraction is our domain, our software logic, our entities: this is what really matters to the business, to our product owner.

This Abstraction is written in a base language (Java, Scala, .NET, Python, JavaScript, and so on). The language must be sufficiently expressive to allow us to create complex logic, like calculating pay to a provider or the total cost for delivery.

Figure 11-1 explains the Abstraction using a simple example.

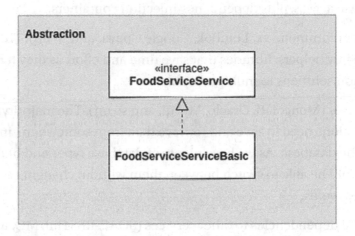

Figure 11-1. *Abstraction concept using the FoodService example*

As we can see from the previous image, for our new Daniel's Delivery website, we defined a FoodServiceService interface and a FoodServiceServiceBasic class. Those objects have operations related to a FoodService business entity. As we can see in the Abstraction, we have the whole core business logic but nothing about details, frameworks, or databases.

The Abstraction usually doesn't change frequently because it is the business core. This only changes if your business core changes.

The Main Concept

The Main is everything else that the Abstraction needs to work in a defined context. Remember, the Abstraction is just business rules, but, how do they connect with each other? Do they need a database to save and retrieve data? Do they need a front-end layer to show data? The Main is who supplies those features to complement the Abstraction.

403

As the Main supplies features to complement the Abstraction, we might find better features through time that work better with our business rules. This means we should be able to change some features by others if we want. To reach this state, we need to decouple the Main and the Abstraction. We are going to talk about this in detail in the following sections.

The following are some examples of features that the Main can have:

- Frameworks (Spring, Jakarta EE, Play, Nodejs, and so on). These are huge frameworks with plenty of features, from RESTful services to database access, plus dependency injection containers.

- Utilities (commons-xx, Lombok, Google Guava, and so on). These are mainly helpers, libraries that save time and effort as they have common solutions to multiple problems.

- Databases (MongoDB, Oracle, MySql, and so on). The majority of applications need to save and retrieve data from somewhere, in this case, the database. As we have plenty of database types and brands, we should be able to switch between them without changing our business rules.

- External dependencies to other services (SOAP, RESTful, MQ, and so on). A software component usually requires other external software components, and the communication is done using multiples protocols like SOAP and RESTful.

- User interfaces (AngularJS, ReactJS, JavaFX, CMD, and so on). Any application needs to be accessed somehow, from the command line to a pretty web UI. Our business rules shouldn't depend on this.

- Infrastructure (Servers, Lambdas, Networks, and so on). Any software project needs a place to run. The infrastructure is vital to create software available to our clients; however, this shouldn't modify our business rules, as they should be decoupled.

In Figure 11-2, we can see an example of the Main in our Daniel's Delivery website.

Figure 11-2. *The Main concept using the FoodService example*

FoodServiceRepositoryJPA class is a good example regarding the Main. That class is pretty specific, detailed, and in charge of persisting a FoodService entity to a database using the JPA framework.

If the FoodServiceRepositoryJPA class belongs to the Main, that means I can change this implementation for others, for instance, using a different access data framework. This will allow our system to be decoupled and evolved to use different technologies.

Understanding the Main and Abstraction Relationship

Well, as the Main and the Abstraction are always present in any software, they have a pretty interesting feature:

Main knows a lot about Abstractions. Abstractions know nothing about Main.

Why? Main can change a lot; however, Abstractions stay the same for a long time.

For instance, if the calculation of the delivery cost knows that it must save that information to an Oracle database, and later, we want to change the database to a MongoDB, we will need to change our delivery cost algorithm to adapt to the new database.

Main is the glue between the details (frameworks, databases, and so on) and the Abstractions (business rules), and it's responsible for creating, structuring, and composing everything in the application.

Figure 11-3 shows the relationship between the Main and the Abstraction.

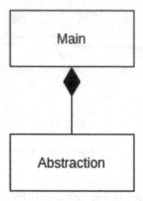

Figure 11-3. *The Main and the Abstraction relationship*

As we can see in the previous image, the Main component is composed of the Abstraction component: this means that the Main cannot exist without the Abstraction. This makes sense as the Abstraction component is the most important component in our system: the business rules. In other words, the Main knows everything about the Abstraction, but the Abstraction knows nothing regarding the Main.

Note   When we said "component," it can refer to a class, module, package, or library.

Now, why is the relationship between the Main and the Abstraction important? Well, you can do something like what is shown in Figure 11-4.

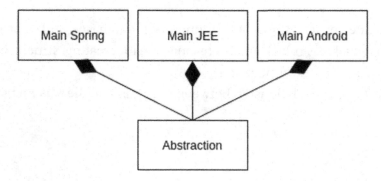

Figure 11-4. *Multiple Mains and one Abstraction*

If you decoupled your Abstraction component from the Main component, that means you can have multiple Main components, using the same Abstraction component. This moves you to choose other options, frameworks, databases, and your core business logic, but it won't need to be changed.

Note   For more information regarding Main and Abstraction, you can check here: `https://coderstower.com/2019/04/02/main-and-abstraction-the-decoupled-peers`

Now that we understand the relationship between the Main and the Abstraction, which best practice can I use to decouple them in a real system? Well, let's talk about dependency inversion.

Using the Dependency Inversion Principle to Decouple Main and Abstraction

We now know that Main and Abstraction should be decoupled, but, how can we do that? Well, let's talk about the Dependency Inversion Principle.

Dependency Inversion Principle (DIP) is one of the SOLID concepts described by Uncle Bob in his book *Clean Code*. He defined the Dependency Inversion Principle as follows:

Depend on abstractions, not on concretions.

There, concretions are the same as the Main component, and Abstractions, well, it is the same as the Abstraction component.

Now, let's see how this applies to our new Daniel's Delivery website (Figure 11-5).

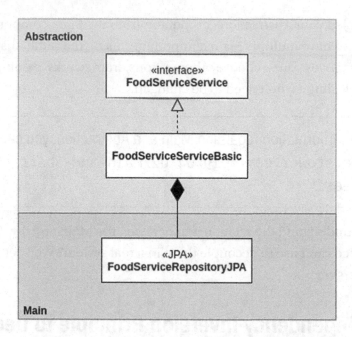

Figure 11-5. *Using the Main and Abstraction without dependency inversion*

As we can see, we have in the Abstraction component the FoodServiceService interface, and the FoodServiceServiceBasic class, and both are related business rules. Besides, we have the FoodServiceRepositoryJPA class in the Main component.

However, FoodServiceRepositoryJPA class has a direct dependency on FoodServiceServiceBasic class. This approach has drawbacks:

- FoodServiceServiceBasic and FoodServiceRepositoryJPA are fairly coupled.

- If we change the FoodServiceRepositoryJPA class and compile it, you must compile the FoodServiceServiceBasic too.

- FoodServiceServiceBasic depends on a concrete class, database access implementation.

- We cannot deploy FoodServiceServiceBasic without FoodServiceRepositoryJPA.

- If we need to later change the JPA for any other framework, you must change FoodServiceServiceBasic to adapt to the new class.

These drawbacks told us that our FoodServiceServiceBasic class is depending on concretions, on the FoodServiceRepositoryJPA class. Now, we need the FoodServiceServiceBasic class to depend on abstractions, so, in Figure 11-6 we invert the dependency.

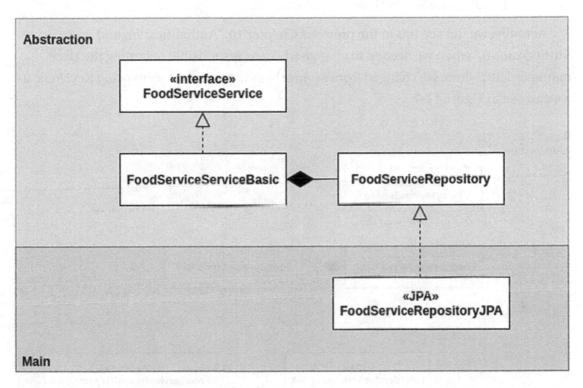

Figure 11-6. *Using the Main and Abstraction with dependency inversion*

Now we have the FoodServiceRepository abstraction. This one helps us to invert the dependency.

This approach has advantages:

- FoodServiceServiceBasic doesn't know anything about it.

- FoodServiceRepositoryJPA (concretions), it only knows about an abstraction (FoodServiceRepository).

- You can use the FoodServiceServiceBasic class without depending on FoodServiceRepository implementations.

- You might have multiple FoodServiceRepository implementations, and you could exchange one by another without affecting FoodServiceServiceBasic.

Actually, we did see this in the previous Chapter 10, "Authentication and Authorization," when we needed to change who was responsible regarding the User management, where we changed from saving them in the database, to using Keycloak, as we can see in Figure 11-7.

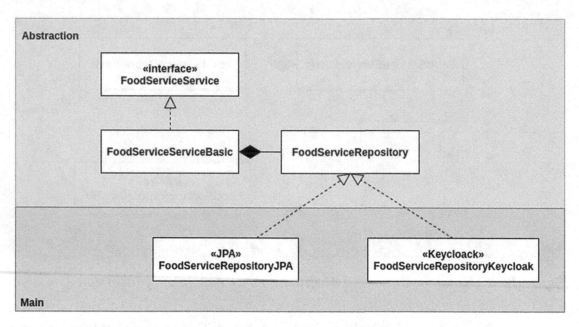

Figure 11-7. *Adding multiple implementations in the Main*

There, we decoupled the Main and the Abstraction through inverting the dependencies using the FoodServiceRespositoryInterface. Besides, we have two different implementations of the FoodServiceRepository interface. However, the FoodServiceServiceBasic class is not aware of them, as it just depends on the FoodServiceRepository interface.

Now, like everything, this has disadvantages:

- More code to maintain, as we need to add interfaces to our application, like the FoodServiceRepository interface.

- It is a challenge to find good implementation names. Naming things in software development is hard.

- And yes, more work. You will need to think regarding interfaces and how to connect them.

Note   For more information, you can check here: `https://coderstower.com/2019/03/26/dependency-inversion-why-you-shouldnt-avoid-it/`

Finally, as we understand how the dependency inversion helps us to decouple the Main and Abstraction, we need a way to put them together; in this case, we are going to use the CDI container in the following section.

Putting Together the Main and the Abstraction Using the CDI Container

Well, we just saw how the Main and Abstraction concepts can be decoupled, but we are missing something: When and how do those two concepts get together? Who is responsible for doing that? Well, the short answer is the CDI container.

As we want to have the Main and Abstraction decoupled, this means that we shouldn't instantiate a class implementation directly, for instance (Listing 11-1).

Listing 11-1. FoodServiceServiceBasic class coupled against the FoodServiceRepository

```
public class FoodServiceServiceBasic{
  private final FoodServiceRepository foodServiceRepository;

  public FoodServiceServiceBasic(){
    this.foodServiceRepository = new FoodServiceRepositoryJPA();
  }

  //More code
}
```

411

In the preceding code, we are using Dependency Inversion as the foodServiceRepository attribute is an interface; however, we are instantiating the FoodServiceRepositoryJPA directly, which means we just couple again the Abstraction against the Main.

To fix this issue, we need to apply the Inversion of Control pattern. This pattern gives the responsibility of object creation to someone else, in the Main component, and not in the Abstraction component.

Note   For more information regarding Inversion of Control, you can read this: `https://coderstower.com/2019/04/09/inversion-of-control-putting-all-together/`

Inversion of Control has different implementations, like using the Abstract Factory pattern or Dependency Injection. For the purposes of this section, we are going to focus on the Dependency Injection solution using the CDI container we have in Jakarta EE.

Note   For more information about Dependency Injection, you can see this: `https://coderstower.com/2019/04/15/dependency-injection-solving-the-inversion-of-control-complexity/`

The idea behind the Dependency Injection pattern is giving the responsibility of object creation plus injection to someone else, in this case, the CDI container. So, our design changes, as shown in Figure 11-8.

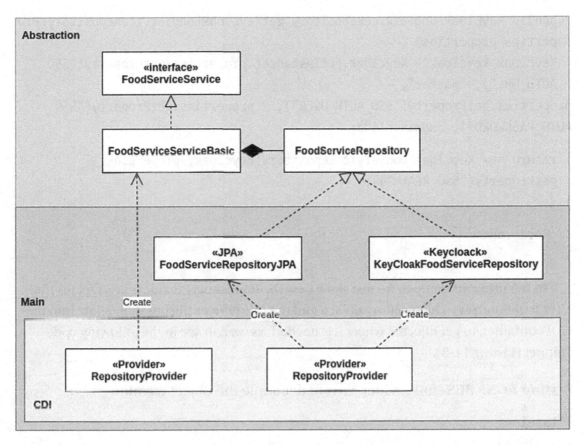

Figure 11-8. *Using dependency injection to inject objects from the Main to the Abstraction*

There, we added the CDI container layer, with the RepositoryProvider and RESTful Provider classes. Those are in charge of creating and injecting the objects we need. See what the RepositoryProvider looks like in Listing 11-2.

Listing 11-2. RepositoryProvider class to decouple the object creation

```
@Stateless
@LocalBean
public class RepositoryProvider {

// More code

  @Produces
```

```
  public KeyCloakFoodServiceRepository getKeyCloakFoodServiceRepository(Pro
  perties properties) {
  Keycloak keycloak = Keycloak.getInstance( properties.getProperty("SSO_
  AUTH_URL"), "master",
properties.getProperty("SSO_AUTH_USER"),    properties.getProperty("SSO_
AUTH_PASSWORD"), "admin-cli");

  return new KeyCloakFoodServiceRepository(keycloak, properties.
  getProperty("SSO_REALM"));
}

// More code
}
```

In the previous snippet, we just show how the RepositoryProvider class creates the KeyCloakFoodServiceRepository object, and the @Produces pushes that object into the CDI container, to get injected where it is needed, as we can see in the following code snippet (Listing 11-3).

Listing 11-3. RESTfulProvider class to decouple the object creation

```
@Stateless
@LocalBean
public class RestfulProvider {

// More code

  @Produces
  public FoodServiceService getFoodServiceService( FoodServiceRepository
  foodServiceRepository) {
  return new FoodServiceServiceBasic(foodServiceRepository);
}

// More code
}
```

There, the CDI container realizes that there is a need for an implementation of a FoodServiceRepository interface, so, it finds one available in its context, and injects it there later to create the FoodServiceServiceBasic object and push it into the CDI context.

As we can see, the CDI container does the work for us, and our Abstraction doesn't know which implementations we are using.

This strategy uses a Factory Method pattern because we have a method to build an object. In this case, this method is under the control of the CDI container.

Note   For more information regarding the Factory Method pattern to decouple the Main and the Abstraction, check this out: `https://coderstower.com/2019/04/23/factory-methods-decoupling-ioc-container-abstraction/`

Finally, we learned that the Main and Abstraction concepts work together to create decoupled systems, using techniques like dependency injection and a CDI container. In the following section, we are going to focus on the stateless servers and why they are a good idea.

Stateless Servers as a Priority

Servers have been around since the beginning of software development. The idea of having someone who asks questions (request), solve problems (transform), and give you outcomes (response) is the final goal of any software. In Figure 11-9 we illustrate the concept.

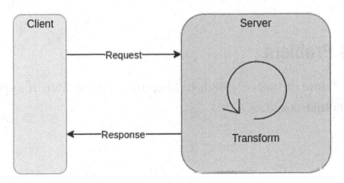

Figure 11-9. *Client and Server relationship*

There, we can see a client requesting information to a server, the server transforms/processes the data, and then it returns a response to the client.

415

In this section, we are going to focus on just one feature regarding servers: its state. We can have two state models:

- Stateful: The server needs to keep some information somewhere (memory, disk) to track multiple things like sessions, common data, and so on.

- Stateless: The server's responsibility is just processing a request and returning an outcome; it doesn't need to track data by itself.

We are going to talk about these models in detail in the following section.

Why Stateful Servers Are Not Cool to Scale

Today's software requirements are pretty different than they were 10 years ago. The needs regarding scaling are huge, and any company that wants to have a good relationship with its clients needs to guarantee availability and responsiveness.

As the number of users a software can have, could be millions, servers' resources where that software is deployed are more relevant, like:

- How much memory do I need?

- How much storage do I need?

- Can I scale horizontally or vertically?

Regarding those resources, we are going to focus on how a server can handle sessions.

The Sessions Problem

A session is a set of data the server needs to keep track of the state of a specific logged user. Figure 11-10 illustrates that.

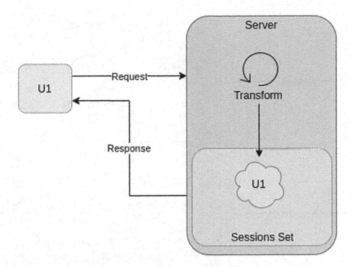

Figure 11-10. *Handling session in the server side*

The previous image has the following flow of events:

1. The user U1 accesses our application and logs in.

2. The server creates a session in memory, named U1, to track the user logged in.

3. The user U1 requests some process to the server

4. The server needs to validate if U1 has a valid session, so, it checks the sessions set and grabs some information he needs to process the request, like the user's name and id.

5. The server applies the transformation and returns an answer.

Now, let's imagine that our application usually needs to support 1,000 concurrent sessions, so, it will look like Figure 11-11.

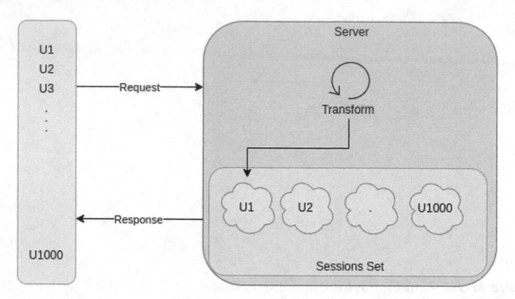

Figure 11-11. *Handling multiple sessions in the server side*

There, we can see the sessions set of 1,000 sessions, if we need 2 Megabytes to save each session, we need at least 2 MB x 1000 = 2 GB to support the typical day of our application.

Well, what if my business is a success, so, my users' numbers double to 2,000, which means, I will need to scale my server vertically, increasing its memory from 2 GB to 4 GB, at least?

Scaling vertically is not the best solution; actually, it has a limit where you cannot scale more. So, as our software architect realizes that, he decides to add a load balancer and scale horizontally adding a new server as we can see in Figure 11-12.

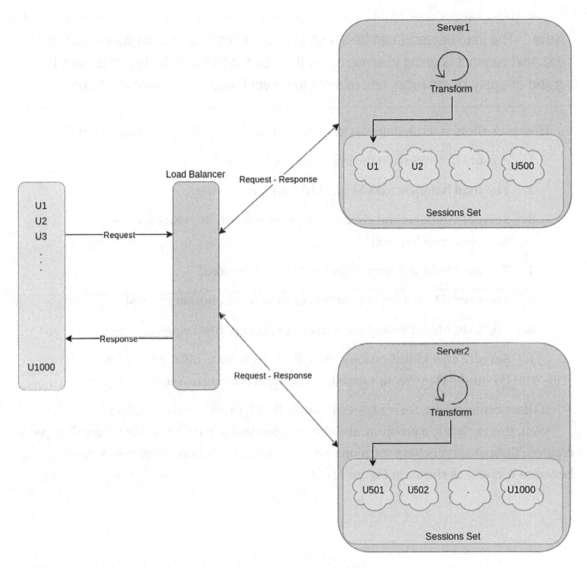

Figure 11-12. *Scaling horizontally the servers and their sessons horizontally*

That solution seems to work, and we have now two servers, Server1 and Server2, behind a load balancer that balances requests in the available servers. Each server will handle 500 users, and the memory of each of those are under control to just 1 GB. If we need to increase our users' number, we just add another server.

Note   The load balancer can be set up in multiple ways to decide which server the next request is going to arrive on. In this case, let's think the load balancer is going to apply round robin, one request to server1, one to server2, and so on.

However, there is a missing part here. Let's find it using the following scenario:

1. A user U1 requests to the load balancer to log in.

2. The load balancer asks Server1 to log in as that user.

3. Server1 validates and creates the users' session in its Sessions set and response "created."

4. The load balancer responses the "session created."

5. The user U1 asks the load balancer to process another request.

6. The load balancer asks the Server2 to process that request.

7. Server2 checks its Sessions Set to find the session information for U1, and if they doesn't find it, the session is living in Server1.

If that scenario fails, Server2 doesn't know that U1 was already logged in.

Well, this is clearly a problem, and the sessions will live in the server where they were created. Robust servers have solutions for this, like serialization of the user's session between servers, as shown in Figure 11-13.

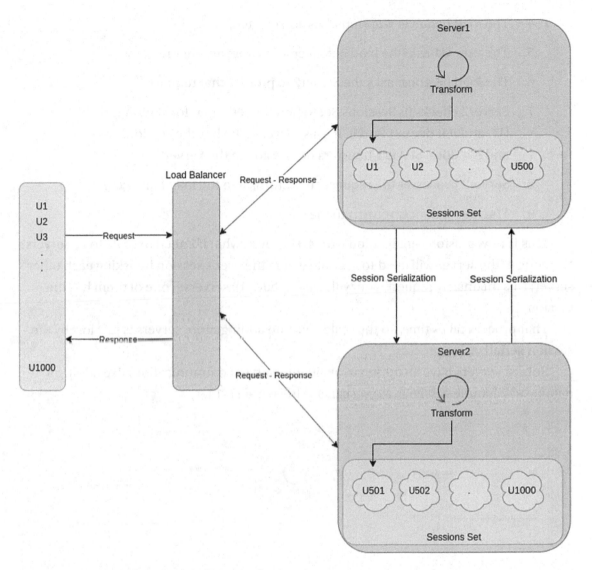

Figure 11-13. *Session serialization between servers*

As we can see, now our two servers need to send back and forward the session, depending on where the session was created and where it is needed. The following scenario illustrates it:

1. A user U1 requests to the load balancer to log in.

2. The load balancer asks Server1 to log in that user.

3. The Server1 validates and creates the users' session in its Sessions set and responds "created."

421

4.   The load balancer responds "session created."

5.   The user U1 asks the load balancer to process another request.

6.   The load balancer asks the Server2 to process that request.

7.   Server2 checks its Sessions Set to find the session information for
     U1, and if it doesn't find it, it asks Server1 if he has the session,
     and if it does, Server1 transfers the session to the Server2.

8.   Server2 processes the request and returns it to the load balancer.

9.   The load balancer returns to the user.

This is how session serialization works. However, what if I need to scale to 20 servers? By request, the server will need to validate where the user's session is, asking each other server; this means, by request, you will need to have 19 servers if one of them has the session.

That process takes time, so the scale you gain adding more servers is just lost by the session serialization process.

Robust servers have an option to avoid interserver communication, like adding a database to handle sessions, as you can see in Figure 11-14.

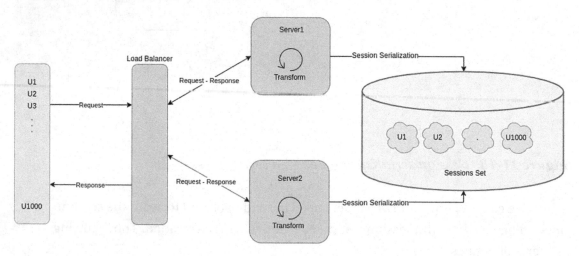

Figure 11-14. *Session serialization using a database between servers*

There, we find that the sessions are saved into a central point, in this case, a database. The servers won't need to ask other servers about the session, they just need to query the database searching the current user's session.

The database solution works fine, but, if the database is down, the users won't be able to connect; moreover, if you have plenty of users, your database could transform in a bottleneck.

In the following section, we will see a better approach.

Delegating Sessions to Another Party

The best idea is to avoid handling sessions by a user in our servers, so the server will be stateless. However, we still need to know who is logged in, and we still need sessions and someone must track them; in this case, we can use an Identity Provider. Figure 11-15 illustrates that concept.

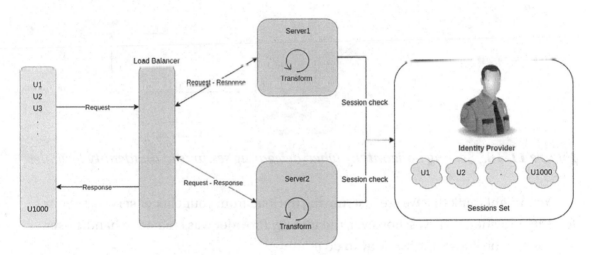

Figure 11-15. *Delegating session to an Identity Provider*

There, we can see that our servers are not in charge of sessions anymore. The sessions are handled by the Identity Provider now, and it saves and tracks them. That means we can add more servers to scale horizontally as we can see in Figure 11-16.

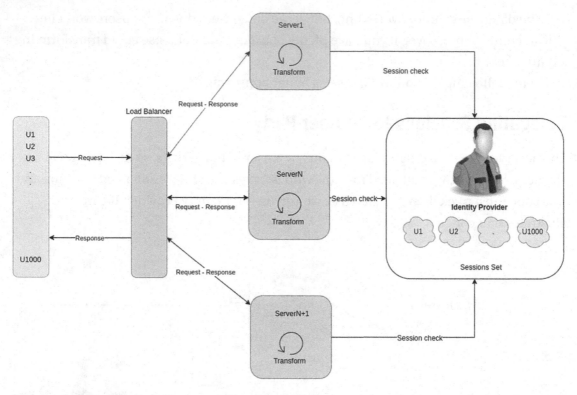

Figure 11-16. *Scaling horizontally when delegating sessions to an Identity Provider*

You might think that we are just moving the load from your cluster servers to your Identity Provider. Well, yes; however, the Identity Provider was created to handle user sessions, so he knows the best way to do it.

Note   Is there a limit regarding how many servers can I cluster? Well, that depends on your cluster strategy. You can add as many as you want; however, that doesn't mean you are going to improve your system capacity in the same measure. Remember, you will need a load balancer controlling everything, so the more servers, the more control it needs to have, and more resources are going to be consumed. Here it is important to think about how much your system needs to support it, measure it, and make a call regarding the best design. A Reactive approach could be pretty useful when the load needs to be huge. You can read more here: https://www.lightbend.com/blog/understand-reactive-architecture-design-and-programming-in-less-than-12-minutes

---

Now, how can I use the Identity Provider to handle sessions? Well, we talk about that in Chapter 9, "Securing Your Full-Stack Application" and Chapter 10, "Authentication and Authorization," where we can use the OpenID Connect protocol plus JWT, as shown in Figure 11-17.

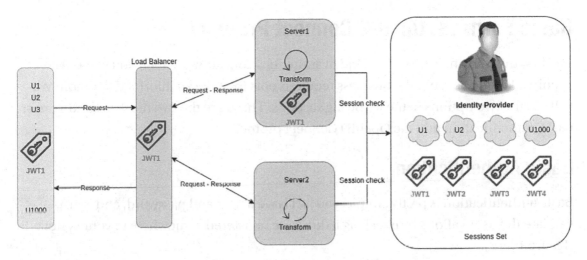

Figure 11-17. *JWT flowing through the system until the Identity Provider*

As we can see, the JWT token flows through the whole system and we use the Identity Provider to check if the token is valid.

Note Remember, there are several ways to validate the token, from a local validation using JWK to an introspect endpoint.

In this section, we learned why a stateful server couldn't be a good idea for a high demanding system, and how we can create a stateless system using an Identity Provider to handle the sessions. In the following section, we will see best practices related to security.

Defining What Kind of Security You Want

Security is pretty important in any application, and it is a must-have for any business.

There are different ways to secure an application, from just a basic login form to more advanced techniques like the OpenId Connect protocol. Besides, we need to define who is it that is going to handle that security? You or a third party? In this section, we are going to focus on some trade-offs regarding security.

Basic Form vs. OpenID Connect Protocol

The first thing to analyze is what kind of authentication/authorization you want. We should take into account the business requirements to make an informed decision. We will see the two options in the following sections. These are the two most common ones: basic authentication and the OpenID Connect protocol.

Basic Authentication

Basic authentication is pretty simple: you just have a user and password, and you validate the user validity by checking if those are registered somewhere in your system (Figure 11-18).

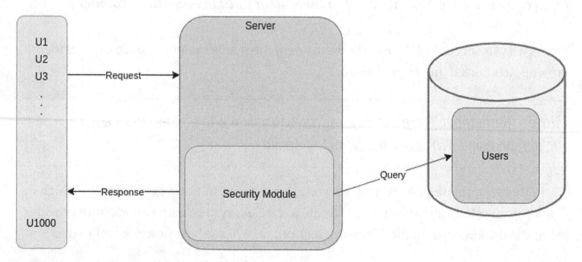

Figure 11-18. *Basic authentication architecture*

As we can see from this image, the security module is handled by us, into our server/application logic. We usually save the user and password in a database and query it when we need to validate if our user exists or not.

Tip   The password should be opaque in the database to avoid being read by database administrators or an attacker.

Application servers like GlassFish usually have options to override the security module to add that basic authentication and automatically create a session into the server, tracking it using Cookies, for instance. As we control the security module, that means we need to handle the user sessions into our servers, and our servers cannot be stateless.

The following are some advantages of basic security:

- Easy to set up. You are in control of the whole flow and the validation is simple; just check if the user and password are valid.

- Good for testing purposes. As you just need a user and password, creating testing against secured environments is easy; you just sent those two data to the system.

- Good for applications that handle noncritical information like payments or sensitive personal data, plus simple designs, like monolithic.

There are some disadvantages as well:

- You should add other security layers to avoid XSS and CSRF in the login process. You can find more information regarding XSS here: https://www.owasp.org/index.php/Cross-site_Scripting_(XSS) and CSRF here https://www.owasp.org/index.php/Cross-Site_Request_Forgery_(CSRF).

- Not applicable to high-critical information systems.

- Difficult to apply a single sign-on option over other applications. You need to handle the password encryption by yourself.

- You will handle the whole user management, from registration to deletion, from updates to sessions.

- Not fit for transferring security through different services, like in a microservice architecture.

OpenID Connect Protocol

We talked extensively about OpenID Connect protocol in the security chapter. This protocol allows us to delegate to an external Identity Provider part of the security module (Figure 11-19).

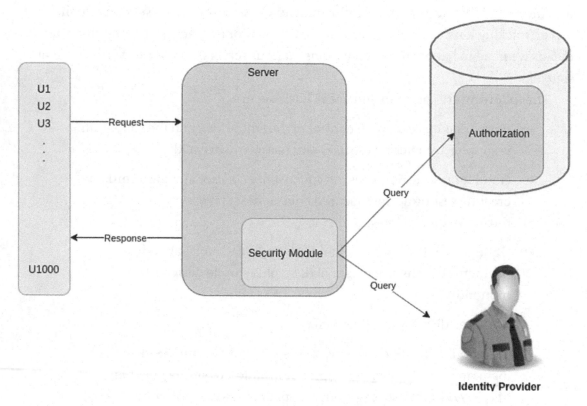

Figure 11-19. *Security module into the server to talk with an Identity Provider*

The main goal of the Identity Provider is to provide security and sessions, which means our security module is going to be smaller than before, as we delegate those features to the Identity Provider.

Now, this doesn't mean you shouldn't handle any security part; you might need to handle the authorization internally to your application, for instance.

The following are some advantages of the OpenID Connect protocol:

- Extensively tested and used, so, we have a degree of certainty that it works fine. Besides, we can find multiple implementations over multiples languages and frameworks.

- Multiple Identity Provider options, from open sources to paid. There are plenty of options out there, for instance, we used Keycloak in previous chapters. For a Service as a Service, you can find OKTA and Auth0.

- Identity Providers are created to be experts handling security and avoid normal pitfalls like XSS and CSRF.

- Good for single sign-on environments, as the token can be transferred and validated in other places different than the source of the token.

- Multiple setups using JWT, like access tokens, refresh tokens, timeouts, life spans, encryption, and so on.

- Multiple libraries to help you to handle the whole protocol and JWTs over multiple languages.

The disadvantages are:

- Difficult and time-consuming to set up for the first time.

- As OpenId Connect is a protocol, we need to follow it well; otherwise, we will open security holes.

- You might need a third party to control the security like an Identity Provider.

Finally, as we can see, there are more advantages using the OpenId Connect protocol than the form of basic security. With that in mind, we need now to choose if that OpenId Connect protocol will be implemented by an external or by an internal Identity Provider. We talk about this in the following section.

External vs. Internal Security Delegation

We just saw that delegating security is the best alternative; now, the question is, do you want to handle that security by yourself or do you want to have an external entity?

This means you can have an internal Identity Provider or use an external one. We are going to detail the features of both options in the following sections.

Internal Identity Provider

An internal Identity Provider is a software module you handle and maintain, and it is inside of your company. For instance, installing Keycloak as the Identity Provider to handle the security of your application means that you have an internal Identity Provider.

Tip   This doesn't mean you need to install the identity provider in your infrastructure; you can contract SaaS identity providers like OKTA or OAuth2.

The following are some advantages regarding an internal Identity Provider:

- Your credentials and information are yours. As the Identity Provider is handled and maintained for you, you control how and when the data is used or deleted.

- You control the setup of that identity provider. You can configure anything you want to install the Identity Provider as your requirements force you.

- You can extend or remove any plugin you need. An Identity Provider usually can be extended adding plugins, but if the Identity Provider is handled by you, you can choose which plugins to use and which to not.

Of course, there are some disadvantages:

- The access to this identity provider is just internal, which means you might need to be into the intranet of your company.

- This strategy is good for internal users, as they might need a corporate email to access the identity provider.

- You will need to maintain the Identity Provider, scaling it, checking its behavior, and fixing it.

External Identity Provider

An external Identity Provider is an Identity Provider that you don't handle, like Google, Facebook, Twitter, and so on.

They work as an Identity Provider using their database information to allow access to other applications. For instance, StackOverflow allows us to log in using different an external Identity Provider like Google, GitHub, or Facebook (Figure 11-20).

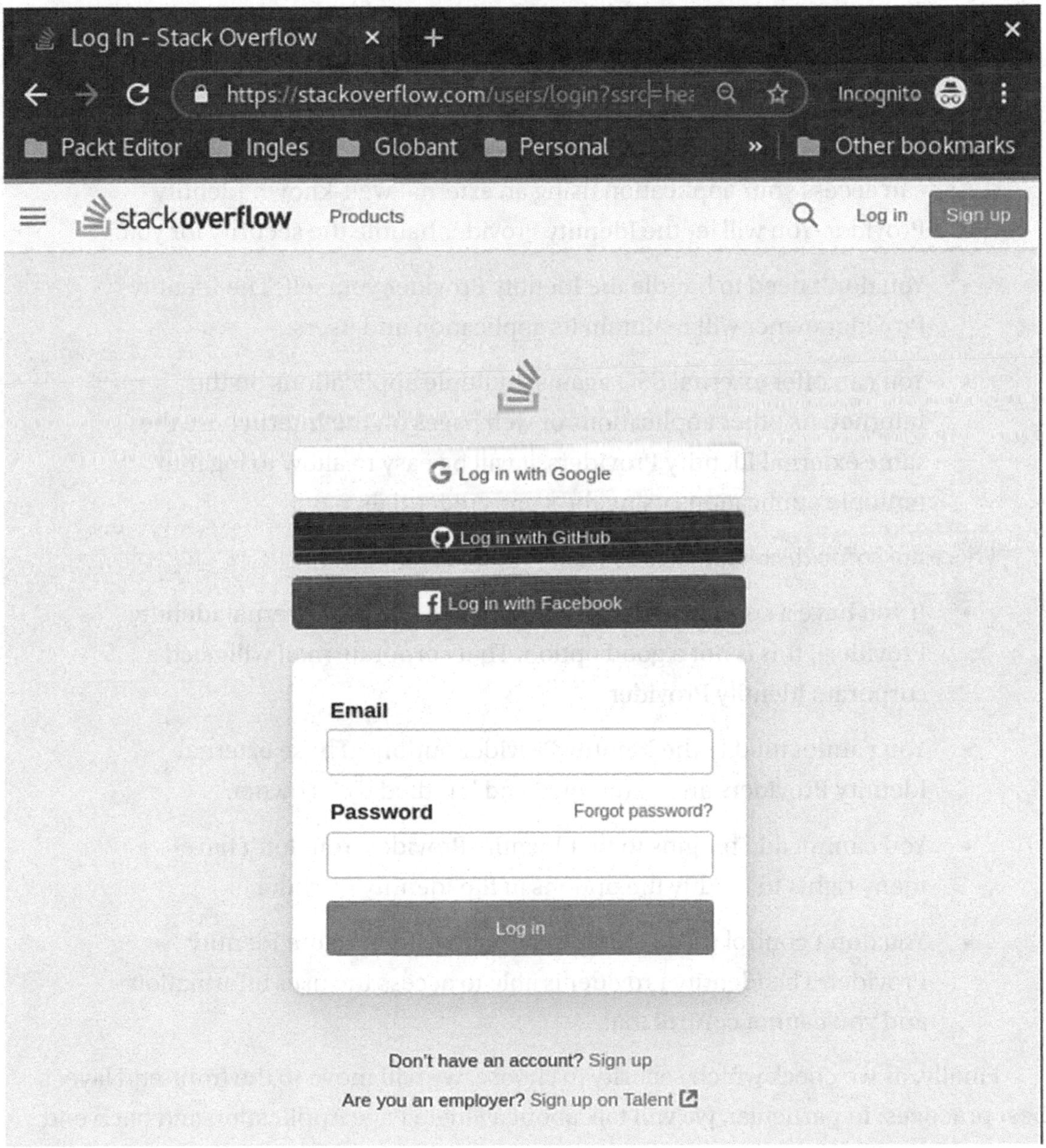

Figure 11-20. *Multiple Identity Provider in the same page like StackOverflow*

The external Identity Provider strategy has the following advantages:

- As you have multiple external Identity Providers, you can provide multiple ways.

- To log in for your users. This is going to remove blockers for your users to join your application, as they can have different Identity Providers accounts.

- Easy access for external users. Users outside of your organization can access your application using an external well-known Identity Provider. You will let the Identity Provider handle the security for you.

- You don't need to handle the Identity Provider yourself. The Identity Provider owner will maintain its application and users.

- You can offer external SSO against multiple applications on the Internet. As other applications or web pages on the Internet use the same external Identity Providers, it will be easy to allow to log into multiple applications using the same credentials.

There are some disadvantages as well:

- If you have a corporate email (different like from an external Identity Provider), this is not a good option. That corporate mail will need a corporate Identity Provider.

- You cannot modify the Identity Provider options. Those external Identity Providers are maintained and handled by its owner.

- You cannot add plugins to that Identity Provider. You don't have many rights to modify the options in the Identity Provider.

- You don't control the user information register into the Identity Provider. The Identity Provider is able to access the user information and you cannot control that.

Finally, as we check which security to choose, we will move to the front-end layer best practices; in particular, we will talk about a Single Page Application and back-end pages.

Single Page Application vs. Back-End Pages

The user interface is basic in any system; that is the way our final users use the system. In this section, we are going to talk about how the user interface worked 10 years before, and how they work now, and where they are tending to return to where we were before.

Some Time Ago... JSP

Java Server Pages was one of the first technologies created to build user interfaces using Java, HTML, and JavaScript. This technology doesn't differentiate between HTML and Java, so, we mixed both to create dynamic web pages, as we can see in Figure 11-21.

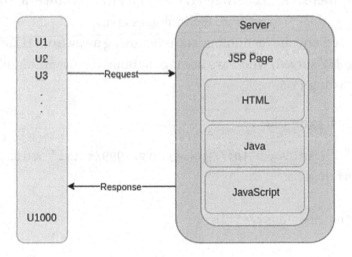

Figure 11-21. *JSP architecture*

There, we see how a JSP page contains everything (HTML, Java, and JavaScript). Besides, that page is server-side rendered.

The following is an example of how a JSP looks (Listing 11-4).

Listing 11-4. JSP example

```
<html>
  <head>
    <title>JSP Example</title>
  </head>
```

```
<body>
  <% double num = Math.random();    if (num < 0.80) {  %>  <h2>Well, bad
  luck now</h2>

    <p>(<%= num %>)</p> <% }    else { %>    <h2>You are a luck   person
    now!</h2><p>(<%= num %>)</p> <% }    %>
  <a href="<%= request.getRequestURI() %>">
    <h3>Ups,something wrong happens</h3>
  </a>
</body>
</html>
```

As we can see, there is a mix between HTML and Java, of course, and there is some special syntax using the <% to get both technologies apart.

The years passed and the technology started moving away from HTML and Java code, so JSTL and JSF surged, where we use tags to build the user interface, free of Java code like that in Listing 11-5.

Listing 11-5. JSTL example

```
<html lang="en"    xmlns="http://www.w3.org/1999/xhtml" xmlns:h="http://
java.sun.com/jsf/html">
  <h:head>
    <title>Using now Tags</title>
  </h:head>
  <h:body>
    #{hello.delivery}
  </h:body>
</html>
```

There, we abstract the HTML to tag components and use templating with #{} to inject values from Java to the JSF page. Those improvements helped a lot to split responsibilities; however, at the end of the day, the server is in charge of serving the HTML page ready to be consumed by the web browser (Figure 11-22).

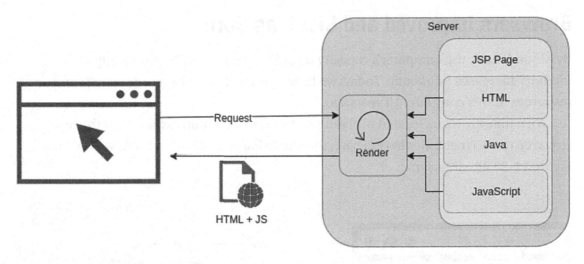

Figure 11-22. *JSP-rendering architecture*

This means the server has the entire responsibility of processing the logic and generating the web page.

Now, this approach has the following advantages:

- The browser receives the page ready to render, so it won't consume many resources in the client machine.

- The development team usually has the capacity to work with HTML and Java. You can scale your web server; therefore, you scale the render process.

And some disadvantages:

- The HTML render frameworks are not customizable; you need much effort for that. Those frameworks were built in Java and generate HTML from behind, hiding complexity but blocking any easy extension.

- You mix HTML and Java in the worst case if you use JSP. Mixing responsibilities cause the application to be difficult to maintain.

- Your development team must be aware of HTML and Java to work on the project. You cannot have team members focused just in HTML, as it is mixed with Java code.

- As it is the server is who renders the web page, he needs more machine resources. The feedback in the development phase is slow because we need to deploy the changes regarding pages to the server before testing changes.

435

Browsers Improved and SPA Was Born

By Moore's Law, the computer's capacity regarding resources like processing and memory increases frequently. Today, we have in our cell phones more capacity and resources than a computer 10 years ago.

With this, browsers located in client machines can do more work, using the new resources those machines have. There, the Single Page Application (SPA) was born. Figure 11-23 illustrates that.

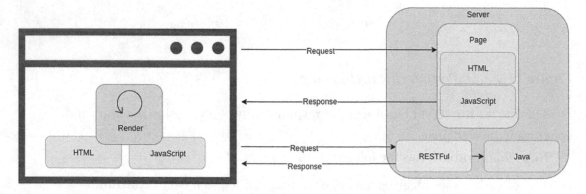

Figure 11-23. *SPA-rendering architecture*

As we can see, the Server just provides HTML templates and JavaScript definitions, and the browser is in charge of rendering the whole page, joining those two with the data it queries from the back end. That data usually is retrieved from the Server using RESTful services.

This is called Single Page Application as the Server just provides the index.html, and JavaScript does the rest of computations into the browser, using HTML templates to create new pages, elements, and fill data to show the final user.

Note   When we talk about JavaScript here, it is not just native JavaScript: it should be a JavaScript framework like Angular, React, or Vue.js.

This approach has the following advantages:

- The back-end server doesn't need to render the page. This means that the resource that was used to render pages is now free to be used for other processes.

- The development team can consist of a mix of front-end developers and back-end developers.

- As the web page is rendered by the browser, the feedback is faster; you just need a lightweight server or the same browsers can show you little changes in your HTML and JavaScript code.

- You don't mix HTML and JavaScript with Java.

- JavaScript frameworks are pretty robust and can handle complex requirements. You can compose UI components, call RESTful services, and process complex logic.

Now, of course, there are some disadvantages:

- The JavaScript framework is usually monolithic, so you cannot split it into smaller parts. So, if the project is huge, you might need multiple teams to handle that layer.

- Browsers improve in terms of performance, however, if you didn't design well your front-end app, you can use a lot of machine resources, causing the client application to seem slow.

- You usually need those with expertise in your project, one for the JavaScript framework and another for the back-end layer.

Single Pages Application is a pretty good solution for most of the business problems; however, there are some cases where a middle ground could better fit the requirements. We will talk about that in the following section.

Micro Front Ends: Mixing the Two Worlds

As the need for divide and conquer in the software industry arrived with the microservice architecture, the front-end layer shouldn't be behind this approach, so, micro front ends were borne.

The idea behind micro front ends is to split a complex UI in multiple pieces, so, each piece can be maintained and deployed by on team, with low coupling between them. Figure 11-24 shows what a micro front-end architecture looks like.

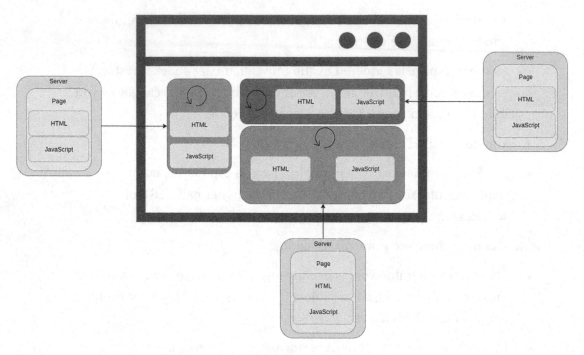

Figure 11-24. *Micro front-end architecture*

As we can see, the front-end layer is composed of multiple micro pages, each of them rendered by a different Server. The browser takes those pages and creates a large one. To the final user, the page looks like just one.

In the micro front-ends approach, the front-end layer is split by domains, so one microservice (and team) is in charge of everything regarding that domain, from the UI to the data.

Tip   To orchestrate this kind of front end, there are different ideas around, and you can find more information at `https://martinfowler.com/articles/micro-frontends.html`

Finally, choosing between a server-side render, a client-side render, or a micro front end should be a decision based on your own requirements.

In the following section, we will focus on the database's best practices.

Choosing the Right Database

Storage has been around from the beginning, saving information in disks, cards, and bands. The database was a huge advance where the data is saved in a "structured" manner, easy to access and process.

However, as time passed, more databases were borne and choosing the right one for our requirements is difficult.

In this section, we are going to talk about databases, focusing on the relational and non-relational databases, and validating when we should use which.

Relational Databases

Relational databases store the information in tables and rows. Those tables can have properties and relationships with other tables. For instance, for our new Daniel's Delivery website, we have the following entity relation model shown in Figure 11-25.

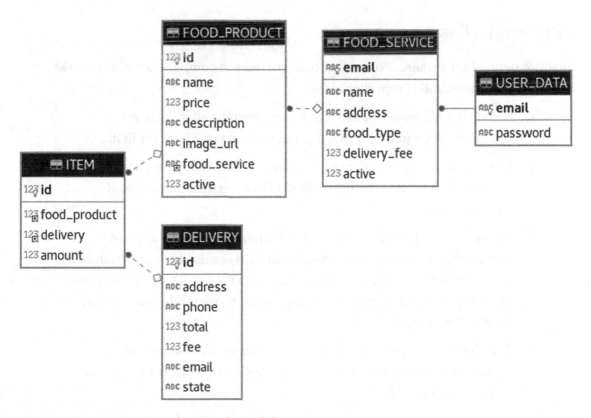

Figure 11-25. *Entity relational model*

There, we have the following information:

- Tables:

  - ITEM, FOOD_PRODUCT, FOOD_SERVICE, USER_DATA, DELIVERY

- Relations:

  - A DELIVERY can have many ITEM

  - A FOOD_PRODUCT can have many ITEM

  - A FOOD_SERVICE can have many FOOD_PRODUCT

  - A FOOD_SERVICE just can have one USER_DATA

As we can see, we have a set of tables and relations. Those tables and relations are the core of any relational database.

Now, relational databases have some specific features, and those are named ACID properties.

ACID Properties

First, we define that a transaction is a set of steps/tasks to complete a whole process. Now, we can define ACID properties as follows:

- Atomicity: A transaction must finish completely, all tasks or none, which means, a transaction is a single unit, so you cannot split it.

- Consistency: Any modification in the data must comply with the database constraints like data types, so that the data is consistent through time.

- Isolation: One transaction cannot see other transactions that are executed at the same time. Transactions just see the current database state. If transaction A is running at the same time that transaction B is and modifies data, transaction B cannot see those modifications until transaction A has finished.

- Durability: Any operation against the database is persistent, which means that if the database is turned off and turned on again, the data you save before is there.

ACID is pretty important, and hundreds of systems today rely on it.

Non-Relational databases

Non-Relational databases are databases that don't have the typical format of tables, properties, and rows. Figure 11-26 shows an example of a Documental database.

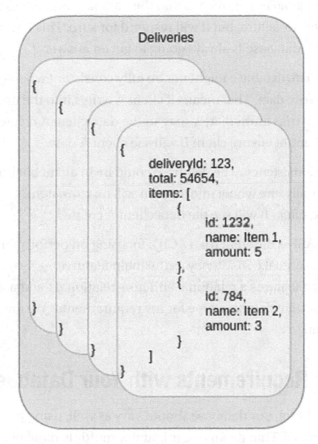

Figure 11-26. *Non-relational data in a Deliveries database*

There, we model the information as JSON documents.

There are plenty of non-relational database types, like key-value, documental, columnar, graphs. Each of them has different features and strategies to handle data, so, depending on your use case, one of them could work better than others. Now, those databases share a set of features, like the relational ones have ACID, and the non-relational databases have BASE.

BASE Properties

We can define BASE as Basically Available Soft State Eventual Consistency. The following points explain it in detail:

- Basically Available: This means that the database is going to respond with success or failure, but it will respond for sure. This implies the client of the database is always going to get an answer.

- Soft State: The database might not be fully consistent when you read and write data. That means if client A writes into the database, and client B tries immediately to read the data client A created, the database cannot ensure client B will see client A data.

- Eventual Consistency: The database could be in an inconsistent state, but, eventually, the whole information will be consistent. This means, eventually, client B will see the data client A created.

As we can see, BASE is different than ACID, focusing on performance and scalability, using soft state and eventual consistency as the main features.

We just saw which features a relational and non-relational database have, however, how can I choose the right database type for my requirements? We are going to use the CAP theorem for that.

Aligning Your Requirements with Your Database

As requirements vary a lot, our database should vary as well, using its best features to solve those requirements. That means we might use multiple databases to solve multiple problems in the same system. Here, the CAP theorem is what we should use to make a call regarding which database we should choose.

CAP Theorem

CAP theorem stands for Consistency, Availability, and Partition tolerant. We will see each one in detail:

- Consistency: A read from any server/node in the system gets the same result. That means, it doesn't matter which node you choose to query information, the information is going to be the same.

- Availability: Any read or write is always going to have a response, and it doesn't matter if it is successful or not.

- Partition tolerant: The database system can be split into multiple parts, and if some parts have outages, the system still has the capacity to respond.

Now, as anything is software, those three features cannot be done at the same time, so we should choose two of them; and those two will affect the behavior of the third. In Figure 11-27, we can see the relationship between the features.

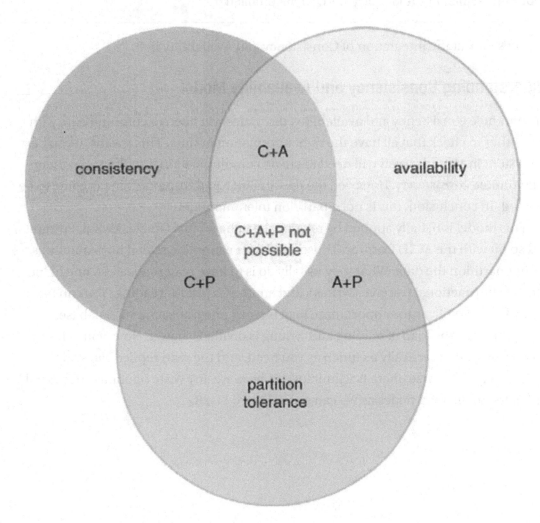

Figure 11-27. *CAP theorem*

As we can see from the previous image, we have the CAP features together. Those overlap each other in some parts: consistency connects with availability and partition tolerance; partition tolerance connects with consistency and availability; availability connects with consistency; and finally, the three overlap in the middle.

In the following sections, we are going to discuss each combination of the CAP features, avoiding the overlapping of the three.

Tip   Implementing Consistency, Availability, and Partition tolerance all at once is not impossible, but it is pretty hard to accomplish

---

Let's look at the integration of Consistency and Availability first.

Understanding Consistency and Availability Model

To guarantee consistency and availability, the nodes will need to communicate with each other to check that all have the right information in time. This means, if you part the system in 10 nodes, you will need to create communication links between them to guarantee consistency. However, the performance and response time is going to be affected. In conclusion, this is not a partition tolerant model.

This model is usually applied by relational databases like Oracle, MySql, Postgress, and so on with the ACID features. Those databases cannot be scaled horizontally as we cannot partition the data. What they usually do is to have read replicas, so one of the nodes is transactional (receives writes), and another is just for reading. You can have multiple read replicas to support more load but just one transactional database.

In this way, the load of reading and writing is divided/shared. Now, you can scale your writing node vertically as much as you need, and the read replica can scale horizontally. Of course, there is a limit for this because any write operation needs to be replicated to the read nodes as we can see in Figure 11-28.

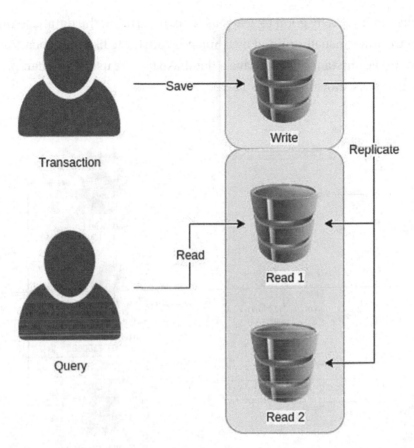

Figure 11-28. *Consistency vs. availability in CAP theorem*

There, we show the model of one transactional node (Write) and two read replicas (Read 1 and Read 2). A transactional operation arrives only to the transactional node; however, a query operation arrives at any read replica node.

Remember, as we need to be consistent, we expected the read replicas to have the up-to-date data, so the writer node is going to replicate by each write operation the information to its read replicas. Therefore, the response time to the client is going to be affected if you have many read replicas

This model is pretty good when you need to guarantee consistency across sensitive information; meanwhile, it is available, like money transactions.

Understanding Availability and Partition Tolerance Model

If we need availability and partition tolerance, that means we cannot guarantee consistency, as we might have different versions of the same data over the nodes.

These features are pretty good to scale, as we can partition the database multiple times. This partition is usually guided by a business attribute like data location, data types, and so on. For instance, if you have a database to save users, you can partition by the ID of the users, as shown in Figure 11-29.

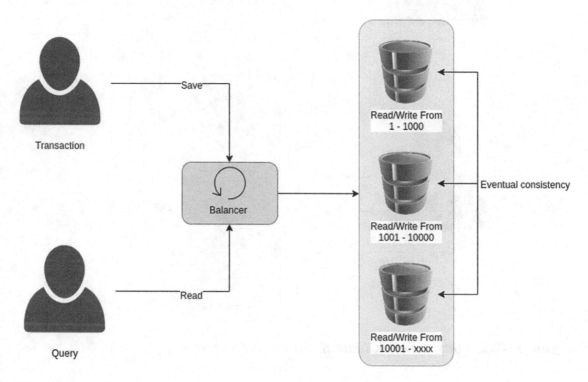

Figure 11-29. *Partition tolerance vs. availability in CAP theorem*

In the preceding image, we can scale horizontally as many times as we want. Here, the BASE features apply, so the system is going to be eventually consistent through time; meanwhile it continues being available. The non-relational databases bring by default a similar partition strategy, like MongoDB, Cassandra, and Gemfire.

As we are eventually consistent, this approach is good for systems where the users don't care about consistent data, like a user Facebook feed, where the user doesn't care if his post appears right now or in 5 seconds. However, if we talk about money, it is pretty important to me to see my account state updated right now with my latest transaction, so that use case is not good for this approach.

Understanding Consistency and Partition Tolerance Model

When a consistency and partition tolerance model is needed, the nodes cannot always be available, responding to requests, because we need to stop them for a while; so meanwhile we apply consistency to them. Figure 11-30 illustrates this concept.

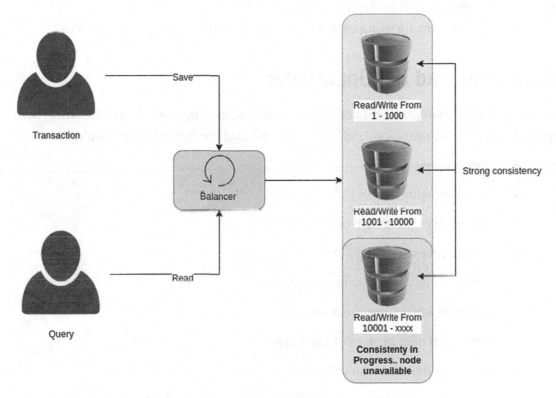

Figure 11-30. *Partition tolerance vs. consistency in CAP theorem*

As we can see above, to have the three nodes consistent, we need to stop one for a while, until the data is replicated completely through the system.

This approach is pretty good for large systems with plenty of data, where partition tolerant is important, and besides, the data must be consistent.

Finally, as systems are large and complex, with multiple use cases, you should choose your database depending on your needs, so, for instance, you can have parts of your system with MongoDB and others with Oracle. Remember, this is not about choosing one for everything. Use cases vary a lot, so, you should have multiple databases addressing multiple requirements.

In the following section, we are going to focus on the RESTful API best practices.

Defining Your RESTful API

RESTful APIs are everywhere today, as they are over HTTP, which is a standard, and lightweight, using JSON to exchange data.

However, as RESTful is built over HTTP protocol, we should design our APIs thinking in that standard, using resources and not operations.

In this section, we are going to talk about RESTful API design good practices.

Resources and Not Operations

First, we should change our conception regarding system operations. For instance, in a system that is in charge of food deliveries, we can find the following operations:

- Create a new delivery

- Get an existing delivery

- Delete an existing delivery

- Update an existing delivery

- Add an item to an existing delivery

- Get an existing item into a delivery

- Update an item in an existing delivery

- Delete an item from an existing delivery

Now, to map those operations to RESTful services, we can find different approaches. The first approach is the operational focus, which we discuss as follows.

First Approach: Operational

The operational approach focuses on using verbs to describe RESTful operations through the URL path. For instance, the following are the operation of the food delivery service using that strategy (Listings 11-6 to 11-13).

Create a New Delivery

Listing 11-6. Create a new delivery operational request

```
---REQUEST---
POST /api/createDelivery
{
.... Delivery data
}

---RESPONSE---
HTTP Status OK
```

There, we define that operation as /api/createDelivery; besides, we use the POST HTTP method without any particular meaning.

Get an Existing Delivery

Listing 11-7. Get an existing delivery operational request

```
---REQUEST---
GET /api/getDelivery
{
deliveryId = 1234
}

---RESPONSE---
HTTP Status OK
{
.... Delivery data
}
```

There, we define that operation as /api/getDelivery; moreover, we use the GET HTTP method to define a query operation, in this case, querying a delivery.

Delete an Existing Delivery

Listing 11-8. Delete an existing delivery operational request

```
---REQUEST---
POST /api/deleteDelivery
{
.... Delivery data
}

---RESPONSE---
HTTP Status OK
```

There, we define that operation as /api/deleteDelivery and we use the POST HTTP method again, meaning that for any query method, we should use GET, otherwise, we use POST.

Update an Existing Delivery

Listing 11-9. Update an existing delivery operational request

```
---REQUEST---
POST /api/updateDelivery
{
.... Delivery data
}

---RESPONSE---
HTTP Status OK
```

There, we define that operation as /api/updateDelivery and we use the POST HTTP method again as this is an update operation.

Add an Item to an Existing Delivery

Listing 11-10. Add an item to an existing delivery operational request

```
---REQUEST---
POST /api/addItemToDelivery
{
.... Item data
}

---RESPONSE---
HTTP Status OK
```

There, we define that operation as /api/addItemToDelivery . From here, it is interesting how we are using one operation to link two business entities, Item and Delivery.

Get an Existing Item into a Delivery

Listing 11-11. Get an existing item into a delivery operational request

```
---REQUEST---
GET /api/getItem
{
itemId = 12344
}

---RESPONSE---
HTTP Status OK
{
.... Item data
}
```

There, we define that operation as /api/getItem; moreover, we use the GET HTTP method to define a query operation, in this case, querying an Item.

Update an Item in an Existing Delivery

Listing 11-12. Update an item in an existing delivery operational request

```
---REQUEST---
POST /api/udpateItemToDelivery
{
.... Item data
}
---RESPONSE---
HTTP Status OK
```

There, we define that operation as /api/udpateItemToDelivery and we use the POST HTTP method again as this is an update operation.

Delete an Item from an Existing Delivery

Listing 11-13. Delete an item from an existing delivery operational request

```
---REQUEST---
POST /api/deleteItemInDelivery
{
.... Item data
}

---RESPONSE---
HTTP Status OK
```

Now, as we can see, we design each food delivery operation as a RESTful operation, without any HTTP protocol feature, like status codes, HTTP methods, and so on. This approach is weak as we are not using the whole HTTP protocol potential.

New Approach: Resources

The HTTP protocol contains some main features that we want to use in our RESTful API design. Those features are described as follows:

- HTTP Status codes: HTTP defines status codes in its responses. Each status code means something related to the result of an operation. For instance, 4xx and 5xx are the most used, any 4xx status code means there was an error regarding the request format, and any 5xx means there was a server error.

- HTTP Methods or verbs: The HTTP methods describe actions. HTTP has different methods, for instance, GET describes a query operation, POST describes a creation operation, DELETE describes a deletion, PUT describes an update, and so on. As we can see, HTTP gives us a way to describe an operation using these verbs.

- Paths and resources: A path is a route, an identifier of an object in a context. A path can have multiple parts split by a slash (/). For instance, a path for a user address could be /user/address. Each of those paths contains parts that are resources. A resource is an object into our system that can be accessed through a path; in this case, we have users and address resources.

Let's rewrite this RESTful API following the best practices, using HTTP status codes, resources, and methods.

Create a New Delivery

Well, the RESTful API for creating a new delivery looks like Listing 11-14.

Listing 11-14. Create a new delivery resource request

```
---REQUEST---
POST /api/deliveries
{
.... Delivery data
}
```

```
---RESPONSE---
HTTP Status Created
Location: /api/deliveries/1324
```

From the previous code, as this is a creation operation, we should use the HTTP method POST. The POST method is like adding a new POST to a blog, increasing the collection of posts that the blog might already have.

Besides, as we need to think about resources, what resources do we have here? Well, we have a delivery. As there is not just one delivery, we should talk in plural, deliveries, as a collection of deliveries. This makes sense with the POST method, as we are going to add new deliveries to the delivery collection.

Now, what should we have as a response? Well, HTTP has status response code, and there is one named HTTP 201 CREATED, and this is pretty meaningful regarding our current operation, as we are creating a new delivery into the delivery collection.

Note   Any resource in a RESTful API should be linkable, which means, any resource must have a unique link to access it.

Besides, we can add the Location header with the URL of the new resources created, in this case, the new delivery.

Get an Existing Delivery

The RESTful API for querying an existing delivery looks like Listing 11-15.

Listing 11-15. Get an existing delivery resource request

```
---REQUEST---
GET /api/deliveries/1234

---RESPONSE---
HTTP Status OK
{
.... Delivery data
}
```

There we can see that this is a query operation, so, we should use the HTTP method GET. The HTTP GET method is pretty clear in its intent. Besides, it is idempotent, so it doesn't matter how many times we call this operation, we get the same result

Moreover, we need to query a delivery from the delivery collection. But what do we need to do that? The delivery unique Id.

> **Note**   Remember, when we created the delivery, we get the unique URL to access it, and that URL is its unique Id.

Now, as the response is the whole delivery, we can use the HTTP 200 OK status code.

> **Note**   What about getting the whole delivery collection? Well, we just need to query /api/deliveries; besides, you can add query params to filter the collection, for instance, /api/deliveries/1234?name=daniel&address="street1".

Delete an Existing Delivery

The RESTful API for deleting a new delivery looks like Listing 11-16.

Listing 11-16.   Delete an existing delivery resource request

```
---REQUEST---
DELETE /api/deliveries/1234

---RESPONSE---
HTTP Status NO CONTENT
```

There, as this is a deletion operation, we should use the HTTP method DELETE. The HTTP DELETE method is pretty clear in its intent.

Besides, we need to delete a delivery from the delivery collection, but what we need to do that? The delivery unique Id again.

Now, as the response is nothing (we are deleting something), we can use the HTTP 204 NO CONTENT status code.

> **Note**   We don't need to send any body content for the request as the unique
> identifier for the delivery is in the URL.

Update an Existing Delivery

The RESTful API for updating a new delivery looks like Listing 11-17.

Listing 11-17. Update an existing delivery resource request

```
---REQUEST---
POST /api/deliveries/1234
{
.... Delivery data
}

---RESPONSE---
HTTP Status OK
```

As this is an update operation, we should use the HTTP method PUT. The HTTP PUT
is idempotent, which means we can invoke the same operation multiple times, and the
result should be the same.

Moreover, we need to update a delivery from the delivery collection, what do we
need to do that? Just the delivery Id.

Now, as a response, we can use the HTTP 200 OK status code.

Add an Item to an Existing Delivery

Here, we need to create a new item, which means that the same concept we saw
regarding creation applies. However, the URL needs to be different.

The delivery resource is a collection of deliveries, and each delivery has a collection
of items. So, the URL is compounded by deliveries and items (Listing 11-18).

Listing 11-18. Add an item to an existing delivery resource request

```
---REQUEST---
POST /api/deliveries/1234/items
{
.... Item data
}

---RESPONSE---
HTTP Status Created
Location: /api/deliveries/1234/item/12345
```

There, we defined a hierarchy regarding deliveries and items. And as we can see, we need to first access the delivery collection to access the item collection.

Get an Item in an Existing Delivery

Here, we need to query a new item, which means the same concept we saw regarding querying applies. However, the URL needs to be different. Now, the RESTful API design is like the one following in Listing 11-19.

Listing 11-19. Get an item in an existing delivery resource request

```
---REQUEST---
GET /api/deliveries/1234/items/12345

---RESPONSE---
HTTP Status OK
{
.... Item data
}
```

Update an Item in an Existing Delivery

Here, we need to update a new item, which means the same concept we saw regarding updates applies. However, the URL needs to be different.

Now, the RESTful API design is the following one in Listing 11-20.

Listing 11-20. Update an item in an existing delivery resource request

```
---REQUEST---
PUT /api/deliveries/1234/items/12345
{
.... Item data
}

---RESPONSE---
HTTP Status OK
```

Delete an Item from an Existing Delivery

Here, we need to delete a new item, which means that the same concept we saw regarding deleting applies. However, the URL needs to be different.

Now, the RESTful API design is the one that follows in Listing 11-21.

Listing 11-21. Delete an item from an existing delivery resource request

```
---REQUEST---
DELETE /api/deliveries/1234/items/12345

---RESPONSE---
HTTP Status NO CONTENT
```

Well, we just defined a good RESTful API using the HTTP protocol.

Summary

We just talked about a lot of good practices we should take into account for any web project, starting from applying good Oriented Object Programming, choosing stateless servers over stateful ones, adding the right security for your use cases, understanding the goals for server-side pages and single page applications, checking different kinds of databases and understanding a method to choose the right one, and finally, designing a good RESTful API.

With those practices in your toolbox, you will be able to create decoupled systems, defining which kind of servers, security, and database fit better for your requirements, and finally, design a meaningful RESTful API using the HTTP protocol.

Now we are ready to move our Daniel's Delivery website to production, using multiple AWS services, like S3, ECS, CloudFront, and so on.

Extended Knowledge

1. Can we apply the main and abstraction concepts to other Java frameworks?

2. How can decoupling one's system help to build a plugin architecture?

3. What is the difference between OpenID Connect and OAuth2.0?

4. How are serverless servers related to stateless servers?

5. Which single page application frameworks are used the most?

6. Provide some examples of non-relational databases.

7. How can we version a RESTful API?

CHAPTER 12

Cloud Architecture Implementation

Ten years ago, creating an application infrastructure was a nightmare. We had the physical servers, where we needed to install step by step each package and application that was needed in our system. There, we needed a lot of detailed knowledge in networking, servers, operative, systems and so on. Moreover, if we needed to create multiple infrastructures for multiple environments, this was pretty difficult as we didn't have all the details regarding how that environment was set up – and besides, we did this manually.

Today, cloud computing helps us to decrease that complexity, creating services easy to manage. We can now define infrastructure by code so that we have a clear view of which services we need and how they are set up.

In this chapter, we are going to define the new Daniel's Delivery website cloud architecture, using AWS as a cloud provider, with infrastructure as code, so we have the ability to automate the infrastructure creation.

The following topics will be covered in this chapter:

- Defining the AWS architecture, from design to the infrastructure as code, using AWS CloudFormation

- Dockerizing and deploying the Jakarta EE back-end into an AWS Elastic Container service

- Deploying the VueJS front-end using AWS CloudFront and S3

- Securing our application using AWS Cognito

© Daniel Andres Pelaez Lopez 2021
D. A. P. Lopez, *Full-Stack Web Development with Jakarta EE and Vue.js*,
https://doi.org/10.1007/978-1-4842-6342-6_12

Technical Requirements

- AWS account

- AWS CLI

We won't cover the AWS account creation and the AWS CLI installation.

Defining the AWS Architecture Using CloudFormation

In this section, we are going to build an AWS architecture for our new Daniel's Delivery website. The main goal is building a basic production (almost) ready environment that accomplishes the goal (Figure 12-1).

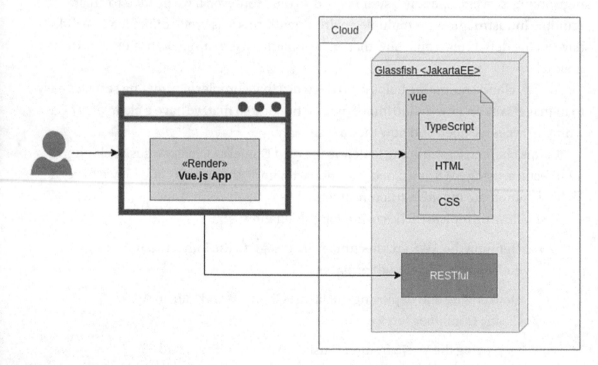

Figure 12-1. *Reference architecture to implement for Daniel's Delivery app*

Note   Production (almost) ready means that we cannot address everything in this book. For instance, the security concern won't be addressed in full, so you will need to get deep into it to have a completely secure production environment.

This was the first design we had in mind regarding the cloud infrastructure. Now, as we have wanted to use AWS as the cloud provider, we are going to translate those needs to its products.

We are also going to use a service called CloudFormation to create the infrastructure as code, which means we will be able to define in a plain text file how the infrastructure is going to be. This has huge advantages, like the possibility of versioning your infrastructure configuration, rebuilding your infrastructure from scratch, or creating infrastructure replicates.

Tip   In the CloudFormation template, you can use variables to be replaced when the template is executed. That format is ${VariableName}. You will find those variables in the following sections.

Let's start with the back-end layer.

Jakarta EE Using ECS, RDS, and Load Balancer

AWS offers different ways to deploy back-end layers using Java. For the purposes of this book, we are going to use the following services:

- S3

- InternetGateway

- VPC

- Subnet

- RouteTable

- SecurityGroup

- ElasticLoadBalancingV2

- LogGroup

- ECS

- Roles

- RDS

In the following sections, we are going to build the infrastructure for the back-end layer by layer, from networking, passing through servers, and finishing with the creation on AWS.

Networking and Security Groups to Isolate Your Infrastructure

We need to define where our infrastructure components will live. In this case, they need to communicate with each other through the network to create the whole picture of the system. To do this, we need to put those components into the same network so they can see each other. Then, we define the following networking architecture (Figure 12-2).

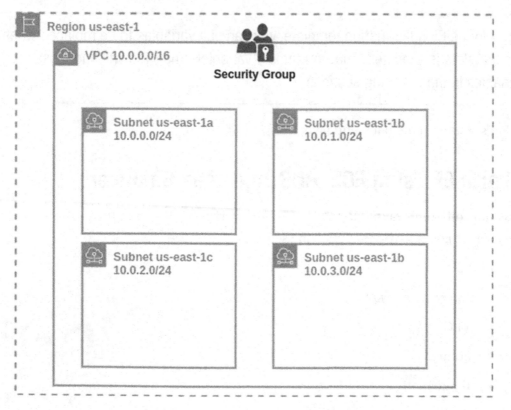

Figure 12-2. *Networking architecture for the new solution*

Let's see what those components mean.

VPC and Region

We define the network, in this case, the AWS service is called VPC (Virtual Private Cloud). We defined a CIDR (Classless Inter-Domain Routing), which defines which IPs will be available to use in this network; in this case, we define 10.0.0.0/16.

Each number is represented by 8 bits, which means the top IP you can have is 255.255.255.255. Adding the /16 means that this network is going to use just the last 16 bits, and the first 16 bits will be static. For instance, the following IPs are valid in this network:

- 10.0.12.75

- 10.0.78.128

- 10.0.250.2

As we can see, 10.0 is static through any IPs in this network.

Also, we choose the AWS region where the network is going to live, in this case, we chose us-east-1. Those regions are important because they are isolated for failures with each other, which means if us-east-1 fails, us-west-1 could be functional.

Tip   If you want to have a disaster recovery strategy, you should replicate your system in different AWS regions so that if one fails, you can still serve your users using a degraded mode in other regions. Of course, this costs more money like everything else in the cloud.

Now, let's see how this service is created using CloudFormation (Listing 12-1).

Listing 12-1. CloudFormation of VPC for Jakarta EE

```
DanielDeliveryJakartaVPC:
  Type: AWS::EC2::VPC
  Properties:
    CidrBlock: 10.0.0.0/16
    EnableDnsSupport: true
    EnableDnsHostnames: true
    Tags:
      - Key: "env"
        Value: !Sub ${Environment}
```

As we can see, we start defining the type as AWS::EC2::VPC. Next, we set the CIDR block, plus we enable the DNS support for hostnames, this is going to give access to a DNS server. This is useful to route into the VPC using the hostnames.

We don't specify the region where the VPC is going to live because that option is done by the subnets definition

Subnets

We create subnets in the network. A subnet is a set of IPs that belongs to the network. These subnets follow the same approach as the network itself, and in our case, we defined the following subnets:

- 10.0.0.0/24: For the first node of GlassFish server

- 10.0.1.0/24: For the second node of GlassFish server

- 10.0.2.0/24: For the master database

- 10.0.3.0/24: For the replica database

As we can see, these subnets belong to the main network, as the main network was defined as /16. These subnets are just using the last 8 bits for the addresses, and the other 24 will be static.

Subnetting is good when you want to split responsibilities in your network, assign efficiently IP addresses, and distribute them in different locations for better failover.

Notice that each subnet belongs to a subregion (availability zone), for instance, 10.0.1.0/24 belongs to us-east-1b. This availability zone is a logical data center that is part of a region. This means you can have multiple services in a region, in different availability zones, to improve the disaster recovery strategy.

Now, let's see how this service is created using CloudFormation (Listing 12-2).

Listing 12-2. CloudFormation of Subnets for Jakarta EE

```
DanielDeliveryJakartaSubnet1:
  Type: AWS::EC2::Subnet
  Properties:
    VpcId: !Ref DanielDeliveryJakartaVPC
    CidrBlock: 10.0.0.0/24
    AvailabilityZone: "us-east-1a"
```

```
    Tags:
      - Key: "env"
        Value: !Sub ${Environment}

DanielDeliveryJakartaSubnet2:
  Type: AWS::EC2::Subnet
  Properties:
    VpcId: !Ref DanielDeliveryJakartaVPC
    CidrBlock: 10.0.1.0/24
    AvailabilityZone: "us-east-1b"
    Tags:
      - Key: "env"
        Value: !Sub ${Environment}

DanielDeliveryJakartaSubnetDBMaster:
  Type: AWS::EC2::Subnet
  Properties:
    VpcId: !Ref DanielDeliveryJakartaVPC
    CidrBlock: 10.0.2.0/24
    AvailabilityZone: "us-east-1c"
    MapPublicIpOnLaunch: true
    Tags:
      - Key: "env"
        Value: !Sub ${Environment}

DanielDeliveryJakartaSubnetDBReplica:
  Type: AWS::EC2::Subnet
  Properties:
    VpcId: !Ref DanielDeliveryJakartaVPC
    CidrBlock: 10.0.3.0/24
    AvailabilityZone: "us-east-1b"
    MapPublicIpOnLaunch: true
    Tags:
      - Key: "env"
        Value: !Sub ${Environment}
```

By each subnet, we define the CIDR block, which VPC belongs to; the availability zone; and finally, MapPublicIpOnLaunch to receive a public IP when a service is launched in this subnet, which in our case will be a GlassFish server or a database.

!Ref is a special operator in CloudFormation that helps to get a reference from another object previously created in the same CloudFormation execution file.

Security Group

Finally, we need to define a Security Group for this VPC. A Security Group is a set of rules and constraints on how the inbound and outbound network traffic works.

Now, let's see how this service is created using CloudFormation (Listing 12-3).

Listing 12-3. Cloud Formation of Security group for Jakarta EE

```
DanielDeliveryJakartaSecurityGroup:
  Type: AWS::EC2::SecurityGroup
  Properties:
    GroupDescription: Security group for loadbalancer
    VpcId: !Ref DanielDeliveryJakartaVPC
    SecurityGroupIngress:
      - CidrIp: 0.0.0.0/0
        IpProtocol: -1
    SecurityGroupEgress:
      - IpProtocol: -1
        CidrIp: 0.0.0.0/0
    Tags:
      - Key: "env"
        Value: !Sub ${Environment}
```

There, we associate this security group with our VPC, plus we define the ingress and egress rules. 0.0.0.0/0 means that this security group allows the inbound and outbound connections from/to any IP, and -1 from/to any port.

You shouldn't do this for the real environments because you are allowing everything. You should restrict the inbound access as much as possible. In the case of the outbound access, typically you let them open as you might need to connect from your VPC to the external world to any IP/port, for instance, to download updated packages or call other services.

An Internet Gateway to Access the World

Now we need to connect our network with the external world (Internet), to have inbound and outbound connections.

For this purpose, we need to create an Internet Gateway. Figure 12-3 illustrates this.

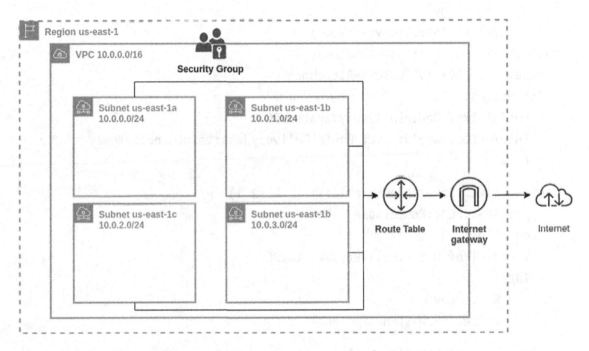

Figure 12-3. *Networking architecture to connect to the Internet*

There, we add the Internet Gateway to our infrastructure. This gateway has a direct connection with the Internet. Plus, we need to associate a routing table to that Internet Gateway.

A routing table is a set of rules regarding what traffic can inbound/outbound into the VPC. It is a firewall at the subnet level.

Now, let's see how this service is created using CloudFormation (Listing 12-4).

Listing 12-4. Cloud Formation of the Internet gateway for Jakarta EE

```
DanielDeliveryJakartaInternetGateway:    # (1.1)
  Type: AWS::EC2::InternetGateway
  Properties:
    Tags:
      - Key: "env"
        Value: !Sub ${Environment}
DanielDeliveryJakartaAttachGateway:
  Type: AWS::EC2::VPCGatewayAttachment
  Properties:
    VpcId: !Ref DanielDeliveryJakartaVPC
    InternetGatewayId: !Ref DanielDeliveryJakartaInternetGateway    #
    (1.2)

DanielDeliveryJakartaRouteTable:      # (2.1)
  Type: AWS::EC2::RouteTable
  Properties:
    VpcId: !Ref DanielDeliveryJakartaVPC
    Tags:
      - Key: "env"
        Value: !Sub ${Environment}

DanielDeliveryJakartaInternetRoute:
  Type: AWS::EC2::Route
  DependsOn: DanielDeliveryJakartaAttachGateway
  Properties:
    DestinationCidrBlock: 0.0.0.0/0
    GatewayId: !Ref DanielDeliveryJakartaInternetGateway    # (2.2)
    RouteTableId: !Ref DanielDeliveryJakartaRouteTable

DanielDeliveryJakartaSubnet1RouteTableAssociation:
  Type: AWS::EC2::SubnetRouteTableAssociation
  Properties:
    RouteTableId: !Ref DanielDeliveryJakartaRouteTable    # (3.1)
    SubnetId: !Ref DanielDeliveryJakartaSubnet1
```

```
DanielDeliveryJakartaSubnet2RouteTableAssociation:
  Type: AWS::EC2::SubnetRouteTableAssociation
  Properties:
    RouteTableId: !Ref DanielDeliveryJakartaRouteTable    # (3.2)
    SubnetId: !Ref DanielDeliveryJakartaSubnet2

DanielDeliveryJakartaSubnetDBMasterRouteTableAssociation:
  Type: AWS::EC2::SubnetRouteTableAssociation
  Properties:
    RouteTableId: !Ref DanielDeliveryJakartaRouteTable    # (3.3)
    SubnetId: !Ref DanielDeliveryJakartaSubnetDBMaster

DanielDeliveryJakartaSubnetDBReplicaRouteTableAssociation:
  Type: AWS::EC2::SubnetRouteTableAssociation
  Properties:
    RouteTableId: !Ref DanielDeliveryJakartaRouteTable    # (3.4)
    SubnetId: !Ref DanielDeliveryJakartaSubnetDBReplica
```

The following is a description of the code sample:

1. First, we create the Internet Gateway and attach it to the VCP.

2. Next, we define the Route Table and attach it to the Internet Gateway. We define a destination block of 0.0.0.0/0 meaning this route will allow every outbound connection to the Internet to any IP address.

3. And finally, we associate each subnet to the Route Table.

Now we have our network configuration ready. Let's add some servers to it.

Elastic Cloud Service (ECS) with GlassFish

Well, we need to deploy our GlassFish server somewhere. The following are the services AWS offers for it:

- EC2 (Elastic Compute Cloud): This service gives us a machine you can run in the cloud. That machine will have a basic operative system, for instance, Linux or Windows. This service is good when you need to have control over everything, from upgrading your operative system, to installing any packages/applications you need. This installation could be done using shell scripts.

- Elastic Beanstalk: This service defines a ready-to-go platform. This means the platform is ready to use and AWS manages it all, from upgrading the operative system to its underline platforms like servers and applications. For instance, you can find ready-to-go platforms for Python, .NET, and Node.js. For GlassFish, it offers a ready-to-go platform with GlassFish 5.0. You can find the supported platforms here: `https://docs.aws.amazon.com/elasticbeanstalk/latest/dg/concepts.platforms.html`

- ECS (Elastic Container Service): This service orchestrates containers. That means you define a container for your application (for instance, using Docker), and ECS will handle it, cluster, restore, and so on. The latest version uses AWS Fargate, and this service allows you to have serverless ECS clusters so that you won't worry about servers, you just will focus on your application. For more information about AWS Fargate, you can see it here: `https://aws.amazon.com/fargate/`

We don't want to use EC2 as the cost of maintenance is high. Elastic Beanstalk is a good option; however, it only offers GlassFish's old versions. So, we choose ECS.

ECS defines a Service and Tasks, and besides we need an ECR (Elastic Container Registry) to save our containers. Figure 12-4 shows how they work together.

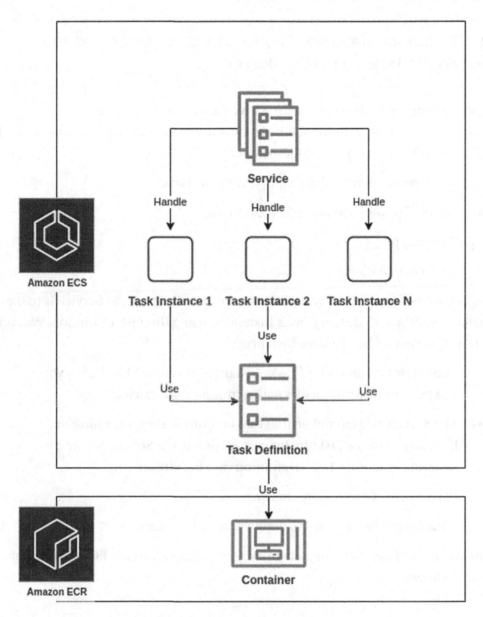

Figure 12-4. *Containers and services using ECS*

First, we have a Docker container. That is a way to encapsulate everything regarding our application, from the operative systems and packages to servers and enterprise applications. For our case, we will have a docker container with our GlassFish server and the new Daniel's Delivery website deployed there.

Note   For more information about Docker containers, you can read here:
`https://www.docker.com/why-docker`.

That container is pushed to the ECR, so we can access it later.

Next, we have a Task Definition. It has how our application is going to work, so there we define the following properties, for instance:

- Machine properties like memory, CPU, and so on.

- Which Docker container you want to use.

- Port mappings.

- Log configuration.

And finally, we have the Service. The main responsibility of the Service is to handle the cluster, creating or destroying Tasks Instances, using the Task Definition. We can define how this Service behaves, for instance:

- The minimum amount of Tasks Instances running: This means you can have a cluster of servers with a minimum of capacity.

- The Service will guarantee that that amount is always running, so, if for any reason a Tasks Instance goes down, the Service is going to instantiate another Tasks Definition into the cluster.

- Percentage of the healthy cluster.

- Which subnets you want to deploy the Tasks Instances.

Now we need to associate the networking infrastructure to the ECS deployments as Figure 12-5 shows.

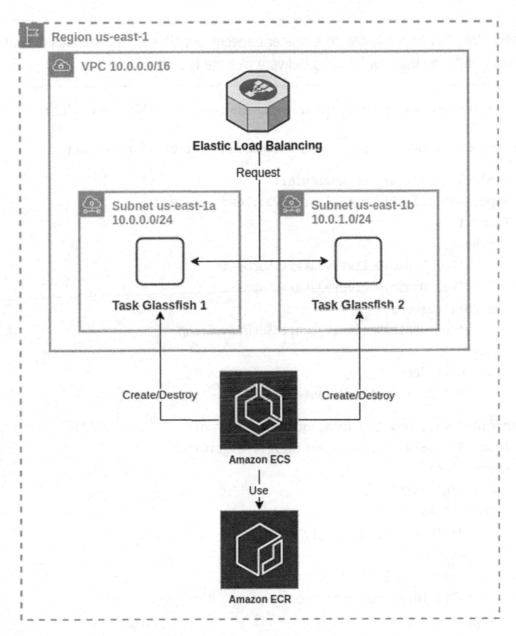

Figure 12-5. *Elastic load balancer and ECS*

There we associate our two previously created subnets to the ECS so that it can use them to create Tasks Instances. Besides, we need load balancing to balance the load between the two GlassFish instances.

> **Note**   We don't need to create a cluster between our GlassFish instances to share session data, as the new Daniel's Delivery website is stateless.

Now, let's see how this infrastructure is created using CloudFormation (Listing 12-5).

Listing 12-5. Cloud Formation of load balancer and ECS for Jakarta EE

```
DanielDeliveryJakartaLoadBalancer:                    # (1)
  Type: AWS::ElasticLoadBalancingV2::LoadBalancer
  Properties:
    Subnets:
      - !Ref DanielDeliveryJakartaSubnet1
      - !Ref DanielDeliveryJakartaSubnet2
    SecurityGroups:
      - !Ref DanielDeliveryJakartaSecurityGroup
    Tags:
      - Key: "env"
        Value: !Sub ${Environment}

DanielDeliveryJakartaLoadBalancerTargetGroup:         # (2)
  Type: AWS::ElasticLoadBalancingV2::TargetGroup
  Properties:
    Protocol: HTTP
    Port: 8080
    VpcId: !Ref DanielDeliveryJakartaVPC
    TargetType: ip
    HealthyThresholdCount: 2
    UnhealthyThresholdCount: 10            # (3)
    Tags:
      - Key: "env"
        Value: !Sub ${Environment}

DanielDeliveryJakartaLoadBalancerListener:            # (4)
  Type: AWS::ElasticLoadBalancingV2::Listener
  Properties:
    LoadBalancerArn: !Ref DanielDeliveryJakartaLoadBalancer
```

```
      Protocol: HTTP
      Port: 8080
      DefaultActions:
        - Type: forward
          TargetGroupArn: !Ref DanielDeliveryJakartaLoadBalancerTargetGroup

  DanielDeliveryJakartaECSCloudWatchLogsGroup:            # (5)
    Type: AWS::Logs::LogGroup
    Properties:
      LogGroupName: !Sub /aws/ecs/daniel-delivery-jakartaee-ecs-
${Environment}
      RetentionInDays: 7

  DanielDeliveryJakartaECSCluster:                        # (6)
    Type: AWS::ECS::Cluster
    Properties:
      ClusterName: !Sub daniel-delivery-jakartaee-ecs-${Environment}
      Tags:
        - Key: "env"
          Value: !Sub ${Environment}

  DanielDeliveryECSRole:                                  # (7)
    Type: AWS::IAM::Role
    Properties:
      AssumeRolePolicyDocument:
        Version: 2012-10-17
        Statement:
          - Effect: Allow
            Principal:
              Service:
                - ecs-tasks.amazonaws.com
            Action: 'sts:AssumeRole'
      Path: /
      Policies:
        - PolicyName: !Sub daniel-delivery-jakartaee-po-${Environment}
          PolicyDocument:
            Version: 2012-10-17
```

```yaml
            Statement:
              - Effect: Allow
                Action: '*'
                Resource: '*'

  DanielDeliveryJakartaECSTaskDefinition:                         # (8)
    Type: AWS::ECS::TaskDefinition
    Properties:
      Memory: 1024
      Cpu: 512
      NetworkMode: awsvpc
      RequiresCompatibilities:
        - 'FARGATE'
      TaskRoleArn: !Ref DanielDeliveryECSRole
      ExecutionRoleArn: !Ref DanielDeliveryECSRole
      ContainerDefinitions:
        - Name: !Sub daniel-delivery-jakartaee-cd-${Environment}
          Image: !Sub ${ECRUrl}:${Environment}
          PortMappings:
            - ContainerPort: 8080
          LogConfiguration:
            LogDriver: awslogs
            Options:
              awslogs-group: !Ref DanielDeliveryJakartaECSCloudWatchLogs
              Group
              awslogs-region: !Ref AWS::Region
              awslogs-stream-prefix: daniel-delivery
      Tags:
        - Key: "env"
          Value: !Sub ${Environment}

  DanielDeliveryJakartaECSService:                                # (9)
    Type: AWS::ECS::Service
    DependsOn:
    - DanielDeliveryJakartaLoadBalancer
    - DanielDeliveryJakartaLoadBalancerTargetGroup
```

```
Properties:
  ServiceName: !Sub daniel-delivery-jakartaee-ser-${Environment}
  TaskDefinition: !Ref DanielDeliveryJakartaECSTaskDefinition
  LaunchType: FARGATE
  DesiredCount: 1
  LoadBalancers:
  - TargetGroupArn: !Ref DanielDeliveryJakartaLoadBalancerTargetGroup
    ContainerPort: 8080
    ContainerName: !Sub daniel-delivery-jakartaee-cd-${Environment}
  Cluster: !Ref DanielDeliveryJakartaECSCluster
  DeploymentConfiguration:
    MaximumPercent: 100
    MinimumHealthyPercent: 0
  NetworkConfiguration:
    AwsvpcConfiguration:
      AssignPublicIp: ENABLED
      Subnets:
        - !Ref DanielDeliveryJakartaSubnet1
        - !Ref DanielDeliveryJakartaSubnet2
      SecurityGroups:
        - !Ref DanielDeliveryJakartaSecurityGroup
  Tags:
    - Key: "env"
      Value: !Sub ${Environment}
```

The following is a description of the code sample:

1. First, we create the Elastic Load Balancing associated with the two subnets we want to use and the security group.

2. We create a Target Group for load balancing. This defines a set of traffic rules to the GlassFish instances. There, we associate the Target Group with our VPC. Besides this, we define the protocol, port, and target type that it is going to use to call the GlassFish server.

The load balancing configuration is important, on one hand, because it is used by the ECS service to verify if the Tasks Instances (the GlassFish server) are healthy or not, so, it can create/destroy instances. For our case, we define a healthy count of 2, meaning that if the load balancing pings a Task Instance twice, and get a response, the load balancing declares that instance as healthy.

On the other hand, we define the unhealthy count to 10, meaning that if the load balancing pings 10 times a Task Instance and gets no live signals, the load balancing declares that instance as unhealthy. The unhealthy instances are destroyed by the ECS service.

3. The default time between pings is 30 seconds. That means, to declare an instance unhealthy, the instance needs to respond with no life for 300 seconds (10 times by 30 seconds). That is 5 minutes - this could be huge for transactional high-reliability applications, so, measure that time carefully.

4. Now, we associate the Target Group with the Load Balancing, defining that any request is going to be forwarded to the Target Group.

5. Of course, we need to save the application logs of our instances somewhere to monitor, so, we create a Group Log in Cloud Watch. We are going to talk about AWS Cloud Watch in the following chapter.

6. Next, we create an ECS cluster: ECS Service needs to create/destroy Task Instance. This means one AWS service needs to create/destroy other AWS services. We need to explicitly tell AWS which AWS service has rights to modify other AWS services, and this is called a Role.

7. There, we define the Role, who (ecs-tasks.amazonaws.com) is going to modify other AWS services. Those rights are specified in the Statement section; in this case, we allow every action to every AWS service.

This is not a good practice; you should restrict as much as you can the right access to the AWS service. For the purposes of this book, we are not going to go deep into this topic.

8. Following that, we define how the Task Definition is going to be structured. We define the tasks as Fargate (serverless service), the Role to execute tasks, the memory, and CPU for the instance; which Docker image we want to use and where it is; plus, a log definition to save any log our GlassFish server creates.

   The memory and CPU here were randomly chosen. You should validate how much memory and CPU your application needs, typically any server requires at least a minimum. You can find some information regarding GlassFish here https://eclipse-ee4j.github.io/glassfish/docs/latest/performance-tuning-guide.pdf

9. Now we define the ECS Service. There, we associate the Task Definition, subnets, security groups, ECS cluster, Docker container image, and load balancing. ECS Service requires at least two subnets,

   DesiredAccount property is important. It defines how many Task Instances the Service must have running at the same time. Also, the Deployment configuration tells how healthy the cluster could be before the Service takes any action to fix it.

With this, our ECS cluster of GlassFish servers is ready. Let's move to create the Docker container repository.

ECR (Elastic Container Registry) to Save the Docker Containers

Docker images are saved in a registry for future use. AWS offers this service through the ECR. We usually need one ECR for the whole organization, so we are going to create that service using the AWS console:

1. Log into the AWS console.

2. Search for the service ECR.

3. Click in the Create Repository option. You will see something like Figure 12-6.

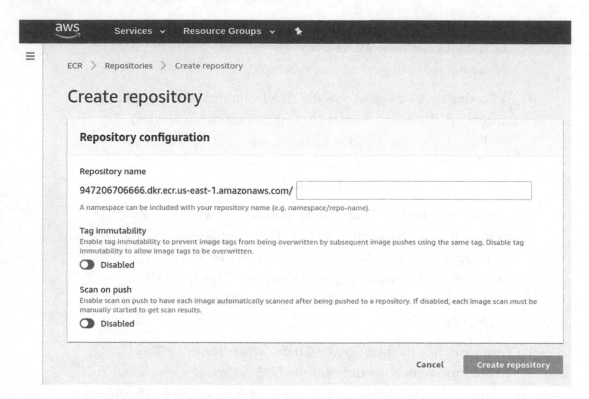

Figure 12-6. *Creating an ECR repository in AWS*

4. Define the name of your repository if you don't want to override
    your tags and if you want a push scan. For the new Daniel's
    Delivery website, we use the repository name newdanieldelivery.

Now, we can move to the MySQL database definition.

Relational Database Service (RDS) with MySQL

RDS is the relational database service provided by AWS. There you can find multiple
relational databases to use. For our case, we are going to use a MySQL database.

Tip   You can find the databases engines supported here: `https://aws.`
`amazon.com/rds/`.

RDS abstracts the maintenance problem of databases. It handles everything from
windows maintenance, upgrades, read replica, storage, snapshots, and so on.

This is how we add the RDS to our architecture (Figure 12-7).

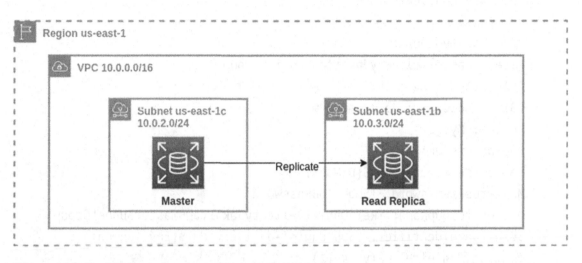

Figure 12-7. *RDS and networking architecture*

A read replica is a database that just serves queries but is not transactional, which means you can create/update any data in a read replica. That is useful to improve the reading performance of your application. However, it is costly as the master database needs to replicate any create/update of data to the read replicate in real time.

Now, let's see how this infrastructure is created using CloudFormation (Listing 12-6).

Listing 12-6. Cloud Formation of RDS for Jakarta EE

```
DanielDeliveryJakartaDBMasterSubnetGroup:        # (1)
  Type: AWS::RDS::DBSubnetGroup
  Properties:
    DBSubnetGroupDescription: DBSubnetGroup for RDS instances
    SubnetIds:
      - Ref: DanielDeliveryJakartaSubnetDBMaster
      - Ref: DanielDeliveryJakartaSubnetDBReplica
    Tags:
      - Key: "env"
        Value: !Sub ${Environment}
```

```
DanielDeliveryMySQL:
  Type: AWS::RDS::DBInstance
  Properties:
    VPCSecurityGroups:
    - Ref: DanielDeliveryJakartaSecurityGroup
    AllocatedStorage: '5'
    DBInstanceClass: db.m3.medium      # (3)
    Engine: MySQL
    EngineVersion: 8.0
    MasterUsername: !Sub ${DBUser}
    MasterUserPassword: !Sub ${DBPassword}
    DBSubnetGroupName: !Ref DanielDeliveryJakartaDBMasterSubnetGroup
    DBInstanceIdentifier: !Sub daniel-delivery-db-${Environment}
    DBName: danieldelivery  # (2)
    Tags:
      - Key: "env"
        Value: !Sub ${Environment}
```

The following is a description of the code sample:

1. We create a DB subnet group where our database is going to live. There, we just associate the two subnets previously created.

2. And we create the master database linking the security group and the DB subnet group.

3. DBName parameter tells RDS which database to create the first time this RDS is created. We also define the user and password for the database.

4. Next we define the database instance as a MySQL 8.0 in a db.m3. medium machine with 5 GB of storage. As we notice for the ECS Task Definition, you should validate those machine needs for your specific needs.

As our database is ready, let's define where we are going to save the images for our new Daniel's Delivery website.

S3 to Save Images

The new Daniel's Delivery website associates images to any Food Service and Food Product. Those images have been saved into the file system of our GlassFish server lives. As we move to the cloud, we want to save those images in another place, and in this case, we choose AWS S3 service.

AWS S3 is a service that allows high availability and "infinite" storage. By "infinite," this means that the services automatically expand when it is needed. It has a set of buckets where you save the files you want.

Now, we need to adapt our new Daniel's Delivery website to support this. Let's talk about it.

Extending the Jakarta EE Application to Support AWS S3

Let's see this step by step. First, we need to add the AWS S3 dependency to the pom.xml (Listing 12-7).

Listing 12-7. AWS SDK Maven dependency

```
<dependency>
 <groupId>com.amazonaws</groupId>
 <artifactId>aws-java-sdk-s3</artifactId>
 <version>1.11.691</version>
</dependency>
```

Next, we create a new implementation of StorageService interfaces: in this case, S3StorageService. There, we are going to use the AmazonS3 client to push and retrieve objects from AWS S3. You can find the whole implementation in the GitHub repository (Listing 12-8).

Listing 12-8. New StorageService implementation using AWS S3

```
public class S3StorageService implements StorageService {
    private final String clientRegion;
    private final String bucketName;
    private final AmazonS3 s3Client;
```

```java
    public S3StorageService(String clientRegion, String bucketName,
    AmazonS3 s3Client) {
        this.clientRegion = clientRegion;
        this.bucketName = bucketName;
        this.s3Client = s3Client;
    }

    @Override
    public String save(String fileName, InputStream inputStream) throws
    IOException {
        try {
            String fileKey = UUID.randomUUID().toString() + "-" + fileName;

            ObjectMetadata metadata = new ObjectMetadata();
            PutObjectRequest request = new PutObjectRequest(bucketName,
            fileKey, inputStream, metadata);

            s3Client.putObject(request);

            return fileKey;
        } catch (AmazonServiceException e) {
            throw new IOException(e);
        } catch (SdkClientException e) {
            throw new IOException(e);
        }
    }

    @Override
    public InputStream load(String fileName) throws IOException {
        GetObjectRequest request = new GetObjectRequest(bucketName,
        fileName);

        S3Object object = s3Client.getObject(request);

        return object.getObjectContent();
    }

}
```

Now, we want to somehow mark this implementation as an AWS implementation, so we create a new alternative named AWSEnvironment (Listing 12-9).

Listing 12-9. New AWSEnvironment stereotype to annotation the AWS classes related with infrastructure

```
@Stereotype
@Alternative
@Stereotype
@Alternative
@Target( { TYPE, METHOD, FIELD })
@Retention(RUNTIME)
public @interface AWSEnvironment {
}
```

This annotation is going to tell Jakarta EE which implementation we want to use depending on the beans.xml configuration. We are going to talk about this in the following sections.

Finally, we instantiate what we need for this new class (Listing 12-10).

Listing 12-10. Setting up the S3 AWS client and the new StorageService implementation

```
@Produces
public AmazonS3 getS3Client(Properties properties){
    return AmazonS3ClientBuilder.standard()
                .withRegion(properties.getProperty("IMAGES_S3_REGION"))
                .build();
}

@Produces
@AWSEnvironment
public StorageService getS3StorageService(Properties properties,
AmazonS3 s3Client) {
    return new S3StorageService(properties.getProperty("IMAGES_S3_
    REGION"), properties.getProperty("IMAGES_S3_BUCKET"), s3Client);
}
```

As we can see, getS3StorageService method is annotated by @AWSEnvironment.

Defining the AWS S3 Bucket

Now, let's see how this infrastructure is created using CloudFormation (Listing 12-11).

Listing 12-11. CloudFormation for a S3 bucket to save images

```
DanielDeliveryImagesBucket:
  Type: AWS::S3::Bucket
  Properties:
    BucketName: !Sub daniel-delivery-images-${Environment}
```

As we can see, creating an S3 Bucket is pretty straightforward.

Creating a Back-End Environment with CloudFormation

Now we are going to create the full back-end infrastructure using CloudFormation for the back end of the new Daniel's Delivery website.

For the purposes of this book, we are going to create a development environment. Although the production environment is pretty similar, you still need to consider more security constraints. As we have a CloudFormation template, we can create as many environments as we want.

Tip   You can find the whole CloudFormation template here: https://github.com/
Apress/full-stack-web-development-with-jakartaee-and-vue.js/
blob/master/CH12-13/aws/jakarta-environment.yaml.

---

1. First, we need to add some headers to the CloudFormation snippets we created before (Listing 12-12).

Listing 12-12. CloudFormation parameters for the Jakarata EE environment

```
Parameters:
  Environment:
    Description: Environment
    Type: String
    Default: dev
  ECRUrl:
```

```
    Description: ECRUrl
    Type: String
    Default: ecrurl
  DBUser:
    Description: DBUser
    Type: String
    Default: MyName
  DBPassword:
    Description: DBPassword
    Type: String
    Default: MyPassword
Resources:
```

There, we define some parameters to be defined when we execute
the CloudFormation. In this case, we define the environment we
want to create, the URL of the ECR, and the user and password
we want to set for the database. Those parameters are used in
the CloudFormation snippets we defined before as ${Variable}
syntaxis. Resources are the whole AWS services we defined in
previous sections.

2. Now, log into the AWS console.

3. Search for the service IAM, section Roles.

4. Check if a role named AWSServiceRoleForECS exists; otherwise,
    you will need to create one using the AWS CLI.

    a. Log into AWS using the AWS CLI.

    b. Execute the following command in your local machine: aws iam
        create-service-linked-role --aws-service-name ecs.amazonaws.
        com This role is required to create ECS services. You can find more
        information here: https://docs.aws.amazon.com/AmazonECS/
        latest/developerguide/using-service-linked-roles.
        html#create-service-linked-role

5. Now, Search for the service Cloud Formation.

6. Click on Create Stack. You will see something like Figure 12-8.

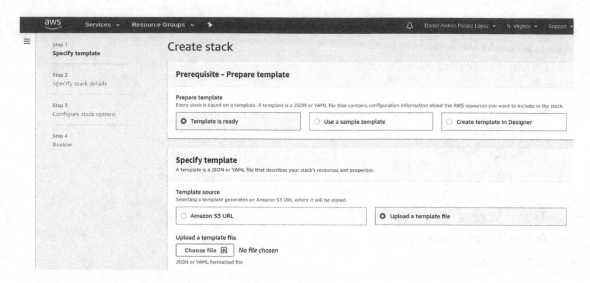

Figure 12-8. *Create Cloudformation stack for the back-end layer*

7. Choose Template is ready and Upload a template file; next, upload
    the template with the options Choose file.

8. Click next. You will see something like Figure 12-9.

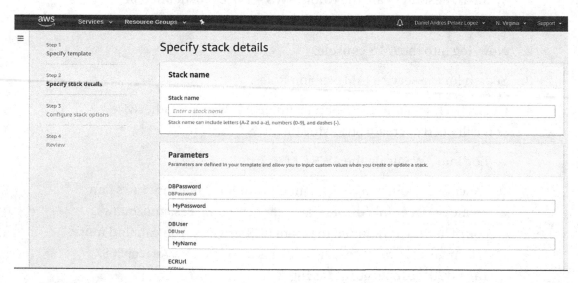

Figure 12-9. *Create CloudFormation stack for the back-end layer with parameters*

9. Set a stack name: in this case, it is jakarta-environment-dev. Set the parameters like database user and password, ECR URL and environment, for example, dev. The ECR URL looks like xxxxxxx. dkr.ecr.us-east-1.amazonaws.com/newdanieldelivery

   After the database is created, you might want to change the password manually to increase security.

10. Click next. You will be able to set tags and extra information for your new stack like reusing Roles.

11. Click next, and you will see the summary of your CloudFormation execution. You will need to acknowledge that you will created roles.

12. Click Create Stack.

13. CloudFormation starts to create the new stack, but it takes time depending on the services you are creating.

14. At some point, CloudFormation is going to be blocked trying to create the ECS Service. This is due to it being an ECS Service; it will try to accomplish the DesiredAccount of 1 Task instance, but, it is going to try to download the Docker image from the ECR and won't find any, so, the Task instance never starts up, and the ECS Service never stabilizes, so CloudFormation never knows that the ECS was created (Figure 12-10).

Events (75)

Q *Search events*

Timestamp	Logical ID	Status	Status reason
2020-04-04 15:23:04 UTC-0500	DanielDeliveryJakartaECSService	ⓘ CREATE_IN_PROGRESS	Resource creation Initiated
2020-04-04 15:23:04 UTC-0500	DanielDeliveryJakartaECSService	ⓘ CREATE_IN_PROGRESS	Not able to add tag on resou new ARN and resource ID fo add tags to the service

Figure 12-10. *CloudFormation blocked by the ECS checkpoints*

15. To fix this, you should do the following:

    a. Search for the service ECS.

    b. Click on your ECS cluster just created.

    c. Click on the ECS Service.

    d. Click on Update.

    e. Update the Number of tasks to 0.

    f. Click on Skip to Review.

    g. Click on Update Service.

16. Return to the CloudFormation and wait for it to pass the block.

17. Return to the ECS cluster and modify the Number of tasks again to
    the number wanted. You can find more information regarding this
    issue here: `https://docs.aws.amazon.com/AmazonECS/latest/`
    `developerguide/using-service-linked-roles.html#create-`
    `service-linked-role`

18. After the CloudFormation finishes, you will see the summary of all
    of the resources it created (Figure 12-11).

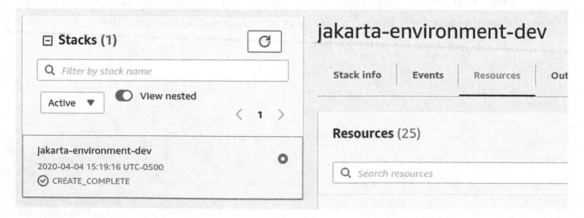

Figure 12-11. *CloudFormation created for the back-end layer*

Now, you will find there all the resources you created, and you can see them through
the console of any of those respective services.

As the back-end environment is ready, let's move to define the front-end infrastructure.

VueJS Using S3 and CloudFront

AWS offers different ways to deploy front-end layers for SPA. As Vue.js just need to be deployed as a static website, we are going to use the following services:

- S3

- CloudFront

Any SPA serves just the index.html plus JavaScript files. That means, we just need a server that serves those files. That server could be a Node.js or a Java one like Apache. Actually, we would be able to deploy a WAR application into the same GlassFish server. However, it is easier to use the more straightforward approach using S3 and CloudFront.

In the following sections, we are going to build the infrastructure for the front end and create them in AWS.

S3 as Static Web Pages Resource

S3 offers "infinitive" storage. That storage can be accessed by external or internal services in AWS.

There, we are going to deploy our Vue.js application. We can configure the S3 Bucket in two ways:

- S3 public static web site: This approach transforms an S3 bucket in a public static web site, so, the web resources can be accessed directly by a URL. This has some restrictions, for instance, we cannot use HTTPs connections, and, you cannot set up cache resources.

- S3 normal bucket: The bucket just saves our Vue.js application and cannot be accessed directly by a URL.

In production environments where we need a high-available front-end layer, it is important to add cache features to the solution, so, we are going to use the S3 normal bucket approach and delegate the cache features to CloudFront. (We are going to talk about this in the following section.)

Now, let's see how this infrastructure is created using S3 (Listing 12-13).

Listing 12-13. CloudFormation to create the S3 backet for the Vue.js app

```
S3Bucket:
  Type: AWS::S3::Bucket
  Properties:
    BucketName: !Sub newdanieldelivery${Environment}
S3BucketPolicy:
  Type: AWS::S3::BucketPolicy
  Properties:
    Bucket: !Ref S3Bucket
    PolicyDocument:
      Statement:
        -
          Action:
            - "s3:GetObject"
          Effect: "Allow"
          Resource:
            Fn::Join:
              - ""
              -
                - "arn:aws:s3:::"
                - !Ref S3Bucket
                - "/*"
          Principal:
            AWS: "*"
```

Well, we just defined where our Vue.js application will live, so now let's open the application to the world using CloudFront.

CloudFront to Serve HTTPS and Cache Services

CloudFront is an AWS service that allows us to have AWS services close to the final users; it is a content delivery service. In our case, we want to serve and cache static resources using the Content Delivery Network of CloudFront.

The Content Delivery Network is a network of regional edge caches that allows to speed up the delivery of static content to the final users. Those edge caches are close to the final users, for instance, if the application is deployed in the United States and you request the web page from Brazil, the first time you request that web resource, the Content Delivery Network of Brazil is going to request the content to the United States, and cache it to have it available for the following requests. The second time you request the web resource, the Content Delivery Network of Brazil will serve what it has in the cache, so, it doesn't need to request the content to the United States.

Figure 12-12 illustrates that use case.

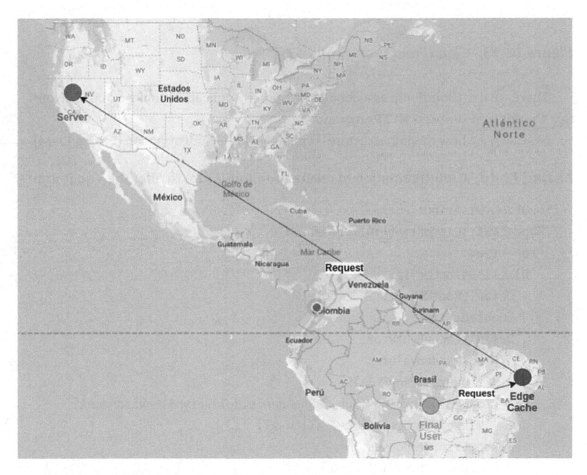

Figure 12-12. *CloudFront strategy*

You can find all of the edge locations here: https://aws.amazon.com/cloudfront/features/

Now, let's see how CloudFront is used with S3 as our front-end environment (Figure 12-13).

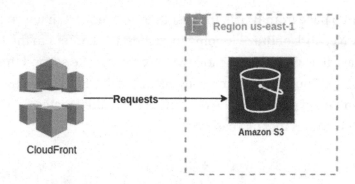

Figure 12-13. *CloudFront strategy and S3*

There we use CloudFront as a door for our Vue.js application deployed on S3. Note that CloudFront supports HTTPs requests.

Now let's see how this infrastructure is created using CloudFormation (Listing 12-14).

Listing 12-14. CloudFormation to create the CloudFront to offer the Vue.js app

```
CloudFrontDistribution:
  Type: AWS::CloudFront::Distribution
  Properties:
    DistributionConfig:
      DefaultRootObject: index.html
      Enabled: true
      DefaultCacheBehavior:
          ForwardedValues:
            QueryString: false
          TargetOriginId: !Sub S3-newdanieldeliveryp${Environment}
          ViewerProtocolPolicy: allow-all
      CustomErrorResponses:
        - ErrorCachingMinTTL: 0
          ErrorCode: 404
          ResponseCode: 200
          ResponsePagePath: /index.html
        - ErrorCachingMinTTL: 0
          ErrorCode: 403
          ResponseCode: 200
          ResponsePagePath: /index.html
```

```
    Origins:
      - Id: !Sub S3-newdanieldeliveryp${Environment}
        DomainName: !Sub newdanieldelivery${Environment}.s3.
        amazonaws.com
        S3OriginConfig:
          OriginAccessIdentity: ''
  Tags:
    - Key: "env"
      Value: !Sub ${Environment}
```

There we define which default object is going to be called by default, in this case, index.html. We also allow all kinds of connections: HTTP and HTTPs.

Next, we define a custom error page. This configuration means that if a 404 error (not page found) occurs, CloudFront is going to redirect to index.html. The goal of this setup is to allow the SPA to redirect always to the index.html as that is how they work.

And finally, we define the origin, who CloudFront is going to connect to. In this case, we set the S3 bucket name we created before as a domain name.

As we can see, the environment for the Vue.js application is less complex than the back-end layer. Now, let's create an environment using this configuration.

Creating a Front-End Environment with CloudFormation

Now, we are going to create the full front-end infrastructure using CloudFormation for the new Daniel's Delivery website.

1. First, we need to add some headers to the CloudFormation snippets we created before (Listing 12-15).

Listing 12-15. Parameters used to the CloudFormation for Vue.js

```
Parameters:
  Environment:
    Description: Environment
    Type: String
    Default: dev
```

There, we just define the environment variable.

2. Now, log in into the AWS console

3. Search for the service CloudFormation.

4. Click on Create Stack. You will see something like Figure 12-14.

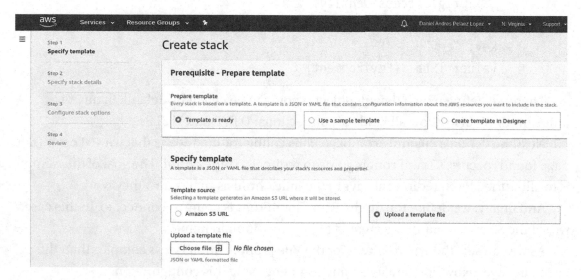

Figure 12-14. *Creating CloudFormation stack for Vue.js*

5. Choose Template is ready and Upload a template file; next, upload the template with the options Choose file.

6. Click next. You will see something like Figure 12-15.

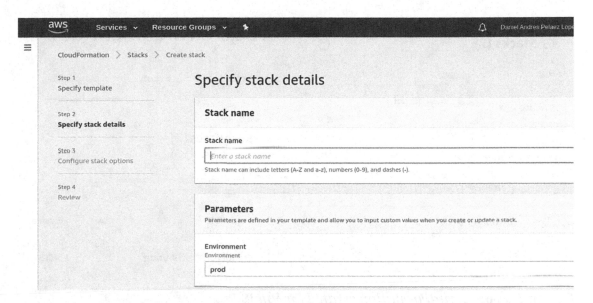

Figure 12-15. *Creating CloudFormation stack for Vue.js adding parameters*

7. Set a stack name: in this case, it is vuejs-environment-dev. Set the environment, for example, dev.

8. Click next. You will be able to set tags and extra information for your new stack like reusing Roles.

9. Click next, and you will see the summary of your CloudFormation execution. You will need to acknowledge that you will create roles.

10. Click Create Stack.

11. CloudFormation starts to create the new stack, and it takes time depending on the services you are creating. In the case of CloudFront, it can take at least 20 minutes to be deployed.

12. After the CloudFormation finishes, you will see the summary of all the resources it created (Figure 12-16).

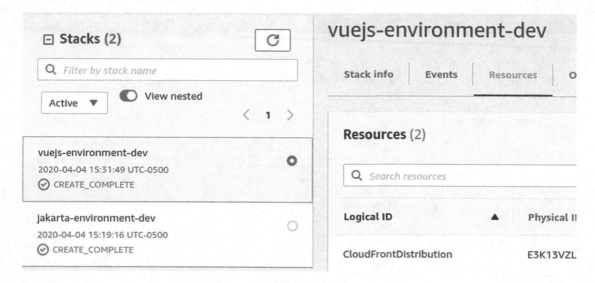

Figure 12-16. *CloudFormation created for VueJS*

You will now find there all the resources you created, and you can see them through the console of any of those respective services.

We just have our back-end and front-end environments ready. Let's create the SSO service using AWS Cognito.

SSO Using Cognito

In this entire book, we used Keycloak as an Identity Provider. Now, as we move to AWS, we want to use the services it offers, in this case, AWS Cognito.

AWS Cognito is an Identity Provider with pretty similar features to Keycloak. We are going to set up a Cognito User Pool and an Application Client for our new Daniel's Delivery website.

A User Pool is a set of features related to users, from their basic data like name, username, password, and address, to multifactor authentication.

An Application Client is an OpenId Connect configuration, where we define scopes, secrets, and so on.

First, we need to add support for AWS Cognito to the new Daniel's Delivery back end:

1. Add the dependency for AWS Cognito into the pom.xml (Listing 12-16).

Listing 12-16. Maven dependency for AWS Cognito client

```
<dependency>
 <groupId>com.amazonaws</groupId>
 <artifactId>aws-java-sdk-cognitoidp</artifactId>
 <version>1.11.693</version>
</dependency>
```

2. Next, we create a new implementation of
    FoodServiceRepository interface. There, we are going to use the
    AWSCognitoIdentityProvider client to modify the User Pool. You
    can find the whole implementation in the GitHub repository
    (Listing 12-17).

Listing 12-17. New FoodServiceRepository implementation to use AWS Cognito
as a source of Food Services

```
public class CognitoFoodServiceRepository implements FoodServiceRepository {

    private final AWSCognitoIdentityProvider awsCognitoIdentityProvider;
    private final String poolId;

    public CognitoFoodServiceRepository(AWSCognitoIdentityProvider
    awsCognitoIdentityProvider, String poolId) {
        this.awsCognitoIdentityProvider = awsCognitoIdentityProvider;
        this.poolId = poolId;
    }

// More code
}
```

3. Now, we instantiate what we need for this new class.

```
@Produces
public AWSCognitoIdentityProvider getCognitoClient(Properties
properties){
    return AWSCognitoIdentityProviderClientBuilder
            .standard()
```

```
                .withRegion(properties.getProperty("COGNITO_REGION"))
                .build();
    }

    @Produces
    @AWSEnvironment
    public CognitoFoodServiceRepository getCognitoFoodServiceRepository
    (Properties properties, AWSCognitoIdentityProvider awsCognito
    IdentityProvider) {
        return new CognitoFoodServiceRepository(awsCognitoIdentityProvider,
        properties.getProperty("COGNITO_POOL_ID"));
    }
```

As we can see, the getCognitoFoodServiceRepository method is annotated by @AWSEnvironment.

Now, let's see how this Cognito configuration is created using CloudFormation (Listing 12-18).

Listing 12-18. CloudFormation to create the AWS Cognito configuration

```
DanielDeliveryCognitoRole:
  Type: 'AWS::IAM::Role'
  Properties:
    AssumeRolePolicyDocument:
      Version: 2012-10-17
      Statement:
        - Effect: Allow
          Principal:
            Service:
              - cognito-idp.amazonaws.com
          Action: 'sts:AssumeRole'
    Path: /
    Policies:
      - PolicyName: AWS-NewDanielDelivery
        PolicyDocument:
          Version: 2012-10-17
          Statement:
```

```
          - Effect: Allow
            Action: '*'
            Resource: '*'

DanielDeliveryCognitoUserPool:
  Type: AWS::Cognito::UserPool
  Properties:
    Policies:
      PasswordPolicy:
        MinimumLength: 8
        RequireLowercase: true
        RequireNumbers: true
        RequireSymbols: true
        RequireUppercase: true
    Schema:
      - AttributeDataType: String
        Mutable: true
        Name: foodType
      - AttributeDataType: String
        Mutable: true
        Name: deliveryFee
      - AttributeDataType: String
        Mutable: true
        Name: imageUrl
      - AttributeDataType: String
        Mutable: true
        Required: true
        Name: address
      - AttributeDataType: String
        Mutable: true
        Required: true
        Name: given_name
      - AttributeDataType: String
        Mutable: true
        Required: true
        Name: family_name
```

```
        - AttributeDataType: String
          Mutable: true
          Required: true
          Name: email
      UsernameAttributes:
        - email
      UserPoolName: !Sub danieldeliveryuserpool${Environment}
      AutoVerifiedAttributes:
        - email

  DanielDeliveryCognitoClient:
    Type: AWS::Cognito::UserPoolClient
    Properties:
      AllowedOAuthFlows:
        - code
      AllowedOAuthFlowsUserPoolClient: true
      AllowedOAuthScopes:
        - email
        - openid
        - profile
      CallbackURLs:
        - http://localhost:8081/auth/
      ClientName: !Sub danieldeliverycognitoclient${Environment}
      GenerateSecret: true
      UserPoolId: !Ref DanielDeliveryCognitoUserPool
      SupportedIdentityProviders:
        - COGNITO
      PreventUserExistenceErrors: ENABLED

  DanielDeliveryCognitoDomain:
    Type: AWS::Cognito::UserPoolDomain
    Properties:
      Domain: !Sub danieldelivery${Environment}
      UserPoolId: !Ref DanielDeliveryCognitoUserPool
```

The following is a description of the code sample:

1. We create a role for the Cognito infrastructure.

2. Next, we define the User Pool.

   There, we define password policies like length and uppercases, custom user attributes like foodTypes and fee. Besides, we define that a user can use its email as a username and a way to verify the email. In this case, Cognito is going to send an email to the User's email address to validate it exists.

3. Now, we create the Application Client. There, we define an auth flow code, add the scopes for email, openid, and profile to define the OpenId configuration. We also define the callback after login. Cognito only accepts as a callback, localhost, or an HTTPs URL.

4. And finally, we set the domain that we want to use to access Cognito.

Creating an SSO Environment with CloudFormation

Now we are going to create the full Cognito infrastructure using CloudFormation for the new Daniel's Delivery website.

You can find the whole CloudFormation template here: `https://github.com/Apress/full-stack-web-development-with-jakartaee-and-vue.js/blob/master/CH12-13/aws/cognito-environment.yaml`.

1. First, we need to add some headers to the CloudFormation snippets we created before (Listing 12-19).

Listing 12-19. Parameters for CloudFormation to create the AWS Cognito configuration

```
Parameters:
  Environment:
    Description: Environment
    Type: String
    Default: dev
Resources:
```

There, we just define the environment variable.

2. Now, log into the AWS console

3. Search for the service Cloud Formation.

4. Click on Create Stack. You will see something like Figure 12-17.

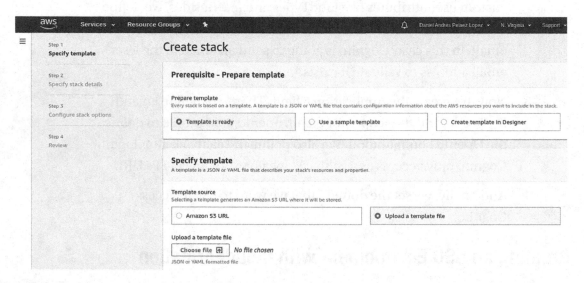

Figure 12-17. *Creating CloudFormation for AWS Cognito*

5. Choose Template is ready and Upload a template file; next, upload the template with the options Choose file.

6. Click next. You will see something like Figure 12-18.

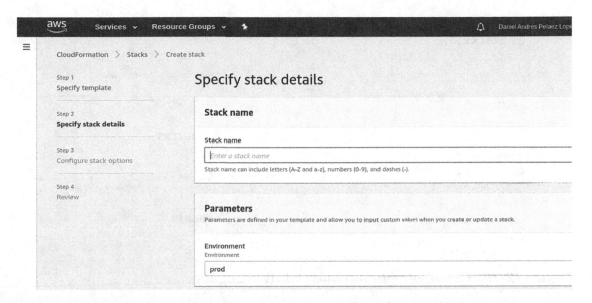

Figure 12-18. *Creating CloudFormation for AWS Cognito adding parameters*

Set a stack name, in this case, it is cognito-dev. Set the
environment, for example, dev.

7. Click next. You will be able to set tags and extra information for
    your new stack like reusing Roles.

8. Click next, and you will see the summary of your CloudFormation
    execution. You will need to acknowledge that you will create roles.

9. Click Create Stack. CloudFormation starts to create the new stack.

After the CloudFormation finishes, you will see the summary of all the resources it
created (Figure 12-19).

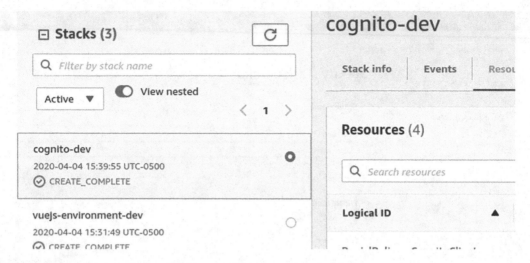

Figure 12-19. *CloudFormation created for AWS Cognito*

Now you will find there all the resources you created, and you can see them through the console of any of those respective services.

Summary

We just designed and implemented a full-stack infrastructure for our new Daniel's Delivery website using different AWS services like ECS, S3, and CloudFront.

Everything was done by infrastructure as code using CloudFormation templates so that we could rebuild our infrastructure as many times as we needed.

With this knowledge, you will be able to build a production-ready full-stack application using VueJS and Jakarta EE in the AWS cloud.

Although we talked about the infrastructure we need, how do we use it? How do we deploy our application in that infrastructure? Well, let's talk about continuous integration and deployment in the next chapter.

Extended Knowledge

- Where can I find the AWS certificates to HTTPs connections?
- How can I use Maven profiles to add/remove files into my EAR file?
- Can I set up my ECS cluster to do blue/green deployments?
- how much does new Daniel's Delivery infrastructure cost?
- Can I use an S3 bucket as a static web site?

## CHAPTER 13

Continuous Integration and Deployment

Continuous integration and deployment are mandatory features in current software projects. These two allow us to build software quickly, with less errors, full testing automation, and control over deployment.

In this chapter, we are going to define the new Daniel's Delivery website continuous integration and deployment pipelines, using AWS CodePipeline. Also, this will be a pipeline as code using CloudFormation, so we can create multiple pipelines for multiple environments.

The following topics will be covered in this chapter:

- Create a continuous integration and deployment pipeline for Jakarta EE

- Create a continuous integration and deployment pipeline for VueJS

Technical Requirements

- AWS account

- AWS CLI

We won't cover AWS account creation and AWS CLI installation.

What Are Continuous Integration and Deployment?

Continuous integration and deployment are strategies to improve the quality of the software products.

© Daniel Andres Pelaez Lopez 2021
D. A. P. Lopez, *Full-Stack Web Development with Jakarta EE and Vue.js*,
https://doi.org/10.1007/978-1-4842-6342-6_13

The idea behind Continuous Integration is to integrate everything the developer team has done so that you guarantee the entire production works as expected. For instance, you can run unit tests, integration tests, static code analysis, and so on. Those tools will give you confidence regarding the quality of the product.

Continuous deployment allows you to deploy your product automatically in environments like development, quality assurance, and so on. The final goal will be to deploy to production automatically. Of course, this step needs to be carefully crafted as it can generate problems for the final users.

To enable these features, we usually define a pipeline. A pipeline is a set of steps executed sequentially/parallel to analyze, build, and deploy our product.

As we have two main layers in our new Daniel's Delivery website, the front end and back end, we are going to create two pipelines for continuous integration and deployment.

Since we are using AWS as a cloud provider, we are going to use AWS CodePipeline to implement those pipelines. We are also going to define CloudFormation templates to create those pipelines on demand. Let's see how they look.

CodePipeline for Jakarta EE

Now, as our new Daniel's Delivery back-end is built using Jakarta EE, we will need to execute some particular steps to build and deploy this application. Let's see what the continuous integration and deployment pipeline looks like in Figure 13-1.

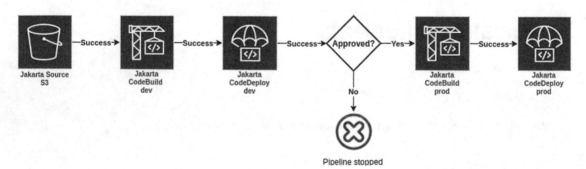

Figure 13-1. *Continuous delivery strategy for Jakarta EE back-end layer*

The whole picture is as follows:

1. Grab the source code for the back end.

2. Build the source code using Maven and create a Docker image for the development environment.

3. Deploy that image in the ECS service in the development environment.

4. If everything goes well, we reach an active approval stage; if you approve, the pipelines continue, otherwise they stop.

5. If you approve, build the source code again using Maven and create a Docker image for a production environment.

6. Deploy that image in the ECS service on the production environment.

Now, let's check those steps one by one.

Source S3

Source S3 is where the Jakarta EE code is from. We use an S3 bucket where we push a zip file with the current Jakarta EE code we want to deploy.

There are other kinds of Sources, like AWS CodeCommit or GitHub repository. This is great as you can define rules like if there is a merge from a develop branch to a master, the pipeline must start. We don't use this source as we have access restrictions to https://github.com/Apress.

Let's see how this is created using CloudFormation (Listing 13-1).

Listing 13-1. CloudFormation to create the Jakarta EE pipeline

```
DanielDeliveryCodePipelineBucket:
  Type: AWS::S3::Bucket
  Properties:
    BucketName: !Sub daniel-delivery-jakarta-pipeline
    VersioningConfiguration:
      Status: Enabled
```

There we define a bucket to save the source code. CodePipeline requires a versioned S3 bucket, which means the S3 service is going to maintain versions regarding the files you put there.

Now, we need to build the AWS CodePipeline with CloudFormation too. Let's see what it looks like in Listing 13-2.

Listing 13-2. CloudFormation to create the Jakarta EE Source stage of the pipeline

```
DanielDeliveryJakartaeeDeployPipeline:
  Type: "AWS::CodePipeline::Pipeline"
  Properties:
    Name: !Sub daniel-delivery-jakartaee-code-pipe
    RoleArn: !GetAtt DanielDeliveryCodePipelineRole.Arn
    ArtifactStore:
      Type: S3
      Location: !Ref DanielDeliveryCodePipelineBucket
    Stages:
      -
        Name: Source
        Actions:
          -
            Name: SourceAction
            ActionTypeId:
              Category: Source
              Owner: AWS
              Version: 1
              Provider: S3
            OutputArtifacts:
              - Name: SourceOutput
            Configuration:
              S3Bucket: !Ref DanielDeliveryCodePipelineBucket
              S3ObjectKey: danieldeliveryjakarta.zip
            RunOrder: 1
```

There we define an Artifact Store that will be an S3 bucket. Any output artifact generated by the pipeline, will be stored there. Next, we define the first Source stage. This stage is defined as a Source, the S3 bucket, searching for a zip file named danieldeliveryjakarta.zip. This stage will read that zip file from S3 and unzip it, and it offers the result as an output artifact named SourceOutput. SourceOutput will be used in the following stages.

CodeBuild in Develop and Production Environment

CodeBuild is going to handle how we build the new Daniel's Delivery website back end. There, we need to use Maven to build the code and Docker to create and push an image for this deployment to the ECR.

In our pipeline, we have two different CodeBuild stages, one for the development environment and the other for the production environment. Both behave the same; it is just changing the configuration regarding the database URL and authentication. We will see how this configuration is changed through this section.

As we are using ECS to deploy our back-end layer, we will need to containerize our application. Let's see how this is done.

Creating a Docker File for Jakarta EE with GlassFish

To containerize our application, we need a Docker file that tells which environment, files, and packages our application will need to execute well. The Docker file requires other files to do its job, so this is the file structure we add to the back-end source code (Figure 13-2).

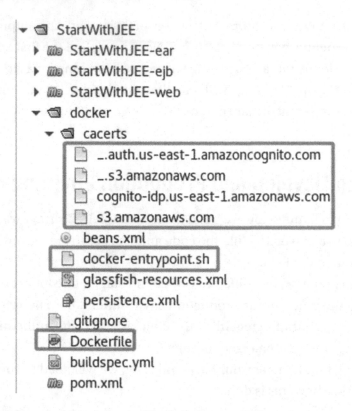

Figure 13-2. *Adding infrastructure file to Jakarata EE project*

For now, let's focus on the cacerts folder, the Dockerfile, and the docker-entrypoint. sh. In the following section, we will talk about the rest:

- cacerts folder: There, we have public certificates from AWS services like S3 and Cognito. We need them to allow the GlassFish server to trust those destinations for HTTPs connections.

- Dockerfile: Tells Docker how to build an image for our application.

- docker-entrypoint.sh: This is a shell script that is executed when the Docker image is executed. We are going to see the details of this file later.

Now, let's start to check how the Docker file works (Listing 13-3).

Listing 13-3. Dockerfile for the Jakarta EE application

```
# (1)
FROM airhacks/java-s2i

# (2)
ENV GLASSFISH_ARCHIVE glassfish5
ENV DOMAIN_NAME domain1
ENV INSTALL_DIR /opt

# (3)
RUN useradd -b /opt -m -s /bin/sh -d ${INSTALL_DIR} serveradmin && echo
serveradmin:serveradmin | chpasswd

# (4)
RUN curl -o ${INSTALL_DIR}/${GLASSFISH_ARCHIVE}.zip -L http://mirrors.
xmission.com/eclipse/glassfish/glassfish-5.1.0.zip \
    && unzip ${INSTALL_DIR}/${GLASSFISH_ARCHIVE}.zip -d ${INSTALL_DIR} \
    && rm ${INSTALL_DIR}/${GLASSFISH_ARCHIVE}.zip \
    && chown -R serveradmin:serveradmin /opt \
    && chmod -R a+rw /opt

# (5)
ENV GLASSFISH_HOME ${INSTALL_DIR}/${GLASSFISH_ARCHIVE}/glassfish
ENV DEPLOYMENT_DIR ${GLASSFISH_HOME}/domains/domain1/autodeploy

# (6)
WORKDIR ${GLASSFISH_HOME}/bin

# (7)
USER serveradmin

# (8)
EXPOSE 4848 8009 8080 8181

# (9)
ARG ENV_ARG
ENV ENV=$ENV_ARG

# (10)
```

```
RUN curl -o ${INSTALL_DIR}/mysql-connector-java-8.0.18.zip -L https://dev.
mysql.com/get/Downloads/Connector-J/mysql-connector-java-8.0.18.zip \
    && unzip ${INSTALL_DIR}/mysql-connector-java-8.0.18.zip -d
    ${INSTALL_DIR} \
    && rm ${INSTALL_DIR}/mysql-connector-java-8.0.18.zip \
    && cp ${INSTALL_DIR}/mysql-connector-java-8.0.18/mysql-connector-
    java-8.0.18.jar ${GLASSFISH_HOME}/domains/${DOMAIN_NAME}/lib/mysql-
    connector-java-8.0.16.jar \
    && rm -R ${INSTALL_DIR}/mysql-connector-java-8.0.18

# (11)
COPY docker .

# (12)
RUN keytool -import -trustcacerts -alias awsidp -storepass changeit
-noprompt -file ${GLASSFISH_HOME}/bin/cacerts/cognito-idp.us-east-1.
amazonaws.com -keystore ${GLASSFISH_HOME}/domains/domain1/config/cacerts.
jks \
    && keytool -import -trustcacerts -alias awsauth -storepass changeit
    -noprompt -file ${GLASSFISH_HOME}/bin/cacerts/_.auth.us-east-1.
    amazoncognito.com -keystore ${GLASSFISH_HOME}/domains/domain1/config/
    cacerts.jks \
    && keytool -import -trustcacerts -alias awss3g -storepass changeit
    -noprompt -file ${GLASSFISH_HOME}/bin/cacerts/_.s3.amazonaws.com
    -keystore ${GLASSFISH_HOME}/domains/domain1/config/cacerts.jks \
    && keytool -import -trustcacerts -alias awss3 -storepass changeit
    -noprompt -file ${GLASSFISH_HOME}/bin/cacerts/s3.amazonaws.com
    -keystore ${GLASSFISH_HOME}/domains/domain1/config/cacerts.jks

# (13)
COPY StartWithJEE8-ear/target/StartWithJEE8-ear-1.0-SNAPSHOT.ear .

ENTRYPOINT sh docker-entrypoint.sh
```

The following is a description of the code sample:

1. First, we define which images are going to be the parent of our image. There, the parent is airhacks/java-s2i. That image was built with Java 1.8.0_191. So, we will have access to Java 8 in our container. You can find the detail of that image here: `https://github.com/AdamBien/docklands/blob/master/java/java8-s2i/Dockerfile`

   GlassFish 5.1 requires Java 1.8.0_144 or later. For more information, see `https://eclipse-ee4j.github.io/glassfish/docs/5.1.0/release-notes/release-notes.html#abpak`

   This GlassFish installation was grabbed from `https://github.com/AdamBien/docklands/blob/master/glassfish/Dockerfile` There are ready-to-use Images named airhacks/glassfish:v5 and airhacks/glassfish:5.1.0; however, they use Java 1.8.0_121, which is not supported by GlassFish 5.1. An issue was reported here: `https://github.com/AdamBien/docklands/issues/30`

2. Next, we add GlassFish 5.1 to our image: it defines some environment variables, in this case, the GlassFish name, the domain, and the installation directory.

3. Adds rights to serveradmin users in the installation directory.

4. Downloads the GlassFish Server 5.1, unzipped, and gives the directory rights to execute.

5. Defines some environment variables for the GlassFish home and the autodeploy directory. The autodeploy directory in GlassFish is a directory where you can put a file to be deployed automatically by GlassFish like WAR or EAR artifacts. GlassFish is listening to that folder for changes.

6. Moves the working directory to the bin folder of GlassFish. In the bin folder we have the GlassFish starters scripts named asadmin.

7. Sets the user of the container to serveradmin.

8. And finally, we expose the GlassFish ports.

9. Following this, we add the ENV environment variable. This ENV_ ARG is going to be injected in the Docker image build time. That ENV variable will save the environment for which we are building this image, for instance, dev or prod.

10. Now, we add the MySQL driver to the lib folder of GlassFish. This is going to be used to connect to the RDS MySQL we created before.

11. After, we need to add the Docker folder to the image.

12. Add the cacerts certificates to GlassFish cacerts.jks.

13. Finally, we add the StartWithJEE8-ear-1.0-SNAPSHOT.ear to our image and define it as an entry point to the docker-entrypoint. hs file. The StartWithJEE8-ear/target/StartWithJEE8-ear-1.0-SNAPSHOT.ear file won't exist, at least until you execute an mvn install. We will see in the following sections when we execute that.

Now, we have our Dockerfile ready. However, we need a way to start our GlassFish server and deploy the StartWithJEE8-ear-1.0-SNAPSHOT.ear.

Let's see the docker-entrypoint.sh file (Listing 13-4).

Listing 13-4. docker-entrypoint.sh for the Jakarta EE application

```
# (1)
PASSWORD=glassfish

echo "--- Setup the password file ---" && \
    echo "AS_ADMIN_PASSWORD=" > /tmp/glassfishpwd && \
    echo "AS_ADMIN_NEWPASSWORD=${PASSWORD}" >> /tmp/glassfishpwd  && \
    echo "--- Enable DAS, change admin password, and secure admin access
    ---" && \
    asadmin --user=admin --passwordfile=/tmp/glassfishpwd change-admin-
    password --domain_name domain1

# (2)
echo "------------------------------------"
echo "asadmin start-domain ${DOMAIN_NAME}"
asadmin start-domain ${DOMAIN_NAME}
```

```
# (3)
sleep 20s

# (4)
echo "AS_ADMIN_PASSWORD=${PASSWORD}" > /tmp/glassfishpwd && \
    asadmin --user=admin --passwordfile=/tmp/glassfishpwd enable-secure-
    admin

# (5)
echo "asadmin --user=admin --passwordfile=/tmp/glassfishpwd add-resources
glassfish-resources.xml"
asadmin --user=admin --passwordfile=/tmp/glassfishpwd add-resources
glassfish-resources.xml

# (6)
echo "asadmin create-jvm-options -DENV=${ENV}"
asadmin --user=admin --passwordfile=/tmp/glassfishpwd create-jvm-options
-DENV=${ENV}

# (7)
echo "-------------------------------------"
echo "asadmin --user=admin --passwordfile=/tmp/glassfishpwd stop-domain
${DOMAIN_NAME}"
asadmin --user=admin --passwordfile=/tmp/glassfishpwd stop-domain ${DOMAIN_
NAME}

sleep 20s

# (8)
cp StartWithJEE8-ear-1.0-SNAPSHOT.ear ${DEPLOYMENT_DIR}

echo "-------------------------------------"
echo "asadmin start-domain --verbose ${DOMAIN_NAME}"
asadmin start-domain --verbose ${DOMAIN_NAME}
```

The following is a description of the code sample:

1. First, we set an admin password for the GlassFish server. There, we are creating a file into the container named glassfishpwd. The created file looks like this:

    ```
    AS_ADMIN_PASSWORD=
    AS_ADMIN_NEWPASSWORD=glassfish
    ```

    And we use the asadmin command to change the GlassFish admin password using that file. This step is necessary to allow us to connect to the GlassFish admin console. Here, we have hard-coded the GlassFish password. You shouldn't do this.

2. Next, we start the GlassFish server. The DOMAIN_NAME was defined in the Dockerfile.

3. After, we wait for the server to start and enable the secure admin feature.

4. enable-secure-admin command allows GlassFish to accept administration messages from remote admin clients such as the asadmin utility, for instance, to create database resources or JVM environment variables. We are going to need this later to create the RDS MySQL data source and set the environment variable for our application, for instance, dev or prod.

5. Now, we create the data source and connection for the RDS MySQL. The glassfish-resources.xml file has a structure to define how a jdbc connection and resource are defined. We are going to see this file in detail in the following sections.

6. Following this, we create the ENV variable into the JVM variables to be read by our application. ENV variable is injected in the Dockerfile. This variable will be accessible into our application using System.getProperty("ENV"). This is going to help us to choose which application.properties file to use depending on the environment.

7. Now, we stop the server to clean the environment and logs.

8. After that, we wait for the server to stop, copy the EAR file into the autodeploy folder, and start the server again. This is it: we now have our script to start a GlassFish server and deploy our application. This whole process could take at least 4 minutes to finish.

Well, we created a Dockerfile with everything it needs to use a GlassFish server. However, when and how do we build our application to generate the EAR file? We are going to talk about his in the following section.

buildspec.yml to Build the Back-End Layer

We need to add a new file to our Jakarta EE code, named buildspec.yml. This file will tell AWS CodeBuild what to do to build the product. Besides this, we need to add new environment files like database connections and application.properties environments to set the right variable values by the environment.

First, we need to define some files that support the buildspec.yml file. Let's start with the glassfish-resources.xml (Listing 13-5).

Listing 13-5. glassfish-resources.xml file to create a datasource into the GlassFish server

```
<?xml version="1.0" encoding="UTF-8"?>
<!DOCTYPE resources PUBLIC "-//GlassFish.org//DTD GlassFish Application
Server 3.1 Resource Definitions//EN" "http://glassfish.org/dtds/glassfish-
resources_1_5.dtd">
<resources>
    <jdbc-connection-pool allow-non-component-callers="false" associate-
    with-thread="false" connection-creation-retry-attempts="0" connection-
    creation-retry-interval-in-seconds="10" connection-leak-reclaim="false"
    connection-leak-timeout-in-seconds="0" connection-validation-
    method="auto commit" datasource-classname="com.mysql.cj.jdbc.
    MysqlConnectionPoolDataSource" fail-all-connections="false" idle-
    timeout-in-seconds="300" is-connection-validation-required="false" is-
    isolation-level-guaranteed="true" lazy-connection-association="false"
    lazy-connection-enlistment="false" match-connections="false"
    max-connection-usage-count="0" max-pool-size="32" max-wait-
```

```
    time-in-millis="60000" name="mysql_rootPool" non-transactional-
    connections="false" pool-resize-quantity="2" res-type="javax.sql.
    ConnectionPoolDataSource" statement-timeout-in-seconds="-1" steady-
    pool-size="8" validate-atmost-once-period-in-seconds="0" wrap-jdbc-
    objects="false">
        <property name="User" value="${DATABASE_USER}"/>
        <property name="Password" value="${DATABASE_PASSWORD}"/>
        <property name="URL" value="${DATABASE_URL}"/>
        <property name="databaseName" value="${DATABASE_NAME}"/>
        <property name="driverClass" value="com.mysql.jdbc.Driver"/>
        <property name="useSSL" value="false"/>
        <property name="allowPublicKeyRetrieval" value="true"/>
    </jdbc-connection-pool>
    <jdbc-resource enabled="true" jndi-name="jdbc/deliverymysql"
    object-type="user" pool-name="mysql_rootPool"/>
</resources>
```

That is a datasource configuration for GlassFish server. As we saw in the docker-entrypoint.sh, we use this to create a datasource in the GlassFish server. As we see, there are some properties like DATABASE_USER, DATABASE_PASSWORD, DATABASE_URL, and DATABASE_NAME, which will be injected through the pipeline execution. We will see this later.

Now, define the right beans.xml configuration (Listing 13-6).

Listing 13-6. beans.xml file to activate the AWS infrastructure using the AWSEnvironment annotation

```
<?xml version="1.0" encoding="UTF-8"?>
<beans xmlns="http://xmlns.jcp.org/xml/ns/javaee"
       xmlns:xsi="http://www.w3.org/2001/XMLSchema-instance"
       xsi:schemaLocation="http://xmlns.jcp.org/xml/ns/javaee http://xmlns.
       jcp.org/xml/ns/javaee/beans_1_1.xsd"
       bean-discovery-mode="annotated">
    <alternatives>
        <stereotype>com.daniel.delivery.main.AWSEnvironment</stereotype>
    </alternatives>
</beans>
```

The beans.xml file tells Jakarta EE how to handle its beans. As we saw in previous sections, we created an annotation named @AWSEnvironment. That annotation is an alternative, which means any annotated bean is going to be active only if you tell Jakarta EE to activate it. So, we activate that alternative in this beans.xml.

And finally, before the buildspec.yml file, define the right persistence.xml configuration (Listing 13-7).

Listing 13-7. persistence.xml file to use the datasource created in the glassfish-resources-xml file

```
<?xml version="1.0" encoding="UTF-8"?>
<persistence version="2.1" xmlns="http://xmlns.jcp.org/xml/ns/
persistence" xmlns:xsi="http://www.w3.org/2001/XMLSchema-instance"
xsi:schemaLocation="http://xmlns.jcp.org/xml/ns/persistence http://xmlns.
jcp.org/xml/ns/persistence/persistence_2_1.xsd">
  <persistence-unit name="deliverymysql" transaction-type="JTA">
    <jta-data-source>jdbc/deliverymysql</jta-data-source>
    <class>com.daniel.delivery.main.repository.delivery.DeliveryData</
    class>
    <class>com.daniel.delivery.main.repository.delivery.ItemData</class>
    <class>com.daniel.delivery.main.repository.foodservice.
    FoodServiceData</class>
    <class>com.daniel.delivery.main.repository.foodservice.UserData</class>
    <class>com.daniel.delivery.main.repository.foodproduct.
    FoodProductData</class>
    <properties>
      <property name="javax.persistence.schema-generation.database.action"
      value="create"/>
    </properties>
  </persistence-unit>
</persistence>
```

The persistence.xml tells Jakarta EE how to handle the persistence layer. There, we define persistence entity beans and database configurations. As we were using this with the default data source to connect to the Derby database, we now need to change it to point to RDS MySQL.

There, we change two main things. First, we define a jta-data-source, and this holds the configuration to connect to the RDS MySQL. As we saw when we defined the glassfish-resources.xml, there we defined the jdbc/danielmysql data source. And second, we tell JPA through a javax.persistence.schema-generation.database. action to create the database tables based on the JPA entities only the first time, as this configuration will be used in lower and higher environments like dev and prod; before, we had the create-drop configuration, but, this will delete and re-create the database each time the application is deployed. That configuration is only desired when you are in a local environment.

With the glassfish-resources.xml, beans.xml, and persistence.xml files in place, we can move to see what buildspec.yml looks like and determine any other required files we need to add (Listing 13-8).

Listing 13-8. buildspec.yml to define the pipeline for Jakarta EE

```
version: 0.2

phases:
  install:
    # (1)
    runtime-versions:
      java: corretto11
      docker: 18
  pre_build:
    commands:
    # (2)
    - echo Logging in to Amazon ECR...
    - $(aws ecr get-login --no-include-email --region $AWS_DEFAULT_
      REGION)
    # (3)
    - echo --- Setup application.properties ---
    - sed -i -e "s,\${SSO_CLIENT_SECRET},${SSO_CLIENT_SECRET},"
      StartWithJEE8-ejb/src/main/resources/application-${ENVIRONMENT}.
      properties
    # (4)
    - echo --- Setup glassfish resources ---
```

```
      - sed -i -e "s,\${DATABASE_USER},${DATABASE_USER}," docker/glassfish-
        resources.xml
      - sed -i -e "s,\${DATABASE_PASSWORD},${DATABASE_PASSWORD}," docker/
        glassfish-resources.xml
      - sed -i -e "s,\${DATABASE_URL},${DATABASE_URL}," docker/glassfish-
        resources.xml
      - sed -i -e "s,\${DATABASE_NAME},${DATABASE_NAME}," docker/glassfish-
        resources.xml
  build:
    commands:
      # (5)
      - echo Build started on `date`
      - mvn clean install -P docker
      # (6)
      - echo Building the Docker image...
      - docker build --build-arg ENV_ARG=${ENVIRONMENT} -t $IMAGE_REPO_
        NAME:$ENVIRONMENT .
      - docker tag $IMAGE_REPO_NAME:$ENVIRONMENT $AWS_ECR_URL/$IMAGE_REPO_
        NAME:$ENVIRONMENT
  post_build:
    commands:
      # (7)
      - echo Build completed on `date`
      - echo Pushing the Docker image...
      - docker push $AWS_ECR_URL/$IMAGE_REPO_NAME:$ENVIRONMENT
      - echo Creating imagedefinitions.json…
      # (8)
      - printf '[{"name":"%s","imageUri":"%s"}]' daniel-delivery-jakartaee-
        cd-$ENVIRONMENT $AWS_ECR_URL/$IMAGE_REPO_NAME:$ENVIRONMENT >
        imagedefinitions.json
artifacts:
  files:
    - imagedefinitions.json
```

The following is a description of the code sample:

1. First, we need to define the version and the environment packages required to build our application. There, we tell AWS CodeBuild to use a JDK named correto11 and the Docker version 18. The JDK is needed to compile and build the source code, and the Docker is needed to build the image and push it to the ECR.

2. Now, we define pre-build commands. In this case, we start with a Docker login into the ECR. We need this to push and pull images from the ECR.

3. Next, we set the SSO_CLIENT_SECRET into the application-{environment}.properties file. SSO_CLIENT_SECRET and ENVIRONMENT variables are injected into the buildspec.yml file from the AWS CodeBuild configuration in runtime. This is to avoid hard-coding secrets into the source code. We will see how this works later. sed command replaces the ${VARIABLE} pattern in a file for a specific value.

   In the source code, we have multiple application-${ENVIRONMENT}.properties files, for instance, this is what the application-dev.properties file looks like:

```
SSO_JWK_URL=https://cognito-idp.us-east-1.amazonaws.com/us-east-1_
IR4AXwO2f
/.well-known/jwks.json
SSO_TOKEN_URL=https://danieldeliverydev.auth.us-east-1.
amazoncognito.com/oau th2/token
SSO_AUTH_URL=https://d152Onyqce9wb6.cloudfront.net/auth/ SSO_
CLIENT_ID=7da9a7ssj4q1v7u1kgvraierrk SSO_CLIENT_SECRET=${SSO_
CLIENT_SECRET}
SSO_CORS_ALLOW=https://d152Onyqce9wb6.cloudfront.net SSO_CLAIM_ID_
NAME=email
IMAGES_S3_REGION=us-east-1 COGNITO_REGION=us-east-1
COGNITO_POOL_ID=us-east-1_IR4AXwO2f
IMAGES_S3_BUCKET=daniel-delivery-images-dev
```

There, we define all of the properties our back end needs to work. Notice that SSO_CLIENT_SECRET is not defined. Also, notice how we add some AWS variables, plus, we modify the URLs to point to the AWS resources we created for the dev environment.

4. Next, we need to create a glassfish-resources.xml file with the RDS MySQL connection information, so we can define those jdbc connections in the GlassFish server. DATABASE_USER, DATABASE_PASSWORD, DATABASE_URL and DATABASE_NAME are injected through the AWS CodeBuild configuration as they are secrets.

5. Following this, we move to the building part. There, we start with the mvn clean install command. This command is going to create the EAR file. -*P docker* means that we need to execute a specific Maven profile. That profile helps us to build an EAR with the beans.xml and persistence.xml files we defined before.

6. After Maven builds our project, we use Docker to create the image based on the Dockerfile. There, we execute the Docker build, which creates the docker image, plus we add the ENV_ARG to define which environment we are building. Besides, we tag the new image with the environment, for instance, the result could be xxxxx.dkr.ecr.us-east-1.amazonaws.com/newdanieldelivery:dev

7. Next, we do the post-build section. We can see how we use Docker to push the image we tagged before to the ECR repository.

8. Finally, we generate a JSON file to let the next stage in the pipeline know which image we just created. We also tell AWS CodeBuild that the output of this stage is going to be the imagedefinitions. json file we create. The following is an example of the file:

```
[
 {
   "name":"----",
   "imageUri":"---"
 }
]
```

CloudFormation for CodeBuild Stage

We just saw that we need to do a lot to build a Jakarta EE application. Now, let's define the CloudFormation for the AWS CodeBuild stage (Listing 13-9).

Listing 13-9. CloudFormation for CodeBuild stage for JakarataEE pipeline

```
DanielDeliveryJakartaeeCodeBuild:          # (1)
  Type: AWS::CodeBuild::Project
  Properties:
    Description: CodeBuild for Jakarta side
    ServiceRole: !GetAtt DanielDeliveryCodeBuildRole.Arn
    Artifacts:
      Type: CODEPIPELINE
    Environment:
      Type: LINUX_CONTAINER
      ComputeType: BUILD_GENERAL1_SMALL
      Image: aws/codebuild/amazonlinux2-x86_64-standard:2.0
      PrivilegedMode: true
    Source:
      Type: CODEPIPELINE
    TimeoutInMinutes: 10
  DependsOn:
    - DanielDeliveryCodePipelineBucket

DanielDeliveryJakartaeeDeployPipeline:
  Type: "AWS::CodePipeline::Pipeline"
  Properties:
    Name: !Sub daniel-delivery-jakartaee-code-pipe
    RoleArn: !GetAtt DanielDeliveryCodePipelineRole.Arn
    ArtifactStore:
      Type: S3
      Location: !Ref DanielDeliveryCodePipelineBucket
    Stages:
      -
        Name: Source
        Actions:
```

```
      # Source Action
- Name: BuildDev
  Actions:

    -

      Name: CodeBuildDev                  # (2)
      InputArtifacts:
        - Name: SourceOutput
      ActionTypeId:
        Category: Build
        Owner: AWS
        Version: 1
        Provider: CodeBuild
      OutputArtifacts:
        - Name: BuildDevOutput
      Configuration:
      ProjectName: !Ref DanielDeliveryJakartaeeCodeBuild
      EnvironmentVariables: '[{"name":"SSO_CLIENT_
      SECRET","value":" not set","type":"PLAINTEXT"},{"name":"
      IMAGE_REPO_NAME","value":" not set","type":"PLAINTEXT"},
      {"name":"AWS_ECR_URL","value":" not set","type":"PLAINT
      EXT"},{"name":"DATABASE_USER","value":" not set","type"
      :"PLAINTEXT"},{"name":"DATABASE_PASSWORD","value":" not
      set","type":"PLAINTEXT"},{"name":"DATABASE_URL","value":"
      not set","type":"PLAINTEXT"},{"name":"DATABASE_NAME",
      "value":"danieldelivery","type":"PLAINTEXT"},{"name":"ENVIR
      ONMENT","value":"dev","type":"PLAINTEXT"}]'
      RunOrder: 1
- Name: DeployDev
  Actions:
    # Deploy dev Action
- Name: ApprovalProd
  Actions:
    # Approval dev Action
- Name: BuildProd
  Actions:
```

```
      -
        Name: CodeBuildProd          # (3)
        InputArtifacts:
          - Name: SourceOutput
        ActionTypeId:
          Category: Build
          Owner: AWS
          Version: 1
          Provider: CodeBuild
        OutputArtifacts:
          - Name: BuildProdOutput
        Configuration:
          ProjectName: !Ref DanielDeliveryJakartaeeCodeBuild
          EnvironmentVariables: '[{"name":"SSO_CLIENT_
          SECRET","value":" not set","type":"PLAINTEXT"},{"name":
          "IMAGE_REPO_NAME","value":" not set","type":"PLAINTEXT"},
          {"name":"AWS_ECR_URL","value":" not set","type":"PLAINTEXT"
          },{"name":"DATABASE_USER","value":" not set","type":"PLAINT
          EXT"},{"name":"DATABASE_PASSWORD","value":" not set","type"
          :"PLAINTEXT"},{"name":"DATABASE_URL","value":" not set","ty
          pe":"PLAINTEXT"},{"name":"DATABASE_NAME","value":"danieldel
          ivery","type":"PLAINTEXT"},{"name":"ENVIRONMENT","value":
          "prod","type":"PLAINTEXT"}]'
        RunOrder: 1
    - Name: DeployProd
      Actions:
        # Deploy prod Action
```

The following is a description of the code sample:

1. First, we define a generic CodeBuild that we will use for the
   development and production environments. There, we define the
   machine we want to use to build our back end; in this case, it will
   be a Linux small with privileges to run Docker.

2. Next, we add a new step (stage) into the CodePipeline for
    CodeBuild in the development environment. There, we took
    the output from the Source stage and referenced the CodeBuild
    we created before. Plus, we defined a set of properties to be
    configured as follows:

    •   SSO_CLIENT_SECRET: The secret for AWS Cognito. IMAGE_
        REPO_NAME: The ECR repository we want to use. AWS_ECR_
        URL: The URL of the ECR repository.

    •   DATABASE_USER: The database user that we want to connect in
        this environment.

    •   DATABASE_PASSWORD: The database user password.
        DATABASE_URL: The database URL for our RDS.

    •   DATABASE_NAME: The database name, in this case, we already
        defined it as danieldelivery.

    •   ENVIRONMENT: The environment we are building, in this
        case, dev.

    These properties are going to be injected into the buildspec.yml
    execution and can be changed by the AWS Console. We will see
    more about this later in this section.

3. Finally, we add a new step (stage) into the CodePipeline for
    CodeBuild in the production environment. As we can see, we
    are reusing the same CodeBuild we used in the development
    environment, and we just need to change the parameters. In this
    case, the ENVIRONMENT is set to prod.

Now, as we build our back end, let's move to deploy it.

CodeBuild in Develop and Production Environment

CodeDeploy is going to help us to deploy our Jakarta EE application. We can use this
stage to deploy in multiple AWS resources like EC2 or ECS. In our case, we will use ECS.

This stage requires a file named imagedefinitions.json that we saw is generated by
the buildspec.yml file. There, we define the image and URL name ECS is going to deploy.
We generated this file in the CodeBuild stage.

Now, let's create the CloudFormation for this stage (Listing 13-10).

Listing 13-10. CloudFormation for CodeDeploy stage for JakarataEE pipeline

```yaml
DanielDeliveryJakartaeeDeployPipeline:
  Type: "AWS::CodePipeline::Pipeline"
  Properties:
    Name: !Sub daniel-delivery-jakartaee-code-pipe
    RoleArn: !GetAtt DanielDeliveryCodePipelineRole.Arn
    ArtifactStore:
      Type: S3
      Location: !Ref DanielDeliveryCodePipelineBucket
    Stages:
      -
        Name: Source
        Actions:
          # Source actions
      - Name: BuildDev
        Actions:
          # Build to dev
      - Name: DeployDev
        Actions:
          - Name: DeployDev
            RunOrder: 1
            InputArtifacts:
              - Name: BuildDevOutput
            ActionTypeId:
              Category: Deploy
              Owner: AWS
              Version: 1
              Provider: ECS
            Configuration:
              ClusterName: not set
              ServiceName: not set
      - Name: ApprovalProd
```

```
      Actions:
        # Approval to prod
    - Name: BuildProd
      Actions:
        # Build to prod
    - Name: DeployProd
      Actions:
        - Name: DeployProd
          RunOrder: 1
          InputArtifacts:
            - Name: BuildProdOutput
          ActionTypeId:
            Category: Deploy
            Owner: AWS
            Version: 1
            Provider: ECS
          Configuration:
            ClusterName: not set
            ServiceName: not set
```

There we define the two stages regarding CodeDeploy, one for the development environment and the other for the production environment. We just need to define two properties:

- ClusterName: The ECS cluster we want to deploy to.

- ServiceName: The ECS service we want to handle the deployment.

For now, we just do not set those properties because we are going to do this through the AWS Console.

Active Approval

Active approval is a special stage that allows us to control the flow of the pipeline. In our case, we are going to use it to approve the deployment to production.

Let's see what the CloudFormation for this stage looks like in Listing 13-11.

Listing 13-11. CloudFormation for ActiveApproval stage for Jakarata EE pipeline

```
DanielDeliveryJakartaeeDeployPipeline:
  Type: "AWS::CodePipeline::Pipeline"
  Properties:
    Name: !Sub daniel-delivery-jakartaee-code-pipe
    RoleArn: !GetAtt DanielDeliveryCodePipelineRole.Arn
    ArtifactStore:
      Type: S3
      Location: !Ref DanielDeliveryCodePipelineBucket
    Stages:
      -
        Name: Source
        Actions:
          # Source actions
      - Name: BuildDev
        Actions:
          # Build actions
      - Name: DeployDev
        Actions:
          # Deploy actions
      - Name: ApprovalProd
        Actions:
            - Name: ApprovalProd
              RunOrder: 1
              ActionTypeId:
                Category: Approval
                Owner: AWS
                Version: 1
                Provider: Manual
              Configuration:
                CustomData: Do you want to deploy to production?
        - Name: BuildProd
          Actions:
            # Build actions
```

```
    - Name: DeployProd
      Actions:
        # Deploy actions
```

There, we just set a question if you want to deploy or not to production. The pipeline is going to wait until you approve or reject it.

Configure the Pipeline through the AWS Console

Now we need to create the pipeline using the CloudFormation template and set up the variables and resources we missed.

1. First, create the new pipeline using CloudFormation. You will see something like this in Figure 13-3.

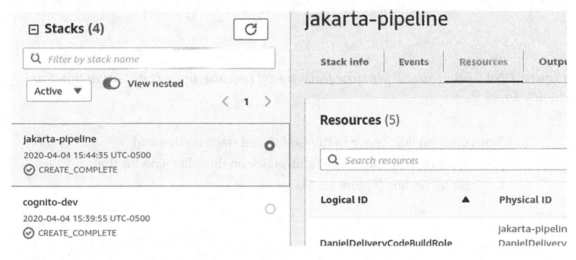

Figure 13-3. *CloudFormation created for Jakarata EE pipeline*

2. Search for the CodePipeline service, and choose the new pipeline you create. You will see something like Figure 13-4.

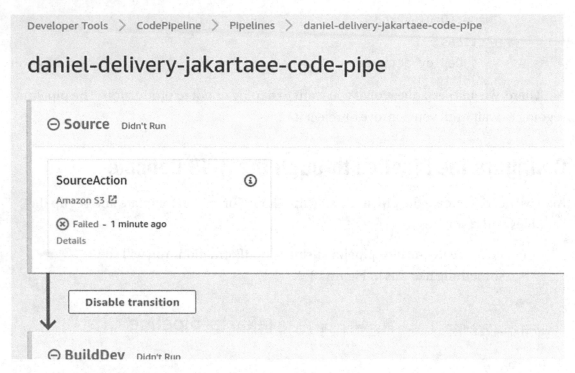

Figure 13-4. *Jakarata EE pipeline fails at first because there is not an artifact to deploy in S3*

3. Now, click on Edit, move to the CodeBuild stage for dev and prod, click on Edit Stage, and finally click on the edict icon for the CodeBuildDev box (Figure 13-5).

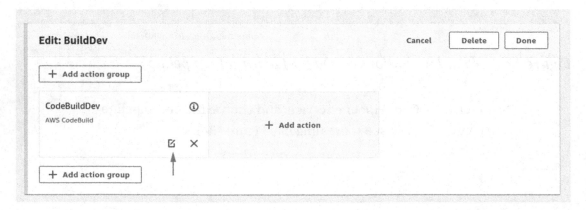

Figure 13-5. *Editing the BuildDev stage in the Jakarata EE pipeline*

4.   There, set the right variables for those environment parameters. For instance, for CodeBuild dev, we can look at Figure 13-6.

Environment variables - *optional*
Choose the key, value, and type for your CodeBuild environment variables. In the value field, you can reference variables generated by CodePipeline. Learn more ☑

Name	Value	Type
SSO_CLIENT_SECRET	5beruh972qu0neiu6dcedj2nui	Plaintext
IMAGE_REPO_NAME	newdanieldelivery	Plaintext
AWS_ECR_URL	████████.dkr.ecr.us-east-1.amazonaws.com	Plaintext
DATABASE_USER	MyName	Plaintext
DATABASE_PASSWORD	MyPassword	Plaintext
DATABASE_URL	jdbc:mysql://daniel-delivery-db-dev.cc80rg7cnp9j.us-east-1.	Plaintext
DATABASE_NAME	danieldelivery	Plaintext
ENVIRONMENT	dev	Plaintext

Figure 13-6. *Setting up the CodeBuild stage for dev with the right values*

As we can see, we can change all of the parameters. As some parameters are secrets, you shouldn't have them here. There are other services you can use, like Parameter store or Secrets Management. You can use them here in the console too. Take into account that the database URL must end with the database name, which in this case is the following: /danieldelivery (Figure 13-7).

Type	
Plaintext	▲
Plaintext	
Parameter	
Secrets Manager	

t-1.amaz

Figure 13-7. *You can grab properties from other AWS services like Parameter Store or Secrets Manager*

5. Now, let's update the CodeDeploy stage for development and
    production. This is what development stage looks like as shown in
    Figure 13-8.

BuildDevOutput

No more than 100 characters

Cluster name
Choose a cluster that you have already created in the Amazon ECS console. O

Q   daniel-delivery-jakartaee-ecs-dev

Service name
Choose a service that you have already created in the Amazon ECS console fo

Q   daniel-delivery-jakartaee-ser-dev

Figure 13-8. *Updating the Deploy dev stage to link the ECS resources*

There, you choose the ECS cluster and service where you want to
deploy. In this case, we chose the development environment.

6. Finally, to get the pipeline running, you need to push the zip file to
    the S3 bucket in the following way. First run mvn clean to remove
    any generated artifact.

7. Zip the source code project. You must zip the content,
    not the folder. For instance, the zip file must be named
    danieldeliveryjakarta.zip (Figure 13-9).

Figure 13-9. *Zipping the source code to deploy on S3 for Jakarta EE*

8. Now, go to the AWS Console and search for the S3 service, and find the bucket you define for this pipeline; in this case, we have daniel-delivery-jakarta-pipeline (Figure 13-10).

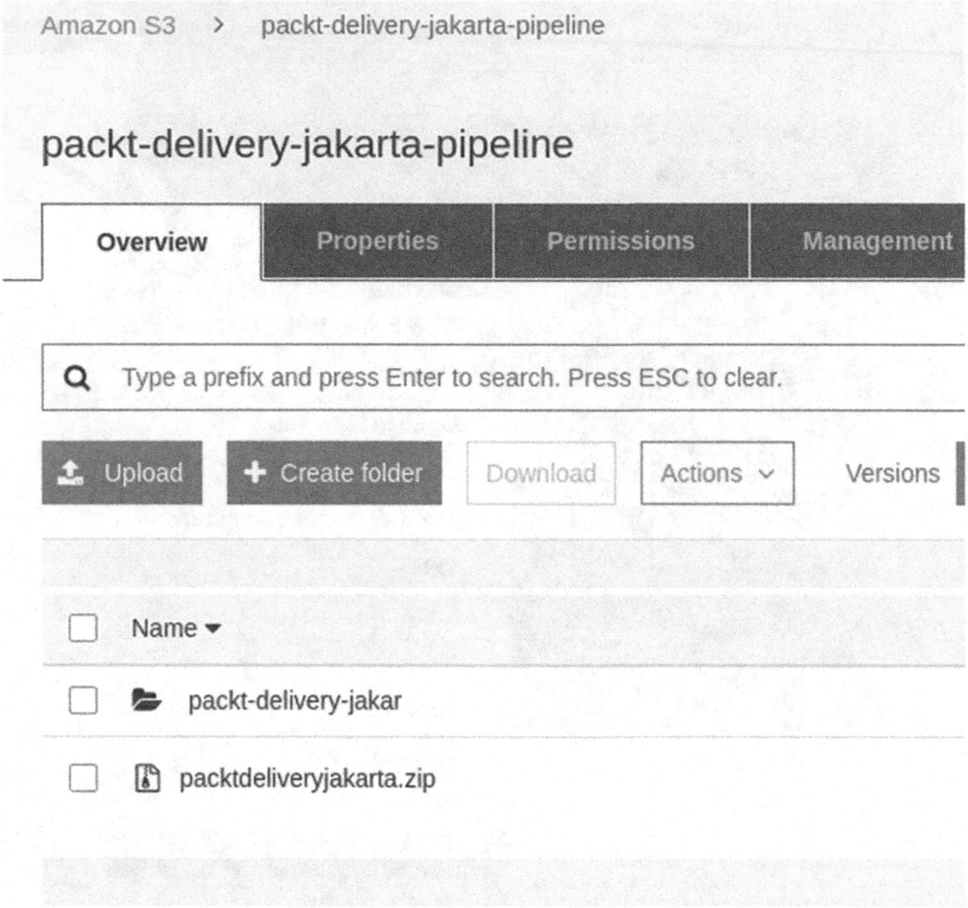

Amazon S3   >   packt-delivery-jakarta-pipeline

packt-delivery-jakarta-pipeline

Overview	Properties	Permissions	Management

Q   Type a prefix and press Enter to search. Press ESC to clear.

↑ Upload   + Create folder   Download   Actions ∨   Versions

☐ Name ▾

☐ 📁 packt-delivery-jakar

☐ 🗜️ packtdeliveryjakarta.zip

Figure 13-10. *Uploading the zip file for Jakarta EE to S3 to deploy*

9.   Drag and drop the zip file into the bucket.

10.   Return to the pipeline and click on Release Version. The pipeline
      will start (Figure 13-11).

Figure 13-11. *Release a change to run the pipeline and grab the zip file from S3*

We just defined the whole pipeline to build and deploy our Jakarta EE back-end layer. Now let's see what the pipeline looks like for VueJS.

CodePipeline for VueJS

Now, as our new Daniel's Delivery front end is built using VueJS, we will need to execute some particular steps to build and deploy this application. Let's see what the continuous integration and deployment pipeline looks like in Figure 13-12.

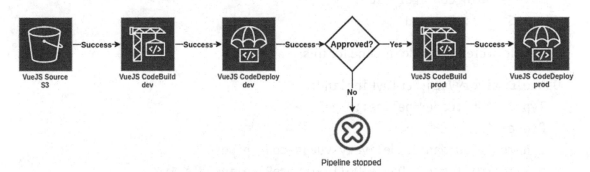

Figure 13-12. *Continuous delivery strategy for VueJS*

The whole picture is as follows:

1. Grab the source code for the front end.

2. Build the source code using NPM for a development environment.

3. Deploy the built VueJS app to a development S3 bucket.

4. If everything goes well, we reach an active approval stage, and if
    you approve, the pipelines continue; otherwise they stop. If you
    approve, build the source code again using NPM for a production
    environment.

5. Deploy the built VueJS app to a production S3 bucket.

Now, let's check those steps one by one.

Source S3

Source S3 is where the VueJS code is from. We use an S3 bucket where we push a zip file
with the current Vue.js code we want to deploy.

Let's see how this is created using CloudFormation (Listing 13-12).

Listing 13-12. CloudFormation for Source stage for Vue.js pipeline

```
DanielDeliveryCodePipelineBucket:
  Type: AWS::S3::Bucket
  Properties:
    BucketName: !Sub daniel-delivery-vue-pipeline
    VersioningConfiguration:
      Status: Enabled
```

Now, let's create a CodePipeline for this:

```
DanielDeliveryVuejsDeployPipeline:
  Type: "AWS::CodePipeline::Pipeline"
  Properties:
    Name: !Sub daniel-delivery-vuejs-code-pipe
    RoleArn: !GetAtt DanielDeliveryCodePipelineRole.Arn
    ArtifactStore:
      Type: S3
      Location: !Ref DanielDeliveryCodePipelineBucket
    Stages:
      -
        Name: Source
        Actions:
          -
```

```
        Name: SourceAction
        ActionTypeId:
          Category: Source
          Owner: AWS
          Version: 1
          Provider: S3
        OutputArtifacts:
          - Name: SourceOutput
        Configuration:
          S3Bucket: !Ref DanielDeliveryCodePipelineBucket
          S3ObjectKey: danieldeliveryvuejs.zip
        RunOrder: 1
  - Name: BuildDev
    Actions:
        # Build actions
  - Name: DeployDev
    Actions:
        # Deploy actions
  - Name: ApprovalProd
    Actions:
      - Name: ApprovalProd
        # Approval actions
  - Name: BuildProd
    Actions:
        # Build actions
  - Name: DeployProd
    Actions:
        # Deploy actions
```

This configuration is pretty similar to the pipeline for Jakarta EE. This is just pointing to a different S3 bucket and the zip file is named danieldeliveryvuejs.zip.

CodeBuild Dev and Prod

CodeBuild is going to handle how we build the new Daniel's Delivery website front end. There, we need to use NPM to build the code.

In our pipeline, we have two different CodeBuild stages, one for the development environment and the other for the production environment. Both behave the same: we are just changing the configuration regarding the .env file, as we want to use to grab the properties.

As we are using S3 to deploy our front-end layer, we just need to build the code and push it to the bucket.

buildspec.yml to Build the Front-End Layer

We need to add a new file to our Vue.js code, named buildspec.yml. This file will tell AWS CodeBuild what to do to build the product. We also need to set which .env properties files we want to use depending on the environment we are building.

Let's see what buildspec.yml looks like in Listing 13-13.

Listing 13-13. buildspec.yml for Vue.js pipeline

```
version: 0.2

phases:
  install:
    runtime-versions:            # (1)
      nodejs: 10
  pre_build:                     # (2)
    commands:
      - echo Installing dependencies...
      - npm install
  build:                         # (3)
    commands:
      - echo Build started on `date`
      - npm run build -- --mode ${ENVIRONMENT}
artifacts:                       # (4)
  files:
    - '**/*'
  base-directory: dist
```

The following is a description of the code sample:

1. First, we need to define the version and the environment packages required to build our application. In this case, we require nodejs 10 to build the front-end layer.

2. Next, we need to install the packages and dependencies we have declared. npm install is going to download everything declared in the package.json file into the Vue.js project.

3. After that, we build our Vue.js application for a specific environment. --mode tells Vue CLI to build the project using that defined environment. That means VueJS CLI is going to use an environment file named .env.${ENVIRONMENT}. For instance, this is what the .env.development file looks like:

```
NODE_ENV=production
VUE_APP_RESTFUL_BASE_URL=http://jakar-daniel-
17laon9qibr2c-391997666.us-east
-1.elb.amazonaws.com:8080/StartWithJEE8-web/api VUE_APP_SSO_
AUTHORIZATION=https://danieldeliverydev.auth.us-east-1.amazoncog
nito.com/oauth2/authorize
VUE_APP_SSO_CLIENT_ID=7da9a7ssj4q1v7u1kgvraierrk VUE_APP_SSO_
REDIRECT_URL=https://d1520nyqce9wb6.cloudfront.net/auth/
```

NODE_ENV is pretty important as it tells VueJS CLI to create a production-ready build for this execution. Despite being in a development environment file, we want to build a production-ready application to deploy on AWS environments.

A production-ready build has advantages like a lower size of code and hashing names for the resources such as images and JS files. This last one is important to cache those files and invalidate them when we deploy a new version.

4. Finally, we tell CodeBuild which resources are outputs of this build. There, we define that every file in the dist directory is going to be the output of this stage.

CloudFormation for CodeBuild Stage

Well, we just saw that we need to do a lot to build a VueJS application. Now, let's define the CloudFormation for the AWS CodeBuild stage (Listing 13-14).

Listing 13-14. CloudFormation for CodeBuild for Vue.js pipeline

```
DanielDeliveryVuejsCodeBuild:                # (1)
  Type: AWS::CodeBuild::Project
  Properties:
    Description: CodeBuild for Jakarta side
    ServiceRole: !GetAtt DanielDeliveryCodeBuildRole.Arn
    Artifacts:
      Type: CODEPIPELINE
    Environment:
      Type: LINUX_CONTAINER
      ComputeType: BUILD_GENERAL1_SMALL
      Image: aws/codebuild/amazonlinux2-x86_64-standard:2.0
    Source:
      Type: CODEPIPELINE
    TimeoutInMinutes: 10
  DependsOn:
    - DanielDeliveryCodePipelineBucket

DanielDeliveryVuejsDeployPipeline:
  Type: "AWS::CodePipeline::Pipeline"
  Properties:
    Name: !Sub daniel-delivery-vuejs-code-pipe
    RoleArn: !GetAtt DanielDeliveryCodePipelineRole.Arn
    ArtifactStore:
      Type: S3
      Location: !Ref DanielDeliveryCodePipelineBucket
    Stages:
      -
        Name: Source
        Actions:
          # Source actions
```

```yaml
  - Name: BuildDev                      # (2)
    Actions:
      -
        Name: CodeBuildDev
        InputArtifacts:
          - Name: SourceOutput
        ActionTypeId:
          Category: Build
          Owner: AWS
          Version: 1
          Provider: CodeBuild
        OutputArtifacts:
          - Name: BuildDevOutput
        Configuration:
          ProjectName: !Ref DanielDeliveryVuejsCodeBuild
          EnvironmentVariables: '[{"name":"ENVIRONMENT","value":
          "development","type":"PLAINTEXT"}]'
        RunOrder: 1
  - Name: DeployDev
    Actions:
      # Deploy actions
  - Name: ApprovalProd
    Actions:
      # Approval actions
  - Name: BuildProd                     # (3)
    Actions:
      -
        Name: CodeBuildProd
        InputArtifacts:
          - Name: SourceOutput
        ActionTypeId:
          Category: Build
          Owner: AWS
          Version: 1
          Provider: CodeBuild
```

```
        OutputArtifacts:
          - Name: BuildProdOutput
        Configuration:
          ProjectName: !Ref DanielDeliveryVuejsCodeBuild
          EnvironmentVariables: '[{"name":"ENVIRONMENT","value":
          "production","type":"PLAINTEXT"}]'
          RunOrder: 1
    - Name: DeployProd
      Actions:
          # Deploy actions
```

The following is a description of the code sample:

1. First, we define a generic CodeBuild we will use for development and production environments. There, we define the machine we want to use to build our front end. In this case, it will be a Linux small with no privileges as we don't need to access the low levels of the system like Docker commands.

2. Next, we add a new step (stage) into the CodePipeline for CodeBuild in the development environment. There, we took the output from the Source stage and referenced the CodeBuild we created before. Plus, we defined the ENVIRONMENT as development.

3. Finally, we add a new step (stage) into the CodePipeline for CodeBuild in the production environment. As we can see, we are reusing the same CodeBuild we used in the development environment; we just need to change the parameters. In this case, the ENVIRONMENT is set for production.

Now, as we build our front end, let's move to deploy it.

CodeDeploy Dev and Prod

CodeDeploy is going to help us to deploy our VueJS application. In this case, we are going to deploy to an S3 bucket.

Now, let's create the CloudFormation for this stage (Listing 13-15).

Listing 13-15. CloudFormation for CodeDeploy stage for Vue.js pipeline

```
DanielDeliveryVuejsDeployPipeline:
  Type: "AWS::CodePipeline::Pipeline"
  Properties:
    Name: !Sub daniel-delivery-vuejs-code-pipe
    RoleArn: !GetAtt DaniclDeliveryCodeP1pelineRole.Arn
    ArtifactStore:
      Type: S3
      Location: !Ref DanielDeliveryCodePipelineBucket
    Stages:
      -
        Name: Source
        Actions:
          # Source  actions
      - Name: BuildDev
        Actions:
          # Build actions
      - Name: DeployDev
        Actions:
          - Name: DeployDev
            RunOrder: 1
            InputArtifacts:
              - Name: BuildDevOutput
            ActionTypeId:
              Category: Deploy
              Owner: AWS
              Version: 1
              Provider: S3
            Configuration:
              BucketName: not set
              Extract: true
      - Name: ApprovalProd
        Actions:
          # Approval actions
```

```
  - Name: BuildProd
    Actions:
        # Build actions
  - Name: DeployProd
    Actions:
      - Name: DeployProd
        RunOrder: 1
        InputArtifacts:
          - Name: BuildProdOutput
        ActionTypeId:
          Category: Deploy
          Owner: AWS
          Version: 1
          Provider: S3
        Configuration:
          BucketName: not set
          Extract: true
```

There we define the two stages, one for development and the other for production. We configure which S3 bucket we want to deploy to; in this case, we are not set on the value. We will do that through the AWS Console. We set Extract to true as we need to unzip the result of the build stage and push those files to the S3 bucket.

Active Approval

Active approval is pretty much the same as we configured it in the back-end pipeline.

Configure the Pipeline through the AWS Console

We now need to create the pipeline using the CloudFormation template and set up the variables and resources we missed.

1. First, create a new pipeline using CloudFormation. You will see something like Figure 13-13.

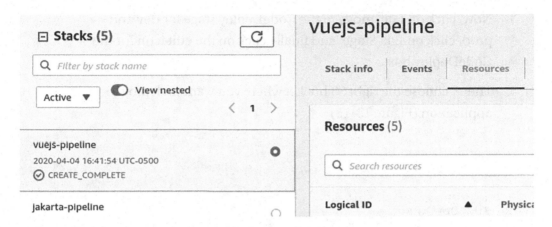

Figure 13-13. *Creating the CloudFormation for Vue.js pipeline*

2.   Search for the CodePipeline service, and choose the new pipeline you create. You will see something like Figure 13-14.

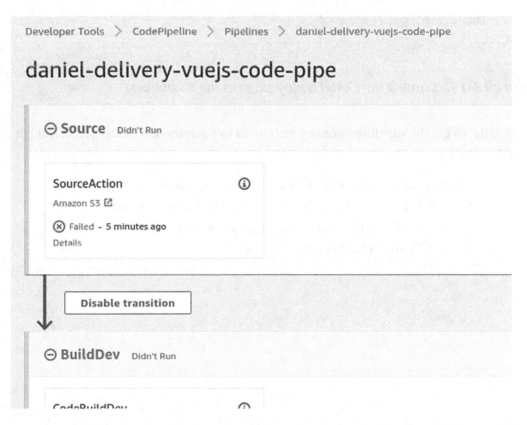

Figure 13-14. *Pipeline for Vue.js fails as there is not an artifact to deploy on S3 yet*

3. Now, click on Edit, move to the CodeDeploy stage for dev and prod, click on Edit Stage, and finally click on the edit icon for the CodeDeploy box.

4. There, choose the right S3 bucket where you want to deploy the application (Figure 13-15).

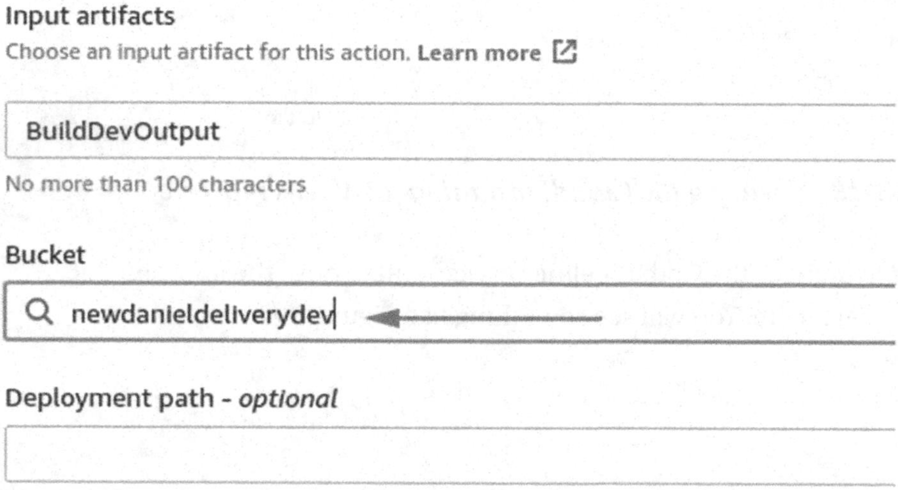

Input artifacts

Choose an input artifact for this action. **Learn more** ⤴

> BuildDevOutput

No more than 100 characters

Bucket

> 🔍 newdanieldeliverydev ⬅————————

Deployment path - *optional*

>

Figure 13-15. *Linking the CodeDeploy stage to the S3 bucket*

Finally, to get the pipeline running, you need to push the zip file to the S3 bucket in the following way:

1. Zip the source code project. You must zip the content, not the folder, avoiding dist and node_modules. Careful, do not forget .env files, for instance: The zip file must be named danieldeliveryvuejs.zip (Figure 13-16).

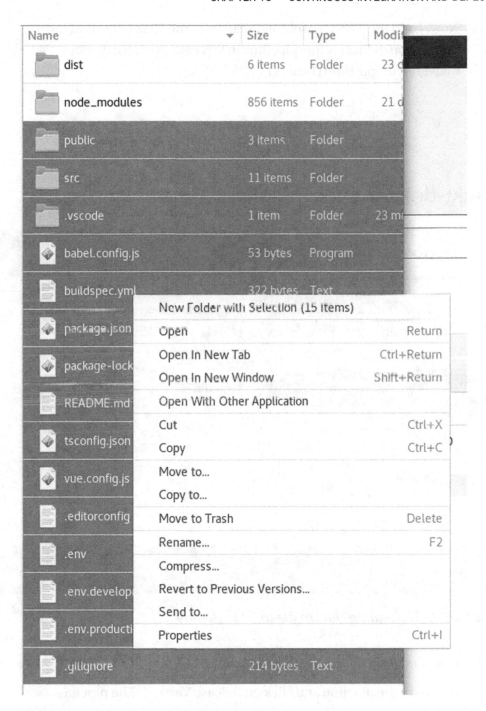

Figure 13-16. *Zipping the source code for Vue.js*

2. Now, go to the AWS Console and search for the S3 service, find the bucket you define for this pipeline; in this case, we have daniel-delivery-vue-pipeline (Figure 13-17).

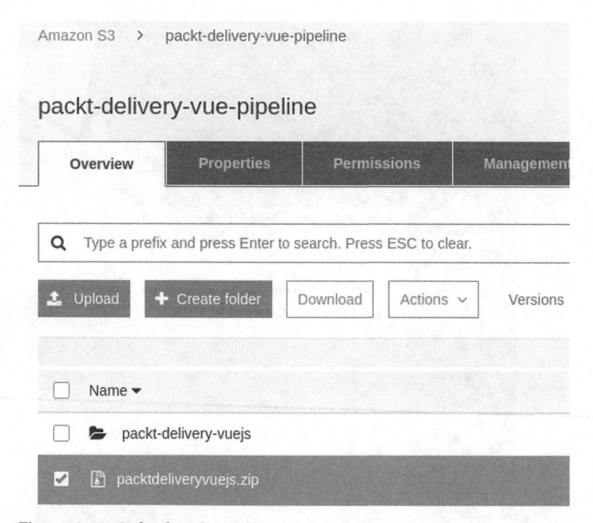

Figure 13-17. Uploading the zip file to S3 to deploy

3. Drag and drop the zip file into the bucket.

4. Return to the pipeline and click on Release Version. The pipeline will start.

5.   After the deployment to the environments is done, you must invalidate the CloudFront cache.

   a. Search for the CloudFront service in the AWS Console.

   b. Click on the CloudFront distribution you want to invalidate.

   c. Move to the tab Invalidations.

   d. Create a new invalidation like that shown in Figure 13-18.

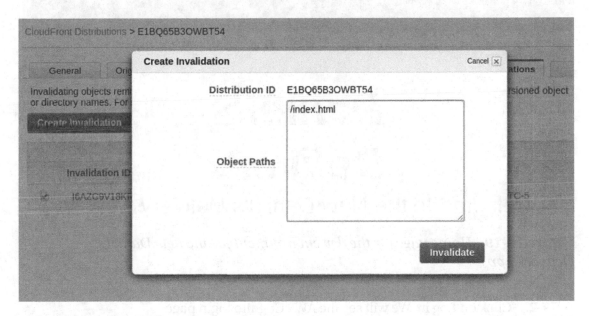

Figure 13-18. *Invalidation for the index.html in CloudFront to delete from Cache*

This is going to remove the index.html from any Edge Cache in CloudFront. The next time a user tries to access that page, CloudFront is going to grab the resources from the origin, in this case, the S3 bucket. As the index.html file links to JS and images resources through hashing names, the browser is going to request the new resources to CloudFront, and it is going to grab them from the origin too.

We just defined the whole pipeline to build and deploy our VueJS front-end layer. Now, let's see how the new Daniel's Delivery website works in AWS.

AWS Daniel's Delivery Website

We just created a whole infrastructure in AWS for our new Daniel's Delivery website. Let's see this website actually working:

1. Access the CloudFront URL of the front-end application (Figure 13-19).

Daniel's Delivery
Welcome to the New Daniel's Delivery website

Figure 13-19. Home page for the dev environment for the new Daniel's Delivery app

2. Click on Log in. We will see the AWS Cognito login page (Figure 13-20).

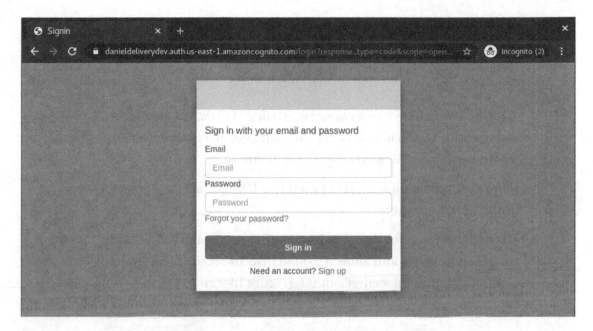

Figure 13-20. *Using AWS Cognito to log into Daniel's Delivery*

3. Log in or Sign up. After either of those is a success, you will find an error like that shown in Figure 13-21.

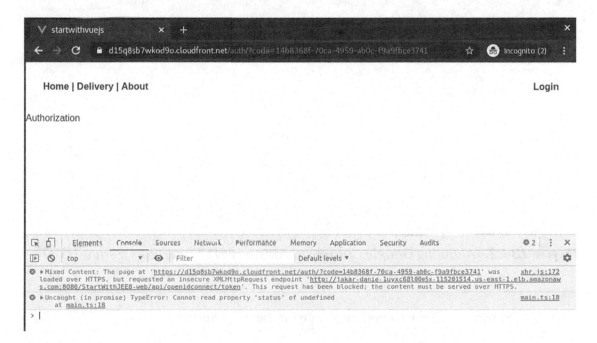

Figure 13-21. *Error trying to consume http services from an https domain*

The mixed content error means that we have an HTTPs page trying to call an HTTP service. In this case, our CloudFront for VueJS is using HTTPs, and our ECS load balancing for Jakarta EE is using HTTP.

The ideal is to have every connection using HTTPs; however, to secure your ECS load balancing, you will need to create a domain and a certificate. We won't cover that in this book.

AWS Cognito requires an HTTPs redirect URL, so, we cannot use full HTTP everywhere.

4. To skip this issue, for Google Chrome, click on the right top corner of the address bar, and allow it to load insecure scripts (chrome:// settings/content/insecureContent) (Figure 13-22).

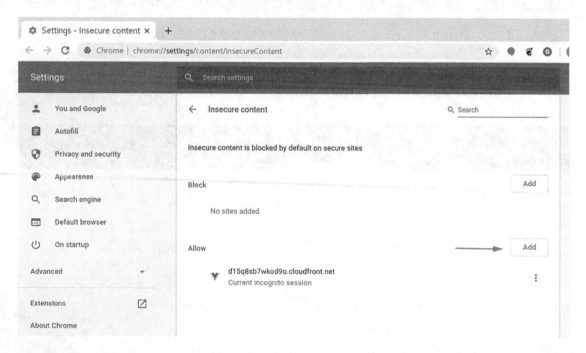

Figure 13-22. *Allowing Google Chrome to consume HTTP services from a HTTPs domain*

5. Now, you will see the settings page for the Food Service.

Well, we just created an entire full-stack application using Vue.js and Jakarta EE in AWS (Figure 13-23).

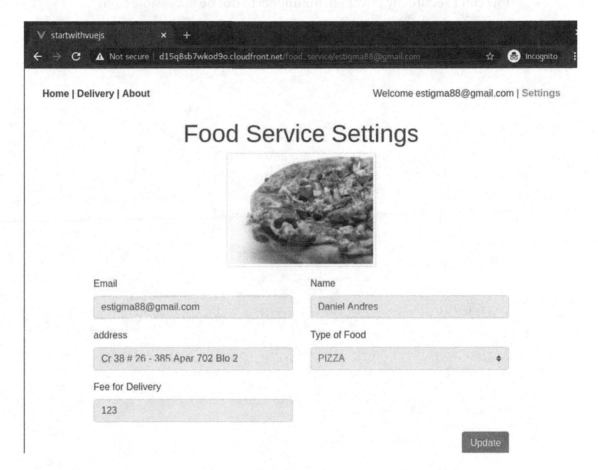

Figure 13-23. *Settings for the Food Service*

Summary

We just designed and implemented a continuous integration and deployment process for our new Daniel's Delivery website using different AWS services like CodePipeline, CodeBuild, CodeDeploy, and S3, for both Jakarta EE and Vue.js.

Everything was done by pipeline as code using CloudFormation templates, so we can rebuild our pipeline as many times as needed.

Now, as we have the Daniel's Delivery website deployed, we should check how it behaves. You will see this in the next chapter about monitoring.

Extended Knowledge

- How can I secure my lower environments to not be accessible from the external world?

- Can I use a different source type than S3 for the AWS CodePipelines?

CHAPTER 14

Testing and Monitoring

Testing and monitoring are two important processes that we need to follow to guarantee the quality of any application.

In this chapter, we are going to see how we can use AWS monitoring tools to check our AWS services; in addition, we will define a load testing process using JMeter to guarantee that our application accomplishes the scalability metrics we want.

The following topics will be covered in this chapter:

- AWS monitoring focusing on RDS and ECS Fargate metrics, plus GlassFish logs to trace our back-end layer

- Using JMeter to define a load testing strategy

Technical Requirements

- AWS account. JMeter 5.2.1

We won't cover the AWS account creation and JMeter installation in this chapter.

You can check the whole project and code at `https://github.com/Apress/full-stack-web-development-with-jakartaee-and-vue.js/tree/master/CH14`

AWS Monitoring

Cloud computing gives us a lot of services out of the box so that we can focus on what really matters: our business. However, cloud computing cannot guess everything our application needs by default: we need to monitor how our application behaves so we can adapt to those changes using cloud computing services.

In this section, we are going to talk about monitoring the basics of the AWS resources we use for our new Daniel's Delivery website, from the database to the cloud front.

RDS MySQL

Databases are pretty important in any business as they save the more important assets in a company: the data. As the data must be accessible for our application, we must guarantee it is always available. Let's see what we can monitor in our RDS database.

Monitoring

AWS RDS gives us multiple metrics regarding the performance of the database. Those metrics are pretty useful to tune the database to the requirements we have.

Let's start with the statistics AWS gives us.

1. Log into the AWS console.

2. Search for RDS service.

3. Choose the DB Instance you want to check.

4. Move to the Monitoring tab. You will see something like Figure 14-1.

Figure 14-1. *Monitoring view in RDS*

There we will find some preconfigured CloudWatch metrics. Let's discuss some of them.

CPU Utilization

CPU Utilization shows how the CPU percent has been used over time. Figure 14-2 is an example.

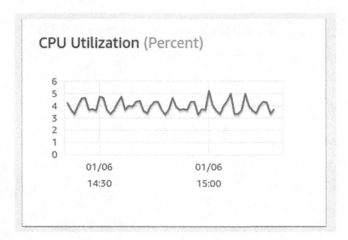

Figure 14-2. *RDS CPU Utilization*

As we can see, our database is not in production or being used by a lot of clients; the CPU just reaches 6%. When the CPU utilization reaches more than 80%, we might need to move our database to a greater AWS instance. Those features set are instances of classes.

There are plenty of database instances classes, mixing CPU, GPU, storage, and memory requirements. Depending on your needs, you should choose one of those. For instance, we use db.m3.medium; this means we have just 1 virtual CPU and 4 GiB of memory. For more information, you can find the whole list here: `https://docs.aws.amazon.com/AmazonRDS/latest/UserGuide/Concepts.DBInstanceClass.html`.

DB Connections

DB connections tell us how many connections are currently active. This metric helps us to understand how many clients would use our database. For instance, let's look at the current behavior of our database (Figure 14-3).

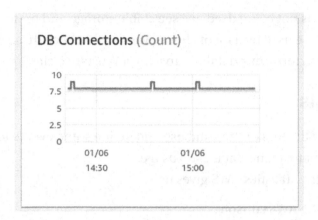

Figure 14-3. *RDS DB connections over time*

There we see 8 concurrent connections. The reason for this is because our GlassFish server has a database connection pool, so it maintains a set of live connections. This is a normal strategy to improve the performance of a database connection, as they cost a lot to be created, so the connection pool reuses connections instead of creating new ones.

Now that this should be measured, as we have a fixed set of connections. If we have more than 8 concurrent clients, the 9th client will need to wait for a connection to be released. You can set this connection pool to grow as we need it to, but you might want to define a limit; otherwise, your database can blow up.

Free Storage and Memory

This metric is clear: we measure how much storage and memory our database is using. Figure 14-4 shows how they behave in our application.

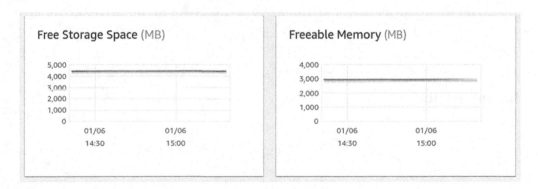

Figure 14-4. *RDS Free storage space and memory*

As our database is not being used, we see stable storage and memory. When the application starts to be used by a lot of clients, we should check these metrics and evaluate if we need to move our database to a bigger instance class.

Logs and Events

AWS RDS lets us see the logs of the database and define some events to validate the limits we want to ensure in the database's usage.

Let's start with the statistics AWS gives us.

1. Log into the AWS console.

2. Search for RDS service.

3. Choose the DB Instance you want to check.

4. Move to the Logs and Events tab. You will see something like Figure 14-5.

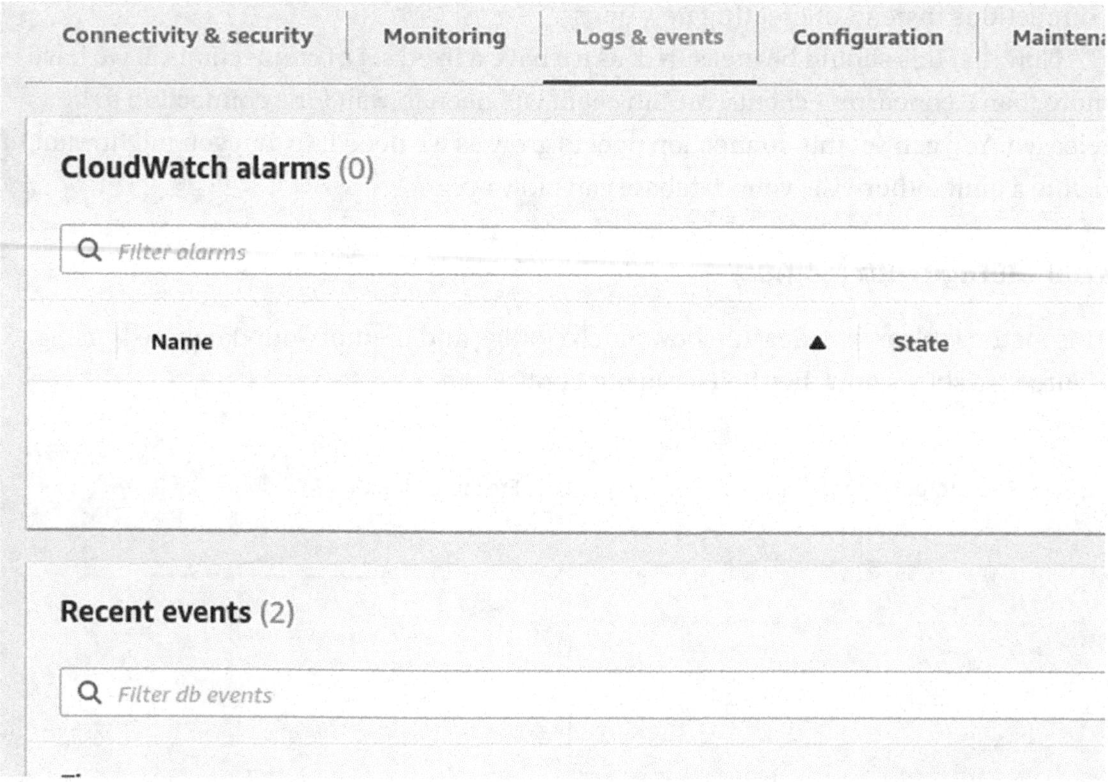

Figure 14-5. *RDS logs and events*

There, we will find three main sections: CloudWatch alarms, Recent events, and logs. Let's see them one by one.

- CloudWatch alarms: CloudWatch is an AWS service that is in charge of monitoring and warning regarding any AWS service. There we can create alarms, for instance, if my database storage reaches 80%, it will notify the database owner. This is pretty useful when you don't want to have surprises regarding how your system behaves.

- Recent events: There, we usually find RDS-related events, like snapshots or maintenance windows. For instance, we have the following events in our database (Figure 14-6).

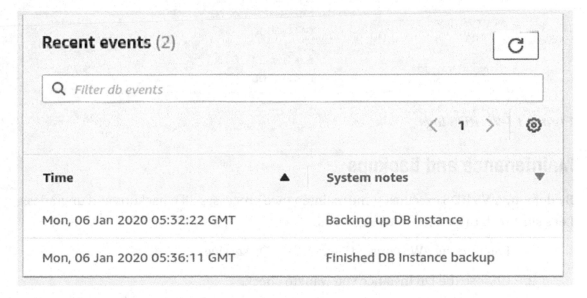

Figure 14-6. *RDS events*

AWS RDS defines by default a maintenance window where the database will be unavailable. This is for different reasons, like taking snapshots of the database, to upgrading the latest security patches. You must be aware of when those maintenance windows occur to prepare your system.

- Logs: We see the logs of the database. In our case, we have a MySQL database, so, we see the following logs (Figure 14-7).

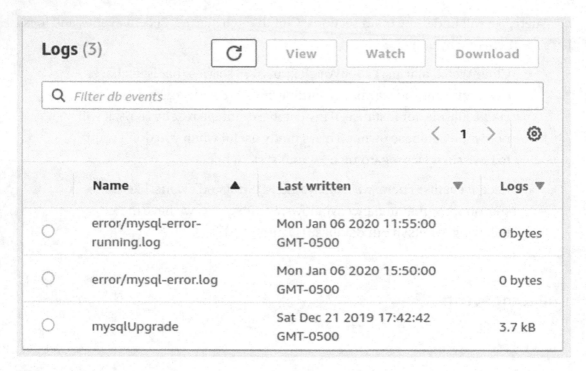

Figure 14-7. *RDS logs*

Maintenance and Backups

By default, AWS RDS executes some maintenance processes, like backups and upgrades. Let's start with the statistics AWS gives us.

1. Log into the AWS console. Search for RDS service.

2. Choose the DB Instance you want to check.

3. Move to the Maintenance and Backups tab. You will see something like Figure 14-8.

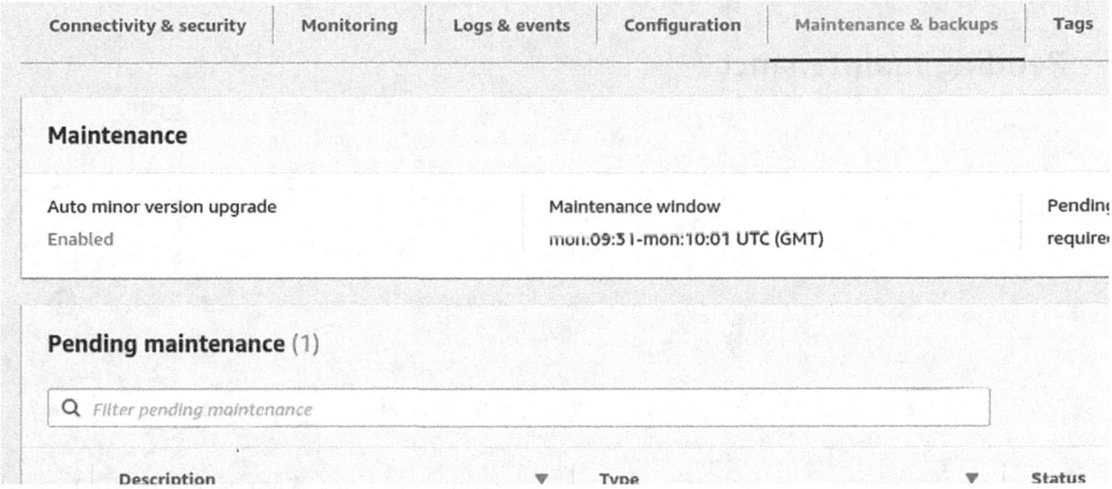

Connectivity & security	Monitoring	Logs & events	Configuration	Maintenance & backups	Tags

Maintenance

Auto minor version upgrade	Maintenance window	Pending
Enabled	mon:09:31-mon:10:01 UTC (GMT)	require

Pending maintenance (1)

🔍 Filter pending maintenance

Description	▼	Type	▼	Status

Figure 14-8. *RDS backups*

There we will find four main sections: Maintenance, Pending maintenance, Backup, and Snapshots. Let's see them one by one.

- Maintenance: This section shows us the configuration of maintenance windows.

- Pending maintenance: This shows us what the next maintenance is going to be about. For instance, our database has a certificate update soon (Figure 14-9).

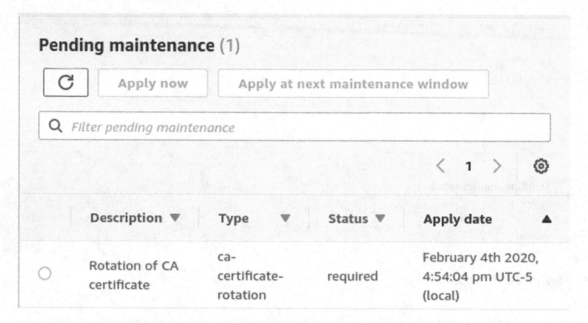

Figure 14-9. *RDS pending maintenance*

- Backup: Here, we have the backup configuration, for instance, we have an automated backup once a day (Figure 14-10).

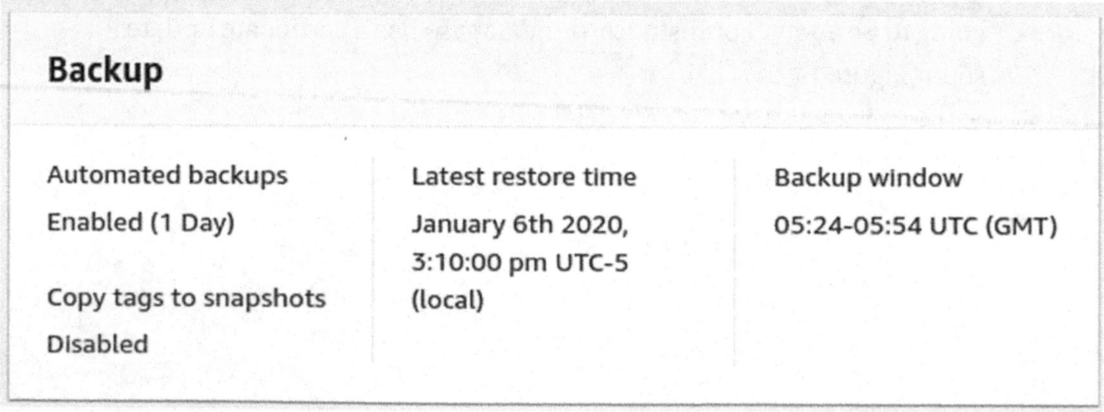

Backup

Automated backups	Latest restore time	Backup window
Enabled (1 Day)	January 6th 2020, 3:10:00 pm UTC-5 (local)	05:24-05:54 UTC (GMT)
Copy tags to snapshots Disabled		

Figure 14-10. *RDS backups*

- Snapshots: There, we see the snapshots that AWS RDS has taken from our database. Besides, you can take a snapshot now.

ECS Fargate Cluster

AWS Fargate is a new serverless service for containers. To monitor those services, we are going to use CloudWatch Insights.

1. First, we need to activate this service in our current cluster. So, use the following awscli command:

   ```
   aws ecs update-cluster-settings --cluster daniel-delivery-
   jakartaee-ecs-dev
   --settings name=containerInsights,value=enabled --region us-east-1
   ```

   There, we set the containerInsights property to enabled.

2. Now, move to our ECS cluster, Metrics tab. You will see something like Figure 14-11.

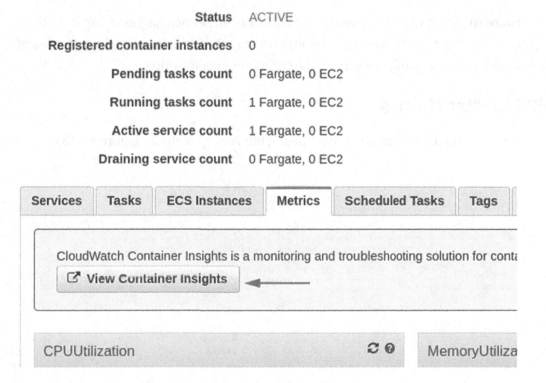

Figure 14-11. *ECS container insights activation*

There we will see a button View Container Insights. Click it, and you will see the following Figure 14-12.

Figure 14-12. *ECS container insights*

There we will find a lot of metrics, by ECS Cluster, Service, or Tasks. We have the default ones, like CPU Utilization, Memory Utilization, and so on. For the purposes of this section, we are going to focus on the container-specific ones.

ECS Cluster Metrics

For the ECS Cluster, we can see the following interesting metrics (Figure 14-13).

Figure 14-13. *ECS cluster metrics, task count, and service count*

Now we can see the following statistics:

- Task Count: How many tasks we have running, in this case, just 1.

- Service Count: How many services we have running, in this case, just 1 too.

ECS Service and Tasks Metrics

For the ECS Service and Tasks, we have the following metrics (Figure 14-14).

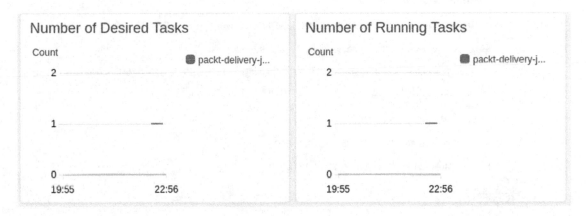

Figure 14-14. *ECS cluster metrics, number of desired tasks, and number of running tasks*

These tell us how many tasks we need running vs. how many we have running. This helps us to understand if our application is stable regarding the scalability requirements.

GlassFish Console Logs

Of course, we need our application server logs. Those logs are pretty important to detect errors in our application deployed in the ECS cluster.

As we saw in the previous section, we attached CloudWatch logs into our ECS cluster using CloudFormation. To find those logs, follow the following steps:

1. Log into the AWS console.

2. Search for ECS service.

3. Choose the ECS cluster you want to check.

4. Move to the Tasks tab and click on the tasks you want to see. You
    will see something like Figure 14-15.

Figure 14-15. *ECS task details*

5. Expand the Containers section, and at the bottom, you will see the links to the logs (Figure 14-16).

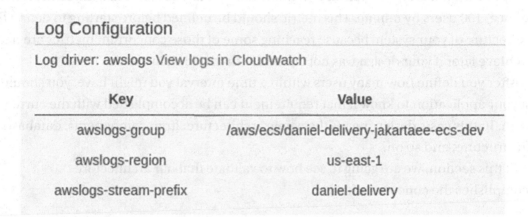

Figure 14-16. *ECS task logs description*

6. After you click View logs in CloudWatch link, you will see the full log text for those tasks (Figure 14-17).

Time (UTC +00:00)	Message
2020-01-03	
	No older events found at the moment. Retry.
15:01:56	[#|2020-01-03T15:01:56.357+0000|WARNING|glassfish 5.1|javax.enterprise.ejb.container|_ThreadID=28;_ThreadName=http-listener-1(1);_Ti
15:01:56	A system exception occurred during an invocation on EJB DeliveryRepositoryEJB, method: public java.lang.Object com.packt.delivery.main.re
15:01:56	[#|2020-01-03T15:01:56.357+0000|WARNING|glassfish 5.1|javax.enterprise.ejb.container|_ThreadID=28;_ThreadName=http-listener-1(1);_Ti
15:01:56	javax.ejb.TransactionRolledbackLocalException: Exception thrown from bean
15:01:56	at com.sun.ejb.containers.EJBContainerTransactionManager.checkExceptionClientTx(EJBContainerTransactionManager.java:642)
15:01:56	at com.sun.ejb.containers.EJBContainerTransactionManager.postInvokeTx(EJBContainerTransactionManager.java:487)
15:01:56	at com.sun.ejb.containers.BaseContainer.postInvokeTx(BaseContainer.java:4576)
15:01:56	at com.sun.ejb.containers.BaseContainer.postInvoke(BaseContainer.java:2084)
15:01:56	at com.sun.ejb.containers.BaseContainer.postInvoke(BaseContainer.java:2054)
15:01:56	at com.sun.ejb.containers.EJBLocalObjectInvocationHandler.invoke(EJBLocalObjectInvocationHandler.java:196)
15:01:56	at com.sun.ejb.containers.EJBLocalObjectInvocationHandlerDelegate.invoke(EJBLocalObjectInvocationHandlerDelegate.java:64)
15:01:56	at com.sun.proxy.$Proxy214.save(Unknown Source)
15:01:56	at sun.reflect.NativeMethodAccessorImpl.invoke0(Native Method)

Figure 14-17. *ECS task logs in Cloud Watch*

There you can see the whole log based on the time of retention you set up, for instance, if it is 7 days, you will only see the last 7 days of logs.

JMeter Load Testing

Any application has an estimate of how many users could be active in a time interval, for instance, 100 users by minute. This metric should be defined before starting to define the architecture of your system because reaching some of those concurrent metrics are hard to achieve later if your design was not created with that limit in mind.

After you define how many users within a time interval you might have, you should test your application to know if that requirement can be accomplished with the current design. In this case, design means the whole architecture: from components, database, infrastructure, and so on.

In this section, we are going to see how to validate that our architecture accomplishes the concurrent load.

What Is Load Testing?

Load testing is the process of executing multiple use cases in your application in a time interval. Those use cases can be simple as just logging in or complex like creating a delivery request in our new Daniel's Delivery website.

Let's define a scenario, for instance, our new Daniel's Delivery website should be able to process 20 delivery requests per minute. A delivery request is composed of the following flow:

1. Open the Daniel's Delivery website.

2. Click on the Delivery menu.

3. Set a delivery email.

4. Choose Food Service.

5. Choose a Food Product of that Food Service, setting the amount as 1.

6. Add that Food Product to the cart.

7. Set the address and phone of delivery.

8. Request the delivery.

There we can see a complex use case, where we have a defined flow and need to fill some data to finish the use case.

Now, as we define that our application should support 20 delivery requests per minute, we need to execute the delivery request use case to 20 times per minute.

This can be done manually, using 20 people in different computers running the use case at almost the same time. However, doing this manually doesn't scale. What if we need to scale to 100 people? 1,000? 1,000,000? Besides, we need this to be replicable, and ideally, we should integrate this test in our continuous integration and delivery pipeline, so that we can guarantee a level of quality in each deployment.

We can find plenty of tools for this purpose, and one of those is JMeter. In the following section, we will use JMeter to execute a use case in our application.

Using JMeter

Apache JMeter is an open source tool used for load testing. JMeter allows you to record the requests you make on a web page, save them, and execute them again in a repeatable way.

For the purposes of this book, we are going to show how to record the delivery request use cases.

First, let's create a basic recording structure using the recording template:

1. Open JMeter.

2. Go to Files | Templates.

3. Choose Recorder.

4. Then click on Create. You will see the following structure (Figure 14-18).

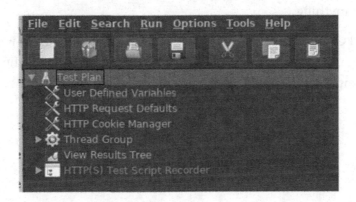

Figure 14-18. *JMeter basic project*

Now, let's see what each of these nodes mean:

- Test Plan: It contains the whole plan of recording.

- User Defined Variables: Those are variables we can use through the whole tests, and usually we use them in the request we do in our application. For instance, we define the following variables (Figure 14-19).

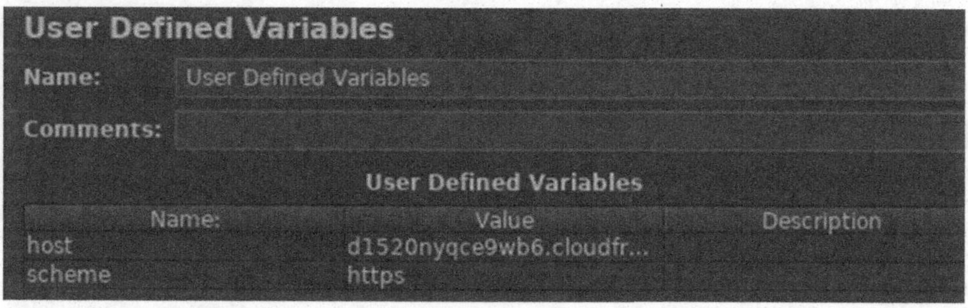

Figure 14-19. *JMeter user variables*

There, we have the scheme we are going to use by each request, in this case, https. We also define the default host we are going to use for each request, in this case, we have the AWS Cloud Front URL.

- HTTP Request Defaults: Here, we define the default features we will have in each request; in our case, we didn't set anything.

- HTTP Cookie Manager: This is where we define how to save and use the cookies that JMeter finds in the request. In our case, we didn't define anything.

- Thread Group: This is one of the more important parts. Here we define our load testing configuration. For instance, we have the following (Figure 14-20).

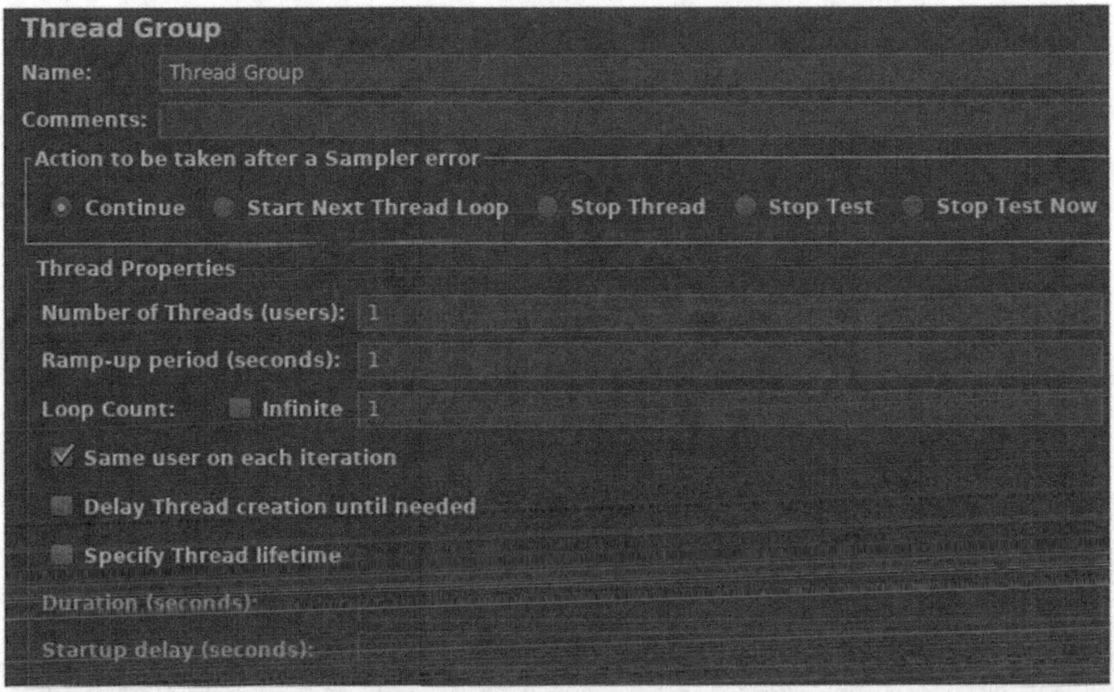

Figure 14-20. JMeter thread group

Here we can set up the number of threads we want; make sure that each thread is a concurrent user; determine how much time you want to start one of those threads, how you want to handle delays, and the duration of the test. In this configuration, you can simulate a kind of real scenario with plenty of users calling your application.

- View Results Tree: This is where we will have a results tree view, in this case, we will see each request executed by the test and its state.

- And finally, HTTPS Test Script Recorder. This node is going to help us to record the request in our delivery request use case. We defined the following configuration as shown in Figure 14-21.

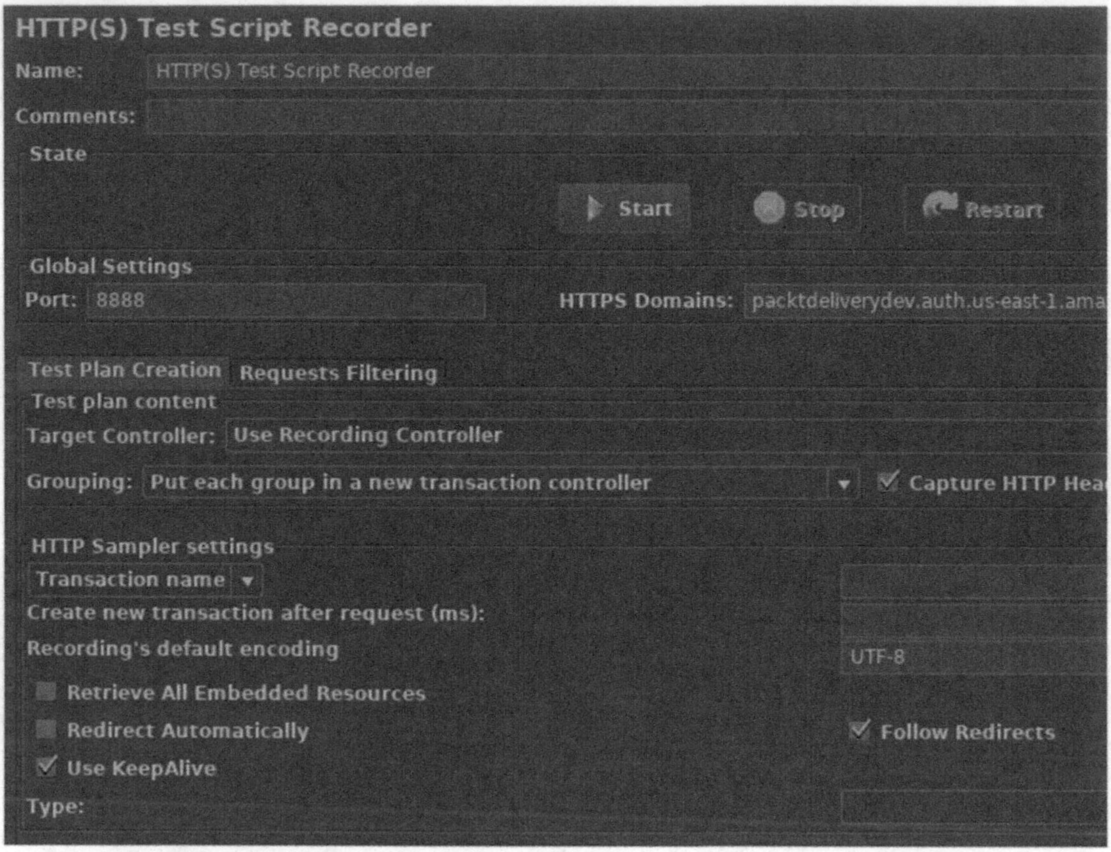

Figure 14-21. *JMeter script recorder*

There we define a port and the HTTPs domains we might call in this process. We need a port because the Script Recorder is a server that intercepts the requests we make in a browser. Now, let's see how to record a user case.

Recording a User Case

To record a use case, let's follow these steps:

1. Change the proxy settings of your browser. For the Chrome case, you will find it in the next step.

2. Go to chrome://settings/

3. Search for Proxy, and click on Open your computer's proxy settings; there you will see your computer proxy configuration.

4. Set your HTTP and HTTPs proxy settings to localhost and port 8888; this port is the same port we set up in the HTTPS Test Script Recorder node in the JMeter configuration.

5. Start your HTTPS Test Script Recorder by clicking on the Start button (Figure 14-22).

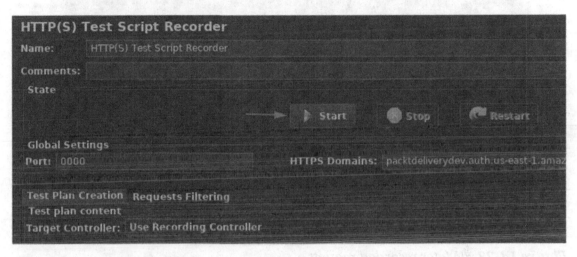

Figure 14-22. *JMeter script recorder start*

6. Now, open your browser, open the new Daniel's Delivery website, and start the flow regarding the delivery request.

7. When you finish, stop the HTTPS Test Script Recorder.

8. After that, if you expand the Thread Group node, you will find the recorded requests (Figure 14-23).

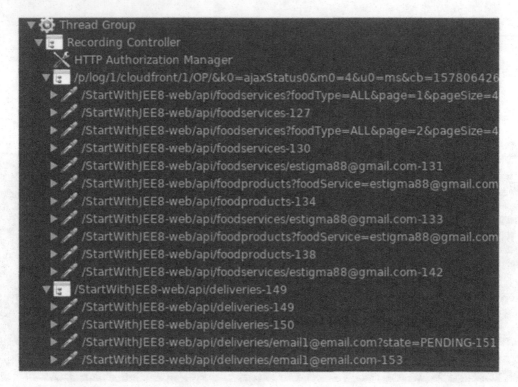

Figure 14-23. JMeter recorded requets

As you can see, we have requests to the GlassFish server as a back-end application.

9. If you want to rerun this use case, you can click on Run | Start. This is going to run the Thread Group configuration you defined, so if you set up 1,000 users, JMeter is going to create 1,000 threads and run this use case. For instance, if we execute the use case with only 1 user and 1 iteration, we get the following in the View Results Tree (Figure 14-24).

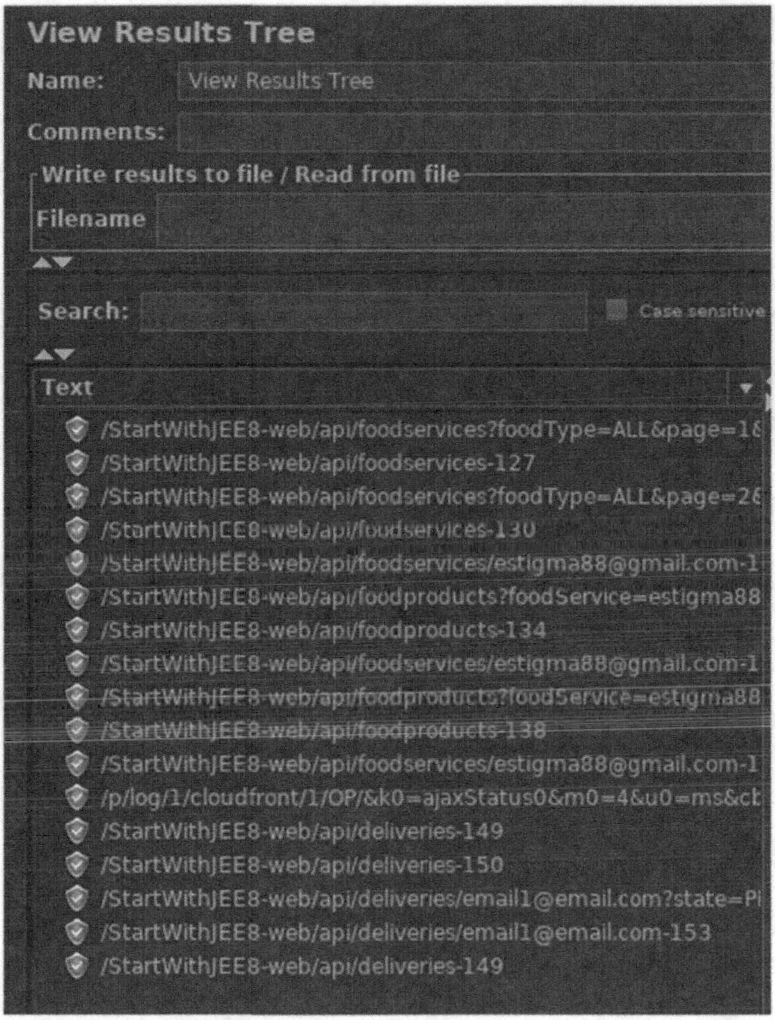

View Results Tree

Name: View Results Tree

Comments:

┌─ Write results to file / Read from file ──────────────
│ Filename
▲▼

Search: ☐ Case sensitive
▲▼

┌─ Text ─── ▼
│ ● /StartWithJEE8-web/api/foodservices?foodType=ALL&page=18
│ ● /StartWithJEE8-web/api/foodservices-127
│ ● /StartWithJEE8-web/api/foodservices?foodType=ALL&page=28
│ ● /StartWithJCE8-web/api/foodservices-130
│ ● /StartWithJEE8-web/api/foodservices/estigma88@gmail.com-1
│ ● /StartWithJEE8-web/api/foodproducts?foodService=estigma88
│ ● /StartWithJEE8-web/api/foodproducts-134
│ ● /StartWithJEE8-web/api/foodservices/estigma88@gmail.com-1
│ ● /StartWithJEE8-web/api/foodproducts?foodService=estigma88
│ ● /StartWithJEE8-web/api/foodproducts-138
│ ● /StartWithJEE8-web/api/foodservices/estigma88@gmail.com-1
│ ● /p/log/1/cloudfront/1/OP/&k0=ajaxStatus0&m0=4&u0=ms&cl
│ ● /StartWithJEE8-web/api/deliveries-149
│ ● /StartWithJEE8-web/api/deliveries-150
│ ● /StartWithJEE8-web/api/deliveries/email1@email.com?state=Pi
│ ● /StartWithJEE8-web/api/deliveries/email1@email.com-153
│ ● /StartWithJEE8-web/api/deliveries-149

Figure 14-24. *JMeter results tree view*

10.   As we can see, JMeter just executes the requests it recorded in the
      same order. For instance, the HTTP request to create a delivery
      request in our new Daniel's Delivery website looks like Figure 14-25.

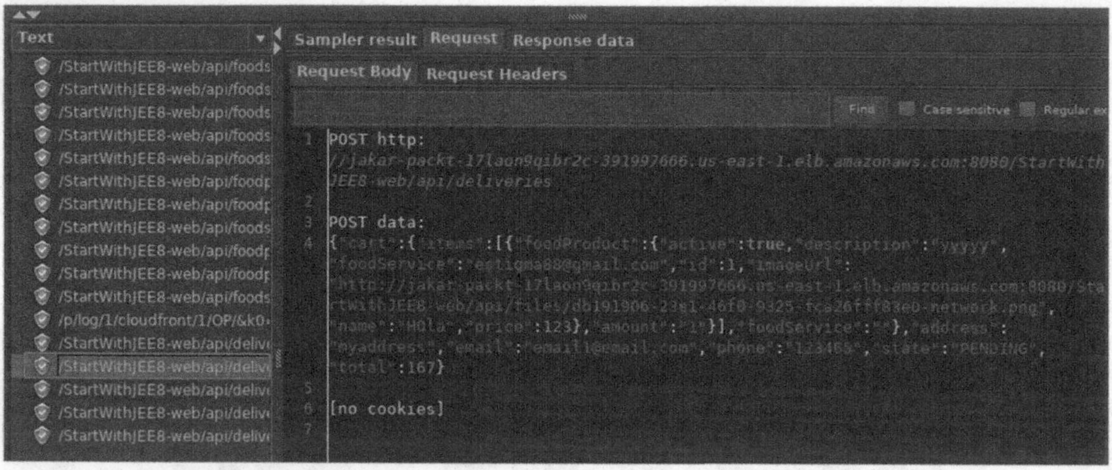

Figure 14-25. *JMeter results tree view detail*

Okay, but, what can I do with this execution? Well, you can check the AWS metrics we saw in the previous section to see how your application reacts to this load and define if it accomplishes what you expect or not.

Now, we can create load testings to guarantee our application accomplishes quality attributes like scalability and performance.

Summary

In this chapter, we covered how to use AWS monitoring services plus JMeter to define a load testing strategy, oriented to validate our architectural decisions, taking into account components, databases, and infrastructure.

After this chapter, you will be able to validate any AWS application using JMeter and its monitoring services. This is the last step to be confident in a production deployment, where we know how our system is going to behave in high-load scenarios.

Extended Knowledge

1. What other load testing tools exist?

2. What if I need to record HTTP requests using JMeter?

3. How can I change the data I use in load testing, for instance, using multiple emails to request the delivery?

Index

A

access_token, 346
Agile methodologies, 127–130
AWS architecture, 462
    CloudFormation, 488–492
    networking, 464
        ECR, 481, 482
        ECS, 472–476, 478, 479, 481
        Internet Gateway, 469–471
        RDS, 482–484
        Security Group, 468
        subnets, 466, 468
        VPC, 465
    reference, 462
    S3, 485
        defining, 488
        extending, 485, 487
    services, 463
    SSO, Cognito, 500–502, 504
        CloudFormation, 505–508
    Vue.js, 493
        CloudFormation, 498–500
        front-end infrastructure, 497
        HTTPS, cache services, 494–497
        S3 as static web page, 493, 494
AWS RDS monitoring, 563
    backups, 569, 570
    CPU Utilization, 563, 564
    DB connections, 564, 565
    logs/events, 566–568
    maintenance processes, 568, 570
    storage/memory, 565
Axios
    definition, 319
    DeliveryService component, 320
    FoodProductNew.vue, 327
    FoodProductService component,
        321, 322
    FoodServiceList.vue, 328, 329
    FoodServiceService component,
        323, 324
    installation, 319
    LoginForm.vue, 325, 326

B

Back-end layer, integration
    adding FoodProduct resource, 304, 305
    adding new endpoints, 300–303
    CORS, 312, 313
    exception handling, JAX-RS, 316, 317
    file resource, 306–312
    handling environment properties,
        Jakarta EE, 313, 315
Business entities
    aggregates, 181
    Delivery entity, 180
    diagram, 174, 175
    FoodProduct entity, 177, 178
    FoodService entity, 176, 177

W, X, Y, Z